# The Queen's Marriage

LIBRARIES NI
WITHDRAWN FROM STOCK

D1580326

## LADY COLIN
## CAMPBELL

*Dynasty*
*Press*

Dynasty Press Limited

36 Ravensdon Street

London SE11 4AR

www.dynastypress.co.uk

First published in this version by Dynasty Press Ltd.

ISBN: 978-1-5272-0984-8

Copyright © Lady Colin Campbell 2018

Lady Colin Campbell has asserted her right under the
Copyrights, Designs and Patents Act 1988 to be identified
as the author of this work.

All Rights Reserved. No part of this publication may be
reproduced in any form or by any means without the written
permission of the publishers.

Typeset by Biddles Books Ltd., Castle House, East Winch
Road. Blackborough End, King's Lynn, Norfolk PE32 1SF

Cover Design by Rupert Dixon

Printed and bound in the United Kingdom

# Contents

This book is dedicated to my beloved sons Dima and Misha, with the hope that they will one day enjoy the true blessing of good and durable marriages.

# Acknowledgements

MANY OF THE MOST penetrating insights and information in this book were provided by people who had no idea, as they were providing them, that one day their comments would see the light of day in a written work. Others generously provided me with information in the knowledge that it would be used literarily, while still others have given me the benefit of their wisdom on terms of confidentiality. I would like to thank them all. They include my old neighbours at the Cundy Street Flats, Lord Charteris of Amisfield and Lord Home of the Hirsel, the 3rd Lord Glenconner, HRH Princess Margaret of Hesse and the Rhine, Ned Ryan, the Hon. Shaun and Mrs Plunket, Robin Dalton, James Buchanan-Jardine, Anne de Courcey, Liz Brewer, Lady Sarah Spencer-Churchill, Lady Caroline Waterhouse, Peter Kares, Elaine Trebek Kares, Lady Jean Campbell, Margaret Duchess of Argyll, Clare Duchess of Sutherland, Major Ronald Ferguson, Helene Cordet, Larry Adler, Feliks Topolski, the Rajmata of Jaipur, the Hon. John Pringle, Mark Sykes, Dr. Michael Davies, Susan Grindling, Vida Menzies, Gary Pulsifer, Jacqueline Lady Killearn, Sonia Palmer, Diana Princess of Wales while still HRH The Princess of Wales, Richard Adeney, Burnet Pavitt, Dame Barbara Cartland, and all those still living whose positions and confidence I undertook not to jeopardise with revealing their identities.

I would also like to thank my publisher David Hornsby for his patience and editorial skills, as well as his understanding as the manuscript proved reluctant to emerge owing to ill health and the more immediately pressing demands of Castle Goring; to Rupert Dixon for the cover design; to David Chambers for the author photograph; and to Nigel Mitchell at Biddles for his care and attention to the book's production.

# Introduction

WRITING BOOKS ABOUT any marriage is a difficult task. It has been said that the only people who *might* know the truth of a marriage are the two people in it, and even then, one or the other could easily be labouring under an illusion.

If one uses that hypothesis as the starting point, getting to the truth of any marriage is challenging. The Queen's marriage is no exception. Indeed, because it is so public, and because there are so many rumours surrounding it, I have had to sift between fact and fiction, hoping, sometimes against hope, that I would hear when the truth bells ring.

I have always found that healthy open-mindedness allied to scepticism is an invaluable tool when dealing with human beings, whether it be in a personal, professional, or literary capacity. Possibly because my own life has been so filled with unexpected twists and turns, I have always found people to be the most fascinating thing on earth. Truth really is stranger than fiction and there is nothing more intriguing than the human condition. However, it is only worthwhile if you aim for the heart of the matter, if you reach as close to the truth as it is possible to get. That is possible only if you remember that all human beings are first and foremost human. That means they have an amalgam of traits and qualities, consisting in varying degrees of the emotional, spiritual, physical, intellectual and material.

Of course privilege, power and position - or their lack - all play their part as influences in the life of an individual, whether it be a public figure or a private person, and it does not behove a writer to forget that the people he or she is writing about are first and foremost human beings, with all the variability and uniformity attendant upon that innate and inescapable condition. I have read too many biographies of public figures that bury the subject in a wealth of trivial detail that obscures, rather than enlightens, the reader, as to the essence of the subject, to want to stray down that dead-end. For that reason, I have carefully chosen the facts which I convey, limiting them in the hope that the characters in the work which follows are illuminated, rather than providing a dazzling array of facts, some trivial, others less so, which would impress the reader with a cornucopia of facts that actually obscure the essence of the personalities being examined.

The Queen and the Duke of Edinburgh have led extraordinary lives. Their marriage has been at the core of their way of life since early adulthood. In their own way, each of them has become an extraordinary person. This did not need to be so. One or the other or both of them could have made much less of the hands destiny dealt them than they have done. The fact that they did not, that they chose a nobler path, lies not only in the conscious choices they made as adults, but also in the influences they had from childhood, and sometimes, from before birth. Being cousins several times over, both of them have common ancestors, some of whom were remarkable, others of whom were anything but, and these, together with the ancestors whom they did not share, but whose influence bore down so powerfully upon their lives, have helped to shape their characters, belief systems, and destinies.

I realised, while writing this book, that I had a choice. I could write yet another version of the many versions of the lives of the Queen and Prince Philip which already exist, focussing on what they did on, say, 27th February, 1957, as they went about their royal duties, or I could delve more deeply, trying to get a snapshot of the core of the woman and the man about whom so much has been written, but so little explained. I have deliberately taken a different path from any of the many books which have been written about them as individuals or a couple in the hope that, by ferreting out facts and travelling down byways and up highways that have seldom been explored, I will take the reader on a journey that is richer, fuller, and more interesting, and hopefully more enlightening, than the regular royal book. For instance, I have never read a book which details the undoubtedly important political factors which resulted in Prince Philip, born a prince of Greece and Denmark, becoming a French, British and German schoolboy. His checkered past, often remarked upon but seldom explored, actually dovetails with many of the important political features of European history in the late nineteenth and early twentieth centuries. Some of these events reverberated, sometimes tragically, into the latter twentieth century.

These events were not only important to Prince Philip, but to Western Civilisation as a whole, and I have therefore touched upon them. In so doing, I am not only laying the ground for the man Philip became, but also to give the reader a sense of the context of the world as it was, royalty aside, and how the past became our present. The past, it should be remembered, was once the present, and before that, the future, and the only way to make sense of our world today, and to get an idea of who the two individuals at the core of this work really are, is to travel far and wide enough to collate the influences that made them what they are, and, in so doing, show how the world into which they were born, and in which they have functioned, became their, and our, world of today.

CASTLE GORING
11th April, 2018

# Chapter I

ANY MARRIAGE THAT LASTS for seventy years is noteworthy, but a marriage of that duration, which both parties regard as a success, is outstanding indeed. Queen Elizabeth II and Prince Philip, Duke of Edinburgh, are both on record stating that they regard their marriage a great success, and this is more than mere public relations. "To see them together is heart-warming. Theirs has been a good marriage, and like all good marriages, it shows in many, tiny ways," Princess Margaret of Hesse and the Rhine, a close friend and relation who had known them well since the 1930s, confided to the eminent flautist Richard Adeney at a concert at Buckingham Palace in honour of Diana's grandmother Ruth, Lady Fermoy, in the early nineties. This was shortly after the Prince and Princess of Wales were separated, and Princess Margaret was actually contrasting the marriage of Charles and Diana with that of his parents.

Notwithstanding what common knowledge it is in royal circles that Lilibet and Philip's marriage is strong and successful, there have been rumours about it. From the very outset, before people even knew Prince Philip, there was gossip. Some was informed, a lot not. The reality is that there is always speculation about the private lives of public figures, so the fact of those rumours was, in itself, nothing out of the ordinary. What turned out to be exceptional was the persistence of some of the stories swirling around about the state of the royal marriage. How close to the truth some were, while others were wildly wide of the mark, only fed the speculation, until stories that had started at Court and in the drawing rooms of Belgravia and Mayfair ended up in the popular press.

Of course, all marriages have their ups and downs. The Queen and Prince Philip's has been no exception. Intermingled with the speculation has been the visible proof of a strong and vibrant, albeit ostensibly restrained, union, leading people to wonder where the personal truth lies. The reality of the marriage is still open to speculation, even among their inner circle, but the truth of its success, according to people close to the couple, can be found in the extraordinary degree of accommodation both Lilibet and Philip have demonstrated to keep their union alive and viable. In many ways, they are polar opposites. She is, by nature, reserved, almost timid personally, while he is outgoing, brave and, some would say, brash. She suffers everyone, even fools, with commendable forbearance, while he has never been known to suffer fools gladly or at all, and sometimes seems to have difficulty tolerating even the ordinarily intelligent. She loathes confrontation and goes to considerable lengths to avoid it, while he has always confronted things and people without hesitation, indeed with alacrity. While everyone who crosses paths with her commends her equable patience and tolerance, many of his critics say that he has a brutal aspect to his personality. Certainly, where she is soft and pliable, he is hard and inflexible. She is traditionalist and conservative by nature, while he has always been an open minded innovator. She is no intellectual, while his vast library and wide range of interests betray an intellectual bent. She is fundamentally and traditionally feminine, in demeanour as well as attitude, while he appears to be, and is, fundamentally and traditionally alpha male, though, on closer examination, his personality betrays the erudite, open-minded exposure to the variety of schools of thought, including Freudian analysis, to which he was exposed from a young age. This means that, beneath that masculine veneer lurks a variety of highly developed qualities often regarded as feminine.

Beneath the differences, however, the couple shares profound similarities. These are what have bound them together through thick and thin. Both are family orientated. Both are, or were, intensely sexual. Both are fundamentally spiritual. Both are responsible by nature and driven by duty. Both are fun-loving. Both always had an interest in physical fitness. Both have good senses of humour. And both have genuinely felt that, if they utilised all their training, inclinations and advantages, their calling could improve the lot of others and of the country they love and were destined to reign over.

The fact that the Queen is now the most revered head of state in the world, and Prince Philip is respected for considerable achievements which have benefitted not only the British, but the natural word internationally, shows that they have lived up to their potential in a way that was unimaginable when they first married in 1947.

# Chapter II

LIKE THEIR PERSONALITIES, the backgrounds of Lilibet and Philip are a curious mixture of tremendously different and uncannily similar.

When Princess Elizabeth of York was born by Caesarean section at 17 Bruton Street, Mayfair, the London house of her maternal grandfather the 14th Earl of Strathmore, on 21st April 1926, no one could have imagined that she would one day ascend the British throne. Her father was merely the second son of King George V, and a second son, moreover, who was generally acknowledged in Court circles to be something of a dolt, albeit a decent one.

Contrasted with his elder brother David, the glamorous, popular, charismatic, articulate and enchanting Prince of Wales, then the most popular young man on earth, Bertie, the Duke of York, cut a very lacklustre figure. He could barely get out three words in as many minutes owing to a terrible stutter. He suffered from chronic ill-health, unlike his sportive elder brother, whose robustness was much commented upon as he flew over high jumps while jeopardising his life hunting. Bertie was old-fashioned in inclination and attire, while David was the archetype of forward-looking fashion, both politically and as a trend-setter, whose clothes were copied far and wide. He had even invented a new way to tie ties, and the Prince of Wales knot would remain renowned as the Windsor knot.

Bertie, on the other hand, was generally acknowledged to be a deeply flawed, inadequate personality who was propped up by his charming wife Elizabeth. Even as a couple, though, the Yorks did not enjoy the approbation that David and his paramour, Freda Dudley Ward, did. They were viewed within Society, as it was then called, as also-rans. While they did receive their fair share of invitations, within the most chic and desirable social circles they were regarded as dull, accepted because of their rank rather than sought after for their cachet.

Although Elizabeth was bright and witty, she dressed so unfashionably that she cut a ridiculous figure and was regarded as dowdy. While her later success as queen would render her style acceptable, albeit not in fashionable circles (her daughter Princess Margaret would openly ask her why she insisted upon wearing such 'ridiculous clothes'), at the time of her elder daughter Lilibet's birth, indeed until her accession to the throne, Elizabeth, Duchess of York was viewed more as a figure to be mocked and pitied than one to be emulated and admired. Amongst the royal families, British as well as foreign, she was dismissed as 'common', an 'arriviste' who 'smiled too much', and whose 'fabled charm' denoted not admirable qualities but a disconcerting degree of ambitiousness allied to pathetic attempts to be accepted as royal by trying too hard. Nor did she fare better within aristocratic circles. She was laughed at for being more royal than the royals, for wearing silk dresses, hats and gloves around swimming pools, while everyone else went hatless and gloveless and wore swim suits or the silken lounge costumes that were then all the rage.

Even among the British royal family Elizabeth was gibed at, though not by the king and queen. Old fashioned in the extreme, George V and Mary found her style and attitudes reassuring, indeed commendable. Elizabeth took full advantage of the predisposition her parents-in-law, her father-in-law especially, showed towards her. By judicious attentiveness, she developed a close and loving relationship with both of them. She wrote them endless letters, agreed with them at every turn, catered to their every opinion, and, most important of all, created a cosy, loving, convivial atmosphere of homeliness, both at home and in the royal palaces she visited. This seduced both of the king and the queen, neither of whom, prior to this, had displayed any inclination towards family life.

However, both George V and Mary were obsessed with family, as only royalty and the aristocracy can be. Having distorted their own children's lives with rigid, inflexible and affectionless parenting, they relished the happy family atmosphere Elizabeth created and, even before Lilibet was born, they had grown closer to Elizabeth and Bertie than they would be to any of their other children or children's families. Nevertheless, David, as the Prince of Wales was known within the family, remained his mother's favourite child.

Elizabeth had a knack for creating a happy home. She was also good company, albeit within the regimented confines of an ultra-traditional way of life. There was nothing risqué or daring or challenging about her. The least rebellious person, she had an unquestioning respect for the established order, but she liked to laugh, and being both bright and well read, could hold her own with far better educated people than she was. She also had a loving nature, and when Lilibet came along, she ensured that her daughter grew into a sweet, obliging and well-behaved child. This further seduced the old king, who developed such affection for his granddaughter that his greatest pleasure became having Lilibet stay with him. Indeed, the king, fearful that his eldest son, whom he actively disapproved of, would marry and have children, went so far as to say that he hoped nothing would come between Bertie, Lilibet and the throne.

By the time Lilibet was a toddler, her mother Elizabeth had worked herself into a position of considerable regard with the king and queen. This she enhanced further by developing excellent relations with senior courtiers, such as her father-in-law's private secretaries, and the Archbishop of Canterbury, Cosmo Gordon Lang, who was then one of the most influential figures in the land.

While Elizabeth's reputation in Court circles grew ever stronger, the Prince of Wales's plummeted accordingly. By the time she produced her second daughter, Margaret Rose, in 1930, the unthinkable was being articulated, albeit discreetly at first. The crown would be safer with Bertie and Elizabeth and their adorable Lilibet than with the Prince of Wales, whose inclination towards modernity and all things American, was regarded by the king and senior courtiers as a grave threat to the future of the monarchy.

The favour shown the Yorks by George V's senior courtiers had dual roots. On the one hand, the king's health was precarious. A heavy smoker who was prone to the pulmonary troubles that had killed his father in 1910, the king nearly died in late 1928 when he developed septicaemia owing to a pulmonary abscess. Although he recovered sufficiently to be functional after a recuperation of several months, some of which were spent at Bognor Regis with Queen Mary and Lilibet, he was never the same again. The imminence of his death was thereafter treated as an unwelcome reality that was likely to take place sooner rather than later, and this focussed the minds of his senior courtiers in a way that had unforeseen effects for the York family as well as for the popular Prince of Wales.

George V's three Private Secretaries during the 1930s were Sir Clive (later Lord) Wigram, Sir Alexander Hardinge (later the 2nd Lord Hardinge of Penshurst), and Sir Alan Lascelles. Fortuitously for Elizabeth, Alec Hardinge was married to one of her oldest and closest friends, the former Helen Cecil. Both Hardinge and his wife regarded Elizabeth as being sound, solid and supportive of their views of the way the monarchy should be run. They all sympathised with the opinion of the most junior of the three Private Secretaries, 'Tommy' Lascelles, who had been the Prince of Wales's Assistant Private Secretary before resigning in 1929. He regarded the heir to the throne as feckless, superficial and a dangerous innovator whose approach could destabilise the monarchy once he became king.

In January 1936, King George V died. The wildly popular Prince of Wales ascended the throne as King Edward VIII and proved to be even more popular with the people than he had been prior to his accession. He had the common touch, and his predilection for liberal modernity being well known, the people thought that he was in touch with their needs and would influence the less sympathetic politicians positively. What played well with the public, however, did not go down so well with the politicians and courtiers. For instance, when Edward VIII toured the stricken mines of Wales and said 'something must be done' to alleviate the suffering plainly visible everywhere, the Prime Minister, Stanley Baldwin, and the new king's own private secretaries, took the view that he was meddling in politics and grandstanding irresponsibly. Not once did it occur to them that he was simply reacting with the degree of empathy that his subjects required of their king, and that far from behaving irresponsibly, his display of empathy was an appropriate response that gave succour to the masses when they needed it the most.

The Royal Archives are littered with adverse comments from the senior courtiers and, to a lesser extent, senior politicians such as the Prime Minister, about King Edward VIII's conduct during the ten months he sat on the throne. There was grave concern, especially amongst his private secretaries, that he was unmanageable; that he was not sufficiently deferential to them; that he was intent on instituting changes which would alter the institution of the monarchy into something new and unrecognisable, and that his approach threatened their very existence. Some of these complaints might seem anodyne today, but they were symptomatic of a larger problem in the making. For instance, the private secretaries were outraged that he had ordered the clocks at Sandringham changed back to real time from the artifice of Sandringham time (Greenwich Mean Time plus 30 minutes, instituted by his grandfather King Edward VII to give extra shooting time at the end of the day, and maintained by his father). The more expected and rational viewpoint would have been for them to be in favour of this action, but there was such antipathy towards the new king that as early as 25th January 1936, only five days after the death of the late king, Charles A Selden was writing in the *New York Times* that the British Establishment was 'anxious about the new monarch.' The concerns of the private secretaries, who had been briefing against the king before he had even succeeded to the throne, were only too evident as Edward VIII was criticised for being too radical and unconventional. Moreover, the criticism continued, he lacked friends among the politicians; he was too outspoken about denouncing the hard lot of his poorer subjects, and he lacked a wife. His brother Bertie and sister-in-law Elizabeth were then advanced as more suitable candidates for the throne. 'There has never been a breath of scandal about him or his family. As far as the public knows neither he nor his wife ever made a single false step to impair their usefulness or popularity.'

4

# Chapter II

The only difficulty was: Bertie was not a candidate for the throne. The crown was not elective, and it had a rightful occupant; one, moreover, who had not yet been tainted with scandal. That, of course, was a problem that could easily be solved by the judicious planting of further damaging stories, and within days the *New York Times* London correspondent, Frederick T. Birchall, was reporting that the king had received Foreign Minister Baron Constantin von Neurath and the new German Ambassador Leopold von Hoesch so warmly at his very first State reception that Germany no longer needed to regard itself as 'isolated and friendless, (as) here unexpectedly a new and powerful friend may have come into her orbit.' Edward VIII was reported to be 'more Left and less Conservative in his predilections than any British monarch within living memory.'

Before the old king's corpse had been properly interred, the new king's body was being prepared for burial under a slurry of innuendo, using two political tenets most unpopular at that time in the US – liberalism and Nazism. The fact that liberalism was more acceptable in the UK, and indeed at the time most segments of the British Establishment were either in favour of or indifferent towards what the Nazis were doing in Germany, rendered such criticism inappropriate on native soil. However, the ground was being laid for the actions of the new king to be questioned, and where better to start than in America, with its press responsive to briefings that could never have been made to English publications? It was a brilliant tool for striking at the essence of the new king, for once those reports had been published, they existed. This gave them a life of their own which rendered them capable of being referred to as evidence of existing public opinion. The fact that they had also been printed by such reputable organs as the *New York Times* gave them a *gravitas* they would never have had, had they been printed in lesser publications. The ground was being laid for his private secretaries to rein Edward VIII in.

It only remained for Edward VIII to play into the hands of these adversaries with a guilelessness that would have been remarkable had he not been born royal, and therefore naïve in the extreme about the methods used by the ambitious as they employ subterfuge to achieve their objectives. In that, the king was as gullible as his equally naïve brother Bertie, though Bertie's wife Elizabeth had a degree of clear-sightedness that would have been remarkable in anyone, be they royal, non-royal or even wily politician. She would hoe a path over the next few months that would, in the eyes of her admirers, preserve the monarchy, though her brother-in-law would come to believe that her machinations, more than anyone else's, were responsible for the crisis which led to his departure from the throne.

Had King George V's Principal Private Secretary, Lord Wigram, remained in the saddle, events might well have taken a more measured course, but, feeling unequal to dealing with the struggle that a monarch of Edward VIII's leanings would inevitably precipitate, he retired in a matter of days after David's accession. Hardinge and Lascelles therefore both moved one rung up the ladder, the former becoming the Principal Private Secretary, the latter the Assistant Private Secretary. The difficulty here was that neither man liked or respected his new boss.

Lascelles positively deplored David, a view which he had been at some pains to impart to his employer when he resigned as his Assistant Private Secretary in 1929. Now here he was, seven years later, back in the same position, except that David was no longer the heir to the throne, fulfilling ceremonial duties, but the king, with all the influence and power implicit in that role.

Nor did Lascelles respect Edward VIII any more than Hardinge did. David would later state that it did not occur to him until after the fact that his two Private Secretaries would betray their monarch by ganging up on him with the Prime Minister, Stanley Baldwin, the Archbishop of Canterbury, Cosmo Lang, and the Editor of the Times, Geoffrey Dawson, to create a political crisis which would induce him to abdicate. He had honestly believed that both Hardinge and Lascelles would put their personal feelings to one side and remain loyal to the man they deplored, because he was their king and they owed him a duty of loyalty as a result of his station.

He also came to believe that the part Elizabeth played was crucial to the successful orchestration of the political crisis that led to his abdication. In his view, his sister-in-law was the prime mover behind the scenes. He blamed her 'ambition' as well as her 'jealousy', asserting that she had tried to marry him before she settled for Bertie, and what she could never forgive was that he wanted Wallis and not her. His view is not as widely accepted as the alternative, promulgated by Elizabeth and her supporters, that she reluctantly took the throne with Bertie, and made a success of it at great personal sacrifice to themselves. History, of course, is written by the victor, and there is no doubt that Bertie and Elizabeth proved to be superb sovereigns at a time of dark need, but now that enough time has passed for the dust to settle it is likely that increased examinations of the roles of all the participants in the Abdication Crisis will result in the Duke of Windsor's interpretation being given greater weight than it has hitherto enjoyed.

The role Elizabeth played would impact upon her own position as well as that of her husband, children and brother-in-law. At present it is a truism that Edward VIII had to vacate the throne in 1936 in order to marry Wallis Simpson. In fact, much has happened since then to call that point of view into question. The monarch did not need then, and does not need now, any politician's permission to marry a divorcee, nor has he or she ever needed to consult anyone, politicians and advisors included, before agreeing to a royal marriage, whether it be his own or someone in line of succession to the throne. This was demonstrated irrefutably in 2005 when the Queen assented to the marriage of the present Prince of Wales despite the feared unpopularity of his choice of spouse. The monarchy being less powerful in 2005 than it had been sixty-nine years previously, logic dictates that Edward VIII needed no one's permission to marry the woman he loved. The marriage of the present Prince of Wales also proves how readily the Government and public will accept accommodations, even those they do not particularly like, when there is the political intent for them to do so.

Another truism which buckles under close examination is the assertion that Wallis Simpson was so beyond the pale that, not only was she unacceptable as a consort of the king, but her deficiencies had rendered her unsuitable for a relationship of any length, depth or substance with any member of the royal family. In the early 1930s, when the Simpsons first entered the royal circle through Wallis's friendships with David's mistress Thelma, Viscountess Furness and her sister Consuelo Thaw, they were totally accepted by Bertie and Elizabeth. They would all lunch, dine, swim and ice skate together. The two households were on dropping-in terms, which in fact is where the antipathy between Wallis and Elizabeth arose. One afternoon the Duchess of York dropped in at Fort Belvedere and caught Wallis, by now David's *maîtresse-en-titre*, mimicking her. Unaware that she was often mocked by her peers, thereafter Elizabeth evinced a dislike of Wallis which festered the closer Wallis got to sitting on the throne that she coveted, according to Edward VIII.

From the moment David ascended the throne, until he died in Paris thirty six years later, Elizabeth was resolute in asserting that Wallis was unfit for inclusion in the royal family, or even to be received by the family in any capacity whatsoever. She was 'the lowest of the low', and after the Duke of Windsor married her Elizabeth made sure she would never be accepted within royal circles in Britain by freezing out anyone who received the Windsors. Later on, after Bertie died of lung cancer in 1952, Elizabeth decreed that Wallis was the reason why Bertie's life had been cut short. By this time, even Queen Mary was taking steps to bring this 'silly feud', as she described it, to an end. But Elizabeth remained resolute.

However, once David was dead, Elizabeth did a complete *volte face*. She evinced a humanity she had never shown while such a course of conduct would have made a difference to the lives of the Duke and Duchess of Windsor. She sent flowers to Wallis on a regular basis, and wrote her little notes expressing good will and good wishes. Wallis's reaction? To bin the flowers and keep the notes, which she would then show to friends as irrefutable proof of Elizabeth's hypocrisy and skill at gamesmanship.

Irrespective of whether Elizabeth's or the Duke of Windsor's version of how he came to be manoeuvred off the throne is accepted as factual, the ten months of his reign were conducted against a febrile background of ever-increasing intrigue. This, however, had no impact upon the life of the two York princesses. Elizabeth was as resolute in her determination to have a happy home life as she was in keeping her American sister-in-law off the British throne. She tolerated no unpleasantness. Around her, everything was happy, and joyous, and joyful, and fun. She also cloaked herself in a high moral tone; all the better to exclude those whose conduct or habits she did not approve of, though when she liked someone she could be surprisingly tolerant of their foibles. Indeed, her younger brother David was a rampant homosexual best known for his love of intrigue, and some of her closest friends, such as Lady Plunkett or the Hon. Mrs (Maggie) Greville, were illegitimate, in a day and age when bastardy often rendered someone *persona non grata*.

What struck people when they met Elizabeth was how 'charming' or 'nice' she was. Bertie came across as a very decent, worthy, but uninteresting personality; someone who sheltered under the shade of his wife's broad tree. Their daughters were third and fourth in line of succession to the throne, ranking immediately behind their uncle David the king and their father. Luckily for them, the tenor of their childhood was set by their mother as aristocratic rather than royal, and Elizabeth had herself benefitted from a happy, aristocratic childhood where fun and laughter were intermingled with decorum and decorousness. Their mother Elizabeth was determined that they would enjoy a happy home life like hers had been, rather than suffer the deprivations which their father, his brothers and sister, had endured.

Joyousness, however, was underpinned by order. The York household replicated that of the Strathmores, both of which were run by a small army of staff. Life revolved around food as much as fun and duty. There was breakfast, followed by luncheon, followed by tea, followed by dinner and, if it was a particularly late night or they had been entertaining, there was a cold supper to tide one over till breakfast. Both Bertie and Elizabeth were sporty. He had been an avid tennis player who had actually competed at Wimbledon when he was a bachelor; she loved fishing and riding. They spent much of their time in entertaining or being entertained. They also had some official duties, though neither of them could be fairly credited with being over-taxed by these obligations. This left much room for family life. They saw a lot of both their families, though less of their children than a modern family.

A month after her birth, Lilibet, who had been under the charge of her mother's maternity nurse Nannie B, was handed over to the care of her full-time nurse. This was Clara Knight, always known within the family as Alah. The daughter of a tenant farmer on the Hertfordshire estate of the Earl of Strathmore, she had been Elizabeth's nurse from the age of a month until eleven years old, at which time she had shifted sideways to take care of the children of the eldest Bowes Lyon daughter, Mary, Lady Elphinstone. She returned to nurse Lilibet in 1926, and would thereafter spend the rest of her life within the royal family, nursing Princess Margaret as well. She would die on 2nd January 1946 at St. Paul's Walden, the place whence she had originated.

Alah was an excellent nanny: solid, trustworthy, affectionate but firm. Her nursery ran like clockwork. Partly, this was due to her personality - Elizabeth once told Lady Astor she had never known Alah to display enthusiasm about anything, but such level-headedness was much appreciated in a world where regularity was more necessary than enthusiasm – and partly due to the able assistance of the under-nurse and the nursemaid. These were two Scottish sisters, Margaret 'Bobo' Macdonald and Ruby Gordon, and in many ways they were the girls' true nurses, for Alah was more of an overseer. They slept with the royal siblings. They played with them. They bathed them. Alah kept order; they kept the girls company, with the result that Bobo and Ruby remained with Lilibet and Margaret into adulthood, two of the very few people outside of their immediate family circle who were allowed to address them by their own names instead of using the more formal 'Your Royal Highness' and 'Ma'am' that even the husbands of cousins were obliged to.

If Lilibet and Margaret Rose, as Princess Margaret was invariably known until she was a teenager, had settled and peaceful lives during the reign of their uncle David, the same could not be said of the adults within the family. There was mounting concern about King Edward VIII's relationship with Mrs Simpson. This escalated once the family discovered early in 1936 that the Simpsons were divorcing. Later that year there was an ugly scene at Balmoral when Wallis, who had been acting as David's hostess for the previous two years, greeted Elizabeth, who had been asked to dine with the king. Snubbing the woman who she feared would supplant her as the leading lady in the land, Elizabeth sailed past Wallis, declaring loudly that she had come to dine with the king. In so doing, she threw down the gauntlet publicly. Thereafter all opponents to the king had a focal point to which they could look.

By the time Wallis's divorce was heard in Ipswich in October, Elizabeth and her close friends Alec Hardinge and Cosmo Lang were asking each other whether something could not be done to deflect the king from the patently obvious path of marriage upon which he was embarked. Feelers were put out, suggesting to the king that he either keep Wallis in the background as his mistress or give her up entirely. According to the Duke of Windsor, Elizabeth already knew that neither course of action would be acceptable to him.

Irrespective of whether Elizabeth sought to divert David away from matrimony because she was concerned for the monarchy, as she maintained, or because her 'vanity' would not allow her to be outranked by someone who had mocked her, as well as occupying the role Elizabeth had once wanted for herself, as the Duke of Windsor maintained, is immaterial. While Lilibet and Margaret Rose enjoyed their enchanting childhoods at 145 Piccadilly, the London residence of their parents, Bertie and Elizabeth were aware of the strong possibility that they faced the massive upheaval that being king and queen would entail.

There is no doubt that Bertie did not want the throne. By his own admission, he broke down and cried like a baby in his mother's arms when he realised that the inevitable would happen. Although Elizabeth disclaimed a desire for the throne as well, her husband's sister the Princess Royal condemned her for displaying unseemly pleasure at her new-found lot. 'Her delight was too evident. She looked like the proverbial cat that had got the cream,' she said. 'I do wish she'd at least make an effort to conceal her delight. All that smiling simply won't do. Is she a Cheshire cat or a Scots' lassie? A bit more of the dour Scot would be preferable to all that skinning of the teeth.'

In October 1936 Wallis was granted a decree nisi. The earliest she and the king could marry would be six months later, when her decree absolute came through. David's coronation was scheduled for May 1937, and it emerged at this time that he wished to have Wallis crowned with him. Many supporters of the lovers counselled him against this course of action, which had the potential to turn a private matter into a public, and official, one. However, he had the bit between his teeth, and like his younger brother Bertie, whose determination to marry the woman he loved had overcome such insurmountable obstacles as disinterest from the intended – Elizabeth had told her friend Helen Hardinge, by now wife of the king's private secretary, that she found Bertie repulsive – David would brook no opposition until he had achieved the object of his desire. Such singlemindedness was a characteristic of the Hanoverian royal family, and Elizabeth knew it only too well from personal experience. There is little doubt that others who knew the brothers well, such as the Hardinges and Lascelles, were also aware that all attempts made by them or by the politicians to deflect the king from his declared intention would increase, rather than decrease, his ardour. It was therefore only a matter of putting sufficient obstacles in Edward VIII's path before he carried out his threat to vacate the throne, at which time the troublesome and unmanageable monarch would be replaced by his more conservative younger brother, who was in thrall to his even more conservative wife, their friend and firm supporter.

As the abdication crisis built to its *dénouement* in December 1936, Lilibet as well as Margaret Rose still remained oblivious to the supreme changes that were imminent in their lives. By this time, the girls had a capable Scottish governess, Marion Crawford, whom Elizabeth had employed in autumn 1933. Crawfie had been a child psychology student working for Lord Elgin when her path crossed Elizabeth's. In her book *The Little Princesses*, this intelligent, well-educated, physically attractive and personable woman gives a vivid and insightful picture into the lives of her charges and their parents. Elizabeth did not believe that either daughter needed to be either well, or even adequately, educated. She felt that her daughters needed no more education than she had received, which was tantamount to none. She was a firm believer that all they needed to get through life with the success she had achieved was to follow the format laid down by her mother Cecilia, whose daughters were not taxed with book knowledge, but encouraged to develop their social skills and deploy their femininity with guile and determination. As Elizabeth herself admitted, the velvet glove should conceal the iron fist, but should not be limited to the fist. Girls even more than boys needed backbones of iron, as they would have to manage the men in their lives the way she managed her husband Bertie and her mother managed her father Claude. That is not to say that they should be overtly domineering. On the contrary, they should be quintessentially feminine, apparently soft, kindly (Crawfie remarks on how '*nice*' Elizabeth was), and jolly, working behind the scenes to achieve their objectives. The only trouble with that attitude was that, while it might well prepare Princess Margaret successfully for the life of a working princess and wife (it did not: in adulthood Margaret often complained about her lack of education), it would not do so for Lilibet, the heiress presumptive to the throne. She would need all the knowledge that a man would need to be a successful monarch, otherwise she would be prevented from exercising her responsibilities adequately. This, Crawfie saw only too clearly, and she quickly discovered that she had an ally in the girl's grandmother, the intelligent, well-educated and worldly dowager queen. The result was that, by the time of the abdication, Lilibet was being educated sufficiently well by Crawfie and Queen Mary that her eyes were open to her surroundings.

Once the story of her uncle's possible vacation of the throne hit the newsstands, Lilibet started to ask whether the banner headlines meant that her father might become king. Upon being told that they did mean that, she figured out that that meant she would most likely become queen one day, and there is a rather cute vignette in Crawfie's book of the six year old Margaret consoling her ten year old sister about such an onerous possibility.

When the Duke of York became King George VI and his duchess Queen Elizabeth, their lives, as well as their daughters' lives, changed out of all recognition. One major issue that is often overlooked is the loss of their Uncle David from the lives of his nieces. Although to a certain extent they were protected from the full personal consequences of the loss by being so close to their parents, throughout their lives he had been one of the few people closest to them. Like his younger brother Bertie, David relished home life. As a bachelor, with no family of his own, he had got his 'fix' of family life from two sources: the two daughters of his *maîtresse-en-titre* Freda Dudley Ward in the 1920s into the early 1930s, and even more so from Bertie and Elizabeth's family unit. The York's London residence, 145 Piccadilly, was in walking distance from his London residence, St. James's Palace, while their country house Royal Lodge was on the Windsor estate, as was his own Fort Belvedere. He dropped in to see his nieces several times a week, romping with them as only a bachelor desperate for his own children would. While the frequency of his visits tapered off once Elizabeth had caught Wallis mimicking her and Elizabeth's coolness towards his American *inamorata* became obvious, David nevertheless remained a frequent visitor to his nieces, who adored him. This was true even after he succeeded to the throne. Inevitably, as the abdication crisis built and Elizabeth cast herself in the role of opponent to his relationship to Wallis, his visits became ever fewer, but once he abdicated and sailed into exile aboard the *Fury*, there was a rupture. Although Princess Margaret was too young to feel the loss acutely, Lilibet was not, and it is interesting to observe the residue of regard she displayed towards her favourite uncle towards the end of his life.

As so often happens in life, what is perceived as a disadvantage at one time and in one circumstance becomes a positive advantage in another. While the ten year old Lilibet was now the heiress to her father's throne, the very insecurity of fifteen year old Prince Philip of Greece's position – predicament might actually be a better word - would work in his favour to make him a more suitable consort for the future queen.

Like Lilibet, Philip had been born on the periphery of a throne. The only son and fifth child of Prince Andrew (known as Andrea) of Greece, his father was the fourth son of King George I of the Hellenes and the former Grand Duchess Olga Konstantinovna of Russia, so Philip was sufficiently far down the line of succession to have little, or no chance, of acceding. The Hellenic throne was Salic, meaning that only sons could accede, and this increased his chances somewhat. His father's three older brothers, King Constantine I, Prince George and Prince Nicholas, were alive at the time of his birth at the Greek royal family's summer residence at Mon Repos, Corfu, on 10th June 1921 and although Nicholas only had three daughters, (one of whom, Marina, would marry Lilibet's uncle and become Duchess of Kent), George had a son, Peter, and Constantine had two living sons, so there were relatively few males before Philip in the line of succession.

The Greek monarchy was convoluted in the extreme. Following it was like having an egg beater in your brain. By the time of Philip's birth, it was a template for insecurity. For example, Constantine's eldest son would succeed to the throne as King George II the year after Philip's birth, and the youngest son, Prince Paul, would ultimately succeed to the throne in 1947. But what made Greece remarkable was that King Constantine I's second son, Alexander, had been placed on the throne while his father and elder brother were exiled from Greece between 1917 and 1920. This meant that Alexander actually became king before his elder brother, in defiance of the ordinary rules of succession. However, Alexander died of sepsis following a bite from a pet monkey, resulting in the repatriation of his father to both Greece and the throne in 1920, which in turn led to George II assuming his rightful place on the throne. But only for a short while.

Although Lilibet and Philip were both born in politically troubled times – her birth coincided with the General Strike of 1926 and his took place during the Greco-Turkish War of 1919-1922 – the British monarchy was stable, while the Greek was anything but. It was also a relatively new crown, imported from abroad, as so many of the Balkan thrones were, in an attempt to appease the Continental powers while also blocking the ascendency of any one powerful local family over its competitors.

Although Philip's grandfather Willie would end up a Greek king, reigning as King George I of the Hellenes, Vilhelm was born a relatively obscure princeling, Christian Vilhelm Ferdinand Adolf George of Schleswig-Holstein-Sonderburg-Glücksburg, in Copenhagen on Christmas Eve, 1845. His parents, Prince Christian of Glücksburg and the former Princess Louise of Hesse, had tenuous claims to the thrones of Denmark as well as the duchies of Schleswig and Holstein, but neither was a prince or princess of Denmark, and the chance of their being monarchs of one country and their son becoming sovereign of another was beyond contemplation. Yet, within a few short years, both father and son would be sitting on the thrones of Denmark and Greece.

Because both Philip and Lilibet descend from the Grandfather of Europe, as Prince Christian would come to be called, and as his influence would spread far and wide throughout the monarchies of Europe, it is interesting to see how serendipity and misfortune paved his way from penurious insignificance to the throne of Denmark. Christian was a distant cousin of the childless Danish King Frederick VII, the last of the line of the House of Oldenburg, while Princess Louise was the monarch's paternal first cousin by virtue of being his late father King Christian VIII's niece. Although other relations had better claims to the Danish throne, for one reason or another, many linked to the divisive issue of the duchies of Schleswig and Holstein, each of these claimants was deemed unsuitable by one Great Power or another.

The Schleswig-Holstein Question was one of the thorniest political problems of the period, and the Great Powers were keen to avoid going to war over it, or to having the Danish throne occupied by a monarch who would tip the scales of the balance of power in favour of one or another of them. Prince Christian was deemed the most likely candidate to maintain the balance of power in favour of the *status quo*, so was designated, under the *London Protocol of 1852*, heir presumptive to the Danish throne. This was ratified the following year by the *Danish Law of Succession*, known more correctly as the *Royal Ordinance settling the Succession to the Crown on Prince Christian of Glücksburg*. Once this was promulgated, the whole family moved exponentially up the royal ladder, becoming princes and princesses of the kingdom of Denmark, rather than remaining the scions of a ducal house. The path was now cleared for the family to achieve the ascendency it would reach in the second half of the nineteenth century.

Previously the Glücksburg family's way of life had been relatively ordinary by royal standards. In real terms, it was resolutely upper-middle-class. Although it remained so even after their elevation – the Danish royal family was notoriously penurious by the standards of the day – thereafter they enjoyed the status and recognition that went along with being heirs to a crown. Their upward trajectory was helped considerably by the family being good-looking, the girls especially so. Their combination of good looks, grandeur and ordinariness had some unexpected side effects, for the family was cosily domestic in a way royal families were not. This was one of the things that appealed to the heirs to the great empires whom the girls subsequently married.

Most royals at the time were deliberately starved of affection by their parents in the mistaken belief that this would strengthen their characters and toughen them up in preparation for their obligation-ridden futures, with the result that they had no idea how to create the happy family atmosphere for which most people yearn. The Glücksburgs were a notable exception to the rule: a gift they shared with the Strathmore family, whence Lilibet's mother Elizabeth originated. The importance of this quality cannot be exaggerated. On it hinged the fate of several crowns.

Although the domesticity the Danish royals enjoyed enhanced their own private lives, this down-to-earth way of life ultimately had a tremendous impact upon the lives of their descendants and the subjects of those descendants, including Philip and Lilibet. This was the first time bourgeois values and the appreciation of personal satisfaction had featured as a valid alternative in the way of life of regnant royal families. The consequences would turn out to be both positive and disastrous, depending on what monarchy was involved.

Within a few years of the Glücksburg elevation, it was clear that all the major royal families of Europe were going to be affected by the bourgeois tastes of the Danish Royal Family. This was because the house of Schleswig-Holstein-Sonderburg-Glücksburg began forming a series of marital alliances, some of which culminated before Christian had even become king, with the three leading European Empires – the British, the German, and the Russian – as well as with several lesser powers. Christian and Louise's eldest son, the future King Frederick VIII, married the King of Sweden's sole child, Princess Louise, while their eldest daughter Alexandra married Queen Victoria's heir Bertie, the Prince of Wales, on 10th March 1863. This preceded Christian's ascension to the Danish throne by eight months, by which time the second son, 17 year old Prince Vilhelm, was already a king in his own right, having been elected King George I of the Hellenes by the Greek Assembly on 18th March OS [30th March NS] 1863, one day shy of three weeks after the marriage of his sister Alexandra to the heir to the British throne.

A year later, the second daughter, Dagmar, was betrothed to the Russian Tsarevitch, Nicholas Alexandrovitch, and when he lay dying of meningitis in 1865, he asked that his fiancée marry his younger brother Alexander, which she did in 1866. Yet another daughter, Thyra, married Ernst Augustus, Crown Prince of Hanover and only son of King George V of Hanover. However, her father-in-law was deprived of his crown in 1866, when he sided with Austria in the Austro-Prussian War. Following Prussia's victory, Hanover was annexed by Prussia. Although Thyra was styled as HRH The Crown Princess of Hanover, and became Queen Consort of Hanover in pretence upon the death of her father-in-law, she was also a British duchess twice over through her husband, who remained the Duke of Cumberland and Teviotdale, as well as the Duchess of Brunswick-Luneburg. The family entertained hopes that the German Emperor would restore her father-in-law's throne. This would have meant that Christian IX would have five of his six children positioned to sit on thrones. While that was not to be, Thyra's son George William did marry Kaiser Wilhelm II's only daughter, Victoria Louise, and, to complete the circle, their daughter Frederica would marry Prince Philip's cousin Paul, and reign with him as his queen consort, justly earning Christian IX his title of Father-in-Law of Europe.

Throughout the nineteenth century, Greece's monarchy appeared to flourish under the able and committed hand of King George I. Greece was the first state in Europe to have its Assembly elected by secret, direct, universal male suffrage. This came about when the eighteen year old king sent an ultimatum to the National Assembly, which had itself elected him to the throne, after their deliberations about a new constitution stalled, to the effect that he would abdicate unless it passed the liberal constitution under which he had been elected to rule. The new constitution was duly passed, and on 28th October 1864 he took the oath to defend the constitution he had done so much to have installed. Thereafter, Greek policy was dictated by the Megali Idea, the objective being to unify all Greeks within a single state. Some of the Greek islands and important cities of Ancient Greece such as Smyrna and Thessaloniki were still in the possession of the Ottoman Empire, and there was much toing and froing for the remainder of the century as the Greek king and his people sought to gain autonomy over such islands as Crete. Usually his close ties to the British and Russian thrones worked in Greece's favour, such as when that country crossed the Macedonian border in 1897. The Ottoman Sultan, Abdul Hamid II, declared war, overrunning the Hellenic Army with a celerity which was paradoxically its saving grace. Both Britain (where his sister Alexandra was Princess of Wales) and Russia (where his sister was Dowager Empress and his nephew Nicholas II Tsar) intervened to ensure that the worst consequences of Greece's defeat were mitigated, for Greece's weakness was so apparent that punishing it severely would have been viewed as remiss.

Although Greece had to turn over Crete to an international administration, within a year there was such unrest there that Britain was able to use that, and the murder of its Vice-Consul, to back the installation of Prince George of Greece as Governor-General of Crete under the suzerainty of the Ottoman Empire. Bit by bit, Greece was achieving its objective of Greek national unification, with the assistance of its king's relations.

By the end of the century Greece was enjoying unprecedented prosperity, with an electorate that enjoyed rights few possessed in any other state. Greece now also began putting to tangible use the lessons learnt from its defeat at the hands of the Ottomans in 1897, following the election of Eleftherios Venizelos as Prime Minister. Like King George I, he understood the necessity of having a well-trained standing army, and, though all the royal males had been forced to resign their commissions in the army by a military league known as the *Stratiotikos Syndesmos*, in a precursor to a military coup that would fail when the king supported the Hellenic Parliament, Venizelos nevertheless agreed to Crown Prince Constantine being reinstated as Inspector-General of the Army, and subsequently Commander-in-Chief, following his electoral victory in 1910.

Greece, of course, was intent on modernising, and with British and French help, the Greek navy was subjected to the same degree of improvement as the Greek army. The French contribution would turn out to be something of a mixed blessing for the crown, as the French advisors fostered the nascent republican movement within the Hellenic armed forces. This was not an altogether unwelcome consequence for the Prime Minister, who, tangential to Russian foreign policy, also had ambitions to unite the Christians in the Balkans against the Ottoman Empire. This aim of the pan-Christian movement made him immensely popular in Greece, and gave him tremendous prestige in Greek Orthodox circles, but he was playing with fire, for the Balkan Question was not as straightforward as the politicians and religious leaders who sought to exploit it for their own benefit perceived.

In part this was because some of the Balkan territories had a heavy preponderance of Muslims within their borders, so the aim of unifying the Christians of the Balkans was redolent of possibilities for present as well as future conflict. The world would witness this time and again during the twentieth century, with Slav turning against Slav, Christian against Moslem, Christian against Christian, Moslem against Christian.

Putting aside, for the moment, the ambitions of the Pan-Slavic movement, which would ultimately result in Prince Philip of Greece spending most of his life outside of his homeland and which would also help trigger the First World War, the conduct of the King of Serbia is a case in point which shows how acceptable rampant Slavic territorial aggrandisement was to such Great Powers as Britain, France, and Russia, even when it conflicted with every moral and legal ethic. Serbia had triggered the First World War when in 1914 it assisted Gavrilo Princip to assassinate the heir to the Austro-Hungarian throne, Archduke Franz Ferdinand, and his morganatic wife Sophie, Duchess of Hohenberg. Notwithstanding its complicity in the start of history's largest bloodbath, at the end of the war this king nevertheless managed, with the connivance of the Allied Powers, to expand his territory to become the king of the Serbs, Croats and Slovenes. In so doing, he gobbled up the Hapsburg territories of Croatia and Slovenia, despite his government's hand in the assassination of the Austro-Hungarian heir to the throne. As if this were not enough, the Allied Powers rubber-stamped his acquisition of the kingdom of Montenegro, a disgrace when one considers that King Nicholas of Montenegro had been an ally and should have been rewarded by the Allies rather than dethroned by them.

The Balkan Question did not get any less convoluted as the 20th century evolved. Nor did the rights of the people and their legal representatives enjoy greater protection than they had earlier. Even when the Great Powers no longer had a motive to exploit Balkan conflict for their own gain, as France had done in the run up to the First World War with its objective of regaining Alsace and Lorraine after its loss to Germany at the end of the Franco-Prussian War in 1871, their conduct as the century closed was unedifying in the extreme. In 1995 the region contributed to one of the greatest of all human atrocities, when the Moslem Bosniaks of Srebrenica were annihilated by their Christian, Serbian brothers, while being sheltered in a nominally safe area under UN protection. The world watched in horror. But it did nothing to protect the very people who had been encouraged to seek refuge under UN protection, as UN troops stood by impotently and the massacre progressed unimpeded.

This high-risk strategy of Balkan affiliation, which would work so well for France during the First World War, but so disastrously for Russia and the Greek king, was very much in the future in 1911, as Prime Minister Venizelos sought to exploit the instability in the Balkans to Greece's advantage. Under his aegis Greece formed the Balkan League, along with Montenegro, Serbia and Bulgaria, all countries with crowns connected to Philip and Lilibet's ancestors. The outbreak of the First Balkan War in 1912 saw those four Balkan nations achieve significant gains against the Ottoman Empire. Greece alone conquered much of Greek-populated Macedonia, but less than three weeks after signing the Treaty of London on 30th June 1913, Greece and Serbia repudiated significant particulars of the pre-treaty and continued to occupy territory they had agreed to forego. Bulgaria (whose Tsar was a member of the Saxe-Coburg-Gotha dynasty along with Lilibet's grandfather King George V) felt justifiably aggrieved at being double-crossed by its allies, so attacked them. Montenegro (whose two princesses were married to Russian Grand Dukes), Romania (whose Crown Princess was born Princess Marie of Edinburgh and was George V's first cousin), and the Ottoman Empire, then attacked Bulgaria, which was forced at the ensuing Treaty of Bucharest to surrender most of its gains from the First Balkan War.

By this time, Philip's grandfather, King George I, had decided to abdicate in favour of his son Constantine following the celebrations planned for his golden jubilee for October 1913. The year before, he had enjoyed the triumph of riding into Thessaloniki, the great and ancient second city of the Greeks captured from the Ottomans, with Crown Prince Constantine and Venizelos. This was one of the most glorious moments of his reign, but it would also lead to his death.

At first, George was left to enjoy his triumph. Tahsin Pasha, the city's Ottoman ruler, had surrendered it to Greek forces on 26th October OS (8th November NS) 1912. The Bulgarians also coveted this great and ancient city of the classical world, and this Ottoman functionary put the Bulgarian army in its place when they arrived the day after the Greeks, and sought, nevertheless, to gain a right to Thessaloniki by having him surrender it to them. 'I have only one Thessaloniki, and I have already surrendered it,' he stated ironically, causing them to have to turn tail and depart without the jewel they sought so dearly for Bulgaria's crown.

George I, however, would not live to witness the annexation of this major city of classical antiquity, along with the rest of Greek Macedonia. This took place when the Treaty of Bucharest concluded the Second Balkan War in 1913, by which time Philip's grandfather had been assassinated.

On 18th March 1913, George I was taking his afternoon constitutional when, at 5.15 pm, a failed political activist named Alexandros Schinas came up behind him. The monarch had always walked about Athens without meaningful police protection, which had earned him the respect and regard of his people. Seeing no reason to change the habit of a lifetime when he was surrounded by his fellow Greeks in this newly acquired city, he was an unprotected target. From a distance of no more than two paces, Schinas shot George I in the back. The bullet entered below the shoulder blade, pierced his heart and lungs, and Greece's longest-serving king died almost immediately.

Schinas was immediately taken into custody. When asked whether he had no 'pity' for his country, he replied that he was against all government. Police enquiries revealed that he was an alcoholic as well as a visionary who had set up a school for anarchists which had been closed down by the authorities and resulted in two of his colleagues being imprisoned, though he had somehow managed to slip through the net. He was tortured to reveal the names of any accomplices, but failed to give up any, and on 6th May he was either hurled from or jumped out of the window of the *gendarmerie* in Thessoloniki. His death was ruled suicide, though there was the suspicion that he might have been silenced before trial because he was patently unstable and might have been a figure of sympathy despite his actions.

George I's assassination, together with the way the authorities dealt with the assassin, was symptomatic of the incendiary nature of Balkan politics. The Balkans were by then regarded as the world's number one trouble spot. As the world was being sucked into the Great War, and Greece and its royal family were being propelled into ever-increasing instability, what was truly exceptional was how committed each of the neophyte sovereigns was to the interests of the country which had nominated him to be its king. This was to the exclusion of all family considerations, because of course they were all related to one another. Loyalty to country figured way before loyalty to family, or indeed to the county of origin. This was as true of the Greek monarchy as it was of the Bulgarian or Romanian. It therefore explains why the Bulgarian Tsar did not allow family considerations, or indeed a previous alliance with Greece and Serbia, to influence him when Bulgaria attacked those two countries on 16th June OS/29th June NS, 1913.

The *casus belli* for what became the Second Balkan War was straightforward enough. Bulgaria had agreed to a reduced share of the spoils at the end of the First Balkan War on the understanding that Greece and Serbia would give up territory they had occupied during the war. When Greece continued to occupy Macedonia and Thessaloniki, and Serbia remained in occupation of the land it had grabbed, Bulgaria felt it had no option but to go to war against its former allies. Montenegro, the fourth of the Balkan states which had formed the Balkan League, now joined forces against Bulgaria with its two other allies and their former adversary the Ottoman Empire. Romania, which had claims of its own against territory Bulgaria had won in the First Balkan War, joined the fight. Bulgaria was quickly trounced, losing most of the territory it had won in the Treaty of Bucharest at the end of the First Balkan War. It also had to surrender territory to the Ottomans in the Treaty of Constantinople to conclude this latest war. This reversal only added to the instability in the Balkans, for now Bulgaria had a grouse against its former allies and neighbours.

Although the throne King Constantine I inherited following his father's assassination appeared to be secure, the volatility in the Balkans destabilised it. The Balkan Question had by now supplanted the Schleswig-Holstein Question as a primary source of danger to the Great Powers. The fact that the lesser powers were seeking to exploit its intractability to their own advantage only added to an already incendiary situation. To his credit, King Constantine was one of the few European heads of state or government who saw the dangers inherent in what became the Third Balkan War, when Austria declared war against Serbia in the summer of 1914. It was inevitable that the war would spread far and wide as a result of the series of interlocking treaties that obliged the various countries to go to war in the event that one state was attacked by another. This was no matter how justified the initial source of the conflict was.

Within days of Austria's ultimatum to Serbia, which was a direct result of Serbia's unofficial involvement in the assassination of their heir to the throne Archduke Franz Ferdinand, the Third Balkan War had become the Great War. Although now known to us as the First World War, it remained known as the Great War until 1939, when the German invasion of Poland equally quickly resulted in the Second World War.

The Great War would prove to be disastrous for the Greek royal family. Without it, there is every possibility that Prince Philip of Greece's fate would have been different. Certainly, the many issues which arose to destabilise the Greek monarchy and ensure that his life be led outside of Greece, would not have existed. It is a truism that the whole course of history would also have been different, but the Great War did happen, and the effects it had upon Philip's family put him on the path that would take him from Mon Repos in Greece to Buckingham Palace in England.

Few even-handed historians would disagree that Austro-Hungary had an unequivocal and absolute right to issue Serbia with the ultimatum it did on 23rd July 1914. State sponsored terrorism ending in the death of an heir to the throne was indefensible under any code of ethics, as well as unlawful under international law. Regrettably for Western Civilisation, those series of interlocking treaties, designed to protect the interests of each state, had the opposite effect, assuring the transmogrification of a local, Central European conflict, into a world war. In his excellent study *The Sleepwalkers: How Europe Went to War in 1914*, (Sir) Christopher Clark, the Regius Professor of History at the University of Cambridge, shows how the toxic alliances between France, Great Britain and Russia on the one hand, and Germany and Austria-Hungary on the other, ensured that once Austria-Hungary issued its ultimatum, and the Serbians failed to satisfy the demands made therein, an almighty conflagration was all but inevitable. Serbia's ally Russia, lured into the conflict under the fallacy that the state of Serbia needed protection on Pan-Slavic grounds, despite its sponsoring of terrorism on a state level, honoured its treaty with Serbia, and came to its aid by putting the Russian army on alert on 25th July 1914. This was before the ultimatum had even had a chance to expire. Although the Russians had not technically mobilised their army, it was so massive, and the distances so vast, that there was little actual difference between a general mobilisation, which threatened war, and an alert, which was not supposed to do so. The Germans and the Austro-Hungarians were therefore under the impression that their territories were being threatened by the Russian army being mobilised, and reacted accordingly. By the time Austria-Hungary declared war against Serbia at 11am on 28th July 1914, the coming conflagration had become unavoidable.

Kaiser Wilhelm II, who would be demonised by Allied propaganda, articulated a point of view that, with time, has come to find favour with many unbiased historians. On 1st August 1914, he wrote in a lengthy commentary, 'For I no longer doubt that England, Russia and France have among themselves – knowing that our treaty obligations compel us to support Austria-Hungary – to use the Austro-Serbian conflict as a pretext for waging a war of annihilation against us.'

Not fully appreciating the way in which French policy had been pursued over the previous forty three years in an attempt to regain its lost provinces of Alsace and Lorraine, the Kaiser ignored France's goal, and continued laying more blame on Britain than was warranted, while allocating less to France than it deserved. 'Our dilemma over keeping faith with the old and honourable Emperor has been exploited to create a situation which gives England the excuse she has been seeking to annihilate us with the spurious appearance of justice on the pretext that she is helping France and maintaining the Balance of Power in Europe, i.e. playing off all European states for her own benefit against us.'

French exploitation of the Balkan Question, which Professor Clark brilliantly addresses in his treatise, had, over the four previous decades, been that nation's objective for creating a *casus belli* whose sole purpose was to regain the provinces of Alsace and Lorraine that it had lost to Germany at the end of the Franco-Prussian War. French foreign policy objectives had been executed between 1871 and 1914 with the sophistication and cold-blooded realpolitik which explained why France had been The Great Nation for the length of time it had. These objectives required an alliance between Russia and France, which the French spent the intervening decades cultivating. Only through such an alliance could France take advantage of the parallel alliance between Germany and Austria. British involvement was an accidental by-product, the icing on the cake which turned out to be a welcome, but unpredictable and uncalculated-for, bonus.

The French intended to, and did, take advantage of those four decades of instability in the Balkans. Their aim was to create a situation whereby Russia, as the leading Slavic nation, would feel compelled to come to the aid of its weaker brethren in the Balkans. This could only be accomplished by fomenting trouble between the minor Balkan states and the Austro-Hungarian Empire. This the French did by a series of dextrous moves. Ironically, the British, who prided themselves on possessing a degree of insight second to no other European power, would take the remainder of the twentieth century before they too began to discern what French foreign policy objectives had been. Meanwhile the Russians, who were generally viewed as being less perceptive, discerned what was going on at the time. In his informed and fascinating memoirs, Tsar Nicholas II's cousin and brother-in-law Grand Duke Alexander Mikhailovitch, who had created the Russian air force following a distinguished naval career, asserted that one of the major reasons for the First World War was France's determination to regain the provinces of Alsace and Lorraine which it had lost in the Franco-Prussian War. Grand Duke Alexander saw clearly how France exploited Serbian ambitions to become a pan-Slavic Balkan state. This would ultimately bring about the assassination of Archduke Franz Ferdinand, which in turn triggered the Austro-German treaty whereby one Germanic empire would come to the assistance of the other in the event that either was threatened by a third party. This in turn would trigger the treaty between France and Russia, whereby Russia would come to the assistance of France in the event that she was threatened by Germany.

The dye was cast as a result of Serbian involvement in Archduke Franz Ferdinand's assassination in June 1914. Germany then found itself threatened by Russia's armed forces massed on its eastern border. France's long-term goal remained the hope that Alsace and Lorraine would be returned to it at the end of any ensuing war between itself and Germany.

In reality Germany had no argument with Russia at that time. Such argument as existed was actually between Austria and Russia, which was supporting Serbia. However, once Russia threatened Germany as a result of its alliance with Serbia, Germany would be threatened by the prospect of being attacked on its western borders by France, as a consequence of France's alliance with Russia, and by Russia itself on its eastern borders. Germany's most likely response, as all the chancelleries in Europe supposed, was to strike pre-emptively against the perceived threat.

This is precisely what happened to trigger the First World War. Faced with the possibility of a war on its eastern and western borders, Germany implemented the Schlieffen Plan. This required it to occupy Luxembourg as a precursor to entering France via Belgium and knocking that enemy out before turning its attention to its eastern front. The Germans were only too aware that Russia, with its vast natural resources and manpower, was the enemy to watch, irrespective of the present state of its armed forces. These were well known to be woefully inadequate as a result of Russia having lost the Russo-Japanese war a decade earlier, but it was nevertheless an empire of such vastness that its very inexhaustibility would ultimately assure it of success in any war of protracted duration.

Declarations of war between the various antagonists, the Triple Entente on the one hand, and the Central Powers on the other, therefore clattered down on the various chancelleries in Europe during the month of August 1914. The scale was truly unprecedented. France and Russia were joined by the United Kingdom, Serbia, Montenegro, Belgium and Japan against Germany, Austria-Hungary and, in November, the Ottoman Empire. The following year Italy and San Marino would join the Allied side, while Bulgaria joined the Central Powers. In 1916 Romania and Portugal would declare for the Allies, and in 1917 the United States, Cuba, Bolivia, Greece, Siam, Liberia, China, Peru, Uruguay, Brazil, Ecuador and Panama, concluding in 1918 with Guatemala, Nicaragua, Costa Rica, Haiti, and Honduras.

Aggrieved, Kaiser Wilhelm II said, 'To think that George (King George V of the United Kingdom) and Nicky (Emperor of All the Russias) should have played me false! If my grandmother had been alive, she would never have allowed it.' In that he might well have been right. It is inconceivable that Queen Victoria would have sat back and failed to find a solution to the conflict which saw her grandson's British Empire pitted in tandem with her granddaughter's Russian Empire against her other grandson's German Empire.

No one was more aware of the potential for trouble that existed as a result of the interconnections of the European royal houses than the Greek king. Constantine was married to the Kaiser's sister, Sophie. His mother was the Russian Grand Duchess Olga Konstantinovna. His close cousins were respectively Empress of Russia, King of Denmark, King of Norway, Queen of Roumania, Queen of Spain, and British King-Emperor. He was also connected to the kings of Montenegro, Italy, Bulgaria and Belgium. His brother George was married to the French Princess Marie Bonaparte; his brother Nicholas to Grand Duchess Elena Vladimirovna of Russia; his other brother Andrew to Queen Victoria's granddaughter, Princess Alice of Battenberg; and his sister Marie was the wife of Grand Duke George Mikhailovitch of Russia. If it was inevitable that cousin would end up fighting cousin, brother, brother, friend, friend, what would prove surprising to the uninitiated was how utterly committed each royal house was to its country. No one put family or personal feelings above their nation's interests, though, as the war progressed, and attrition followed, many would be unfairly suspected of doing so. Although few people appreciated that Western Civilisation as it had evolved up to that point was about to come to an end, not everyone was blind to the consequences that a general European war would bring in its wake. There was significant and justifiable opposition to the war in each country, though once the declarations were made the opponents were silenced by the enthusiasts. King Constantine I of the Hellenes, however, would prove to be one of the few heads of state or government who understood the dangers inherent in such interlocking turmoil. He resolved to keep Greece neutral. This had little to do with family feeling and all to do with protecting Greek interests, which were threatened irrespective of which side Greece took in the conflict.

Although Queen Sophie was the Kaiser's sister, they had never had a close relationship. Their parents, Emperor and Empress Frederick (the British Princess Royal, Victoria, always called Vicky in the family), had had a genuinely happy marriage, but their children were divided into two groups. Neither Frederick nor Vickie nor their children benefitted from the cosy, bourgeois domesticity of the Danish royal family, for though both their families would end up being allied to them martially, neither the German Crown Prince nor the British Princess Royal was a descendant of Christian IX of Denmark. Frederick, Vickie and their children had all had resolutely traditional royal upbringings, with the result that Kaiser Wilhelm II had a disastrous relationship with his parents, his mother in particular.

Wilhelm and his two younger siblings Charlotte and Heinrich, fell under the sway of their paternal grandparents, King Wilhelm of Prussia, later Emperor Wilhelm I of Germany, and his wife, the former Princess Augusta of Saxe-Weimar-Eisenach. Wilhelm and his Minister President, Otto von Bismarck, were out of sympathy politically with the children's parents. Frederick and Vickie were decidedly liberal, in favour of constitutional monarchy, workers' rights and parliamentary democracy. They had been much influenced by the political ideals of her father, Prince Albert of Saxe-Co-burg-Gotha, the Prince Consort, all of which were, in varying degrees, antipathetic to Wilhelm I and Bismarck. Their goal was to achieve German unification under Prussian rule. This they did in 1871, when Bismarck unified the disparate German states and the German Empire came into being following the Franco-Prussian War.

Germany's political direction was a hotly disputed issue while Frederick's father Emperor Wilhelm I was on the throne. Otto von Bismarck was even more conservative than his conservative sovereign, and both he and Wilhelm I set about forming the political ideals of the heir's heir, Wilhelm II, and the spare, Heinrich. To do so, they had to counter the influence of the boys' parents. The couple's three eldest children were therefore removed from the day to day control of their parents into the custody of the aged monarch and his Chancellor, as Bismarck became following Prussia becoming the leading state of the German Empire. Many would argue that their success was absolute, for Wilhelm II fully imbibed the militaristic culture of his grandfather and Bismarck, with tragic consequences for the empire that those two men had created.

Queen Sophie of Greece (always known as Sossy within the family), being one of the younger children, was left to the care of her parents, along with the two other daughters, Margaret (Mossie) and Viktoria (Moretta), who was named after her mother and grandmother, Queen Victoria. There were two other brothers, Sigismund and Waldemar, the former dying before Sophie was born, the latter at the age of 11 when she was 8. All those children were deemed unimportant politically because they were, in the case of the males, far enough down the line of succession to stand no chance of acceding to the throne, and in the case of the females, too young to be companions for their two eldest brothers, whose proximity to the throne made it imperative that their characters and beliefs be moulded to fit the militaristic ideal that the Emperor and his Iron Chancellor believed imperative for the future success of the great empire they were intent on creating.

Crown Prince Frederick and Crown Princess Victoria were loving parents as well as formidably intelligent. She had made herself unpopular within Court circles in Berlin because she made no secret of her belief in the superiority of all things British, including, indeed especially, British constitutional democracy. That meant that the Crown Princess and her husband, who shared her political beliefs, were out of step with Germany's prevailing culture at the time. However, they were blithe to criticism, for they believed their day would come when Frederick succeeded to the throne. In the meantime, they bided their time and brought the younger children up to have a high regard for liberalism and all things British. Sophie frequently visited her grandmother, staying with Queen Victoria for long periods, especially at Osbourne House, where she and her siblings would spend days collecting shells by the seashore. They were all devastated when their favourite brother and their parents' favourite son Waldemar died of diphtheria. Thereafter, Vickie clung even more strongly to Sophie and her sisters Mossie and Moretta, whom their mother took to calling 'my trio'.

It was inevitable that there would be conflict within a family that was, on the one hand, militaristic, autocratic and suspicious of all things British (to include British Parliamentary democracy), and on the other liberal, parliamentarian and lovers of all things British (to include the self-same Parliamentary democracy). When Sophie was seventeen, she came to England to celebrate Queen Victoria's golden jubilee. The old queen was encouraged by her granddaughter's growing relationship with the Greek Crown Prince Constantine, writing, 'Is there a chance of Sophie's marrying Tino? It would be very nice for her, for he is very good.' The romance gathered pace the following year when Constantine represented Greece at the funeral of Sophie's grandfather, Emperor Wilhelm I, in Berlin in March 1888. Sophie's father was now the German emperor, but the relationship developed at a particularly trying time, for Frederick was dying painfully of throat cancer, and with him were also dying the hopes and ambitions he, his consort, and the liberals in Germany had harboured for the empire.

The Emperor Frederick died on 15th June 1888, and Sophie's engagement to Constantine was announced on 3rd September. Despite Queen Victoria's approval, the match was not universally applauded. Her brother Wilhelm II was hardly pleased by it, nor was the Greek Queen. While Queen Olga had reservations because Sophie was Lutheran and she and the Greek Royal Family were Greek Orthodox, Wilhelm II's concerns were not merely limited to religion. He took his position as Head of the Evangelical State Church of Prussia's older provinces seriously, but, as long as Sophie did not convert, the religious differences could be accommodated. Rather more serious, however, was Germany's ever-increasingly close relationship with the Ottoman Empire and Greece's antipathy towards its former suzerain. Nor were the French pleased, considering the marriage a step in the wrong direction just when their influence in Greece was growing as they gained another important foothold in the Balkans by assisting with improvements in the Greek army and navy (and in the process, encouraged the budding republican movement).

Where the Greek public were concerned, however, the marriage was a cause for celebration. Two years later, Sophie produced a son, George, and decided to convert to Orthodoxy after gaining the support of her mother, now known as the Empress Frederick, and of her grandmother Queen Victoria. When she informed her brother of her decision, Wilhelm II threatened to exclude her from membership of the Prussian Royal Family, then banned her from entering Germany for three years. Sophie's feelings are neatly encapsulated in a telegram she sent to her mother, which ended with the words, 'Mad. Never mind.'

Sophie and Constantine would go on to have five more children. Amidst the turmoil of Greek politics, she remained a constant. She opened soup kitchens, led various initiatives in the field of education, founded and developed hospitals and orphanages, and in 1896 founded the Union of Greek Women, for the benefit of refugees from the Ottoman Empire.

The following year, Greece was defeated in the Thirty Days' War against the Ottoman Empire. Damagingly for Sophie and the monarchy, her brother Wilhelm II and his government vociferously supported the Ottomans and, when approached to act as mediator at the end of the war, demanded humiliating concessions from the Greeks. His actions gave a spur to the burgeoning republican movement, causing Sophie and Constantine to leave the country until the dust settled.

The couple returned and settled into useful occupation in a country that was intrinsically and extrinsically volatile. Greek domestic politics had always been such, but the external pressures caused by the various powers seeking to exploit Balkan instability for their own benefit aggravated an already inflammatory situation. Nevertheless, no one expected Constantine and Sophie to ascend the throne at the moment of one of modern Greece's greatest glories, the return of ancient Thessaloniki to Greek control, but they did, as a result of King George I's assassination.

Although feted in the country at the time of their accession, Constantine and Sophie's popularity would be put to the test with the advent of the Great War. Their internationalism gave them greater insight into the realities of Greece's predicament than that possessed by its politicians, with their narrower, more nationalistic perspectives. They knew from their personal knowledge of Kaiser Wilhelm II how reliable an enemy he would be, and could see no advantage to Greece entering the war on either side. In their opinion, the only viable course of action for Greece was neutrality. However, Prime Minister Venizelos wanted to attack the Ottoman Empire and thereby make further territorial gains in advancement of the Megali Idea, which had become something of an obsession with him. Constantine and Sophie, however, appreciated the danger in such a high-risk strategy. What would happen if Germany came to the aid of the Ottoman Empire? Greece might well find itself occupied. This turned out to be a prescient perspective, for within months of the first declarations of war the Ottoman Empire had indeed entered the fray on Germany and Austria-Hungary's side. Had

Greece attacked the Ottoman Empire, Germany would have occupied Greece.

Greece was simply too strategically important to the Allies for them to allow it to remain neutral. The Allied governments and Venizelos did everything in their power to force Constantine to enter the war on their side. Following the debacle at Gallipoli, when Britain and its Anzac troops had to withdraw ignominiously from what had been sold to the people as an assured success to capture the Dardanelles Straits, Constantine's neutral stance appeared to be vindicated. This, however, only led the Allies and Venizelos to resort to greater lengths to force Greece to enter a war which was not going so well for them as they had imagined it would, but which they discerned would be easier to prosecute if they could use Greek territory and troops. Although the Greek populace were supportive of the neutralist policies of their king, the ensuing split between the political elite was so severe that it became known as the National Schism.

The Allied press were vociferous in portraying the Greek king and queen as traitors to the Allied cause, with the French going so far as to accuse the queen of regularly providing fuel to German submarines from the beaches of Phalerum. On 3rd October 1915 the Greek Prime Minister even went to the extreme of inviting the Allies to occupy Thessaloniki. This caused a permanent rupture with the king, who regarded Venizelos's action as tantamount to sedition.

Nor were the French passive. They were behind a series of plots to kidnap or assassinate the king and queen, and were strongly suspected of being behind the fire that started on Bastille Day 1916, in the forest surrounding Tatoi. The royal family was in residence. Several members of the royal family, including the king, were injured. Sophie saved her youngest child, Princess Katharine, from certain death by running two kilometres into the forest with the baby in her arms. Tatoi was largely destroyed and sixteen or eighteen, depending on sources, soldiers and palace staff were killed.

At the time, Constantine's sister-in-law, Princess George, the former Princess Marie Bonaparte, was conducting an open affair with Aristide Briand, France's Prime Minister. By December 1916, the French navy was shelling Athens and Briand was suspected, alternately, of having seduced Marie to bring about Greece's entry into the war on the Allied side, or of hoping to replace the neutral king with his mistress's husband.

Although the Germans behaved more correctly, there was also pressure from them for Greece to enter the war on their side.

It was inevitable that, under such overwhelming pressure from the warring Great Powers, and a Prime Minister who was actively promoting Greece's entry into the war on the Allied side, something would give. Constantine and his heir George, who was also unfairly suspected of harbouring German sympathies, were sent into exile while the second son Alexander became a puppet king. The remainder of the family was then expelled, with the exception of the newly-proclaimed King Alexander, who was effectively a prisoner of the Allies and Venizelos. He was banned from having any contact with his family, a ban which persisted for the duration of his reign.

Greece was now at war with the Central Powers. Following the end of the Great War in 1918, Greece increased in size by about a third. At the Paris Peace Conference its territorial conquests were acknowledged through the treaties of Neuilly (1919) and Sevres (1920).

Venizelos's gamble had paid off, but he now made the fatal mistake of unleashing his battle-weary troops against Turkey. He invaded Anatolia beyond the Greek protectorate of Smyrna, in the hope of taking Ankara, the present-day capital of Turkey, as a precursor to occupying and annexing Constantinople, then the Turkish capital, in the hope of fulfilling the Greek ideal of the Megali Idea. The Turks under Mustafa Kemal Pasha, later the Father of Modern Turkey known as Ataturk, resisted fiercely, in the knowledge that failure to repulse the Greeks would result in the destruction of what remained of their state, which was still known as the Ottoman Empire although its fate was still being decided by the victorious Allies, who were apportioning, sometimes conflictingly, its territories.

Although the French wanted Greece to be a republic, the British saw that dethroning the king would decrease their influence while increasing that of France. To maintain the balance of power, Alexander was allowed to remain on the throne even after he married a commoner, Aspasia Manos, much to the disapproval of the Greek government as well as of his own family. She was not made queen, received no royal title (she was known as Madame Manos), and prevented from taking part in any official functions. However, she was allowed back into Greece with the king and became pregnant. But he remained a virtual prisoner. For instance, when he had been visiting Paris and his mother telephoned to speak to him, not only was she not put through, but he was not even informed that she had called. He was not allowed to write to or receive letters from any other member of the Greek royal family, all of whom had been sent into exile following the expulsion of King Constantine I.

# Chapter II

Tragedy, however, was about to bring about dramatic changes. Within months of Alexander's return to Greece with Aspasia Manos, he was bitten by the pet Barbary macaque of the steward of the palace's grapevines, when he intervened to break up a fight between it and his pet Alsatian dog. The wound turned septic and it became apparent that he was dying. He started crying out for his mother, but the Greek government refused to allow her to return from exile in Switzerland. Finally, they agreed to allow in the Dowager Queen, Olga, who regrettably arrived twelve hours after her grandson's death shortly after 4pm on 25th October 1920.

The rest of the royal family was refused permission to attend the funeral. Alexander's tombstone shows that the family never recognised his reign as being legitimate. Unlike all the other Greek kings, whose tombstones bear the inscription 'King of the Hellenes, Prince of Denmark,' his reads 'Alexander, son of the King of the Hellenes, Prince of Denmark. He ruled in place of his father from 14 June 1917 to 25 October 1920.' The use of the word 'ruled' drove the point home. Had there been any recognition of the legality of his occupancy of the throne, the word used would have been 'reigned'.

Alexander's death, however, brought matters to a head. With the country still at war with the Ottoman Empire, and the British not in favour of a republic, despite Venizelos's support for one, and the Greek government finding King Constantine and Crown Prince George unacceptable, the Greek parliament sought to appease the conflicting parties by offering the throne to Prince Paul, the youngest son. He refused it, and the ensuing legislative elections of 1920 became a bitter fight between the pro-republican Venizelists and the supporters of King Constantine. Venizelos was roundly defeated and he left the country of his own accord, and the Dowager Queen became regent until Constantine could return. This return was overwhelmingly ratified by a referendum, demonstrating the degree of support the old king and the monarchy possessed amongst the people. The rest of the royal family also returned, though Prince George and his wife, Marie Bonaparte, still spent most of their time in France, where her affair with Aristide Briand petered out.

Prince Philip's parents Andrew and Alice, however, returned with the intention of making Greece their permanent home once more. Of all the Greek royals, Andrew was the most assertively Greek. He regarded himself as Greek, spoke in no other language unless he had to, and had originally entered the Greek Army with the intention of serving his country through it for the remainder of his life. When he was reinstated in the army with the rank of major-general, he was happier than he had been in years, but the joy would be short lived.

Greece was still pursuing its war against the Turks, which was going badly, partly, as Andrew stated, because of the incompetence of his superior officers, but also because the Ottomans understood that this was one war they could not afford to lose. Andrew was given command of the II Army Corps during the Battle of Sakarya and he was ordered, on 19th September 1921, to attack Turkish positions, an order which he judged 'ill-conceived panic'. He refused to follow an order which he foresaw would result in the pointless loss of the troops under his command, and pursued his own battle plan, to the consternation of his commanding general, Anastasios Papoulos. The Turks then attacked and Andrew's troops were forced to retreat. The prince was made to go on leave for two months, after which he was posted elsewhere while General Papoulos was replaced by General Georgios Hatzianestis. Foreseeing the debacle that would inevitably ensue if the government continued conducting the war the way it had been, Andrew was then transferred to the Supreme Army Council before being given command of the V Army Corps in Epirus and the Ionian Islands. He left behind his wife and infant son, Philip, who was born in June of that year just as the turmoil in Greece was reaching its height. After four daughters, Philip's parents were delighted to have a son, but the celebration of his birth was quickly followed by a series of national and personal crises, which culminated in the defeat of the Greek Army by the Turks in August 1922.

Notwithstanding the fact that the Greek royal family had been in exile when the Greco-Turkish War started in 1919, and it was the anti-royalist, pro-republican politicians such as Venizelos who were responsible for the war, the royal family was tainted by the defeat. The populace had been whipped up from the beginning with promises of assured victory against the Turks, and when the end came, it was inevitably followed by recriminations. A cabal of pro-republican army officers, sensing that this afforded them an excellent opportunity to undermine the monarchy and move against their political opponents, staged a coup known as the 11 September 1922 Revolution.

The Revolutionary Committee was headed by Colonels Nikolaos Plastiras and Stylianos Gonatras, along with the Venezilest Lieutenant General Theodoros Pangalos, who demanded the resignation of the government and the abdication of King Constantine. He was to be replaced by the less prestigious and more malleable Crown Prince George, as the first step to the declaration of the Second Hellenic Republic. They also organised a show trial, known to history as the Trial of the Six, of the former Commander-in-Chief of the Asia Minor Campaign, General Hatzianestis, along with three former royalist Prime Ministers and two former royalist Ministers of State. This began on 31st October 1922. Unsurprisingly, the six men were found guilty of high treason, and were summarily executed by firing squad a few hours after the verdicts were handed down, before the verdicts were published, thereby preventing the possibility of clemency. Tellingly, the Greek Courts reversed the convictions for high treason against the six in 2010, when the grandson of one of the Prime Ministers reopened the case.

Meanwhile, Andrew had been summoned from Corfu to Athens. To demonstrate to the populace that the royal family was heavily implicated in the military defeat, and, with it, the *Megali Idea* which would hereafter never come to fruition now that Smyrna, one of the largest Greek cities in the world, would always remain Turkish, the Revolutionary Committee ordered the arrest of the prince as soon as he arrived in the capital. He too was charged with high treason, his trial scheduled to begin on 2nd December 1922.

Andrew's youngest brother Christopher recounted, 'No one was allowed to go near Andrew except his valet. Guards kept strictest watch and confiscated all letters and parcels. Finally, I hit on the expedient of writing a letter on cigarette paper, rolling it tightly and putting it with cigarettes in his valet's case. Andrew answered with a short note full of courage, but I knew he had no hope of regaining his freedom. Andrew had just had a conversation with a former school-fellow, Pangalos, now Minister for War and instigator of his trial, that left him small grounds for optimism. "How many children have you?" Pangalos asked suddenly, and when my brother told him he shook his head: "Poor things, what a pity, they will soon be orphans."'

According to Prince Christopher, the brothers' nephew, the newly installed King George II of the Hellenes was powerless to intercede, but Princess Andrew swung into action, moving heaven and earth to save her husband from the firing squad. Leaving baby Philip and the other children behind in Corfu with Nanny Roose, Alice headed for Athens to orchestrate a campaign to save her husband's life. She wrote letters to the Pope, the President of France, her cousin Ena of Battenberg's husband the King of Spain, her brothers George and Dickie, the former Princes George and Louis of Battenberg but now known as the 2nd Marquis of Milford Haven and Lord Louis Mountbatten. Dickie was at that time a close friend of David, the Prince of Wales, and the young men approached King George V, who was also Andrew's first cousin. Having stood still and allowed his other first cousins, the Tsar and Tsarina, to be murdered five short years beforehand, George V was not prepared to repeat that mistake. He organised for Dickie Mountbatten to see his prime minster, Andrew Bonar Law, who turned the matter over to the Foreign Secretary, Lord Curzon, under whose jurisdiction it fell. Curzon ordered Commander Gerald Talbot, the former Naval Attaché in Athens, to go to that city and do what he could to save Andrew's life. So necessary was secrecy that Talbot entered Greece under fabricated papers, wearing a false beard.

In what would turn out to be a moment of magnificence for George V, he now utilised his position as Commander-in-Chief of the Armed Forces, and ordered the Admiralty to send a cruiser to Athens to back Talbot up. The *Calypso* arrived in the Bay of Athens under the command of Captain H.A. Buchanan-Wollaston on the evening of 29th November, shortly before the trial was due to begin.

At the very moment of the cruiser's arrival, Talbot was at a meeting with Pangalos, whom he knew from the days of his posting in Athens. Talbot had been seeking compassion, while Pangalos had been adamant that Andrew would be executed just like the other 'royal traitors'. No amount of pleading worked, until a functionary entered the office with the news that the British cruiser had entered the harbour with its guns trained on the shore. Memories of the outcome of the French shelling Athens during the war, which had resulted in the downfall of King Constantine, were still fresh in the minds of all, with the result that Pangalos immediately saw the sense of clemency. Talbot was then able to return to the British Embassy and telegraph London that he had 'obtained this evening promise from Minister of War and also from General Plastiras, the two leaders of the government, that Prince Andrew will not be executed but allowed to leave the country in charge of Talbot.'

Show trials, of course, are theatrical productions whose outcome is previously scripted. Andrew's was no exception. Found guilty, he was stripped of his rank, turfed out of the army, deprived of his citizenship, and, as the verdict stated, 'consideration being given to the extenuating circumstances of lack of experience in commanding a large unit, he has been degraded and condemned to perpetual banishment.'

Alice was already on board the *Calypso* when Andrew arrived under cover of darkness, escorted from prison personally by Pangalos. As soon as the prince was on board, the cruiser weighed anchor and headed for Corfu, where they picked up the five children the following day. Philip was famously taken ashore in an old orange crate, which was used as his makeshift crib. The day after, they arrived in Brindisi, where the family, and such trusted retainers as Nanny Roose, disembarked. Although Andrew was distraught at being exiled from the country and profession he loved, the family used humour to bolster their spirits – a family characteristic Philip has utilised throughout his life.

Captain Buchanan-Wollaston, who escorted them out of Greece, recounted how they 'were rather amusing about being exiled, for they so frequently are.'

Beneath the humour, however, the family was painfully aware of how unenviable their lot was, though also poignantly aware of how much worse it could otherwise have been. They therefore stopped off in Rome to thank the Pope for his support, before heading for London.

In London, the family found shelter at Kensington Palace with Alice's mother, Victoria of Hesse and Battenberg, Dowager Marchioness of Milford Haven. Feeling the need for a break, Andrew and Alice left the five children with their grandmother and crossed the Atlantic to stay with Andrew's youngest brother Christopher and his American wife, the fabulously rich Nancy Leeds.

Christopher's story is in itself an illustration of how adversity had loosened up the Greek royal family's strictures. He had fallen in love with the twice married widow, who was ten years his senior – he admitted to four – and their engagement was announced in 1914. However, the royal family remained opposed to the union until exile and penury eroded their objections. On 1st February 1920, they were married in Vevey, Switzerland. The following year, the new Princess Christopher's nineteen year old son William Bateman Leeds Jr. married her husband's eighteen year old niece, Princess Xenia Georgievna of Russia. In two short years, the Leeds family had therefore become intertwined with the royals, though by the time of Andrew and Alice's visit, their sister-in-law Nancy was living on borrowed time. She would die the following year of the cancer from which she had been suffering for four years.

Andrew and Alice were an attractive couple, well-connected but relatively unimportant in the royal pecking order. Alice herself was a granddaughter of Queen Victoria and a niece of the assassinated last Tsarina of Russia as well as the murdered Grand Duchess Serge (Elizabeth Feodorovna, known in the family as Ella) and of the deposed Grand Duke of Hesse, who lost his throne following the fall of the Germany empire in 1918. Her parents, Prince and Princess Louis of Battenberg, had lost their royal titles during the war when George V prevented the further use of German titles by members of the British Royal Family. They were converted into the merely aristocratic Marquis and Marchioness of Milford Haven, but the Battenberg family as a whole proved surprisingly buoyant. Alice's sister Louise became Crown Princess and later Queen of Sweden, her Battenberg double cousin Ena was already Queen of Spain, and of course her son Philip would end up a British prince, duke, baron and consort to the queen.

At the time of their flight from Greece, however, Andrew and Alice were virtually penniless. They had a second wealthy sister-in-law, Princess George of Greece, and she came to their rescue when they returned from visiting Prince and Princess Christopher in New York. Being the granddaughter of Francois Blanc, the principal property developer of Monte Carlo and the owner of 97% of the shares of the *Société des Bains de Mer et du Cercle des Étrangers*, which controlled gambling and just about everything else in Monaco, Marie possessed one of Europe's great fortunes and lived in some style at St Cloud near Paris. A bright, generous, open-minded woman, who was a student of Sigmund Freud and would go on to become one of the two lay female Freudian psychoanalysts acknowledged by Freud (his daughter Anna was the other), Marie happily turned over the lodge, near the big house on her estate, to the family.

The world that the young Prince Philip of Greece grew up in was both privileged and deprived. His earliest memories include magical times at Cotroceni, Sinaia and Constanza with his exact contemporary, the boy-king Michael of Roumania, whose mother was his first cousin Princess Helen of Greece, and in Romania and Venice with Helen's niece Princess Alexandra of Greece, whose father King Alexander had died of the monkey bite before either Philip or Alexandra was born. Madame Manos, by now known as Princess Aspasia of Greece following her elevation by her brother-in-law, had a house in Venice. When not staying by the Black Sea or in Italy, Philip could also be found by the Baltic, at the Greek royal family's holiday home at Panka, or visiting his sisters, especially Cecile at Darmstadt, where her father-in-law, his grandmother's brother Ernst, the Grand Duke of Hesse, lived in regal splendour as if he were still the official sovereign and Hesse still a monarchy.

Although Prince and Princess Andrew had no money, they were surrounded by the creature comforts of great wealth without actually possessing the ability to dispose of any of them. They had butlers and cooks and Nanny Roose, and they had many relations living in or near Paris. But many of these were exiles themselves, trying to maintain a degree of dignity while living off hope of restoration and the sale of jewels. Disposable income was so tight that Andrew and Alice could not even afford clothes. Her other rich sister-in-law, the former Edwina Ashley, granddaughter of the Jewish financier Sir Ernest Cassel, had married Alice's brother Dickie, Lord Louis Mountbatten, and Edwina thoughtfully instructed her couturiers to make her dresses with extra-large seams. These garments she would pass on to Alice at the end of the season, to be let out by a seamstress and worn by the exiled princess or her four daughters. Once known as one of the most

Chapter II

beautiful princesses in Europe, Alice might have been beautifully arrayed in couture garments, but these were nevertheless hand-me-downs.

Marie, the other benevolent sister-in-law, willingly paid the school fees of the girls and Philip, when he was enrolled in 1927 at the American school, the MacJannet Country Day and Boarding School, run by Donald MacJannet at St. Cloud. The irony is that Marie did not agree with private education, and sent her own two children to state schools. Nevertheless, she judged it ethically correct that she should put her prejudices against private education to one side and provide Andrew's children with the education they would have received had they not been exiled and still had the means to pay.

Philip's first headmaster has left an illuminating account of his young pupil. He was a 'know it all, smarty person, but always remarkably polite with it' – a description that some people would say has remained true throughout his life. However, it should not come as a surprise to anyone that Philip was confident and had a high opinion of himself. Aside from being a bright little boy, he was his family's golden child, the only boy after four girls. He was truly the adored child, beloved not only by his parents, but also by his sisters. He was gregarious by nature, something of an imp, but a lovable one, and so naturally intelligent that few things had to be explained to him more than once for him to have a genuine understanding of them.

Catherine Pegg Levitsky, Philip's grade III teacher, remembered him as not only bright and cheerful but also a helpful young man with exquisite manners. 'He would sit on my right hand at the dining table, not as an honoured guest but because he was particularly agile and a careful carrier of hot dishes. He would never wait for the maid to carry in the different courses, for, as he explained to me, his mother had taught him that a gentleman does not let a woman wait on him.'

'Give me a boy till the age of seven, and I will give you the man for life,' the Jesuits have always said, and the boy whose character was being shaped by his surroundings would remain remarkably true to his formative experiences throughout his life.

One of the decisive factors in shaping the young Philip was the mother who adored him, and whom he adored in return. Alice was severely handicapped. Like just about every other handicapped person who learns, from early youth, how to cope with adversity, Alice was no weeping willow. She was loving and positive and tough, without being hard. Life had dealt her a stacked hand, in that she became deaf at the age of four. Throughout their lives, she and Philip would have such frank interchanges that onlookers would be taken aback, without realising that beneath the lack of superficial sentiment lay deep love, understanding, respect and compassion. Tellingly, Philip has never once been known to criticise his mother – not to friends, relations, or anyone else, whether on or off the record. His was not the easiest of childhoods, in part because of his mother's mental health issues, for added to the handicap of deafness was an extended period of mental ill health. But she had a well-developed streak of compassion, and this he evidently inherited. Like her, however, he is tough. He has no truck with sentimentalism, plainly viewing it as meaningless piffle, but he does have a deep sensitivity where genuine human distress is concerned, and, like his mother, can be truly compassionate.

Helene Cordet was a childhood friend of Philip's. 'Prince Philip and I have known each other all our lives,' she told me. 'I remember their lives in Paris very well. He was much younger than his sisters, by about eight years. He was very much loved by the whole family. Because the age gap was so big, he was very close to his mother. She was a wonderful woman. Very, very nice and kind and very good with him. He was also close to his father. Prince Andrew was very nice too. He was dashing and elegant. They really were a very nice family.'

Philip's father does not appear to have had the stalwartness of character his wife did. Like many children born into comfortable circumstances, he was, by all accounts, a charming, fun-loving, and agreeable personality. But nature had not cut him out for adversity, and when it struck, he was too old to develop the coping mechanisms that youths develop when confronted with life challenges at an early age.

Although Philip's birth was eagerly-anticipated, and he was much loved by his entire family, his parents' marriage began to unravel under the strains of exile. Andrew was a vigorous, engaged young man who found the enforced inactivity of his banishment difficult to cope with. When I broached the subject of his philandering with Helene Cordet, she explained, 'The grown-ups talked, but he was no more naughty than anyone else.' In those days, few men of rank, substance and stature failed to keep mistresses. His wife Alice, however, did not help matters, for rather than confront her husband's problems, and deal with them realistically, she sought refuge in religion. Being deaf, Alice was no stranger to adversity, and she had developed coping skills early on, in that she could lip read in several languages and speak them so well that strangers had no idea of her disability. Coping with her husband's issues, however, seems to have been beyond her ken. Andrew's other consolation, the gaming tables, put even more strain on the marriage, especially as the political turmoil in Greece increased.

The Revolutionary Committee had asked Constantine's son and heir King George II to leave the country in 1923, and he had complied, though he had refused to abdicate, following which a republic had been declared on 25th March 1924. This had had a profound effect upon Andrew and Alice as well as the rest of the family, for George II was officially deposed, stripped of his citizenship, his property confiscated, with the rest of the Greek Royal Family once more finding itself *persona non grata* in and exiled from their own country.

Trying to create something positive out of the ashes, Andrew wrote a book, *Towards Disaster: The Greek Army in Asia Minor in 1921,* justifying his conduct and explaining the disastrous policies which had led to the national, and his own, disgrace. Alice translated it into English for him, but by the time it was published in 1930, she was well and truly in the grip of religious mania, claiming to receive divine messages and to be in possession of healing powers. She was diagnosed as suffering from paranoid schizophrenia, first by Dr Thomas Ross, then by Sir Maurice Craig, a diagnosis which was confirmed at Dr Ernst Simmel's sanatorium at Tegel, Berlin, which she went to voluntarily. Her sister-in-law Marie Bonaparte's colleague Sigmund Freud, a medical figure of the greatest eminence at the time, was called in. Freud diagnosed her delusions and agitation, which manifested themselves in hyper-activity followed by listlessness, and had resulted in weight loss, as stemming from sexual frustration. This diagnosis was supported by her gynaecologist, who came from Athens to examine her. Alice seems to have become infatuated with a man, but could not consummate the union owing to her strong religious feelings. She and Andrew, now estranged, were no longer sleeping together, which did not help matters, so a recommendation was made that her ovaries be X-rayed in order to kill off her libido by inducing a premature menopause. This was done, and she did regain some of the weight she had lost, and was released. Her symptoms, however, persisted, doubtless aggravated by the induction of an early menopause, and, Andrew having relegated all control to her mother, Victoria Milford Haven took the decision to have her committed to an institution for the mentally ill. While she and Philip were staying with Cecile, and the children were out for the day, she was forcibly taken to Dr Ludwig Binswanger's sanatorium in Kreuzlingen, Switzerland.

Alice protested her sanity, and demanded to be released. Andrew did go and visit her once, as did Philip, who accompanied his grandmother. She was deeply unhappy there, and once escaped through a window, but she was soon found locally and returned to the asylum. She was luckier, however, than a fellow inmate, the celebrated ballet dancer Vaslav Nijinsky. Two years after what she regarded as imprisonment at the Swiss clinic, and after a brief stay at another in Meran, she was released, while the dancer would be in and out of sanatoria for the rest of his life.

Alice found her incarceration both mortifying and frightening. When she learnt that she had not been committed at the behest of the doctors, but of her own mother, she was indignant.

Quite what Prince Philip made of his mother's disappearance from his life, is open to speculation, for it is one of the many subjects upon which he refuses to be drawn. It would appear, however, from what his relations and friends have said, that he simply accepted it as something he had to cope with, so he just got on with it. But it must have been troubling, on some level, for a child who had been so close to his mother, to have her wrenched away from him. What indubitably aided his ability to cope was that he was already at boarding school, so was already somewhat used to being away from her. But the fact remains that, for the first nine years of his life he was exceedingly close to his mother, and for the next five he had no contact with her.

Following Alice's release, she kept well away from her family. Although she corresponded with her mother, and needed to keep in with her enough to be maintained, her movements suggest that she was intent on avoiding her family and, with that, the possibility of being re-interred. She clearly felt vulnerable and was determined that she would never be returned to a sanatorium no matter what. She also appears to have felt that her family had not been as understanding of her predicament as they could have been. Her marriage had been unravelling slowly since they had been banished following Andrew's escape from the firing squad. While she had sought comfort in religion, he had done so in the companionship of various female friends and the thrills of the gaming tables. His more conventional reaction appeared to find more favour with her family than her own less orthodox solution, notwithstanding the fact that extreme religiosity ran in her mother's family. Her aunt Ella had even founded an order of nuns following the assassination of Grand Duke Serge, and is today a saint in the Russian Orthodox Church.

What lessened the blow of his mother's disappearance from his life was that, in 1929, the eight year-old Philip of Greece had been sent to Cheam Preparatory School, the school Alice's brother George had been to and which his heir David attended. This was less to avoid the developing tensions within the home, which were not readily evident to the children, than to further his education in keeping with his status. Although many royal families still did not educate their children at school, preferring to retain the traditional method of home-schooling with tutors, exiled royals like Andrew and Alice were no longer in a position to incur such expenses. Necessity having forced their hands, they soon discovered that the aristocratic tradition of sending boys to boarding school at the age of eight had many merits. These children developed independence, confidence, had less patchy educations, formed social ties which could and often did last a lifetime, and left school able to function more easily in the world at large than children who were tutored at home.

Cheam had a good reputation and had produced some venerable old boys, including the early nineteenth century Prime Minister Henry Addington, 1st Viscount Sidmouth, and, later in the century, Lord Randolph Churchill, Chancellor of the Exchequer and Leader of the House of Commons, whose son, Winston Churchill, had been President of the Board of Trade and Home Secretary prior to the Great War, and First Lord of the Admiralty until the Gallipoli debacle during it. He would, of course, go on, during the Second World War, to be the revered Prime Minister who steered Britain to victory against Nazi Germany.

Philip's home from home in England, when he was not at school, was his maternal grandmother Victoria Milford Haven's apartment at Kensington Palace. In those days, that palace was known as the 'Aunt Heap' by the then Prince of Wales and the younger generation, for the number of royal widows and spinsters who were housed in it. The Dowager Marchioness of Milford Haven occupied one of the less extravagant apartments, being only a granddaughter of Queen Victoria, unlike her two aunts, Princess Louise, Duchess of Argyll, and Princess Beatrice (known as HRH Princess Henry of Battenberg until 1917), who lived in some style.

Philip's accommodation was almost Spartan, but that in itself was not unexpected, for royal children seldom had luxurious bedrooms. Their Spartan sleeping quarters usually contained plain furniture, simple, sometimes hardy beds, and the minimum of creature comforts, the thinking being that they should be toughened up while young so their characters would not be weakened by too much luxury. That same level of simplicity was replicated in the bedroom he used at his maternal uncle George, 2nd Marquis of Milford Haven's house, Lynden Manor in Bray, Berkshire. There was one important difference between Kensington Palace and Lynden Manor, however. At the latter, as at school, he had the company of his cousin David, Earl of Medina, heir to his father the 2nd marquis and his near contemporary, David being two years Philip's senior. The two boys became close friends, their only-son-in-the-family status fostering a bond that being first cousins, who got along well with each other, cemented further. Robin Dalton, who lived with David Milford Haven for five years prior to his first marriage, and knew them intimately, told me that each was effectively the brother the other had never had.

Prince Philip was a boy of nine, back home on holiday in France from school in England, when his mother was taken away to what the aristocracy has always called 'the looney bin'. He was not present while she was removed, and when he returned home and asked for his mother, was fobbed off with an excuse of her having gone away for a while. If his own and other accounts are to be believed – and there is no reason why they should not be – he accepted the explanation phlegmatically. Clearly, the young prince already had a pronounced degree of equanimity which might well have been innate in part, but must certainly have been fostered by having learnt, from babyhood, that life went on, irrespective of the tumultuousness that was interwoven with being an exile and the treasured child in a large, loving family with strong values.

In fact, from birth Philip had been exposed to a glittering array of characters, many of whom were deeply unconventional beneath conventional exteriors. The Greek royal family, it must be remembered, was a collateral branch of the Danish royal family. All the Greeks were therefore not only princes and princesses of Greece but also of Denmark, which was mightily convenient during periods of exile, when they could travel on Danish passports rather than suffer the indignities of their Russian relations, who were stateless. Prince Philip himself is on record as having stated that he thought of himself primarily as Danish. Beside the cosy, bourgeois way of life of the Danish royals, there co-existed a streak of acceptance of human fallibility that went beyond conventional morality and was characteristic of genuinely sophisticated people such as Philip's family.

The most unconventional of Philip's near relations were undoubtedly his Uncle George (known in the family as Big George) and Aunt Marie, with whom the family lived in Paris, and Big George's paternal Uncle Valdemar. Prince Valdemar of Denmark could himself have become a king like his two brothers the Danish and Greek monarchs, having been offered the thrones of Bulgaria and Norway, but he wisely opted for a less splendid life. His private life was unconventional, to say the least. Having joined the navy as a fourteen year old he quickly rose in the ranks, becoming a lieutenant by the age of twenty one and ultimately an admiral. Aged twenty four, he was living at Bernstorff Palace, effectively the tertiary residence of the Danish royal family, when his sister-in-law Queen Olga of the Hellenes brought her fourteen year old son Prince George of Greece to live with him. The Greek king wanted his second son to have a naval education and judged it wise to have this in the Danish navy, which was more established and stable than the Greek.

Big George, however, felt abandoned by his father, and developed what he would later describe to his wife as a profound and ever-lasting attachment for his uncle from that day forward. Undoubtedly, uncle and nephew were completely devoted to each other. They shared an unbreakable bond of love, about which they were open. This would later lead to speculation that they were involved in an incestuous homosexual relationship, but theirs was not the only unshakeable bond between an uncle and a nephew in royal circles. In Britain, there was considerable gossip about Princess Louise's husband John (always known as Ian within the family), Marquis of Lorne and later 9th Duke of Argyll, and his sister the Duchess of Sutherland's son, Lord Ronald Leveson-Gower. In 1907, when the Irish Crown Jewels were stolen and Police enquiries led to the innocent Lord Ronald as a result of several of his patently guilty homosexual circle, the authorities were assiduous in taking steps to keep the names of both nephew and uncle from surfacing, lest they, and the Royal Family, be involved in a scandal which was already uncomfortably sensational.

By this time, it was supposed in smart social circles that both the duke and his nephew were homosexual. This might well have been so, but whether their extraordinarily close relationship was because they were lovers, which they were commonly supposed to be, seems less likely. Their closeness can as readily be explained by the affinity of any two people sharing a great deal of common interests as by a sexual predilection which was, in the nineteenth century, frowned upon socially as well as being illegal. I for one do not believe that Princess Louise would have been quite so ready to be seen out and about with her husband and his nephew *à trois* with the frequency and regularity that they were, had there been an incestuous relationship to conceal. She was always careful to conduct herself in such a way that the stories remained unverifiable about her affairs with such men as Arthur Bigge, her mother Queen Victoria's assistant private secretary who would ultimately become, as Lord Stamfordham, Private Secretary to Victoria and King George V, and the famous sculptor Joseph Edgar Boehm, who is supposed to have died on top of her. She maintained decorum by keeping a discreet distance socially when there was something to hide, and the idea of her openly cavorting around England, Scotland and Europe, as part of an incestuous , homosexual *ménage à trois*, hardly seems credible when one examines the personalities and conduct of the individuals concerned, Louise especially.

Had there been something to hide, it is more likely that the two princesses married to Valdemar of Denmark and George of Greece would have been more motivated to tolerate and cover-up the *ménage à quatre* than to treat the relations between their husbands as something acceptable. However, neither woman gave the slightest indication that her husband shared a bed with the other man, though they were both open about the strength of the love each husband possessed for the other. Over the years, I have often had cause to say to friends, when speaking about the rumours that have swirled around about the personal conduct of people I know well enough to know the truth about, that many an onlooker sees sexual activity where there is none. Onlookers frequently misrepresent real passion for sexual desire, innocent fun for prurience, and seem incapable of understanding that many a close relationship is powered by genuine non-sexual affection, not lust. Often, it is the lack of sex which keeps the relationship on the even keel that makes it a lasting one, for lust often invites turbulence, and once slaked, disinterest often follows only too quickly in its wake.

While there is evidence to support the view that Prince Valdemar had a healthy interest in the carnal, and Prince George of Greece might well have been homosexual, there is much to indicate that Big George was more than likely asexual. In her unpublished writings, Marie Bonaparte articulates the deeply unsatisfactory nature of her sexual relations with her husband. He expressed distaste at the sex act with her, stating that he knew neither of them wished to do it, but had to, to procreate. He pointedly refused to kiss her, ever. There was no physical affection between them. She concluded that he was cold, disinterested in sex with her and with any other woman, but would grit his teeth occasionally to get the job done, so they could have children. They did indeed produce two, a son Peter and a daughter Eugenie, but Marie Bonaparte was starved of the affection she needed, as well as the sexual satisfaction, which she sought elsewhere once her children were born. Reading between the lines of what she wrote, it is not unreasonable to infer that George was homosexual, but, for the prurient, there is a disappointing lack of evidence to suggest incest between him and his uncle.

If, however, they did have a lifelong love affair, both their wives displayed commendable tolerance, and this was a characteristic which many members of Prince Philip's family possessed. Indeed, Valdemar's wife, Princess Marie d'Orléans, went to some pains to explain the closeness of their husbands to Marie Bonaparte when she was newly wed, recommending that the men be given what we would now call 'space' to pursue their relationship without undue spousal interruptions. Marie-Valdemar also prepared Marie-George for the cataclysm of emotions that the men's partings always caused. After each of the several visits a year that Big George made to Bernstorff, the younger prince would break down, weeping uncontrollably, while Valdemar would take to his bed.

Marie Bonaparte had a great deal of respect for her aunt by marriage, whom she described as having more brains, pluck and character than any other member of the extended Danish/Greek royal family. How these wives coped with their husbands is instructive of the way Prince Philip's family, in his and the previous generations, behaved. In that day and age, when marriage was for life, and your life wasn't your own to dispense with as you pleased, accommodations within it nevertheless were. Philip and all Valdemar's relations would have known that Princess Valdemar had a warm and friendly relationship with her husband, and an affair with his stable-master. Believing in social equality, she was informal, with Bohemian tastes and interests. She did exactly as she pleased, even down to getting a tattoo of an anchor on her upper arm to show solidarity with the navy, which horrified her mother-in-law, the Danish queen, whenever it was exposed at state functions. She wrote to the Danish author Herman Bang, 'I believe that a person, regardless of her position, should be herself.' At a time when no royal lady went out unaccompanied, she required the right to go out and about without her lady-in-waiting, and, when she was criticised for her unconventional behaviour, she declared, 'Let them complain, I am happy nevertheless.' When moves were made to curtail her conduct by institutional-ising her, she decamped from Denmark to her native France until the threat was removed.

Another role model the young Prince Philip had regarding the exercise of individuality, within the strictures of the royal way of life, was his other Aunt Marie: Marie Bonaparte. She was vociferous in denouncing her husband's family as being ' all royal bourgeois, Danes, bourgeois virtues and defects, united, honest, good, simple, kind, desperately treading the common path.' Although having no interest in family life the way all the other bourgeois Greek and Danish royals did, Marie Bonaparte nevertheless assiduously followed their custom of taking lovers. She spent most of her time in France on her estates while her husband Big George was often away for months at a time, travelling between his many royal relations throughout Europe. Following the restoration of the Greek monarchy in 1935, he could often be found in Greece, but Marie limited her visits there.

Marie and Big George had a friendly *modus vivendi* like their aunt and uncle, but it was significantly less affectionate than Uncle Valdemar and Aunt Marie's, for while both women had warm temperaments, Big George's was altogether less warm than his uncle's. Nevertheless, there was a sub-text to these relationships which everyone who knew them well accepted, and by which the family was permitted to live. Personal satisfaction was not only a quest to be undertaken, but an objective to be achieved. In Prince Philip's world, there was nothing untoward about his father moving to the South of France to be near to his mistress, Comtesse Andrée de La Bigne. Conventions should be adhered to when they furthered the interests of civilised conduct, but their existence should never be a preventative to the pursuit of human fulfilment. Just because something was new and/or untried did not mean it should be avoided. Indeed, new ground could and should be broken when there was the possibility that it might enhance one's life, or the lives of others.

A case in point was Princess Marie Bonaparte's clitoris. Unable to climax, she sought to free herself from sexual frustration with various solutions. Having tried lovers and therapy, both of which had failed, she undertook a scientific study of the role the clitoris plays in orgasm. She examined 243 women, taking measurements of the distance between the vagina and the clitoris, and came to the conclusion that those who climaxed easily had clitorises positioned less than 2.5 cm from the vagina (*paraclitordiennes*), while those with a greater distance (*teleclitordiennnes*) found orgasm more difficult or impossible. Those in between, she categorised as *mesoclitordiennes*. In 1924 she published her findings under the nom de plume A.E.Narjani, presenting her theory in the respected Belgian medical journal, *Brux-elles-Medical*. Putting her money where her mouth was, she approached the surgeon Josef Halban to have her clitoris repositioned closer to her vagina, and when the outcome did not result in the desired effect, had him repeat the procedure on two separate occasions. In the finest scientific tradition, having diagnosed herself as being a *teleclitordienne,* she published an account of the procedure, calling it the Halban-Narjani operation.

This was the open-minded world in which Prince Philip grew up. The contrasts with Lilibet's world were not quite so great as might appear to be the case. Although the English Court, as conducted by King George V and Queen Mary was stiff, old-fashioned and appeared to uphold staid morality, if the respected historian A.N. Wilson is correct, George V had a taste for ladies of the night, though he always slept in the same bed as his wife. Lilibet's paternal Uncle David, the Prince of Wales, was but one of many men in Court circles who had a mistress. Women with lovers also proliferated, including both Mountbatten wives, and Lilibet's maternal Uncle David (the Hon. David Bowes Lyon) was an acknowledged homosexual, albeit, like many of his peers, married. In Britain, appearances counted for more than what really went on behind closed doors, except with young women. Maidens were expected to be virgins, and to remain faithful while producing heirs and spares. That aside, there was tolerance in elevated social circles, but British decorum – some would say Anglo-Saxon hypocrisy – required that the façade of high moral probity be rigidly maintained, thereby giving the onlooker a misleading impression of what went on in private.

If there was tolerance sexually, there was little acceptance of people who openly broke the codes of acceptable behaviour. There was therefore no tolerance of people who 'bent the rules', which meant that people who were emotionally disturbed or mentally ill received no sympathy. Mental illness, along with the chaos it generated, was something that was shied away from in horror. Its existence could taint families who suffered from it. For instance, Lilibet's mother Elizabeth's two nieces were quietly institutionalised so that no one would learn that they appeared to be mentally ill (in fact they suffered from Huntingdon's Chorea, a hereditary condition that presents to the uninitiated as mental illness but isn't). Everyone thought the two girls had died, and it would only be five decades or so later that it emerged that they had in fact been institutionalised.

The prejudice against the mentally ill accounts in part for why Alice was carted away quietly and firmly to a discreet Swiss sanatorium when her stay at Tegel did not 'do the trick', and why all four of her daughters were married off within the space of ten months shortly after her interment. The first of the daughters to be married off was the youngest daughter Sophie, married age 16 to her second cousin once removed via Queen Victoria, Prince Christopher of Hesse, a grandson of Kaiser Wilhelm II, on 15th December 1931, at Kronberg, Berlin. Two months later, on 2nd February 1932, Alice's third daughter, nineteen year old Cecile, was married off to her maternal first cousin once removed, George Donatus of Hesse at Darmstadt, the family seat so beloved of the couple's common ancestress, Queen Victoria. Ten weeks later, Alice's eldest daughter Margarita was married to Prince Gottfried of Hohenlohe-Langenburg, another great-grandchild of Queen Victoria, in Langenburg, Germany, at the family's palace, which was on a par with Buckingham Palace. Four months later it was the turn of Alice's third and final daughter Theodora, who married her paternal second cousin, Berthold, Margrave of Baden on 17th August 1931 at Neues Schloss, Baden-Baden.

This last marriage would have a lasting effect on Prince Philip for reasons which will soon become evident. Suffice it to say, Berthold's family had a legacy politically. His father, whom he had succeeded as Margrave in 1929, is better known to history as Prince Max of Baden, the liberal Chancellor of Imperial Germany who ensured the creation of the Weimar Republic at the end of the First World War when he took it upon himself to announce the abdication of Kaiser Wilhelm II, despite the fact that the emperor had not actually abdicated. In so doing, he forced the Kaiser's hand as well as the collapse of monarchy in Germany, but assured a defeated Germany a smoother transition in keeping with the tenets of the victors, American President Woodrow Wilson's Fourteen Points in particular.

Family life, as the ten year old Prince Philip of Greece had known it, was at an end once his mother was institutionalised and his four sisters were married off. The family figuratively scattered to the winds, with each member of it living in a different place. To drive the point home, Philip no longer had a home to go to in France, as his father had decamped to the South of France and was leading a bachelor's existence with his mistress that was, in plain English, unsuitable for a growing boy, even one from so open-minded a family as the Greco/Danish Royal Family. Thereafter, until Prince Andrew's death on 3rd December 1944, at the Hotel Metropole in Monte Carlo, father and son saw each other on only a handful of occasions, though they did correspond frequently.

Tellingly, Prince Philip has never criticised his father for the choices Andrew made. Possibly this is because he never had any doubt that his father loved him even when he was no longer physically present. Even from a distance, Andrew still took an active interest in his son's activities. He had to approve all Philip's main activities, including his travel plans, and this practice seems to have conveyed a feeling of care. Nevertheless, this way of doing things caused logistical difficulties for the family. Philip's maternal grandmother Victoria handled most of the arrangements, and her letters reveal her frustration in having to wait for word from her son-in-law before she could finalise Philip's holiday plans.

Whether Philip was aware of this difficulty is open to question, but if he was, he did not allow it to colour his attitude towards his father. Whenever he has spoken about him, he has done so with affection. Where others might have considered themselves to be victims of a cruel fate, Philip accepted the disintegration of his family with a surprising degree of equanimity, displaying genuine empathy for the difficult predicament in which his parents found themselves. Nevertheless, his cousin Gina Wernher (later Philips and then Lady Kennard) said, 'He never saw his parents and he minded that terribly. He told me so.'

In some ways, Philip's saving grace was that he was away from home, at boarding school in England, when the family disintegrated. This undoubtedly cushioned the blow, as did his close friendship with his cousin David, whose parents became his *in loco parentis*. There is a common misapprehension that Philip was always closer to his other maternal uncle Dickie (Lord Louis Mountbatten), his wife Edwina, and their daughters Patricia and Pamela, than he was to Dickie's elder brother Georgie, the 2nd Marquis of Milford

Haven, and his wife Nada. This is not true, as Philip himself confirms. He was much closer to David's parents.

If Dickie and Edwina Mountbatten were an exceptional couple, so too were Georgie and Nada Milford Haven. She especially was another of Philip's colourful relations. Born Countess Nadejda Torby on 28th March 1896, her story was the stuff of fiction, except that it was fact. The daughter of Grand Duke Michael Mikhailovitch of Russia and a descendant of the great Russian poet Alexander Pushkin, in 1934 she was exposed as a lesbian, the lover of Gloria Vanderbilt Sr., one of the most famous women of her day. This happened during the famous custody battle between Gloria and her late husband's sister Gertrude Vanderbilt Whitney, who had applied for custody of her niece Baby Gloria on the grounds that Big Gloria was an unfit mother. The Vanderbilt custody case was front page news throughout the world, and when the maid testified that she had seen Lady Milford Haven kissing Mrs Vanderbilt I in an unmistakably sexual manner, the scandal was monumental.

To add to the wheels within wheels, Gloria Vanderbilt Sr. had once been engaged to Prince Gottfried 'Friedel' von Hohenlohe-Langenburg, who was now married to Prince Philip's sister Margarita, while Gloria's identical twin sister, Thelma, Viscountess Furness, was then the established mistress of David, Prince of Wales. That is, until she was ill-advised enough to ask her friend Wallis Simpson to look after her prince while she was away in New York propping up her sister, whose health had collapsed under the strain of being the central character in the most sensational trial of its day.

The unmasking of his aunt was Philip's first real experience of how damaging adverse publicity could be. Gloria Vanderbilt Sr. never recovered from being outed the way she was (she ended up suffering from hysterical blindness and was ostracised socially), though Nada Milford Haven rose above the scandal as the whole family closed ranks to protect her. Margarita and Friedel even flew to New York to testify on behalf of Gloria. Afterwards, as Gloria crumbled, Nada travelled all over the world with her sister-in-law Edwina, who was equally notorious for her lovers, though they were all male, and sometimes even black, Paul Robeson, the famous American bass, and Leslie 'Hutch' Hutchinson, the nightclub singer/pianist, being the two most renowned. Ironically, Edwina's greatest love, Harold 'Bunny' Phillips, whom she wished to marry, would desert her to marry Nada's sister Lady Zia Wernher's daughter Gina in the last of the wheels within wheels.

Nada's *sang froid* doubtless had much to do with her family having had practise for generations in rising above inconvenient facts. She was the younger daughter of Grand Duke Michael Miklailovich of Russia and his morganatic wife, the former Countess Sophie von Merenberg. After their marriage, Sophie's uncle Adolphe, the Grand Duke of Luxembourg, ennobled her in her own right as Countess Torby, so that she and her children would be titled. The Tsar had forbidden the marriage, not only because she was not of royal blood, but because she was, in his eyes, a 'Negress', and therefore unsuitable for inclusion in the Russian Imperial Family. He exiled Grand Duke Michael and banned Sophie from ever entering his empire. She never did.

Sophie's mother was herself the product of another morganatic union, this time between Prince Nikolaus Wilhelm of Nassau and Natalya Alexandrovna Pushkina. Thereby lay the double rub. Mademoiselle Pushkina had been unsuitable as a royal bride, partly because she was not of royal blood, but also because she was the celebrated poet Alexander Pushkin's granddaughter. And Pushkin was famous throughout Europe not only as Russia's greatest poet, but also as possessing an African heritage. His ancestor, Abraham Petrovich Hannibal (sometimes spelt Ganibal) had been a black slave, most likely from Chad, purchased in Constantinople by the Russian Ambassador, Savva Ruguzinski, on the instructions of Peter the Great to add 'a few clever little African slaves' as exotica at the Tsar's Court.

Hannibal, however, was highly intelligent and Peter took a shine to him, even standing as his godfather when he was Christened (hence the patronymic Petrovich). So began the rise of this extraordinary man, who ended up registered as a nobleman and a major-general in the army of Peter's daughter Empress Elizabeth. His descendants continued his extraordinary ascendancy, marrying, as we have seen, into various royal families and becoming established under so many guises that nowadays they include the head of the Mountbatten family (George, 4th Marquis of Milford Haven), the present Duke of Westminster, and the future 6th Duke of Hamilton.

The year before Nada's private life featured on the front pages of newspapers all over the world, Philip was moved from school in England and sent to Schule Schloss Salem in Germany. This institution of learning had the merit of being free, for it was housed in the castle of his brother-in-law Berthold, whose father Prince Max of Baden had founded the school in 1920 as an experiment. Republican German's first Chancellor was firmly convinced that Waterloo had been won on the playing fields of Eton. Seeking to educate the future leaders of Germany in humanist rather than militarist values, he founded a school in his castle at Salem. It began with four pupils, one of whom was his son Berthold. As it grew, Prince Max entrusted its running entirely to his former Private Secretary, Kurt Hahn, who would go on to achieve a reputation as one of the greatest educators of the twentieth century.

## Chapter II

Hahn was of the opinion that civilisation, as it stood at the time, was sick. Young people were in danger of being exposed to five areas of decay: the decay of fitness, the decay of initiative and enterprise, the decay of care and skill, the decay of self-discipline, and the decay of compassion. Salem's syllabus was calculated to counteract each of these instances of decay, not only scholastically, but through sport, behaviour, attitude and awareness.

Philip, however, lasted only two terms. The Nazis had come to power in 1933. This presented the Salem school with problems on several fronts. Firstly, Hahn, who was a renowned anti-Nazi as well as Jewish, was arrested and imprisoned following Hitler's order on 5th April for the boycott of all Jewish establishments. Berthold orchestrated a campaign for the headmaster's release, which included an appeal from the British Prime Minister, Ramsay MacDonald, to the German president, Field Marshal von Hindenberg, who ordered Hahn's release. Hahn immediately fled to Britain, with the intention of opening up the British branch of the school in Scotland.

Philip's presence at Salem was actually a declaration by Berthold that Salem would continue its educational purpose irrespective of the change of government. His young brother-in-law's contempt for the Nazis, however, quickly became a real problem: one which was liable to get him and the rest of the family into trouble. Philip regarded them as preposterous, their theatricality a tasteless joke. He openly mocked them at every turn. On one occasion, he goose-stepped through the market square at Uberlingen, giving the Nazi salute time and again, each time acidly commenting on how the Cheam boys did the same thing whenever they needed permission to go to the lavatory.

When the school broke up for the summer holidays, Philip was transferred to its new offshoot at Gordonstoun, which Hahn was founding in Scotland. It was situated in the Highlands near Lossiemouth, birthplace of Britain's first Labour Prime Minister, Ramsay MacDonald, on a three hundred acre estate whose main residence was called Gordonstoun House. Renamed the British Salem School of Gordonstoun, Philip became one of the first thirty pupils. It was a hardy existence, and the students, all boys, had to do everything, from emptying the garbage, to converting stable blocks into dormitories, to building a dining room and even huts. They slept in unheated dormitories, had cold showers, and went for early morning runs in shorts, come rain or shine. Philip states that he would not have traded one moment of the experience, and though Gordonstoun was hardier than Salem and he had to endure the inevitable period of adjustment, he did so without regret and with remarkable success.

Although Hahn had been a true intellectual, who had read Greats at Oxford and studied at the universities of Berlin, Heidelberg, Freiburg, and Gottingen, Philip was not. He displayed a 'determination not to exert himself more than was necessary to avoid trouble,' but he did absorb Hahn's love of books, as is evident by the extensive library of well-thumbed books he would collect in the coming decades. He also absorbed Hahn's belief in the power of the great outdoors, which both men would put to excellent use in later years through the Outward Bound Trust and the Duke of Edinburgh's Award Scheme. Hahn stated, 'My best schoolmaster is the Moray Firth,' and Philip said that though he was, 'wet, cold, miserable, probably sick, and often scared stiff,' he would not have missed the experience of sailing on the Moray Firth 'for anything'.

According to Hahn, 'When Philip came to Gordonstoun his most marked trait was his undefeatable spirit. He felt the emotions of both joy and sadness deeply, and the way he looked and the way he moved indicated what he felt. That even applied to the minor disappointments inevitable in a schoolboy's life. His laughter was heard everywhere. He had inherited from his Danish family the capacity to derive great fun from small incidents. In his schoolwork he showed a lively intelligence.'

Although Philip's academic record was never better than middling, Hahn ended up having a high opinion of the teenager. He made him the head boy, or Guardian in Gordonstoun parlance, and said in his final report, 'Prince Philip is universally trusted, liked and respected. He has the greatest sense of service of all the boys in the school. Prince Philip's leadership qualities are most noticeable, though marred at times by impatience and intolerance. He will need the exacting demands of a great service to do justice to himself. His best is outstanding; his second best not good enough.' This was a prescient comment, and would be borne out by Philip's admirers and detractors in the coming years, both of whom saw a side of him which Hahn had spotted early on.

From Philip's return to England in 1933 and his departure from Gordonstoun in 1938, life bumbled along in its quixotic yet curiously stable way. He shuffled between his grandmother Victoria Milford Haven at Kensington Palace; his uncles Georgie and Dickie at their country houses in England; his Aunt Nada's sister Lady Zia Wernher, who was married to the immensely rich Harold Wernher and lived in great style at Thorpe Lubenham Hall near Market Harborough and later on at Luton Hoo in Bedfordshire with her two daughters Myra and Gina, and an only son Alexander, who was Philip's exact contemporary. He would be killed, while serving with the 17/21 Lancers in Tunisia in 1942, when his leg and hip were crushed between two tanks which were being towed out of a gully. Without antibiotics, septicaemia set in. The letter Philip wrote to Zia shows what her son meant to him. 'Alex filled a place in my life that was very important to me, he filled a place of a brother and for that alone I am eternally grateful to him.'

Gina, who later became Lady Kennard, described playing with her young cousin Philip. 'There were four of us who played together all the time': Philip, David the brother he never had, Gina, who was known as George, and her younger brother Alex. 'We called ourselves *The Four Musketeers*.' She remembered him being 'very' happy' as a 'little boy', 'very jolly, very lively. As Philip grew older, he became more thoughtful, more introspective.' The fact that he was parentless bothered him. 'He never saw his parents, you know. Never. And he minded that. He told me so,' Gina said. 'He was perfectly happy at school, but he said to me – I remember this clearly – "Everybody has a family to go back to. I don't."

Without his own family to return home to, Philip also spent holidays with other cousins such as Michael of Roumania and his mother, the former Princess Helen of Greece, in Roumania; his uncle King Alexander's widow, the former Madame Manos now known as Princess Aspasia of Greece following Alexander's brother's accession to the throne, and their daughter Alexandra in Venice, where they resided; and his sisters in Germany. His favourite was Cecilie, known within the family as Cecile. She was happily married to the Hereditary Grand Duke of Hesse, by whom she had two sons and a daughter.

Cecile's father-in-law, Ernst Ludwig, Grand Duke of Hesse, was another of the colourful characters in the family whose private life would have raised eyebrows had the public known about it. Brother of their grandmother Victoria, Dowager Marchioness of Milford Haven, as well as of the murdered Tsarina Alexandra and Grand Duchess Serge of Russia, Uncle Ernie, according to his first wife, the former Princess Victoria Melita of Edinburgh (another of Queen Victoria's grandchildren and therefore his maternal first cousin), was a homosexual with whom 'no stable boy was safe'. As soon as their mutual grandmother died, Ducky, as she was known, divorced him and married her paternal first cousin, Grand Duke Kirill of Russia, the man with whom she had been in love all along. Ernie remarried, in keeping with the custom of the day. This time he made a very successful marriage with Princess Eleonore of Solms-Hohensolms-Lich. She was not in love with anyone else, unlike Ducky, and cared nothing about his outside activities, producing two sons, George Donatus (Philip's brother-in-law Don) and Ludwig (Lu). Meanwhile, Uncle Ernie pursued an established relationship with Karl August Lingner, the very rich businessman who marketed Odol, one of the first liquid mouthwashes.

By Philip's own account, his favourite place to stay was with his sister Cecile and brother-in-law Don at Darmstadt. He was a bright boy, humorous and good natured if somewhat bluff. A born leader, he never shirked his responsibilities and was growing into a stunningly handsome young man. He had a shock of white hair and equally startling blue eyes. He was tall, slim, and athletic. He oozed energy, charisma and sex appeal, qualities he would retain even into his tenth decade. The television producer Mike Hollingsworth recounted to me how he came across the 90 year old Philip in a field in the country. He moved to open the gate for the prince, but, before he could do so, Philip had leapt over it and was bounding along in his customarily cheerful and energised way.

The restoration of the Greek monarchy towards the end of 1935 was a material fact in the life of all Greeks, royal or otherwise. Coming as it did following thirteen disastrous years of republicanism, the restoration did make a difference to a wider public. There had been thirteen coups, twenty-three different governments, and one dictatorship in the interregnum. Upon the resignation of the man who would become the last President of the Second Republic, Alexander Zaimis, in October of that year, the last republican Prime Minister of the Second Republic, General George Kondylis, declared himself Regent and called for a plebiscite on 3rd November to determine the fate of the monarchy. The vote was 1,491,992 in favour, with 34,454 against. King George II, Philip's first cousin, was invited to return to his throne, which he did later that month. Ironically, the one person who was least affected by the restoration was the sixth in line to the throne. Although Philip father's financial situation eased somewhat, there was still no great fortune to call upon. His parents were still separated. He remained at school in Britain. He still shuffled between relations during the school holidays. And his mother was still not in touch with him or any of the other members of her immediate family, with the exception of her own mother, for whom she had a pronounced scepticism.

In January of the following year, when Lilibet's uncle David ascended the British throne and hurtled towards his own version of banishment, Philip's father's perpetual banishment from Greece was rescinded. The royal family's confiscated properties were restored, and on Wednesday, 20th May 1936, the London Times reported that Andrew had returned to his native land for a brief visit. By Fall, he had returned to live in the palace as the principal *aide-de-camp* to his nephew, King George II.

In November, to emphasise the permanence which it was hoped the restoration would possess, it was announced that George II was organising the return of the bodies of his parents, King Constantine and Queen Sophie, and his and Philip's grandmother, Queen Olga, from the Russian Orthodox Chapel in Florence, for re-burial at Tatoi, the traditional burial place of the Greek royal family. The British Ambassador, Sir Sydney Waterlow, who had confidently predicted in 1935 that the monarchy would never be restored, reported back to his superiors in London that the complications involved in staging such a spectacle would give the Greeks 'ample opportunity for the confusion that has hitherto been the rule on all ceremonial occasions in Greece.' However, when the time came for the ceremonies, 'not only was there no confusion, but there was presented to the public a series of spectacles which, for seamlessness, order and even magnificence at the appropriate moments, would have done credit to any country. Greece has never seen anything like this before.' Virtually the whole Greek royal family was in attendance, including Philip, whom Hahn had given special leave from Gordonstoun.

This was Philip's first sight of the country of his birth since his father's banishment fourteen years before. He was transfixed by the whole occasion. Caught up in the 'pomp and panoply of royalty', he was eager to learn who was who and what was what to such an extent, as his cousin Alexandra of Greece recalled, that one of their aunts had to ask him to desist from bombarding everyone with questions.

His future now came up for discussion between his father and the king, who wanted him to enter the Greek Naval Academy. Hahn later stated that Philip 'keenly felt' the 'lure of early and undeserved importance'. He was sorely 'tempted by both the hazards and comforts likely to come to a Prince of Greece in Athens.' But Andrew's view, repeated elsewhere to his mother-in law, prevailed: 'Never the Greek Navy. In the Greek Navy after a bit they would throw him out – that's what they did to me, not once....or twice, but three times!' There was also the fact that the Greek royal family in general, and Alice and her brother Dickie Mountbatten in particular, appreciated that Philip was ideally configured for the role of consort to the next British queen. His character, good looks, background, and commitment to service all equipped him ideally for the role, and Queen Mary, with her awe of royalty, was in favour of Philip in a way Lilibet's mother, who wanted British aristocrats like herself for her daughters, would never be.

Fortunately for the ambitions of the Greek royals, Lilibet was well known to have a close and loving relationship with her grandmother, who was schooling her for the role of monarch in a way Elizabeth never could. A stint in the Royal Navy would be preferable to one in the Greek Navy. Philip, therefore, returned to Britain to complete his schooling at Gordonstoun, before taking the necessary steps to enter Dartmouth naval college. He seems to have made his peace quite happily, asserting, 'England is my home,' though he was also tempted by the lure of a Greek future.

Meanwhile Alice, the mother he had not seen for years was making a steady recovery. She was living in a boarding house in the country near Cologne, and though still embittered by the way her family had behaved during her illness, re-established contact gradually. In the spring of 1937, she allowed her mother to see her, and that Easter, while Philip was staying with Cecile and Don at Wolfsgarten, the Hesse hunting lodge outside Darmstadt, she met her son, daughter and son-in-law for lunch in Bonn. None of her children had seen Alice for five years, but the meeting was a great success on all sides. This was followed in the summer by equally successful visits to Theodora at Schloss Kirchberg on Lake Constance, and Margarita at Langenburg, where the family's palace was splendour itself.

That same summer, Philip and his father travelled to Darmstadt to see Uncle Ernie, who was fading slowly but surely from lung disease. In situ was Philip's grandmother Victoria, Dowager Marchioness of Milford Haven and Ernie's eldest sister. She had come over from England to help nurse him. Nursing was something of a vocation in the Hesse family. Their mother, Alice, Queen Victoria's second daughter, had been a nurse and had founded the Alice-Hospital in Darmstadt as well as the Princess Alice Women's Guild, an organisation for training nurses in the grand duchy of Hesse. Her daughter Ella, Grand Duchess Serge, had also been a nurse, and her granddaughter Alice had been mooting the idea of starting an order of nursing nuns.

Uncle Ernie's decline, however, was more precipitate than expected. His death would inadvertently lead to other deaths, because his demise on 9th October came so much sooner than expected that the coming wedding of his second son, Ludwig, to the Hon. Margaret Campbell-Geddes had to be postponed and rescheduled for November.

Although not royal, Peg Geddes, as Margaret was known, had a sufficiently grand background for the Hesse family to approve of the match. Their approval showed to what extent European royalty had altered their standards since the Great War. Her father, the 1st Lord Geddes, had been a member of David Lloyd George's Coalition Government during the war, and had also served as British Ambassador to the United States. Since the British Royal Family had welcomed into its bosom the merely aristocratic Lady Elizabeth Bowes Lyon in 1923 upon her marriage to the second in line to the throne, 'equal birth' had been stretched beyond royalty to include aristocracy, not only for the British royal family but for many other royal families in Europe as well.

Lu's marriage to Peg was postponed and rescheduled for 20th November in London, where the groom was the German Ambassador Joachim von Ribbentrop's secretary. A splendid state funeral was being organised for the deposed Grand Duke in Darmstadt, though Alice was not informed, lest the news unsettle her. In the event, she read about it in the newspapers and attended it on 12th October 1937. There were vast crowds of mourners, who made it clear how much they had respected their late and former sovereign, causing many comments to the effect that it was hard to believe that Hesse was now a republic.

Alice's conduct, both during the funeral and for the week afterwards, was exemplary. She had not seen her brother Georgie Milford Haven for seven years or her sister Crown Princess Louise of Sweden for five, and their mother wrote to Philip, who remained at Gordonstoun, to say that his mother 'spent a week with us all at Wolfsgarten. She was quite her old self again, like before she fell ill.'

Don and Cecile were now the occupants of the defunct grand ducal throne, with his younger brother the sole heir after their two young sons. This was not quite the hollow patrimony one might imagine it to have been. The family was popular in the former grand duchy, and they had retained all their properties. Like most of the dethroned German royals, they were far richer than many of the other dethroned royals who had been forced into exile, leaving their countries and properties behind. This had doubtless been a consideration when Andrew was arranging the marriages of his daughters, all of whom had married German royals with financial substance. Everyone therefore looked forward with confidence and expectation to Don and Cecile sharing the honour, respect, and regality which his father had enjoyed as the occupant of the former grand ducal throne.

It was a happy Hesse grand ducal family who left Darmstadt on 16th November to fly to London for the wedding. The party consisted of Don, his mother Eleonore the Dowager Grand Duchess, his wife Cecile, their two sons Ludwig and Alexander, Cecile's lady-in-waiting Alice Hahn, and the best man, Joachim von Riesdesel, as well as the pilot and two crewmen from Sabena. They left behind their one year old daughter Johanna. Cecile was seven months pregnant, and seems to have gone into labour during the flight, forcing the pilot to try to land at Ostend in Belgium. That city, however, was encased in fog. When the second and third of the emergency guidances failed to reach the pilot, he flew blind, hit a factory chimney some 150 feet high and killed all the occupants. Discovered in the wreckage was the corpse of Cecile's newly-born son. The Belgian enquiry into the crash concluded that the pilot had been trying to make an emergency landing despite the bad weather, owing to the medical emergency.

The wiping out of a young family is a tragedy, and the shock for their surviving loved ones can be easily imagined. Lu and Peg had gone to Croydon Aerodrome to meet the party, who were due to stay with Dickie and Edwina Mountbatten at Brook House, their palatial London residence in Mayfair. After being advised that the flight was delayed, a Sabena official informed the prince of what had happened. Devastated, he and Peg returned to her father's house, where a 'ghastly' family meeting took place. According to Dickie, 'My mother said the wedding ought to go ahead, not in four days' time with all the formality and publicity, but the very next day, while they were still in a state of shock.'

Although the marriage had been scheduled for 20th November, it was duly brought forward. Ludwig was the sole surviving male in his branch of the family, as well as the sole adult survivor. He needed the support of a wife more than ever, so the following day he and Peg took their vows at St. Peter's Eaton Square. The bride wore black instead of the Bavarian national dress she had intended to wear, everyone else was in mourning, and Dickie Mountbatten stood in for the dead best man.

Rather than a celebratory bridal night, the bride and groom left London to make a choppy crossing to Belgium, where they had the sad task of identifying the remains of the family. The eleven coffins were loaded onto a train back to Darmstadt the following day.

No one was harder hit by the tragedy than sixteen year old Prince Philip. Cecile had been his favourite sister and Don his favourite brother-in-law. He says, 'I spent most of my holidays with them in Darmstadt or at Wolfsgarten,' their hunting lodge near Frankfurt. To lose them so suddenly was a sadness which he took in his stride but has evidently felt for the remainder of his life. Gina Kennard said, 'He loved his sisters very much, and when Cecile was killed in that air crash in 1937, it affected him deeply.' Although he did not wear his heart on his sleeve, he kept as a talisman a small piece of wood from the aeroplane with him at all times. He once showed it to Gina, who was impressed by its symbolism, observing that 'it meant a lot to him'.

Right after the wedding, Philip and his uncle Lord Louis Mountbatten, left London for Darmstadt, where the funerals took place on 19th November. There is a touching picture of the funeral procession, led by Ludwig, with

Philip immediately behind him flanked by his sisters' husbands Prince Berthold of Baden, Prince Friedel of Hohenlohe-Langenburg, and Prince Christopher of Hesse, with the latter's brother, the namesake Philipp of Hesse, on his right.

According to Princess Margaret of Hesse and the Rhine, as Peg now became, the funerals tore at the hearts of all their loved ones.

(Princess Margaret's styling came about because her husband Ludwig was now the head of the family and, though not styled Grand Duke of Hesse the way he would have been before the abolition of the monarchy in 1918, his new wife, as the consort of a would-be sovereign, became HRH Princess Margaret of Hesse and the Rhine. Had George Donatus and his sons lived, she would otherwise have been merely Her Grand Ducal Highness Princess Ludwig of Hesse.

Although Alice had not seen her husband for years, at their daughter's funeral, the couple saw each other again. She made it known that she was prepared to reconcile with him, but he was fully established with Comtesse Andrée de La Bigne, with no wish to reshape his personal arrangements, so afterwards they once more went their separate ways.

The shock of Cecile's death had the most ironic effect upon Alice. Although Dr Binswanger had told Victoria that her daughter would, 'always need to be discreetly watched over & guided', Theodora told him that what he characterised as the 'first curative shock' had 'completely cured' her mother. He concurred that, 'contrary to what was expected it apparently tore her out of everything'.

It would appear that the shock did indeed cure her. There is now some doubt that she was ever a paranoid-schizophrenic. Her symptoms and the development of her illness all dovetail with what we now call bi-polar disorder. The excesses of energy she had displayed, not only while ill, but when setting up her hospitals during the war; the heightened sexuality; the bouts of torpor and lassitude, even the anger at her family's reaction to her condition, all suggest a pattern of fluctuating high and low which medicine now recognises as bi-polar. Shock treatment, whose value as a treatment for mental illness has been much challenged for the last century, is now recognised as being one of the few effective tools that work with bi-polar patients when their systems are resistant to drug therapy.

Cecile's death also resulted in Alice letting go of the last vestiges of cautiousness she had regarding mixing with her family. She had been talking of returning to Greece and setting up an order of nursing nuns even before Cecile's death. This had been cause for concern where Cecile and her sisters were concerned, for they had wondered if this was another sign that their mother, whose religiosity had been a feature of her illness, was in danger of relapsing. It turned out not to be. This really was Alice's calling, the vocation that would give her life definition and purpose, and allow her to live out the rest of her life on an even, if spiritually elevated, keel.

The following January, while Alice was making preparations to move back to Athens, Philip and his father met up in Rome. They then set out for the Greek capital, where Philip was due to act as one of the three supporters (best men in royal parlance) at the marriage of his first cousin Paul to another cousin, Princess Frederica of Hanover. The other two supporters were Peter of Greece and Michael of Roumania, who had been replaced on the throne by his father, King Carol II. Theodora and Margarita also joined the festivities.

Alice then moved back to Athens. 'I have taken a small flat, just for you and me,' she wrote Philip. 'Two bedrooms, each with a bathroom and two sitting rooms. I have found some furniture stored away in various places in the Old Palace, which I had not seen again since 1917, a most agreeable surprise & the family here are giving me things to complete it.' It was well located, near the Benaki Museum, and she concluded with, 'Dickie tells me there is a chance of you having a holiday in Spring so I am looking forward to your living in our flat.' Alice set about founding her charity and working with the poor. She had finally found her calling, and would go on to found an order of nursing sisters. She would ultimately dress as a nun, though at this point she was still clad in mufti. But her lifestyle was hardly luxurious and certainly not at all regal.

Although Philip had not lived with either parent throughout the 30s, he and his father had continually corresponded during their years apart. Once Alice was back in his life, they too wrote each other weekly letters. Life seemed to be settling down to a discernible rhythm when, out of the blue, another death jolted Philip.

If the deaths of Cecile and her family were sudden, the other death which would impact so powerfully upon the young prince was anything but. Nevertheless, it too came like a bolt out of nowhere and proved to be equally shocking. Within weeks of the Hesses' funerals, Uncle Georgie slipped and fell on a marble floor in London, breaking his thigh bone. Bones normally take six weeks to heal, so when it became apparent that his break was not healing, investigations led to a diagnosis of terminal, untreatable bone cancer. Nada and the rest of the family were disconsolate, but they decided to put up a show for the patient's sake and kept his prognosis from Georgie.

## Chapter II

Philip was billeted to spend Christmas with the Wernhers at Lubenham, the Milford Havens being in no position to play host. According to Gina Wernher, it was a 'very sad Christmas'. Philip was grieving for Cecile and Don. 'He was very quiet.' This was uncharacteristic of the normally boisterous young man, who did not display his emotions even as he struggled to contain them.

When Philip returned to Gordonstoun in the new year, Victoria wrote to him to tell him that his favourite uncle had been 'moved to a nicer nursing home, where he can have treatment.' He died on 8th April, still being told he was on the road to recovery. He was only forty five. 'He was one of the most intelligent and brilliant of people,' his cousin Lilibet stated. This was not hyperbole. An accomplished mathematician, who had been a naval officer, he used to work out complicated gunnery problems in his head and read Calculus for pleasure. He left two children, his son David, and Tatiana, his first-born, who was handicapped and would outlive all her immediate family, dying in 1988.

Notwithstanding the accommodations Georgie and Nada had had to make so that their marriage would survive, or possibly because of them, they were a genuinely loving couple and the atmosphere in their family had been warm, inviting, and nurturing, without being excessively demanding. Nada's sister Zia thought her 'louche', and disapproved equally of the other Mountbatten wife, Edwina, but Philip was always happy to be a part of Uncle Georgie and Aunt Nada's family. Georgie's death, though expected, was a tremendous loss to all his loved ones, especially the two boys, David and Philip. Philip was now left with only Harold Wernher as an adult male role model.

The deaths, however, were not yet at an end. Barely eighteen months after the plane crash which killed the rest of her immediate family, little Johanna, who had been left behind at Darmstadt and subsequently adopted by Lu and Peg, was diagnosed as suffering from meningitis. Alice, now fully re-incorporated into the family, had been en route to England to see Philip when the news of her granddaughter's likely death at the Alice Hospital reached her. She immediately diverted to Darmstadt, but soon after arriving, her granddaughter died. She wrote Philip a touching letter commenting upon how much like Cecile little Johanna looked as she lay dying. She felt it was like losing her child a second time, and, showing the affection she still had for her estranged husband, and the way they all gracefully finessed away awkward situations, she said, 'I was thankful that Papa was away travelling, for Papa adored Cecile when she was small and could never bear to be parted from her.'

Throughout the years, there has been a persistent myth, which Prince Philip himself has gone to some pains to squash, that the uncle who nurtured him while he was growing up was Georgie's younger brother Dickie, Lord Louis Mountbatten. The mere fact that Philip has felt compelled to address it shows where his true affections lay. While he has never been known to utter a word against his uncle George, who acted *in loco parentis* in a nurturing, non-dominating way, and he showed his regard for Harold Wernher by continuing to spend holidays with his family at Luton Hoo even after he was married – he and Lilibet always celebrated their wedding anniversary with them - he has often said, and even more frequently implied, that keeping his uncle Dickie in his box required sustained effort. Although Dickie did take over once Georgie was dead, it was the excessive taking over by the overbearing older man, interfering incessantly with the younger, and when not interfering, making inflated claims which appeared, to the young and intelligent prince, to be attempts to boost uncle rather than nephew, that caused friction between them.

There was also the tricky matter of Dickie's rank, which was no longer royal, and of Prince Philip's, which indubitably was. More than Georgie, Dickie had felt the loss of his princely rank acutely, to such an extent that when he was first offered a peerage, he refused on the grounds that, having been demoted from a prince to the second son of a marquis, it was intolerable to expect him to accept a further demotion, second sons of marquises outranking barons in the tables of precedence. With one sister a Swedish crown princess and another a Greek princess, he seemed to be the royal version of the *Ancient Mariner*, forever thirsting for something he was surrounded by but did not possess, except that it wasn't water, water everywhere, with not a drop to drink, but royal titles, royal titles everywhere, with not even one for him.

Dickie was also notorious, in the family and outside of it, for being an arch self-promoter whose ambition knew no bounds. There is little doubt that Philip put as much distance between his uncle and himself as he could, while retaining the family links. Not only was this because Dickie Mountbatten would 'take over', which someone who knew his own mind like Philip found antipathetic, but also because his uncle's reputation could have been injurious to his own interests and ambitions. Dickie was called as straight as a corkscrew, and his machinations antagonised others almost as much as his constant harping on his royal links.

Ironically, however, it was Dickie who helped arrange an encounter between Philip and Lilibet which resulted in the touch-paper of sexual attraction being lit. And, even more ironically, it was Lilibet's mother, Queen

# Chapter II

Elizabeth, who would later become something of an adversary to Philip, who was the other instigator.

# Chapter III

ALTHOUGH PHILIP would later tell his friend and biographer Gyles Brandreth that he would, 'have gone into the Air Force without a doubt' had he been left to his own devices upon leaving Gordonstoun in the summer of 1938, he opted to follow his maternal grandfather, Prince Louis of Battenberg, 1st Marquis of Milford Haven and former First Sea Lord, and his uncle Dickie, 1st Earl Mountbatten of Burma and another, future, First Sea Lord, into the British Navy. Navies generally were something of a tradition in his wider family. His paternal grandfather, King George I of the Hellenes, had been in the Danish navy, as had his great-uncle Valdemar of Denmark and his uncle George of Greece, who also served in the Greek Navy.

At the end of the summer holidays, Philip went to Cheltenham, where he lodged with Mr and Mrs Mercer while the former coached him for the Civil Service examination which he would have to pass before he could be accepted as a cadet at the Royal Naval College at Dartmouth.

This was a fraught and sad time for the young man. He was still coming to terms with the death of his uncle Georgie Milford Haven, whose death, according to his cousin Gina Wernher, 'was another blow for Philip, especially coming as it did, only a matter of months after his sister Cecile and her family were killed in that awful crash. It was a difficult time.'

Like his mother, however, Philip had a streak of indomitability and the resolve to meet whatever challenges life threw at him. He therefore knuckled down to his studies, proving yet again that his combination of natural intelligence and determination would see him through. Nevertheless, Philip was no academic, and expended only as much energy as was required to garner sufficient knowledge to pass his examinations. His gifts lay outside the classroom, not within it, and he came a modest sixteen out of thirty-four cadets in his entrance examinations.

We have an insight into his way of life and the burgeoning relationship with the uncle he so far barely knew and would thereafter do his utmost to 'handle', as a result of a letter Dickie wrote to his wife Edwina in March 1938. 'Philip was here all last week doing his entrance examinations for the

Navy. He had his meals with us and he really is killingly funny. I like him very much.' The tone shows how slightly Dickie and Edwina knew Philip.

At Dartmouth, Philip would show yet again that his brilliance lay not in academe but in how he dealt with the living world. He entered the naval college on 4th May 1939, and resolved to excel, in keeping with the example of his uncle Dickie, who had placed first out of the whole college in his final examinations. But Philip was his own man. He had no desire to follow in Dickie's footsteps, even as he sought to emulate his success. So he applied himself no more strenuously than he had during classes at Gordonstoun, proving Hahn's comment to be true that he only exerted himself as much as he needed to. His written work only ever got average marks, but his oral score, when his presence of mind became a factor, was 95%, demonstrating that when he could bring the brilliance of his personality into play, he excelled. After his first term, he was awarded the King's Dirk as the best all-round cadet of his term and the Eardley-Howard- Crockett Award for the best cadet at the college. This set him up for having as brilliant a naval career as his grandfather had had, and his uncle Dickie would eventually have.

In 1939, however, Dickie Mountbatten was no high-flier the way he would become during the Second World War and thereafter. He had only recently, in June of that year, been given command of the destroyer *HMS Kelly*. Captain Lord Louis Mountbatten was also at that time a relatively humble naval *aide-de-camp* to his cousin, King George VI. His appointment was, in part, a reward for having switched allegiance from David's camp to Bertie's, following the abdication, and while Bertie was fond of him, Elizabeth remained distrustful, and would continue to be for the remainder of his life. But the two princely cousins had both been cadets at Dartmouth, and with the possibility of war looming, a visit to the naval college had been scheduled for Saturday, 22nd July 1939.

King George VI and Queen Elizabeth had only recently returned from a triumphant visit to the United States, which had itself been preceded by an equally triumphant visit to Paris. Both these visits had been attempts to drum up support in the event of a war against Nazi Germany, which seemed increasingly likely, even though people, including the king and queen themselves, still hoped it would not come to that. These two foreign visits had turned the king and queen from rather drab replacements for the glamorous and popular King Edward VIII into genuine international superstars in their own right. Now that they were back in their native land, they were displaying, yet again, solidarity with those who might be called upon to defend the empire, hence the visit to the Dartmouth naval college.

They arrived on the royal yacht, the *Victoria and Albert*, which put into the River Dart. On board with the king and queen were the inevitable *aides-de-camp*, ladies-in-waiting, and the two royal princesses and their governess, Marion Crawford. She provided an extensive account of the visit in her memoir, *The Little Princesses*, which might well have been accurate, but I prefer to rely upon the account given by Queen Alexandra of Yugoslavia, as Philip's cousin and exact contemporary, Princess Alexandra of Greece, became when she married King Peter of Yugoslavia.

The reason why the girls were with their parents was that the family was on its annual summer cruise on the royal yacht. They would need to be entertained, so, according to Queen Alexandra, 'My Aunt Elizabeth and Uncle Dickie put their heads together' and hauled Philip away from his previously assigned duties to keep Lilibet and Margaret Rose company. 'Philip rather resented it, a youngster of eighteen called to help entertain a girl of thirteen and a child of nine.'

Crawfie verifies Alexandra's account in her memoir. Philip, she wrote, was 'rather offhand in his manner. He said, "How do you do" to Lilibet,' as if they had never met before, which they most certainly had. Philip himself places their first meeting as most likely being the wedding of her uncle George, Duke of Kent, to his first cousin, Princess Marina of Greece, on 29th November 1934. While there were other occasional and casual encounters, such as following her father's coronation, there was a world of difference between two children meeting at large family gatherings, and the thunderbolt that struck the adolescent Lilibet, when the gloriously masculine, stunningly handsome, pulsatingly energetic and sexy eighteen year old Nordic god hove into view with his amazingly blue eyes and the shock of white –blond hair slicked back in keeping with the custom of the day.

According to Crawfie, Philip paid more attention to nine year old Margaret than Lilibet. He was, 'quite polite with her, but he did not pay her any special attention.' They partook of ginger crackers and lemonade and Philip, 'spent a lot of time teasing plump little Margaret,' who, even then, was by far the more outgoing and entertaining of the two sisters. After politely enduring the ordeal of playing trains with them, boredom set in. This was understandable from the point of view of any eighteen year old boy. Lilibet and Margaret Rose were, in many ways, an oddity, for the elder sister was being kept artificially young at the insistence of their mother, while the precocious younger girl, dressed identically in childish attire, was encouraged by both parents to run riot openly.

Even as a little boy, Philip had exhibited the dual qualities of politeness and resourcefulness, so he proposed that they adjourn to the tennis courts, to 'have some fun.' They duly walked down to them, and Crawfie, ever protective of her charges, thought he showed off a great deal as he jumped over and over the nets, but the, 'little girls (note the *little* to describe a thirteen year old in the full flush of raging hormones) were much impressed.' Lilibet felt compelled to observe admiringly, as Mike Hollingsworth would do seventy two years later, 'How high he can jump.'

But admiration was only one of the many feelings Philip engendered in his young cousin. Long before Lilibet gave her father's biographer permission to state that she fell in love with Prince Philip on that occasion, Crawfie noticed, 'Lilibet never took her eyes off him the whole time.' Afterwards, she sang his praises. She was well and truly smitten, and, in true Hanoverian style, like her father and uncle David before her, once she had the bit between her teeth, there was no way of getting her to let go.

In royal circles, courtships involving actual or future queens regnant did not follow the same path as in aristocratic, bourgeois, or working class circles. The woman is the one who takes the first steps, who initiates the courtship, then invites the man in question to marry her. Queen Victoria, for instance, had to propose to Prince Albert, even though he was her first cousin and their mutual uncle, King Leopold of the Belgians, had done all he could to promote the match.

Because Lilibet was so young, her early interest passed unnoticed by everyone except Crawfie, and unremarked by all, at least contemporaneously. Later on, such cousins as Patricia Mountbatten, Dickie's elder daughter who succeeded to the Mountbatten earldom as the 2nd Countess Mountbatten of Burma following his assassination in 1979, would confirm, 'She fell in love with him at thirteen and has remained in love with him from that day to this.' But in 1939 her interest was easily mistaken for cousinly affection, so when their correspondence and visits started, it took a while for onlookers to twig as to what was going on.

Moreover, there were other, more momentous, events taking place worldwide than the possibility of a budding romance between the thirteen year old heiress to the British throne and the eighteen year old Greek prince before whose feet girls fell like nine pins. Just four weeks after the Dartmouth visit, on 23rd August, the German Foreign Minister Joachim von Ribbentrop and the Soviet Foreign Minister Vyacheslav Molotov signed a ten-year non-aggression pact on behalf of their respective governments. Known as the Molotov-Ribbentrop Pact or the Nazi-Soviet Pact, this freed the German army from fighting a two front war the way they had had to do in the Great War. This was yet another indication that Hitler was preparing to go to war, so Parliament was recalled from its summer recess on the 24th. The king was in Scotland where there were the most grouse he had ever seen, according to Sir Miles Lampson, later the 1st Lord Killearn and the husband of my late friend Jacqueline, Lady Killearn. An avid gun, George VI had bagged 1,600 brace in two days, and complained that it, 'was utterly damnable that the villain Hitler had upset everything'.

The Prime Minister, Neville Chamberlain, had been so firmly convinced that the peace would not be shattered that he had gone on a salmon fishing trip on 6th August, and encouraged the king to enjoy the shooting season in Scotland. He now reiterated his belief that a reminder that 'Britain meant business' would suffice to check Hitler. Nevertheless, George VI returned to London. On the 25th Britain and Poland signed an Agreement of Mutual Assistance in the event of either country being attacked by another European state. In doing this, the British Government virtually assured war against Nazi Germany.

George VI was as naïve as his politicians and the Poles in believing that, by signing such an agreement, Hitler's bluff would be called. They discovered to the contrary when the German army entered Poland on 1st September. The following day, Britain and France issued ultimata, and when the German Government failed to respond satisfactorily, those two nations declared war on Sunday, 3rd September, 1939.

Lilibet and Margaret Rose were still in Scotland when war was declared. Their mother returned south to be with their father on 28th August, so they could visibly lead the struggle against Hitler, spending their days at Buckingham Palace but their evenings at the more secure Windsor Castle. All the royal palaces were stripped of their valuables. Pictures were removed from the walls and sent for safekeeping along with the more valuable furniture. What remained was covered with dust sheets.

Meanwhile, Crawfie was called back early from her summer holidays, the castle was shut up, and the girls were moved to Birkhall on the Balmoral estate along with Crawfie, Alah, Bobo, and Ruby. It was judged to be safer than having them in London. Every evening they spoke to their parents on the telephone at six o'clock, which helped somewhat, for they missed them. Life, for both girls, continued on its serene way, for Elizabeth instructed Crawfie to adhere, 'to the usual programme as far as you can,' which was relatively easy to do in the early days of the war. There was little fighting, and the calm before the storm would go down in history as The Phoney War.

Nevertheless, there was the occasional incursion which ended badly for the British, such as the sinking of the *Royal Oak* at Scapa Flow with the loss of some eight hundred lives. According to Crawfie, Lilibet responded with fury and disbelief, jumping from her chair in horror and declaring, 'Crawfie, it can't be! All those nice sailors.'

The week before Christmas, the girls were taken to Sandringham to celebrate the holidays with their parents. Frantic preparations were afoot throughout the nation in case the war escalated, for Britain had not been prepared for it and, though there was a determination to fight any invasion, the possibility existed that the Germans might overrun us. There was talk of the two princesses being sent abroad, with Canada the favourite destination, but Queen Elizabeth flatly refused to leave her husband, and the girls would not leave without her. So the girls remained at Sandringham until February, after which they were spirited away to Royal Lodge, the old York family home in Windsor Great Park, where lessons with Crawfie resumed, their whereabouts a state secret. Meanwhile their cousins, Patricia and Pamela Mountbatten, were sent to New York to live with Grace Vanderbilt in case the Nazis invaded. With them it was an absolute necessity, for they qualified as Jewish under the Nazis codification of Aryanism, and had they been seized they would have been exterminated.

By and large, however, the first eight months of the war were quiet, until Germany invaded Denmark and Norway at around 4 o'clock on the morning of 9th April 1940. Denmark capitulated within two hours, its army, navy and air force overwhelmed by the attacking Nazis, who issued the explicit threat that the Luftwaffe would bomb the capital, Copenhagen, killing a large proportion of the country's population as they destroyed it. Denmark was a small country, with a small population, and its flat terrain and common border with Germany meant that further resistance would be suicidal. When only one general suggested resistance, the entire government and king, Christian X, capitulated in exchange for retaining political independence in domestic affairs. The occupation of Denmark, which would last until 5th May 1945, had begun.

Christian X now came into his own, becoming the focal point of national 'mental resistance'. Every day, for the first two and a half years of the war, the aged king, unaccompanied by ADCs or even a groom, rode his horse *Jubilee* through the streets of the capital, waving to and being waved at by his subjects, thereby silently affirming the bond between sovereign and people in the face of the occupying power. There is an account, possibly apocryphal, of one of the occupying Germans questioning whether the king was not endangering his life by going out without a bodyguard, only to be told, 'All Denmark is his bodyguard.'

This activity, however, came to an abrupt end when the old man fell from his horse and injured himself seriously on 9th October, 1942. Thereafter, he was a virtual invalid. By then, however, he had not only managed to become a revered symbol of resistance throughout the occupied kingdom, but had also ensured that his Jewish subjects would not have to wear the Star of David. This he did by the simple expedient of informing the occupying forces, as his diary entry confirms, 'I stated that I could not meet such a demand towards Danish citizens. If such a demand is made, we would best all wear the Star of David.'

Later on, when those self-same citizens were in danger of being rounded up for the Final Solution, Christian X helped finance the smuggling of the Jews of Denmark to their unoccupied neighbour, Sweden, where they were safe from Nazi persecution.

While Denmark was being overrun, its neighbour Norway, whose king, Haakon VII, was Christian X's younger brother Carl, found itself in a different predicament. King Haakon VII of Norway, known in the British, Greek and Danish royal families as Uncle Charles, was the widower of the former Princess Maud of Wales, Bertie's aunt. He was also the nephew of Bertie's grandmother Queen Alexandra and King George I of the Hellenes.

Haakon VII of Norway was another of those Danish princes who had been appointed to thrones. Born Prince Carl of Denmark, he accepted the throne of Norway in 1905 when it was offered, on the condition that the Norwegians have a referendum confirming their choice of monarchy over a republic. This they did by a resounding majority of 79% of the vote, being 259,563 pro and 69,264 contra. He was a popular and respected constitutional monarch. When the Nazis invaded and demanded the replacement of the democratically elected Prime Minister with Vidkun Quisling, leader of the Norwegian fascist party, Nasjonal Samling, Haakon VII, with the consent of the democratically elected Storting (Parliament), refused to appoint someone he knew would never be acceptable to his government or people. When the German envoy to Norway, Curt Bauer, suggested that Haakon accept capitulation the way his brother King Christian X had done in Denmark, he informed him that he could not act without the consent of his government, and they had declined to give it. He did not say that he had also advised his government that he would not stand in their way should they wish to make peace with the enemy, but if they did, he would abdicate. In fact, the royal prerogative did give him the authority to make war or sue for peace, without reference to the government, but his refusal to do so earned him the undying love of his people and the respect of the lawfully elected government, which fled from the capital to the British supported hinterlands, along with the king and Crown Prince Olav, Bertie's first cousin.

Although the Allies were in secure possession of northern Norway, which was mountainous, when the Nazis overran France in May 1940, the Allied High Command took the decision to withdraw its forces from Norway. This meant the inevitable capitulation of Norway. The democratically elected government took the decision to go into exile with the king and continue the fight from England. Crown Prince Olav offered to stay behind with his wife and three young children, Princesses Ragnhild and Astrid, and Prince Harald, who is the present king of Norway, but his offer was declined. On 7th June 1940, the British sent the heavy cruiser *HMS Devonshire* to evacuate the royals and government, along with 461 passengers.

For the duration of the war, Quisling ruled supreme in Norway as its Prime Minister, but at the end of the war he was arrested, tried, found guilty of embezzlement, murder and high treason, and sentenced to death. He was executed by firing squad on 24th October 1945. His name is such a byword for traitor that he and Judas Iscariot share the dubious distinction of being the only two individuals in history whose names are synonymous with treachery in several different languages, English included.

The Norwegian crisis led to the fall of the British Prime Minister, Neville Chamberlain, who had succeeded Stanley Baldwin in May 1937. Wildly popular at the time of the Munich crisis, when he shared the Buckingham Palace balcony with the king and queen having returned waving a piece of paper with Hitler's signature which, he said, promised 'peace in our time', by 1940 his premiership was untenable. He was widely blamed for having appeased Hitler in 1938, and, at a time when a government of national unity was fundamental to the survival of the nation, neither Labour nor Liberal MPs would serve in a government with him at its head. He therefore resigned, to be replaced by Winston Churchill, one of the few British politicians to have systematically opposed Hitler from the very start.

Neither George VI nor Elizabeth wanted Winston Churchill as Prime Minister. He had been one of King Edward VIII's most vociferous supporters – a position that invariably resulted in everlasting hatred from Elizabeth – and Bertie, as usual, was swept up in the wake of his charismatic and strong-minded wife. However, Churchill was the man the nation wanted, so he was called upon to kiss hands with the king.

Meanwhile, Lilibet and Margaret Rose, who had been living at Royal Lodge with Crawfie, Alah, Bobo and Ruby, were moved to nearby Windsor Castle, in the interests of security. They would remain there, with few breaks, for the remainder of the war.

Ever since their move south, the girls had once again been seeing their parents on a regular, usually daily, basis. The king and queen's routine, which had already been established while their daughters were in Scotland, seldom varied. Days were usually spent at Buckingham Palace in London, nights and weekends at Windsor.

Buckingham Palace now became royalty's version of a refugee camp. First to arrive were King Haakon VII and Crown Prince Olav with his family. They were quickly followed by the heiress to the Dutch throne, Princess Juliana, her husband the former Prince Bernhard of Lippe-Biesterfeld, and their two young daughters, Beatrix and Irene. Her mother, the widowed Queen Wilhelmina, was evacuated with the Dutch Government on board the British destroyer *HMS Hereward* the day after her daughter's flight from the Netherlands. Juliana and her children quickly left for Canada, but Wilhelmina and Prince Bernhardt of the Netherlands, as he had become upon marriage, stayed behind.

Relations with the Dutch queen's Prime Minister, Dirk Jan de Geer, quickly deteriorated. He foresaw a German victory and openly advocated opening negotiations for a separate peace. The iron-willed Wilhelmina demonstrated the effectiveness of monarchy by orchestrating his removal with the aid of the anti-Nazi minister, Pieter Sjjoerds Gerbrandy, who replaced him to serve as Prime Minister from 3rd September 1940 till 25th June 1945. Like Haakon VII, who regularly used the BBC World Service radio broadcasts to drum up resistance and inform his people of the conduct of the war, Wilhelmina and her Prime Minister were also soon strengthening resistance in the Netherlands via Dutch Radio Oranje under the aegis of the BBC.

Next to arrive and avail herself of the services of the BBC, while staying at Buckingham Palace, was Grand Duchess Charlotte of Luxembourg. She had escaped from her country with her government when the Germans violated its neutrality on 9th May 1940. Unlike the Dutch and Norwegian royals, who had come directly to Britain, Charlotte, her husband Prince Felix of Bourbon-Parma, their numerous children and her government, took a more circuitous route. First they sought refuge in France, which soon fell. As it was doing so, the Luxembourgers were granted safe passage to Portugal through Spain as long as they did not stop in that country. By 29th August the grand duchess, her family, and her government-in-exile were in London. However, it would be another two years before monarch and government settled in London. She soon left Britain for Canada, where she enrolled her children at school in Montreal, and travelled extensively between Canada, the United States, and Britain, raising the profile of her small grand duchy as she drummed up support for the Allied cause.

As the foreign royals poured into London, taking advantage of the protection offered against the Nazis by the English Channel and the North Sea, the Battle of Britain began. It would run from 10th July to 31st October. Hitler's original intention was to overwhelm British defences from the air, following which Operation Sea Lion, the invasion of Britain by sea and air, would take place. To soften up the calf for the slaughter, day by day the Luftwaffe came over in waves, bombing such essentials as coastal shipping convoys, ports and shipping centres like Portsmouth, RAF airfields, factories involved in the production of aircraft, and other essential war materiel. Buckingham Palace itself was hit on sixteen separate occasions, the first taking place on 8th September. The quadrangle and forecourt received direct hits on the 13th of that month, as did the royal chapel, causing Elizabeth to say, 'I am glad we have been bombed. It makes me feel I can look the East End in the face.'

While the Battle of Britain was raging over the skies of the kingdom, the Blitz began on 7th September 1940. These deadly, large-scale night attacks saw tons and tons of bombs raining down on British targets. On the 14th of that month, Hitler withdrew his directive not to bomb population centres, following which London and many other major cities and their citizens found themselves being targeted. In so doing, the Germans sought to pound the British populace into submission. Their actions, however, had the opposite effect.

With their backs against the wall, the British fought back furiously. RAF Bomber Command began flying night raids into Germany, disrupting the preparation of such invasion essentials as converted barges, while demonstrating that the Luftwaffe's aim of knocking out the Royal Air Force was not succeeding. This forced Hitler to delay, then cancel, Operation Sea Lion.

Many people who lived through the Battle of Britain and the Blitz said that it was the most exciting time of their lives. At Windsor, however, Lilibet, still subject to a child's regimen at the age of fourteen, was cocooned not only from the excitement but the danger inherent therein. She lived with her ten year old sister on a floor in the Augusta Tower known as the nursery.

This was made up of five rooms: three bedrooms apportioned to Lilibet, Margaret Rose, and Alah, as well as the 'day' nursery and the schoolroom. Bobo and Ruby had bedrooms on the floor above, while Crawfie reposed in the Victorian Tower, signifying her superior station. Not only did the sisters do their lessons in the nursery; they also ate there. Breakfast lasted for a maximum of half an hour and was served punctually at nine o'clock by Cyril Dickman, the footman who brought up the food from the castle kitchen, which was some distance away, as kitchens inevitably are in castles. At half past nine the girls were seated in the classroom ready to start their lessons, which lasted an hour and a half, before they took a break for an hour. They frequently rode in Windsor Great Park, Elizabeth and Bertie being great believers in exercise and outdoor living, after which there were more lessons till lunch time, which was from one to two. They then had more lessons, which finished at half past four, following which they had a traditional tea with cakes, scones and sandwiches. Five to seven thirty was their leisure time, which they filled with activities such as the Girl Guides and going for rambling walks, after which they repaired to the nursery to be served simple fare such as shepherd's pie or sausage and 'buttered potatoes', as they called the dish more popularly known as mashed potatoes.

The girls' syllabus was initially created by Crawfie in conjunction with Elizabeth. It included English Literature, Grammar, Writing and Composition, History, Arithmetic, Geography, and Scripture, which were taught before lunch, with Music, Dancing and Drawing in the afternoon, and French classes firstly by Mrs Montaudon-Smith and from 1941 onwards by the stylish Belgian refugee, Vicomtesse Pierre de Ballaigue. Born Marie Antoinette Willemin, 'Toinon' was employed firstly by George VI's Private Secretary, the 2nd Lord Hardinge of Penshurst, to teach his children French, and when this proved a howling success he recommended her to the king and queen, who snapped her up. Toinon de Ballaigue not only taught both princesses French and French Literature, but opened their eyes and minds to a far more sophisticated world than Crawfie and Mrs Montaudon-Smith were capable of doing. She said, 'In our general conversations, I endeavoured to give the princesses an awareness of other countries, their way of thought and customs – sometimes a source of amusement. Queen Elizabeth II has always had from the beginning a positive good judgement. She was her simple self, *très naturelle*. And there was always a strong sense of duty mixed with *joie de vivre* in the pattern of her character.' Toinon, as the girls called her, also functioned in tandem with the Vice-Provost of Eton, Henry Marten (knighted in 1945 upon becoming Provost, till 1949), who would set essays in French for both princesses on continental history subjects which *la baronne* would, at his instigation, teach them.

# Chapter III

Marten was an interesting character. A founder of the Historical Association in 1906, six years later he co-authored with George Townsend Warner one of the most popular school textbooks of the first half of the twentieth century: *The Groundwork of British History*. He next co-authored another school textbook, this time for younger children, which was simply entitled *Histories*, and in 1938 co-produced yet another book called *The Teaching of History*. He not only loved history, but had a capacity for communicating his enthusiasm to his students. His technique was enhanced by his personality, which was colourful to say the least. He had a pet raven, which lived with him in his rooms at Eton and would sometimes, while reposing on his shoulder, playfully nip his ear. He kept lumps of sugar in his pocket, which he would pop into his mouth and nibble while teaching. He never looked at his students, but looked beyond them, Elizabeth included, while he passionately communicated the thoughts, idea and love of history which drove him.

While still Lord Dunglass, the future Prime Minister Sir Alec Douglas-Home (previously the 14th Earl of Home and subsequently the life peer Lord Home of the Hirsel) had been taught at Eton by Marten, and he remembered him as being a racy and enthusiastic teacher who viewed history and historical personalities very much as living things. The ideas in Walter Bagehot's *The English Constitution*, which some people might have found dry reading but which was something of a bible to the British monarchy - to such an extent that both Lilibet's father and grandfather knew it off by heart - came to life with such vivacity when Marten lectured on that weighty tome that Lilibet didn't even need to memorise it to learn it back to front and inside out. In years to come, she would refer back to it when some of her Prime Ministers tried to function beyond it, or get her to do so. Sometimes, Marten would get so carried away with his own enthusiasm that he would forget his sole pupil was his next queen, and address her as 'Gentlemen,' the way he addressed his students at Eton.

Marten had been roped in to teach the heiress presumptive constitutional history at the instigation of her grandmother, Queen Mary, who had been appalled, as had Crawfie, by the standard of education Elizabeth deemed acceptable for Britain's future monarch. He used to come over from Eton in a dog-cart, but this was not eccentricity so much as practicality, for rationing was the order of the day and the Gladstone bag full of books, with which he would lumber the footman as soon as he arrived, would have been far less wieldy on a bicycle, and certainly impossible to carry on foot.

Marten also had a very willing student in Lilibet. From childhood, Queen Mary had instilled a love of history in her favourite grandchild, and one of her favourite activities was to sit and listen to the elder members of the family talk about the past. Once, when Queen Victoria's granddaughter Princess Marie Louise (daughter of Princess Helena and Prince Christian of Schleswig-Holstein) commented how bored she must be listening to a bunch of ancients chattering about the past, she said, 'But Cousin Louie, it's **history** and therefore so thrilling.'

The five years age difference between Lilibet and Philip meant that he had completed his schooling by the summer of 1939, after which he had gone to stay with his mother in Greece. The outbreak of the war found them there. They had arrived shortly before the declaration, having left London on 11th August for Paris, where they spent three days before travelling by train to Italy, then onwards to Greece by boat.

The war presented Philip and his loved ones with a dilemma. He was very pro-British and wanted to play a part in the struggle against Nazism, notwithstanding his three surviving sisters being married to German officers. Greece, however, was neutral, so he would not be able to resist Nazism if he entered the Greek navy. However, he was now closer to the Greek throne than he had ever been. Only the king's brother Paul and his Uncle George's son Peter stood between him and the crown, and that month Peter lost his right of succession when he married his mistress of five years, the twice divorced Russian, Irina Alexandrovna Ovtchinnikova, at the Danish consulate in Madras, without the permission of the king. If Frederica had only girls, Philip would ascend the throne after Paul.

Alice was in favour of Philip staying in Greece, as was her mother Victoria, though their reasons differed. The former espoused the view to her brother Dickie that he was such a stranger to the language and people of his homeland that he needed to establish a bond with them before it was too late to do so, in the event that he became king, while his grandmother believed that war was too dangerous a business for him to put himself in the line of fire unnecessarily, which, she feared, he would do if he entered the Royal Navy. However, his father Andrew remained dead against his entering the Greek navy, and George II resolved the dilemma by recommending that Philip return to the naval college at Dartmouth.

This left Philip in a new quandary. As the citizen of a neutral country, he was prevented by regulations from serving in a theatre of war. Nor could he renounce his citizenship or apply for naturalisation, as all such applications had been suspended for the duration of the war. Ironically, he was already a British subject. The *Act of Settlement* of 1701, which settled the throne on King James I of England and VI of Scotland's Protestant granddaughter

Sophie had been further ratified by the 1705 *Act for the Naturalization of the Most Excellent Princess Sophia, Electress and Dowager Duchess of Hanover, and the Issue of her Body*, stipulating that she and all the non-Catholic issue of her body were English. This automatically made Philip a British subject, although no one, not even the king or his uncle Dickie, appeared to know that fact.

George VI and Dickie Mountbatten knocked heads together and agreed that Philip could serve in the China Station, after the latter's former flotilla commander, H.T. Baillie Grohman, agreed to have him serving as a midshipman on the battleship *Ramillies*. This vessel escorted convoys of Australian and New Zealand troopships heading for Egypt, and, much to Philip's disappointment, was not in danger of entering the fighting.

Philip joined the *Ramillies* on 22nd February 1940, at the Ceylonese capital, Colombo, having travelled out on HMAS *Hobart*. An old vessel, *Ramillies* was swelteringly hot at night once the scuttles were shut, and Philip, as Captain's doggie, was starting at the very first rung of the ladder, having to do such chores as make the cocoa. However, he went about his chores with resolute cheerfulness as the battleship headed first to Sydney, and from there to Aden. After a three month stint, he was transferred to the flagship of the China Station, a county-class cruiser called the *Kent*. He regarded this as a mixed blessing. On the one hand, he was pleased that it was now, 'quite possible to sleep below decks in comfort,' but he bemoaned being unsettled just as he was, 'beginning to settle down and get accustomed to a definite routine.' Although the men had dreaded having a royal on board, Philip soon won them over with his willingness to do whatever was asked of him cheerfully and with a smile.

The *Kent* steamed via the Chagos Islands to Bombay, and escorted troops home via Durban in South Africa, where Philip was impressed by the natives' 'grand unselfish hospitality.' Nevertheless, he remained frustrated by the fighting eluding him, and yearned to see action. It was coming sooner than he realised.

In August, Philip disembarked from the *Kent* in Colombo for a five week stint on a shore station, after which he was posted to its sister ship, the *Shropshire*. This involved convoy duties up and down the east coast of Africa, from the Red Sea to Durban. Two months later, Greece entered the war on the Allied side when Mussolini's forces invaded that kingdom via Albania. The Italian dictator had previously invaded Albania on 7th April 1939, forcing the Albanian king, Zog, into exile, and declaring Albania a part of the Italian Empire. Greece, however, was not Albania, which had capitulated after five days. Although Il Duce had thought that the Greeks would be equally easily defeated, they put up a fierce resistance, which meant that Italy was pushed back into Albania, which the Greeks now occupied parts of.

Now that Greece was in the war on the Allied side, any restrictions placed upon Philip owing to his status as a neutral alien ceased to exist. That December, he was informed that he would join the Mediterranean Fleet on board the recently reconditioned battleship, the *Valiant*. After seeing in the new year at Port Said, he travelled by train to Alexandria, where he boarded his new ship.

The action which Philip had been yearning for was now about to start. Within days of boarding his new ship, the fleet left port to bombard the Libyan coastal town of Bardia. Philip's diary records, 'We went to action stations at 07.30 and at 08.10 the bombardment commenced.' His excitement is palpable as he states, 'the whole operation was a very spectacular affair.' For the remainder of the year, Philip served on that battleship.

In January 1941, he was given five weeks shore leave. He stayed between his mother's Athens apartment and Tatoi, the royal family's summer palace twenty seven kilometres from the capital where George II slept each night, returning to the royal palace in Athens during the day in much the same way that Bertie and Elizabeth commuted between Buckingham Palace and Windsor on a daily basis. Philip's cousin Alexandra provided a glimpse of his activities, which were an intermingling of dancing to gramophone records and the fun of partying with his cousins and 'a whole new group of friends.'

A sudden death interrupted Philip's pleasures on the 29th of the month, when General Ioannis Metaxas, the Greek Prime Minister from 1936, died of toxaemia brought on by a sore throat. A controversial figure, the strongman might have been deplored for his dictatorial tendencies, but he was also respected for having fought off the Italian invasion of Greece, and for creating the fortifications on the Bulgarian border in northern Greece known as the Metaxas Line. These would prove helpful when the Germans and Bulgarians joined the Italians in mounting a second invasion of Greece in April 1941.

Virtually the whole Greek royal family attended General Metaxas's funeral, including Philip, though his father was unable to do so. Andrew had been trapped in Monte Carlo since the fall of France, and was now living on the 167 foot *Davida* with Andrée de La Bigne. His letters convey his frustration at not being able to be in Greece to make a contribution to the war effort, but soon the rest of the royal family, with the exception of his wife and sister-in-law Princess Nicholas, would be forced to flee for their lives when

## Chapter III

German tanks rolled across the border to assist the besieged Italians who had been pushed back into Albania the year before. Following the German conquest of Crete in June, the whole of Greece was under occupation by German, Italian and Bulgarian troops. The government went into exile with the king, to be replaced by an Axis collaborationist puppet government, along the lines of what had happened in Norway the year before.

The only two royals to remain behind in Athens were Alice and her widowed sister-in-law, the former Grand Duchess Elena Vladimirovna of Russia, whose husband Nicholas had died suddenly of a heart attack in 1938. One daughter, Marina, was married to the Duke of Kent, a second, Olga, to the Prince Regent of Yugoslavia, and a third, Elisabeth, to the German mediatised Count Karl Theodor zu Toerring-Jettenbach. Both princesses having daughters whose husbands were serving the Axis cause, they were more or less left alone to pursue the relief work which they undertook in an attempt to alleviate the Athenians' suffering. This was intense. Food was scarce and the occupying forces brutal towards the civilian population.

By this time, Philip had re-joined the *Valiant*. He had done so at the beginning of March, before the invasion, which was anticipated. To bolster Greek defences, British troops had been ferried from Alexandria to the ports of Piraeus and Crete, protected by convoys such as the ones of which the *Valiant* formed a part. Their major threat, *en route*, had been the Italian navy. Although much smaller than the mighty British navy, the Italians were nevertheless a deadly danger to Allied shipping, and the codebreakers at Bletchley Park had been hard at work trying to break the Italian codes.

Towards the end of March, a nineteen year old codebreaker named Mavis Lever happened to notice an anomaly with the letters PERS and duly broke the Italian Enigma code. The first message stated, 'Today's the day minus three,' followed three days later by a message reporting the sailing of an Italian battle fleet consisting of a battleship, two light and six heavy cruisers, together with destroyers to attack the Allied merchant fleet and convoys protecting escorting troops. So that the enemy would not know that their code had been broken, a reconnaissance flight was deliberately sent to 'discover' the approaching battle fleet, which was 'spotted' south west of Cape Matapan.

A further subterfuge was entered into by the Commander of the Mediterranean Fleet, Admiral Andrew Cunningham. He arrived with a prominently displayed suitcase, as if intending an overnight stay, at a golf club in Alexandria, during the afternoon of his fleet's departure. After spending time on the links within sight of the Japanese consul, and spreading rumours about an impending party that evening on his flagship, he surreptitiously made his way back under cover of darkness to his battleship, HMS *Warspite*. Together with the aircraft carrier HMS *Formidable*, his own battleship as well as the *Barham* and *Valiant*, and two flotillas of destroyers, he slid out of port. A second force, under Admiral Sir Henry Pridham-Wippell, was nearby, with the intention of linking up.

The ensuing Battle of Matapan was the greatest disaster ever suffered by the Italian navy. Allied casualties during the battle were one torpedo bomber shot down by the 3.5 inch anti-aircraft guns of the Italian flagship, *Vittorio Veneto*, with the loss of its three man crew, while the Italians lost 2,303 sailors. The Royal Navy also lost the heavy cruiser, HMS *York*, but the Italians lost a whole cruiser division.

Philip's function during the battle was to man the *Valiant*'s midship light. According to him, it, 'picked out the enemy cruiser and lit her up as if it were broad daylight.' He illuminated two Italian heavy cruisers that were escorting the stricken heavy cruiser *Pola*. This ship had been hit earlier in the day along with the *Vittorio Veneto*, and the Italians had made the fateful decision to send back ships which had already slipped way, to escort both stricken vessels to safety. In the event, Philip trained his light on the escorting vessels of the *Pola* so efficiently, holding his light so steadily while all hell broke loose around him, that they were sunk, along with the *Pola*. 'Thanks to his alertness and appreciation of the situation, we were able to sink in five minutes two eight-inch-gun Italian cruisers,' his superior officer noted. He was mentioned in despatches and awarded the Greek War Cross by King George II.

The excitement which Philip craved continued. In May, the *Valiant* was hit, 'twice on the quarterdeck,' according to Philip's journal. It put into Alexandria for repairs, giving Philip a chance to see his Greek relations, who had fled Greece in two tranches, the king staying behind for an additional three weeks in Crete to provide a rallying point. He also linked up with his uncle Dickie, whose K-class destroyer HMS *Kelly* was sunk on the 23rd of the month during the evacuation of Crete. Half its men were lost and Mountbatten had a near-miraculous escape, for he had gone down with his ship, but, according to him, was shot out of the sea like a cork when the bridge collapsed. All the survivors were disconsolate, Dickie memorably consoling them with the thought that, 'we didn't leave the *Kelly*; the *Kelly* left us.' So gripping was the loss of the ship that the following year a movie, *In Which We Serve*, was made of the event, starring Noel Coward and John Mills.

Another relation who, coincidentally, was in Egypt at the same time, was Philip's brother-he-never-had, David Milford Haven. They all had a good time, even though Alexandria was bombed repeatedly. Afterwards, Philip saw the Greek royals off from Port Said when they left for exile in South Africa. Serendipitously, a fortnight later, his ship put into Cape Town, where he linked up with them again, before heading for Portsmouth to sit his sub-lieutenant's exams.

These exams were divided into five separate segments: navigation, signals, seamanship, gunnery and torpedoes. Philip applied himself, gaining the top marks in four (a one) and a two in the fifth. He was then posted in June 1942 to HMS *Wallace*, a Shakespeare-class flotilla leader which had been selected, in 1938, for conversion into an Anti-Aircraft Escort. She was deployed in home waters and took up her war station at Rosyth on the Firth of Forth after the outbreak of the war.

This was no cushy posting. These convoy vessels were the targets of German E-boats, the Schnellboot (fast boat in German) capable of a sustained speed of 43.5 knots (80.6km/h; 50.1mph) and acceleration to 48 knots (89km/h; 55 mph). Their diesel engines gave these vessels, 35 metres (114'10") long by 5.1 metres (16'9"), a range of 700 nautical miles, something which the gasoline fuelled American PT boat or the British Motor Torpedo Boat could not match.

Both the merchant vessels and their convoy protectors were frequently attacked, and not only from the E-boats. German bombers frequently rained down bombs on these convoys, which had very little room for manoeuvre, trapped as they were between the British coast and their own mine barrier during the sixty hour journey from Scotland to Sheerness in England.

The underlying treachery of the situation, together with the frequency of bad weather, fog especially, resulted in accidents as well as losses from the enemy. One such occurred when a merchant vessel sliced into the forward boiler room of the *Wallace*, killing one stoker and scalding two others. Philip acquitted himself nobly, rushing into the damaged boiler room in an attempt to release the men.

By this time, Philip and Lilibet were established correspondents. His cousin Alexandra of Greece believed that his motivation had less to do with romance and more to do with a desire for invitations, which might well have been correct where he was concerned, but Lilibet's interest was altogether more personal. Be that as it may, keeping in touch with cousin Lilibet did result in invitations to Windsor Castle, the first of which took place in October 1941. 'Philip came here for a week end the other day,' George VI wrote to the younger man's grandmother, Victoria. 'What a charming boy he is, & I am glad he is remaining on in my Navy.'

At the time, Philip actually had a girlfriend. She was sharing a flat with Dickie Mountbatten's goddaughter, the Hon. Sarah Norton, daughter of the film-maker Lord Grantley and mother of Samantha Cameron's stepfather, the 4th Viscount Astor. Osla Benning was Canadian beauty to whom Sarah attributed 'dark hair, alabaster white skin, an exquisite figure and a gentle loving nature.' She had made her debut weeks before the beginning of the war, and would go on to be one of the debs of the year. Both girls were sharing a cottage near Slough and working at Hawker Siddeley, the aircraft manufacturer, helping to build Hurricanes, when Dickie asked her to 'find a nice girl' for his nephew. Sarah introduced them and chemistry did the rest.

Sarah was categorical about putting to bed the question of whether Philip and Osla ever slept together. 'We were all ignorant, and if we'd known we would have thought it disgusting. Certainly, I and all my friends would have considered ourselves defiled if we hadn't come to marriage as virgins. Even after you had become engaged, it made no difference. Virginity lasted right up until the wedding night.' That is certainly a view with which my mother, and all the girls of her generation, concurred.

A few months into their jobs at Hawker Siddeley, both girls received letters, at the instigation of Alastair Denniston, head of the Government Code and Cypher School, summoning them to a labour exchange in London where their skills in German were tested. Having passed the test, they were sent to Bletchley Park and assigned to Hut 4. 'Nobody explained anything,' Sarah recalled. 'You were merely told that pieces of paper in German would come through and you had to take out any salient information, put it all on to a filing card with the co-ordinates, and index it. The information we were dealing with was obviously decrypted.'

The work was gruelling, but the girls, who were fortunately billeted, and worked, together, threw themselves into enjoying themselves as well. According to Lord Grantley, even before they were working at Bletchley Park, they drew 'as sharp a contrast as they could between their days in the factory and evenings in the cottage.' They had a busy social life, which included Philip, who, Grantley thought, had a 'forceful intellect' and was 'the best of company.'

As the relationship between Philip and Osla developed, Sarah withdrew slightly, to give them more space, but they nevertheless all remained great friends. According to Osla's daughter Jane, Lady Risby, 'I do know that he was her first love. She never told me about him for years. She just said, "I fell in love with a naval officer." Then I found a wonderful picture of Philip, very young-looking, with his hair all tousled, quite curly.'

# Chapter III

After her mother told her about her first love, Lady Risby immediately saw what they had in common. She felt that neither of them, 'even by the standards of their time, had experienced much emotional warmth or security as children.' They 'were both very much outsiders with no roots in the English milieu in which they moved.' Although 'they were both very good looking, full of life and with a similar sense of fun,' their emotionally deprived, insecure, outsider status, 'gave them a special bond.'

The first person Philip rang, whenever he returned to England, was Osla. Notwithstanding that they were boyfriend and girlfriend, there is little doubt that theirs was a pure relationship. Anne de Courcy, a writer whom I know, like, and respect, recounts how Osla 'caused a mild sensation in a nightclub when she complained loudly that it was very inconsiderate of her boyfriend always to carry his torch in his pocket as it was so uncomfortable when they were dancing.' This was during the days of the blackout, when men did carry torches to find their way around, and though Anne doesn't say it, the timings suggest that the boyfriend in question was Philip. Plainly, if Osla thought what she was feeling was a torch, she had never seen it.

Philip was no 'bounder'. His reputation was that of a young man who was 'safe in taxis'. For all his undoubted charm and sex appeal, there was not a breath of scandal about his conduct. Had there been, you can be sure it would have been used against him in the run-up to his engagement: a time when Elizabeth and her courtier cronies were doing their level best to put barriers in his way. The fact that no specific incident or person surfaced which they could use against him gives the message that no such incident or person existed.

Meanwhile, as the war continued and Philip and Osla saw each other, his relationship with Lilibet went from strength to strength. That is not to suggest that Philip was two-timing Osla. There was nothing untoward between the cousins, who were friends and pen pals. But the bonds between them were strengthening. The more they saw of each other, and the more they wrote to each other, the more they realised how much they liked each other, and, tellingly, the more they respected each other. Philip had an imaginative and worldly side which Lilibet found captivating, while she had a sweetness and steadiness which, for all his bravura performances in drawing and mess rooms, he needed, as only a child of misfortune can. Although, by her own admission, she was already 'in love' with him, and had been since that visit to Dartmouth, there is little doubt that such love as she felt would have disappeared had the suitability of his personality and personal attributes become open to question.

As Lilibet, Queen Mary, and King George VI were discovering the better they got to know him, Philip's suitability did not rest solely, or even largely, upon his being a prince of Greece. Certainly, where grandmother and granddaughter were concerned, Philip's royal station was a decided plus. He was at least as royal as the king, more so than the king's mother, and decidedly more so than Lilibet. However, his personal attributes were what fitted him for the life of consort even more than his royal background. He was intelligent, personable, with an enquiring mind. He was confident and outgoing. He liked people and cared about their welfare. Aside from being breathtakingly handsome and athletic, he had a highly developed spiritual side, which Lilibet also had. He was fun to have around but could be relied upon when needed. He exuded masculinity through every pore, and, put crudely, seemed to promise goodness both in and out of bed. As George VI said, Philip thought 'about things in the right sort of way.' Kurt Hahn had ensured that he would not only want to be of service to others, but that he would develop the abilities to implement this objective. This was of supreme importance to Lilibet, who had also been raised to revere public service. Philip, in short, had everything except money, but that was not necessarily a handicap, for a more financially secure prince might have been less eager to serve country and humanity. In short, he had everything that any woman in her right mind would want and Lilibet, being the sound and sensible creature she was, saw it, appreciated it, and intended to continue her friendship with Philip, doubtless in the hope that he would one day reciprocate some, if not all, of her feelings.

It is a testament to her basic solidity, good sense and firmness of character, that Lilibet saw, at such an early age, what a gem she had found in Philip. And one, moreover, who was thrilling, and would continue to thrill her to the core, even when he shook her to that same core.

Meanwhile, Elizabeth was compiling a short list of men she regarded as being suitable for her daughter. Called the First Eleven, not one of these men was royal. Each of them was a British aristocrat. They included Hugh, Earl of Euston, heir to the 10th Duke of Grafton, whose ultimate wife, Fortune, would become her Mistress of the Robes; Charles, 10th Duke of Rutland, who would marry my step-mother-in-law Margaret, Duchess of Argyll's daughter Frances Sweeny; Walter Francis John Montagu Douglas Scott, known always as Johnny and at the time Earl of Dalkeith, a nephew of Bertie's sister-in-law Alice, Duchess of Gloucester, and son of Elizabeth's childhood friend and sworn enemy Mollie Lascelles, whose husband was the 8th Duke of Buccleuch; and last but by no means least , Henry, Lord Porchester, always known as Porchy and heir to the 6th Earl of Carnarvon, then of Tutankhamun fame, now better known because Downton Abbey was filmed at their seat, Highclere Castle.

Lilibet was happy to have these young men as dancing partners, and might even, for a short while, have had her gaze diverted in Porchy Porchester's direction. Like Philip, he was tall and good looking, though, unlike Philip, he was dark and burly rather than blond and lean. Such interest as might have existed, however, was short lived, though the basic affinity that had brought them together remained intact. Not only were they genuinely compatible as personalities, with similar senses of humour and a love of horses, but they enjoyed each other's company and even, according to one of Lilibet's ladies-in-waiting, 'fancied' each other. The result was that Lilibet and Porchy were genuinely fond of each other and would remain lifelong friends who were so cosy with each other that people who not know them well might have confused their intimacy as having a sexual expression. Indeed, later on, rumours would swirl around about the extent of their relationship. But more of that later.

During the war, while Elizabeth was pushing her First Eleven, and Porchy and Lilibet's liking for each other was attracting favourable comments from her mother and the band of cronies who always enthused about anything the strong-willed Queen Consort liked, George VI took an entirely different view when the news of this potential interest reached him. 'I'll be buggered if my daughter is going to marry any fucking butler's son,' he declared in the fruity language he had been exposed to in the navy, and which he thereafter used when appropriate.

The Carnarvon family was colourful indeed. And not only in the present generation. The two previous ones were quite something as well. The 5th earl's wife had been born Almina Wombwell, daughter of Marie Wombwell, the French wife of a British army officer named Captain Charles Frederick Wombwell. However, her natural father was the immensely rich banker Baron Alfred de Rothschild. Although she was legitimately her mother's husband's daughter by virtue of presumption of legitimacy, Rothschild acknowledged her as his child and left her a vast fortune. This funded the Egyptian excavations of her husband and Howard Carter, who discovered Tutankhamun's tomb.

Two years after marrying her husband, Almina gave birth to a son. By her own account, she could not be sure whether her husband was the boy's father, or whether it was her lover, Prince Victor Duleep Singh, son of the last Maharajah of the Punjab by his half-German, part Abyssinian wife, Bamba Muller. Whoever the biological father of the boy was, he was legally born

Henry Herbert, Lord Porchester (thereafter called Porchy) owing, yet again, to that legal convenience known as presumption of legitimacy.

This Porchy Porchester, later the 6th Earl of Carnarvon, cut a most amorous swathe through society. I remember him well from the seventies, when he was very old and I, very young. He was a charming, convivial and rapacious lover of the girls. There was indeed something of the orient about the cast of his eyes, which had a real twinkle. He never missed an opportunity to flirt with a pretty young thing, and to decorously show his appreciation of a filly's form as his hand brushed over one's arm or passed over one's leg. It has to be said, no one minded in the slightest. We all thought he was a hoot, and he often shared his luncheon table at the Ritz with girls young enough to be his granddaughter. This was before sexual hankering was regarded with anything but compassion and tolerance, and I was but one of many 'pretty young things' who enjoyed his company. The only thing I hold against him is talking me out of backing *Ile de Bourbon* which I knew, just knew, would win the Group Two King Edward VII Stakes, the moment it entered the parade ring at Royal Ascot in 1978.

Irrespective of who his father was, the old rake was most decidedly the *châtelain* of Highclere Castle, which had been brought back to life *gratis* his mother's money. He had been married twice, firstly to Anne Catherine Tredick Wendell, who produced a son and a daughter, and secondly to the beautiful Austrian actress, dancer, choreographer and painter Tilly Losch. She was a friend of my step-mother-in-law Margaret Argyll, and used to go around telling all and sundry that her husband was sterile. According to her, his son, Henry George Reginald Molyneux Herbert, Lord Porchester (Lilibet's Porchy), born on 19th January 1924, and his daughter, Lady Anne Penelope Marian Herbert, born on 3rd March 1925, were both Aaron's babies, the product of one of two helpful gynaecologists in Harley Street to whom aristocratic wives in need of heirs would go when all else had failed.

These Miracle Workers of Harley Street both used the semen of butlers, who would make their deposits in medical trays in one room, while the lady of the manor would be in an adjoining room, feet placed in stirrups ready to receive what everyone hoped would be the beginning of a pregnancy. Adultery played no part in this purely scientific exercise, which was based upon sound demographics.

Butlers were, in the heyday of Western Civilisation, the equivalent of managing directors in today's world. Unlike today's MDs, who might be intelligent but can equally be ugly as sin or as socially unskilled as an Asperger's victim, in the 1920s, butlers in the grander households were invariably tall, physically attractive, personable men of intelligence. They all had impeccable social as well as managerial skills, and really were all-rounders: nature's aristocrats. In other words, they were good mating material. Certainly the 7th Earl of Carnarvon, as Porchy Porchester the younger became upon the lovable old rogue's death in 1987, was a handsome man, while the 6th earl was anything but.

Whether young Porchy caught Lilibet's attention briefly or not, none of the others of the First Eleven did, while the relationship with Philip, who kept in touch via the post when he did not visit, gathered strength.

There is a lot to be said for letter writing. It is both intimate and non-threatening. It gives correspondents time to marshal their thoughts, to put their best foot forward, and, in the gap between writing and receiving a letter, it gives both the writer and the reader time to unfurl. Where intermittent meetings in person can result in awkwardness, letters provide a lubricant that allows the guard to be lowered and emotions to develop safely and comfortably. This is especially true when sexual attraction plays a part. It is even truer when conventions prevent gratification of that attraction, as it would have done with any 'nice young couple' in the 1940s.

While being posted on the *Wallace* gave Philip more of a chance to weekend at Windsor than he would otherwise have had, had he continued to be posted abroad. Osla did continue to be his girlfriend. Another important figure in Philip's life now entered the picture. John Michael Avison Parker, always called Mike, was the second in command on the *Lauderdale,* another ship in the flotilla. He was a big, bluff, no-nonsense Australian who had an 'ambivalent attitude' to authority but took great pride in his work. The two men hit it off at once. They were both gregarious, both competitive, both down-to-earth, with a lust for succeeding in their chosen profession. In October 1942, upon the recommendation of his commanding officer, Prince Philip became first lieutenant of the *Wallace.* Having just turned 21, he had the distinction of being one of the youngest first lieutenants in the navy. He was now also the exact equivalent of his new friend, who was his senior by a year and equally committed to working his way to the top of the navy.

'We were highly competitive. We both wanted to show we had the most efficient, cleanest and best ship and ship's company in the Navy. And instead of pushing us apart, it drew us closer,' Mike Parker said. He also hit the nail on the head when he said that another thing which drew them together was the fact that neither of them had a home to go to. His was on the other side of the world; Philip's didn't exist. After all the other men had rushed off home, leaving the two of them alone on their quarterdecks, with nowhere to go to, Parker thought, 'You're a poor bloody orphan, just like me!'

The two men also had penury in common. 'He was better off than I was,' Parker said, 'but compared with many people he didn't have a brass razoo.'

Dickie would later claim that he gave Philip an allowance of £5 per week. In a day and age when secretaries and shop attendants often didn't each earn as much, it was a significant enough sum to make a difference between being able to go out and have a drink, or being forced to stay home and miss out on all the fun. But it was hardly wealth. With Andrew cut off behind the enemy lines of occupied France, Alice in occupied Athens, neither parent had access to funds of any significance. They would not have been able to spare anything for their son, even if they had had the ability to transfer funds to him, and indeed getting letters to him was a difficulty for Alice, who would nevertheless manage to funnel the odd one to him through her sister Louise, the crown princess of neutral Sweden. As for Andrew, his lot was even worse. Philip's sister Sophie used to beseech the Germans to allow her to visit her father in occupied France, but they systematically refused her requests, even when her husband Christopher of Hesse was a director in the Ministry of Air Forces and the Commander of the Air Reserves.

Moreover, Greece's entrance into the war scuppered any chance Philip had of financial relief from that quarter, as such income as his father had, had ceased. The result was that Andrew's war was even more penurious and lonelier than the rest of his family's, each of whom had at least some of the others, while he had none of them. As he had spent a good deal of his time prior to the war – even while in exile from 1922 to 1936 – travelling between the castles, palaces and houses of his many relations, his was indeed an isolated existence. Philip understood that. He did not expect what force of circumstance prevented, so he managed as best he could on his naval pay and his allowance. It says something about the stoical aspect of his character that he never complained, neither contemporaneously nor later, and never displayed any resentment at the hand the fates had dealt him.

What helped to secure the friendship of Philip and Parker was the latter man's attitude towards his princely status. 'The fact that he was a prince didn't register with me. I gave him deference when it was official, but if it was not official then 'relax' was the order of the day.'

As the war ground on, slowly but surely the chances of Allied victory improved. The first two years of the war had seen reversal after reversal for the Allies, as Hitler's juggernaut crushed all before it. Austria had been wiped off the map during the Anschluss even before the outbreak of the war, as had the Sudetenland of Czechoslovakia. By 1941, the British Channel Islands of Guernsey and Jersey, the Czechoslovak Republic, the Free City of Danzig, France, Luxembourg, Croatia, Belgium, Denmark, Norway, the Netherlands, Yugoslavia, Lithuania, Poland, Estonia, and large parts of the western Soviet Union, including Ukraine and Byelorussia, were occupied. Not since Napoleon had one man had such vast swathes of Europe under his control. Hitler's mistake, however, was Operation Barbarossa.

On Sunday 22$^{nd}$ June 1941, Hitler invaded the Soviet Union in repudiation of the Molotov-Ribbentrop Accord of 1939. Stalin was so taken off his guard that he refused to believe the first reports. As the Germans poured into the western republics, devastating all before them and reaching the outskirts of the Tsarist capital Petrograd, as St. Petersburg had been renamed at the start of the First World War, before it was changed to Leningrad in celebration of the Soviet Union's founding father, Stalin had no option but to realise that his fellow dictator had broken faith with him. It was a tremendous blow to Russian pride when the German's occupied Tsarskoye Selo, location of the Tsars' summer palaces, and carted off the treasure known as the Amber Room from the Catherine Palace. However, Hitler was making the same mistake that Napoleon had made. Russia was ultimately indefatigable. It was so vast, so naturally rich in resources and manpower, that it could afford to lose even its old capital, the way it had with Moscow in 1812. As long as its leadership had the will to resist invasion, it would finally prevail, for it simply wasn't possible to invade and occupy, much less keep, the whole country. Moreover, Russia had one thing on its side that few other nations did: its weather. This had been crucial in the defeat of Napoleon, and would prove equally indispensable in the defeat of Hitler.

Once Stalin accepted that he had been invaded, which he did in a matter of days, the order went out to resist the enemy at all costs. Russian resistance had begun in earnest. The German advance on the former capital was stopped just a few kilometres outside of it. The Germans settled down to besiege the city into surrender. Stalin, however, had ordered that there could be no surrender. The Siege of Leningrad has gone down in history as one of the longest (872 days) and deadliest (over 1 million fatalities, mostly from starvation) sieges of all time, if not *the* longest and most deadly. Surrounded as the city was by the Germans, there was only one route through which supplies could filter, the so-called Road of Life across Lake Ladoga. Although many citizens were evacuated or escaped, Stalin would never have allowed its inhabitants to leave the city open to the Germans. They were condemned to stay and starve. Dead people were a common sight on the street, having dropped dead where they stood or sat. There was cannibalism, and once the siege took hold, dogs, cats and horses were all consumed. Nevertheless, the city held out against the invader.

By the end of 1941, Hitler was in occupation of a significant portion of the Soviet Union's western territories, but his hold on his conquests was considerably less secure than it had been in the free states of western and central Europe. He then compounded his error by ordering the 6th Army under General Friedrich Paulus, who had achieved a major victory at the Second Battle of Kharkov, to occupy Stalingrad and secure the oil fields of Baku and Azerbaijan. The Battle of Stalingrad commenced on 23rd August 1942. Any student of history would have been able to warn the Fuhrer of the folly of launching a campaign so late in the summer. Russian winters come suddenly and lethally, and such chance of success as might have existed had battle commenced earlier, had disappeared by this date.

Not, it has to be said, that there was ever much chance of success. There was never any prospect of the Germans achieving an easy victory over the city which had been named in honour of the Soviet leader. Notwithstanding the contribution of the 4th Panzer Army and the Luftwaffe, which razed much of the city to the ground with bombs, the Russians fought back with magnificence, forcing the Germans to fight hand to hand for every inch of territory.

As both sides poured reinforcements into the city, the Red Army launched Operation Uranus on 19th November. This was a two-pronged attack on the weaker Hungarian and Romanian armies protecting the German 6th Army's flanks. Overrunning these forces, the Red Army managed to encircle the 6th Army, which found itself trapped. Hitler refused to consider retreat, ordering Paulus to stay put and make no attempt to break out. The logistical impracticality of feeding an army from the air was now undertaken, with only limited success, while the Germans tried to breach the encircling Russians from without. When both these solutions proved futile, the 6th Army began to disintegrate under the combined weight of the weather, attacks from the Red Army, illness, hunger, and exhaustion.

On 7th January 1943, General Konstantin Rokossovsky, Commander of the Red Army on the Don front, called a ceasefire and offered magnanimous surrender terms while pointing out the impossibility of the invaders' predicament. The Germans were assured of normal rations, medical treatment for whoever needed it, the right to keep their badges, decorations, uniforms and personal effects. Paulus asked Hitler for permission to surrender before his army was annihilated, not only by the encircling Red Army but by the attrition of the Russian winter. In *With Paulus at Stalingrad* (2015; translated by Tony Le Tissier), Wilhelm Adam and Otto Ruhle quote the order that the Fuhrer demanded the German High Command to pass on, 'Capitulation out of the question. Every day the army holds out longer helps the whole front, and draws the Russian divisions from it.'

Two weeks later, on 25th January, Paulus was again offered a second chance to surrender by the Russians when they overran the last emergency landing strip in Stalingrad. The 6th Army was now indisputably in an inextricable vice, with death the only real alternative to surrender. Paulus again radioed Hitler requesting permission to surrender. Again, the Fuhrer ordered that he hold Stalingrad to the death. By 30th January 1943, it was apparent even to Hitler that surrender was now a distinct and, for him, unwelcome possibility, whether he gave permission or not. To stiffen Paulus's resolve, he promoted him to field marshal, observing that no German field marshal had ever surrendered in the whole of German history. He also issued a raft of lesser promotions to inspire the more junior ranks to fight to the death as well.

According to General Max Pfeffer, Paulus had a view of his promotion. He saw it as an invitation from the Fuhrer to commit suicide. This would have given Hitler scope to lay the blame at his doorstep, rather than where it truly lay, namely his own, but Paulus was a Catholic and opposed to suicide. He also told the general, 'I have no intention of shooting myself for this Bohemian corporal.'

To cut a long story short, by the last day of January 1943, Paulus found himself in the same position Napoleon had been in while retreating from Moscow. Then, the French army, which was being harried by the Russians, had had no choice but to freeze to death. Now, however, there was a choice. When the forces defending the 6th Army's Headquarters were overwhelmed by the Russians and taken prisoner, Paulus's chief of staff, Lieutenant General Arthur Schmidt, discussed surrender terms with officers from General Mikhail Shumilov's headquarters while the newly-created Field Marshal Paulus waited in a room next door. The respected historian, Sir Antony Beevor, observed, 'Whether this was a ploy to allow Paulus to distance himself from the surrender, or a further example of Schmidt handling events because Paulus was in a state of nervous collapse, is not clear.' It seems likely that Paulus refused to dishonour himself further by failing to obey a direct order from his commander in chief, when he was already in the invidious position of having been captured by the enemy, so surrender was now an inevitability, irrespective of who surrendered. Moreover, the vainglorious Fuhrer had put Paulus in the invidious position he now found himself in, by ordering the Battle of Stalingrad to commence when it did, and, as all students of history know, the primary responsibility of a good commander is to spare his men, not sacrifice them. Without surrender, the 6$^{th}$ Army was facing complete annihilation.

By 2$^{nd}$ February 1943, the surrender was final. Some 107,000 Axis soldiers, mostly German, as well as 22 generals and the field marshal, were taken into custody. The Germans having surrendered under far less favourable terms than those offered weeks before, half the prisoners taken would die on the march to Siberian war camps , while most of the remainder would die in captivity. Only 6,000 survived the decade of imprisonment they endured before repatriation to their fatherland.

The surrender infuriated Hitler. Showing his scorn, he asserted that Paulus, 'could have freed himself from all sorrow and ascended into eternity and national immortality, but he prefers to go to Moscow.'

Paulus, however, would have the last word. He testified for the prosecution at Nuremberg.

The failure of the Stalingrad campaign was the turning point of the Second World War. Everyone knew it. Though the war would drag on for over two more years, after Stalingrad the question was no longer if the Allies would survive, but for how long the Axis powers could hold out.

While the captured German soldiers were dying on the forced marches to Siberia, Philip was learning of the latest tragedy to overtake him in his short life when his uncle Dickie sent him a telegram informing him of his cousin Alex Wernher's death. Within months, his own life was on the line as he traversed the Atlantic on the *Wallace*, which was on convoy duty, before heading for Sicily to help with the Allied invasion.

This proved to be the occasion upon which Philip demonstrated what a quick and lateral thinker he could be. The night of 8$^{th}$ July was particularly dangerous because the waxing crescent of the moon, at thirty per cent, was catastrophically illuminating the sea so that every ripple was visible. This included the wake the *Wallace* left as it cut through the water. This was ideal spotting conditions for would-be bombers, and the presence of the ship was detected by a posse of Stukas, who dive-bombed it, hitting one side. When they departed, everyone on board was painfully aware that it was inevitable they would return with the intention of sinking the ship.

First Lieutenant Prince Philip of Greece, who had been overseeing operations from his post on the bridge, came up with a truly ingenious ploy to divert the returning bombers away from the *Wallace*. After consultations with the captain, a wooden raft was hurriedly assembled with a smoke float affixed to each end. Once illuminated, it would look like the remnants of a sunken ship and would hopefully deceive the bombers into thinking that they had fatally hit the *Wallace* on their first foray.

Having launched the diversionary raft, the ship then sailed away at full speed, cutting its engines a safe distance away. In so doing, the incriminating wake was no longer visible as the *Wallace* lurked in stillness under cover of what darkness there was, suggesting that the ship had been sunk. Sure enough, the Stukas returned, screaming overhead as they sped over the ship to close in on the diversionary raft in the mistaken belief that they were merely finishing off the job they had started. According to one of the Ratings, Harry Hargreaves, 'Prince Philip saved our lives that night.'

Time and distance were having their effects upon Philip and his relationships. Although he and Osla continued to be boyfriend and girlfriend throughout 1943, and they would exchange Christmas presents at the end of the year, it is clear, from the way his relationship with Lilibet began to gather pace, and Osla's relationship with the handsome diplomat (later Sir) Guy Millardbecame so serious that they were engaged by the spring of 1944, that his and Osla's relationship had simply run its course. There was no bitter parting of the ways: no recrimination; nothing untoward. They were simply two young people who had come together for a period, enjoyed each other's company, and moved on to other romantic attachments while remaining friends.

The depth of their feeling for each other, and the innocence of their time together, is confirmed by their behaviour once they parted. Osla did not, in fact, marry Guy Millard. Two years later, she married another diplomat, the Hon. John Henniker-Major, heir to the 7th Lord Henniker, who would go on to have as splendid a diplomatic career as his predecessor, both of whom became ambassadors amongst other prestigious posts. When she gave birth to her first child, Mark, the 9th and present Lord Henniker, in September 1947, Prince Philip became his godfather.

Christmas of 1943 was the turning point in Philip and Lilibet's relationship. Philip was asked to stay at Windsor with his cousin David Milford Haven. They were due to see the two princesses in the premiere performance of the royal Christmas pantomime, *Aladdin*, in which Lilibet uncharacteristically showed off her legs, clad in tights, as well as her luscious, womanly figure, with its slender hips, tiny waist and ample bosom, in a figure-hugging costume whose skirt was so short that even Mary Quant would have found it daring twenty years later. But then, she was playing a boy.

According to Crawfie, Lilibet was very excited about Philip's attendance. Disappointingly, however, he missed the first two performances, because he was laid up in London with influenza. He did make the third performance on 18th December, sitting beside the king and queen and his cousin Marina, the widowed Duchess of Kent, whose handsome husband had died in an aeroplane crash the year before, leaving her with a six week old baby, a five year old daughter, and a six year old son.

Philip had grown very close to his cousin who, though fifteen years his elder, had become very much like one of the big sisters to whom he no longer had access. For her part, Marina was happy to have her handsome, enthusiastic, intelligent and fun-loving cousin around. She was proud of her handsome cousin, and delighted in encouraging and promoting his advancement. Proud of her ancestry, and mindful of her position as the most junior consort within the British royal family, despite being the only royal duchess of royal blood, she also took pride in her cousin, her fellow Greek, being mooted in fashionable circles as a possible husband for Lilibet. It was her mother whom Chips Channon used as the source of his diary entry, two years before in Athens, which is the very first recorded mention of the possibility of Philip becoming the future British monarch's husband. In its very discussion, Philip's potential elevation would also boost the prestige of the rest of the Greek royal family. And, exiled yet again, this poorest of European monarchies, sorely needed any elevation which would inflate their status at the bottom of the royal pile. This was especially true of Princess Marina, whose penury only added to the indignity of the sufferance she endured at the hands of what she regarded as her jumped up, competitive, but saccharine sister-in-law.

Although the cynical might have interpreted Marina's advancement of Philip's cause as possessing elements of self-aggrandisement, the fact remains, she was fond of him and had known him all his life. Both branches of the Greek royal family had shared their exile in the 1920s at St. Cloud, near Paris, and both cousins were intelligent, sophisticated and fun-loving. It was only natural that the signature Philip could be found, and would continue to be found, with significant repetitiousness in the visitors' book at *Coppins*, her country house near Iver in Buckinghamshire. George V's favourite sister Princess Victoria had left Marina's late husband George the property in 1935.

It was therefore comforting for Philip to spend that crucial Christmas of 1943 surrounded by loved ones such as Marina and David Milford Haven. Although he had by this time developed the capacity to settle in to new surroundings, and acquit himself well, beneath the bravado there lay a sensitive soul, as many would discover in the years to come. It must therefore have been a relief to be surrounded by such intimates as David and Marina, as well as an unexpectedly 'more animated' Lilibet, who, Crawfie tells us, was displaying, 'a sparkle about her none of us had ever seen before,' to such an extent that, 'many people remarked on it.'

From the outset, the Christmas stay went with a bang. The precocious Margaret Rose, in the process of losing the babyish second name along with her puppy fat, joined in all the festivities, claiming, 'we danced and danced and danced.' Both her parents were excellent dancers and had always liked nothing better than a good party, so Bertie and Elizabeth encouraged David and Philip, and Lilibet and Margaret, and all the other young people in attendance, to roll 'back the carpet in the crimson drawing room' and dance the nights away. Although Margaret was as much a part of the fun as Lilibet, and the younger sister would remain for the next several years almost a third wheel with Philip and Lilibet, there was never any jealousy between the siblings, nor jockeying for position. While Margaret was included in all activities, to such an extent that onlookers might have wondered which of the two sisters had the handsome Greek prince in her sights, the fact that onlookers never did question where each participant's affections lay, says much about the closeness between Lilibet and Margaret, and Philip's generosity of spirit in including the baby sister at all times. It also has to be said, of course, that Margaret was extremely precocious, very gregarious, outrageously entertaining even at that age, and growing into a budding beauty; so the gap in years between the sisters was more illusory than real, in terms of their personalities and sociability.

What fostered good relations within the unit of three which was emerging, was the fact that the three of them, like many other young people of their day and age, were innocents, interested in having a good, clean time rather than pursuing the more sensual and lascivious pleasures to which successive generations would fall prey. They were interested in dancing, playing charades, even hide and seek and blind man's bluff. The idea that any respectable young man and woman would slink off to have sex in some back bedroom, or do drugs in the lavatory, was simply unthinkable.

At the end of the stay, Philip wrote Elizabeth a thank you letter telling her he hoped she did not mind if he added Windsor to his two other favourite places, namely *Broadlands*, where his uncle Dickie now lived in great style, Edwina having inherited Lord Palmerston's magnificent eighteenth century Palladian stately home from her father Lord Mount Temple in 1939, and *Coppins*, Marina's altogether more modest house in Iver.

There is little doubt that Philip hungered for family life, and that one of the appeals of Lilibet, aside from her unswerving and increasingly obvious passion for him, was the close-knit and happy atmosphere which Elizabeth had created within her immediate family. No one misses, or values, family life more than a happy child who has had his own family snatched from him, and in that respect, Philip was performing true to what any psychologist would have expected of him. There was a tremendous lure to the possibility of being included in this magic circle, and Philip made no secret of his regard for it. Later that year, in another bread and butter letter, he would articulate how it, 'is the simple enjoyment of family pleasures and amusements and the feeling that I am welcome to share them,' that meant so much to him.

Of course, there were the additional pleasures of being at the centre of court life, of the 'panoply' of royalty, something his cousin Alexandra of Greece had noticed appealed to him when they were in Greece for the reburial of their respective ancestors.

By this time, Lilibet had shown her interest in Philip sufficiently unmistakably, and he had reciprocated her feelings sufficiently fully, for them to have progressed, from being cousins who corresponded, to boyfriend and girlfriend. Philip, being a prince, knew how things should be done. He therefore approached his cousin George II of the Hellenes, who was in exile in England, having been asked to move on from Egypt by King Farouk, to ascertain of King George VI whether he could press his suit with Lilibet.

On the face of it, the playing field for Philip was more level than it would have been for a merely aristocratic suitor. Consent was being sought from monarch to monarch. There was therefore a degree of equality which, in royal terms, would ordinarily have been welcomed.

This, however, is where the trouble started. According to the Duke of Windsor, Elizabeth was a 'pathologically jealous' woman who brooked no opposition whenever people got in her way. Like most jealous people, she was possessive, and nowhere more so than with her children. She had set out to recreate the happy family of her youth, and in that she had been outstandingly successful, 'Us Four' being the paradigm of a close and loving family. She was therefore never likely to welcome into it any prospective son-in-law who she felt was not easily controllable by her.

Philip, on the other hand, was very much his own person. He had strong opinions, just like Elizabeth, but his outlook often ran counter to hers. Moreover, he was open where she was covert. He conveyed in conversation how much he relished modernism, just like the brother-in-law who now blamed Elizabeth for costing him his throne. Elizabeth, of course, was resolutely old-fashioned and viewed any deviation from the traditional norm as something approaching heresy.

Although Elizabeth and Philip had a love of the outdoors and socialising in common, such profoundly different approaches to life were bound to grate on someone like her. The better she got to know the handsome alpha male, the clearer she saw the threat he would present to her in the long term, should he ever become a part of her family. In reality, they were two cocks of one walk. And Elizabeth was not used to having her ascendency threatened. Nor was she about to begin countenancing it.

The stage was being set for a tussle of wills that would play out over the next fifty-five years. In the future, Lilibet would prove to be extremely skilful at balancing the demands of a dominant husband and an even more dominant mother, but in these early days, the game was in its infancy, and there is no indication that the daughter had any idea of how resolute her mother could be. Nor, it has to be said, did Elizabeth yet have a clue as to how similar her daughter could be to her, when it came to pursuing her objectives. The daughter would prove to be more than a match for the mother: for sheer determination and obduracy Lilibet was every bit Elizabeth's daughter, though unlike her mother, she was not a dominating personality

Fortunately for the ostensible harmony of the family, neither Elizabeth nor Lilibet was one for direct confrontation. Both of them wanted to retain the façade of a loving family living in harmony. In this, they would succeed because both of them were mindful of maintaining an air of harmoniousness behind which all their struggles would take place.

Lilibet was a very agreeable, dutiful personality who never challenged authority. Elizabeth was made of far more challenging stuff, though all her skirmishes had always been conducted behind a hyper-feminine façade of agreeability. Meanwhile, she would lay trip wires in the hope of ambushing her adversaries, deploying her charm to lull potential victims into a sense of false security until they fell into the traps she had set for them. She was such an operator that even Hitler had called her, 'the most dangerous woman in Europe.' Her *modus operandi*, of hiding behind masks of high-minded principle and charm while getting others to do her undesirable work for her, meant that she seldom got her hands dirty. Unlike most other operators, who want their skill acknowledged, she had no desire for recognition, preferring to gather the scalps while others took the credit, or blame, as long as she got the results she wanted. .

Elizabeth now swung into action, starting a *danse fantastique* to achieve her objective of driving enough wedges between Lilibet and the man with whom she was in love, to achieve her over-riding objective: the acquisition of an amenable and malleable husband for her dutiful and loving daughter. She therefore ensured that the flow of eligible young men, mostly officers but all aristocrats of the most eminent lineages, became a flood.

Of course, had Elizabeth had the passionate nature of her husband or her daughter, she would have understood that you do not try to supplant a strikingly handsome, hyper-masculine sex god with a nice, even interesting, but antiseptic heir to a peer whose masculinity is carefully concealed beneath a carapace of what Mummy regards as good breeding. On an atavistic level, Philip held out the promise of excitement in and out of bed; his competitors a clammy hand at the opening of the local fete.

Elizabeth, however, appears not to have known Lilibet's nature or her mettle. She was nowhere near as malleable as her mother thought. She would get what she wanted, and she would do so in such a way that her achievement would not impact adversely upon her relationships with her mother, father or sister. But she could not be moved about on the Elizabethan chess board with quite the ease that her mother seemed to hope.

So began the dangling of every aristocratic heir in the kingdom Elizabeth regarded as desirable. For the next three years this dance would continue until it threatened to become a *danse macabre*. While it was going on, Elizabeth did her utmost to wean Lilibet away from Philip.

Fortunately for the young couple, Elizabeth had not yet shown the antipathy she possessed for Philip. To have done so would have been to give away her game. Only later, after it had been lost, would she, rather pointlessly but only too humanly, do so. This, however, would come later, when she and Philip were butting heads about the direction the monarchy should take. In the meantime, this woman who had understood how to use her brother-in-law's passionate nature against him in the run-up to the abdication, seems not to have understood that Lilibet's passion for Philip could and would be equally lethal to her intentions to replace a real man with one of the chinless wonders who were in awe of her and the monarchy.

One of Philip's great appeals for Lilibet was precisely his lack of awe for her. To him, she was not a princess to be revered and possibly acquired in bland and antiseptic matrimony. He had no awe for her, unlike the other potential suitors whom Elizabeth hoped would supplant him. He did not treat Lilibet with kid gloves. His touch might be gentle, but there was no doubt about the fact that he was a man, and she an equal: a living, breathing woman with whom he was falling more and more deeply in love. He was not one of those stereotypes of good breeding who promised an antisepsis that clearly appealed to Elizabeth but had no corresponding appeal for Lilibet.

On the other hand, the better George VI got to know Philip, the more he liked him. This was not altogether surprising. Both men had many personal traits, characteristics and experiences in common. Both were princes. Both had had difficult youths. Both were naval men with the same sort of down to earth perspective and colourful turn of phrase typical of their profession. Both had similarly jocular senses of humour; both had similarly humane approaches towards humanity. Both were athletes who liked nothing better than robust outdoor activity followed by a good meal with convivial company. Both were straightforward, and the king, like the prince, had no side to him. George VI told his mother that Philip was, 'intelligent, has a good sense of humour, and thinks about things in the right way'.

Queen Mary also liked Philip and heartily approved of him for her granddaughter. This meant a lot to Lilibet, who adored her grandmother and had a real affinity with her, born of the judicious care the dowager queen had taken over the years to inculcate in her granddaughter and the country's future monarch the attitudes necessary for the preservation and continuance of the crown.

Although there is no doubt that Lilibet loved her mother, and that this love was returned in full by Elizabeth, the royals surrounding them have always been at pains to point out, privately, that the more reverential relationship was between Lilibet and Queen Mary. While Elizabeth was accomplished at gamesmanship, the old queen functioned on another level entirely. With her, the monarchy was imbued with spiritual significance. God Himself created monarchs. The calling was a sacred one, the temporal the worldly manifestation of His will. A good monarch lived up to his or her Godly duty. He or she did what was **right** at all times. Self-effacement was not only a guiding principle but imperative if one were to execute one's duty to the fullness of one's capabilities. Although Queen Mary was very aware of the value of publicity, she also possessed undeniable integrity. She did not play to the gallery. She did not court public approbation by smiling the way Elizabeth did, but by being the living, breathing evocation of rectitude and regality.

Queen Mary's influence on her granddaughter would prove to be lasting and is, in some ways, accountable for the way Queen Elizabeth II has conducted herself throughout her long reign. It is just as well that the old queen had the views she did, for Lilibet was far more like her dour, po-faced grandmother than her ineffably charming and personable, but conniving, mother. Had Lilibet not had the encouragement of the grandmother who would strengthen her resolve to perform her duties in a way that allowed her to be true to herself while at the same time being true to the long-term interests of the crown, it is doubtful that Lilibet would ultimately have achieved the respect and approbation she has throughout this earth. Although privately humorous and jolly, she has never put a foot wrong because she has never **acted.** Rather, she has **been.** In so doing, she has conveyed a degree of truthfulness, sincerity, and integrity that she would never have been able to achieve had she tried to emulate her more outgoing mother, whose role, it must be remembered, was only that of consort, never regnant.

There are parallels between the way Lilibet and Philip have performed their public duties, even though he too was only a consort. Both husband and wife have displayed a degree of sincerity and integrity that has earned them respect, even though Philip has leavened the loaf by being rather more forthright, in the process making blunders and causing controversy that his more reserved wife has never made.

It is likely that Philip and Lilibet, having been born royal, did not have the same motivation that Elizabeth did to make her mark on the world stage. They seem to have always been driven by the effect of their accomplishments rather than the effect those accomplishments would have upon their popularity. According to the royals who surrounded her, Elizabeth had something of a complex about not having been born royal. Rightly or wrongly, many of the born royals regarded her as something of an upstart. There is some anecdotal evidence to support the viewpoint that snobbishness was not necessarily at the root of their attitude. Each instance has an alternative explanation, usually that the royals regarded Elizabeth's unseemly delight in her station as something of a putdown to those who ranked beneath her.

One famous instance is when Princess Marina complained that she had to enter rooms, 'behind those two common Scots girls.' It would appear that the self-effacing Duchess of Gloucester, born Lady Alice Montagu-Douglas-Scott, got caught in the cross fire, for Marina's real annoyance was with Elizabeth, whose delight in her position was so pronounced that it had led to mockery on several occasions, including when Wallis Simpson so fatefully mimicked her for what was commonly regarded in royal circles as prissy self-importance run riot.

I know of several royals, some of whom were given refuge by the British royal family, who regarded her as unutterably common, and sneered at her attempts at regal conduct. To them, her fabled charm smacked of insincerity and trying too hard, her constant smiling the simpering of an *arriviste*, and an insincere one at that. Colin Glenconner once told me how he witnessed an argument between Elizabeth and Princess Margaret, who finally shut her mother up with the withering riposte, 'Oh, do shut up. You weren't even born royal.'

Elizabeth's creation of the First Eleven list was therefore motivated as much by her desire to have sons-in-law who would never threaten her in terms of her background, as it was by a desire to have sons-in-law whom she could dominate. She rightly supposed that while aristocrats would be eternally grateful to her for such support as she would give them – this turned out to be the case when Margaret married Antony Armstrong-Jones - royal sons-in-law would not confuse the co-operations of a good mother-in-law with the awe she required from one and all.

Had Elizabeth welcomed Philip with the open arms she displayed towards the future Earl of Snowdon, there is little doubt, amongst people who knew him, that he too, ironically, would have been eternally grateful. Not on the grounds of status, for there was never any doubt in his mind, or the minds of any of his relations, that in terms of lineage there was no comparison between hers and his, but because he yearned to replicate the warm and loving family he had known in his youth, and a welcoming mother-in-law without side would have been his ideal scenario.

So Elizabeth, rather than welcoming Philip as a suitor, convinced her husband that their eighteen year old daughter was too young to 'fix' upon one man. Knowing how much her husband and mother-in-law liked Philip, she was careful to say how much she liked him and shift her objections onto Lilibet's age at the very time she was dangling other bachelors under her nose in the hope of persuading her away from the potently attractive and eminently suitable prince. Sir Edward Ford, who became Assistant Private Secretary to the king in 1946, and whose wife Virginia was the niece of the fabled Nancy Astor, remembered how Elizabeth, 'wanted to introduce her daughter to a wide range of possibilities from the highest flights of the British aristocracy,' so, 'you'd often find three or four of them staying at Sandringham or Balmoral at the same time.'

Around the time that George VI broke the unwelcome news to George II in early 1944 that Lilibet was still too young for Philip to be cast in the role of suitor, his mother Alice was heading, on a mercy mission as a result of the latest tragedy to overwhelm the Hesse royal family, towards Schloss Friedrichshof, the monument that Queen Victoria's daughter Vickie (married age 17) had built to the memory of her beloved husband, the Emperor Friedrich. Situated on the foothills of the Taunus Mountains outside Frankfurt, the empress had left the castle to her daughter Margaret (Mossie), Landgravine of Hesse, sister of Kaiser Wilhelm II and mother of both Princes Philipp and Christopher of Hesse, the latter being his sister Sophie's husband.

Sophie had been living, since the outbreak of the war, with her mother-in-law and the two sons and two daughters she had produced between 1933 and 1939. She was five months pregnant when the children of her brother-in-law Philipp and his wife Mafalda, daughter of Italy's King Vittorio Emanuele III, were ominously deposited into the care of their grandmother in October 1943. In reality, this meant that Sophie would take care of her children's first cousins as well as her own children.

Philipp and Mafalda had disappeared. No one knew where they were, or by whom they had been detained, though the family strongly suspected that their detention was linked to the Armistice of Cassibile which Italy, with the backing of its king, had secretly signed with the Allies on 3rd September 1943. This news was catastrophically made public prematurely on 8th September by the Americans, under General Eisenhower, before the Italians had a chance to make the necessary dispositions regarding their citizens, personnel and troops still in the Axis territories.

Philipp disappeared the very day the armistice was announced. In fact, he had been arrested on Hitler's orders at the Fuhrer's Headquarters at Rastenburg following a dinner the two men had had. Hitler was convinced that Philipp must have had advance knowledge of Italy's capitulation through his father-in-law, King Vittorio Emanuele III, and the prince was taken into immediate custody, stripped not only of his rank, uniform and membership of the Nazi party, but also his name. He would later recall that he was transferred to Gestapo Headquarters in Berlin and handed over to the custody of the head of the Gestapo, SS-Major General Heinrich Muller, who informed him that, 'Prince Philipp of Hesse, who had existed until now, was to be regarded as dead and that all memory of him had to be extinguished.' As an additional insult, he was allocated the Jewish name of Herr Weinberg, but managed to convince Muller to allot him Herr Wildhof instead. This was the travelling incognito of the family, chosen by him because, 'if something should happen to me, my family would always know it was I'. His arrest was kept secret from everyone, especially his family. He was forbidden all outside communication, kept in solitary confinement when he was not being interrogated, prevented from speaking to anyone but his gaolers, and finally escorted south by five criminal policemen dressed as civilians, to Flossenberg concentration camp near Regensburg in Bavaria. He had not been charged with any crime, and naively, 'had always believed that no one could be put in a concentration camp without a good reason. I, however, was locked up without any grounds being given'. As had millions before him, and after him, his wife included.

While Philipp was being secretly detained by the SS, his wife Mafalda was in Bulgaria, attending the funeral of her sister Giovanna's husband Tsar Boris, who had been Hitler's reluctant guest only a few short weeks before, after which he had returned home, fallen ill, and died inexplicably. A slow acting poison administered by the Fuhrer's medical team was suspected, for Boris had been refusing to declare war against the Soviet Union, which Hitler was insisting upon, and with the monarch out of the way, a regency for his six-year old son Simeon might prove more amenable, though Josef Goebbels' diary indicates that he believed that Boris had been poisoned by anti-Axis elements close to him. Hitler was convinced that the Italians had poisoned him to ease their transition to the Allied cause.

Whichever version of the tumultuous turn of events was true, Mafalda found herself in an invidious position once the country of her birth declared for the Allies. She decided to head for Italy, seeking refuge in the Vatican with the help of Monsignor Giovanni Montini, later Pope Paul VI.

As Mafalda was doing so, the Germans not only attacked Italy, but were occupying it with all the brutality of an enemy which was a former ally. Her father, mother and the other members of the Italian royal family fled from Rome, heading towards Brindisi, where Prince and Princess Andrew and their children had been taken in 1922 having been evacuated from Greece. Mafalda's three youngest children, who were technically German and members of the Hesse royal family and not the Italian (Italy's royal house rules were Salic, descent being determined through the male line), were given shelter in his superb residence beside the Sistine Chapel by Monsignor Montini, who was a prominent member of the Holy See's Secretariat of State.

The Vatican was not occupied by the Germans, being a sovereign state whose existence had been recognised through the *Reichskonkordat*, the *Concordat between the Holy See and the German Reich* of 20th July 1933. This had been signed, on the one hand, by the German Vice Chancellor Franz von Papen, and on the other, by the Holy See's then Secretary of State, Eugenio, Cardinal Pacelli, who became Pope Pius XII on 2nd March 1939, and was therefore Pope at the time of these events.

Because the Vatican was only too mindful that Hitler could, at any moment, occupy their state, seize the Pope, even declare the Catholic Church abolished in German-occupied territories, they had been involved in an elaborate balancing act from the very beginning of the war. Christ's admonition, 'Render unto Caesar that which is Caesar's, and unto God, that which is God's,' was never more adroitly followed, as the Church tried to discharge its duty to its Flock without falling foul of the Fuhrer and suffering the fate of France, Norway et cetera et al.

The day after Mafalda arrived at the Vatican, she was tricked into leaving the safety of that state. The Germans informed her that her husband wanted to speak to her urgently on the only secure line then operational throughout Italy, at the Villa Wolkonsky. This magnificent villa, which I have had the pleasure of visiting, had been the German Embassy until it was reconfigured into the German military headquarters in Rome following the announcement of the Armistice of Cassibile on 8th September. As the car carrying the princess approached the Villa Wolkonsky, which is now the British Ambassador's residence, it was intercepted by an SS officer from the Afrikacorps, who informed her, 'Your husband called and said he will soon arrive at the airfield here in Rome and that he wanted to speak with you there.'

When Mafalda arrived at the airfield, she was taken into a room, which she was prevented from leaving when she wanted to eat some breakfast. It was at that moment that she realised that she was no longer a free woman. She was put on a flight, ostensibly heading for Munich, but in reality for Tempelhof airfield outside Berlin. There, she was met by the Gestapo, who took her to their offices near Lake Wannsee. For fourteen days she was interrogated without being allowed even a bed. She was led to believe that her husband had been shot, and though allowed to write letters, none of which ever reached their recipients, but which she wrote when not crying, she was thrown into Buchenwald concentration camp. There, she was billeted to the special Isolation Barracks. This was arguably the most dangerous place in the camp, located as it was near an armaments factory, the Wilhelm-Gust-loff-Works. There was every likelihood it would be blown to smithereens should the camp be bombed. Indeed, it was. Mafalda was gravely injured during a bombing raid, and bled to death from her injuries during the night of 26th-27th August 1944, following the amputation of her arm.

Although by the end of that year there were rumours of Mafalda's death, her family was denied all access to information throughout the war. It was only at its end that they learnt her fate. Historian Jonathan Petropoulos states in *Royals and the Reich: Princes von Hessen in Nazi Germany* (Oxford University Press, 2006), 'There can be little doubt that Hitler himself issued the orders concerning Mafalda: the princess experienced the dictator's rage on a personal level.'

While Mafalda was meeting her tragic end in one concentration camp, her sister-in-law Sophie was now caught up in the drama which Hitler was orchestrating for the whole family, with equally tragic results. To date, Christopher of Hesse had been a director of the Third Reich's Ministry of Air Forces, Commander of the Air Reserves, with the rank of Oberfuhrer in the SS. In May of that year, when Hitler had issued the *Princes Decree*, as the *Decree Against Internationally Connected Men* was popularly known, Christopher had been one of the few princes spared dismissal from the armed forces. While the contemporaneous impression might have been that Hitler still trusted him, subsequent events indicate that the Fuhrer was actually playing a waiting game. Both Christopher and his brother Philipp knew too much, and were too well connected internationally, with both Germany's allies and enemies, for them to be merely dismissed and released back into society, the way most of the other princes were, their brother Richard included.

Because Christopher was a senior ranking officer with access to highly classified information, having retained his positions in the SS and being the nominal head of the Forschungsamt (the agency which intercepted the post and telegraph system), should he return to Germany from his posting in Italy, it was only a matter of time before he discovered the carefully concealed fates of his brother and sister-in-law.

Throughout late September and early October, Christopher remained stationed in Italy with his Fighter Squadron. He was as much in the dark of where they were as anyone else. The documents show that he was treading very carefully, declining to contact Hitler or his other high level connections, lest such an approach should increase the danger to their wellbeing.

According to the later testimony of one of his comrades, Christopher was then 'ordered to leave his squadron and therefore Italy and to report for reassignment in the territory of the Reich.' On 7th October, 1943, the prince and his experienced pilot, Wilhelm Gsteu, checked the weather conditions repeatedly, before flying out of the airport near Rome in a Siebel 204 twin-engine light transport plane. Their destination was the Fighter Squadron's home base near Mannheim in Germany. At 5.30pm their aircraft crashed into a 1,000 metre high part of the Apennine Mountains near Monte Collino, 30 kilometres southwest of Forli in Romagna. The aircraft was so utterly destroyed that it took two days to find the bodies of the men, who were laid to rest in the cemetery in Forli.

Dickie Mountbatten, who had been fond of his cousin, believed that, 'Hitler, distrustful of his loyalty, had him killed by a bomb planted in his aeroplane.' Prince Philip takes a more measured view of the crash, simply saying, 'No one has explained it.' While the Germans presented it as being a straightforward accident, most likely caused by pilot error, the facts suggested otherwise.

Alice provided a vignette of Sophie's grief in a letter she wrote to Philip, 'I went to Tiny (Sophie), who is so brave when she is with her children and us, being her usual self and making jokes but her hours in her room alone are hardly to be endured.' Tellingly, she continued, 'I never suffered after 'the accident' (the crash which killed Cecile and family) as I did those three weeks with Tiny and I will certainly never forget them as long as I live. Her children are perfectly adorable, you would love them, and the new baby is too sweet for words.'

Alice returned in April 1944 to Athens, where she had been tirelessly working through the Red Cross, organising soup kitchens to feed the starving Athenians; the Germans systematically shipped out all agricultural produce, leaving the locals to starve. She had even flown to Sweden, on the pretext of visiting her sister the Crown Princess Louise, but in reality to bring back medical supplies. Early on in the war, she had moved out of her small apartment and taken up residence in her exiled brother-in-law George of Greece's palatial, three storey villa near the city centre. Alice described it as, 'very cold now as there is no means of working the central heating. Upstairs there is a room with a fireplace, so happily I have one warm room in which to sit and dress and eat. Aunt Ellen (Princess Nicholas, Marina's mother) is well and lunches with me very often. We are the only ones and so we became very close friends.'

What Alice told no one was that she was harbouring a Jewish widow, Rachel Cohen, and two of her five children. She would doubtless have shared Mafalda's fate, in being carted off to a concentration camp, had she been caught committing this capital offence. Her reward would come in two stages long after her death. In 1988, the Israeli authorities permitted her to be buried at the Convent of St. Mary Magdalene in Gethsemane on the Mount of Olives near her aunt Ella, the Grand Duchess Serge, by then a Russian Orthodox saint. And in 1994, the Israeli government honoured her at Yad Vashmen as *Righteous Among the Nations*. Her two surviving children, Philip and Tiny, attended the ceremony, the former putting his mother's conduct into perspective when he said, 'I suspect that it never occurred to her that her action was in any way special. She was a person with a deep religious faith, and she would have considered it to be a perfectly natural human reaction to help fellow human beings in distress.'

# Chapter III

One of Philip's relations, who knows him well, told me that the words he used to describe his mother could equally be applied to him. He too has a deep spiritual faith, and he too has never regarded it as extraordinary whenever helping others has been within his grasp. Indeed, much of the good he has achieved through initiatives like the Duke of Edinburgh Awards Scheme has been motivated by the philosophy which he imbibed through Alice and Kurt Hahn. Though neither Philip nor the latter man had the opportunity to test their beliefs to the extent that Alice did, each of the three individuals, in his or her own way, believed strongly that it is the duty of each human being to do what he or she can to better the lot of mankind, in both abstract and personal ways, and each of them did so in exemplary fashion.

Another way in which mother and son would to prove be similar, is the way they would do what they regarded as the right thing, even in the face of opposition which would frighten off less stalwart individuals. Although Philip's struggles with the established order were still to come in 1944, Alice's reaction to the dictates of the British army curfew, when they liberated Athens in October 1944, demonstrated her mettle. She broke the curfew with alacrity as she moved around Athens distributing food parcels to the needy. When neither order nor threats worked, an appeal was made to her sense of self-preservation. 'They tell me you don't hear the shot that kills you, and in any case I am deaf. So, why worry about it?' she observed, as she continued distributing her food parcels while all around her snipers picked holes in buildings.

The year 1944 was a decisive one for the Allies. While preparations continued for the Allied invasion of France in June, other theatres of war had to receive their due attention. That spring, Philip found himself in Newcastle-upon-Tyne, where he helped oversee the completion of his latest ship, the *Whelp*, a W-Class destroyer. Initially assigned to the 3rd Destroyer Flotilla of the Home Fleet, based in Scapa Flow, her commander was G. A. F Norfolk and her first lieutenant Philip. She was then assigned to the 27th Destroyer Flotilla which left for the Far East on 2nd August, covering the Allied invasion of Southern France, Operation Dragoon, in mid-August.

For much of that year, Philip remained embarked in this final posting. In the Mediterranean, the *Whelp* proceeded to Alexandria, whence it would take the Suez Canal to Ceylon, where it was to link up with the Eastern Fleet as part of the abovenamed Flotilla.

Four days after Philip's arrival in Egypt on board the *Whelp*, his uncle Dickie flew into Cairo en route to Karachi to resume his command in South East Asia. Philip was at the airport to meet the uncle whose naval career had taken him to glorious heights since the beginning of the war. War or no war, Dickie still found the time to intrigue in an attempt to maximise his nephew's chances of becoming Lilibet's consort. Dickie told Lord Killearn a cock and bull story about how he was in Egypt to organise for Philip to become British, for George VI was keen for the young man to become an 'additional asset' to the British royal family, now that there were no adult male princes after the Duke of Gloucester, following the death of the Duke of Kent in that plane crash in 1942 and the abdication of Edward VIII. This, of course, was arrant nonsense. The likelihood of George VI needing a Greek prince to assist in the execution of public duties makes no sense, unless, of course, the said prince married into the family. A naturalised Greek prince not married into the British royal family would not be a member of the British royal family. And George VI had made it plain, and would continue to do so, that he and Elizabeth would not countenance any attempts made by Dickie and the Greek royal family to arrange a marriage between their daughter and Philip. They wouldn't even agree to Philip being declared a suitor.

Dickie, however, was a born intriguer. He knew that persistence might win the day, where surrender would inevitably provide the one result he and his family did not want. So he persisted. He raised the subject of Philip's suit with the king in June 1944. George VI suggested that Philip should renounce his Greek citizenship and become British as a precursor to pressing his suit with Lilibet, before backtracking in a letter he wrote stating, 'I have been thinking the matter over since our talk, and I have come to the conclusion that we are going too fast.'

This letter can be interpreted in a variety of ways. Was the king articulating his genuine concerns, or, as seems more likely, was he suppressing his approval of Philip and backtracking after discussing the matter with his strong-minded wife?

Whatever view is taken, Miles Killearn's diary gives no hint of the 'pinch of salt' with which Elizabeth said she took Dickie. Without actually telling the high commissioner that he was doing all he could to position his nephew as the most suitable and desirable consort the future queen could have, Dickie proceeded to tell him that Philip had gone along with idea that he become British, as indeed had King George II of the Hellenes and his heir presumptive, Prince Paul, whose wife Frederika had given birth to a son and heir in 1940. Together with the parlous state of Greece, which had embarked upon the opening stages of the civil war that would tear it apart before the Axis powers had even vacated the country, and before the royal family had even a chance to return to their homeland, the baby Prince Constantine of

Greece meant that there was little point to Philip remaining a Greek prince when he might become a British prince consort. There was now no likelihood of his ever acceding to the Hellenic throne, so he might as well renounce his Greek citizenship and thereby maximise his suitability by way of becoming British. Becoming a British citizen was therefore nothing more or less than a device to render him more acceptable in the event that Dickie's and the rest of Philip's family's machinations worked.

It should be noted at this juncture that Philip himself is, and always was, categorical in his claim, articulated unmistakeably in 1970 to his official biographer Basil Boothroyd, that he did not seriously consider marriage to Lilibet until his stay at Balmoral in 1946. This has the ring of truth. Philip has always been fiercely independent, as Lilibet herself has stated on many occasions. He is also something of an idealist. Although he did become increasingly drawn to the attractive cousin who was very much in love with him, he was not the sort of personality who could be manipulated into surrendering his freedom, nor into altering a large part of his identity, for opportunistic reasons alone. His heart had to be involved. He also had to feel that he was making the decision himself. This meant that Dickie and the rest of the family, his mother Alice included, had to avoid prodding him in the direction that he knew they wanted him to head.

Philip was not foolish. He knew that there was much talk about him being a suitable candidate for the hand of the princess. He is even on record stating that of course there was such talk; there were few candidates available. He was one of a very narrow field. He also knew that his family wanted the match, not only for him, but also for themselves. He would have had to be thoroughly stupid and utterly unsophisticated to have understood otherwise. All well-bred people are brought up from birth to marry as well as they can. Marriage had not yet become the rose-tinted receptacle of unrealistic romanticism which Hollywood would present it as being in the years after the Second World War, with the result that expectations of marriage have changed throughout the western world, including in upper class circles. But in 1944, the war was still being waged and marriage was still a traditional institution. It still had practical and worldly elements to it, though by then all idealists wanted to marry someone they loved. In that, Lilibet and Philip were typical products of their time.

It is important to have the right perspective on the way their relationship developed, otherwise perceptions can be coloured by the talk which already surrounded it. For instance, there are several mentions in Sir Henry 'Chips' Channon's diaries, starting in 1941 and continuing intermittently thereafter every time the diarist or his parents-in-law ran across the Greek royals, that a marriage was being arranged between Philip and Lilibet. This can lead to the mistaken belief that the two parties themselves were like pieces on a chess board being shoved in the right direction, when the opposite is actually the truth. The letters and diary entries for the period show that the couple cocooned themselves against the rumours swirling around about them. Or, to be more accurate, that Philip himself was careful to insulate himself against all talk, refusing to even countenance any incentive than that which Lilibet herself presented him with through the ordinary expedient of being a girl in love with a guy, and one moreover who ultimately seduces the object of her desire through the sweetness of her character and the strength of her love.

An illustration of this fact is a letter Dickie wrote in February 1945 to his sister Alice. She was about to visit Britain from Greece, and he cautioned her against saying anything on the subject of a possible marriage when she saw the George VI and Elizabeth. 'The best hopes are to let it happen – if it will – without parents interfering. The young people appear genuinely devoted and I think after the war it is very likely to occur.'

These two sentences plainly show that Lilibet and Philip had indeed grown close and that outside interference would hinder rather than help. Dickie cannot have been blind to Elizabeth's antipathy towards the match, nor to her attempts to deflect her daughter's gaze elsewhere. It would appear, therefore, that all the talk he and the Greek royals were engaged in, was simply a public relations exercise to establish Philip's suitability by persuading the great and the good of the desirability of the match. It was also a way of Philip's relations boosting themselves. This, of course, was nothing out of the ordinary. It was, and remains, standard fare for people to sprinkle gold dust over themselves whenever the opportunity presents itself. It doesn't matter whether they are newspapermen, royals, television presenters, aristocrats, technocrats, entrepreneurs, artists, actors, middlingly successful or even particularly ordinary. This has always been the way of the world and, had Philip not married Lilibet, he would nevertheless have had the kudos of going down in history as a suitable contender for her hand, in much the same way that Princess Olga Romanoff, Lady Jane Wellesley and Sabrina Guinness are still mentioned as having been early candidates for Prince Charles's hand.

Throughout 1944, the relationship between the young couple remained not only unsure, but distant and intermittent. It was conducted mainly by letter, for Philip's ship took him to the Indian Ocean, where the *Whelp* escorted the aircraft carriers *Indomitable* and *Victorious* while their aircraft attacked Nancowry Harbour and the Nicobar Islands as a part of Operation Millet. By 22nd November 1944, when the British Pacific Fleet was formed, the *Whelp* was transferred to that fleet, its main base being at Sydney, Australia, with a forward base at Manus Island in northern Papua New Guinea. In Australia, Philip would link up with David Milford Haven. He also had the companionship of Mike Parker, who had remained posted in the same flotilla with him.

Now came the latest of the knocks which would colour Philip's life. On 3rd December 1944, his father died suddenly of a heart attack. He had been staying in a villa of the elegant, Belle Epoque Hotel Metropole, built in 1886, with his mistress, Andrée de La Bigne. He had been looking forward to the normalisation of relations now that Southern France had been liberated and the war appeared to be drawing to a sure if slow close. They had been to a party in Marseilles, which the Germans had surrendered on 28th August, and had turned in for the night when he was awoken with chest pains. There was nothing Andrée could do to save her lover. Death was almost instantaneous.

Although only 62, Andrew was old before his time. He had been diagnosed with arrhythmia and arteriosclerosis, possibly the products of a sybaritic existence free of exercise and healthy living. When Alice had last seen him in Germany, she had noticed that he had become deaf and doddery. The war years, with the enforced idleness of days spend wining and dining on board yachts in the harbour of Monte Carlo, had done nothing to improve his health.

Andrée telegraphed Alice in Athens. The day of Andrew's death could not have been more ominous for her, and not only for personal reasons. 3rd December 1944 was literally the day of the opening salvoes of the civil war that would ravage Greece for the next four years. For the following thirty three days, this first of the many battles that would rage in Athens began in the streets surrounding Big George's villa. Of course, Alice was not able to telegraph her daughters, who were all in enemy territory, as Germany had become with the departure of the Wehrmacht from Athens, but she was able to get a message through to her brother Dickie. He sent a wire to Philip on board the *Whelp*. Mike Parker remembered that the news was a 'great shock' to Philip, who 'really loved his father.'

Andrew's funeral took place at St. Nicholas Russian Orthodox Cathedral in Nice. At the conclusion of the war, his body was taken back to Greece, where it was interred in the royal burial ground at Tatoi.

Christmas, however, was not a lonely time for Philip. The *Whelp* put into Colombo and he spent the holidays at the King's Pavilion in Kandy with Dickie, who was now Supreme Allied Commander, South East Asia Command. According to Mike Parker, Philip was cut to the quick by the death of his father. However, as his sister Sophie demonstrated when she lost her husband Christopher, the children of Alice and Andrew had been brought up to put a good face on things and retain an air of normalcy, even of jollity, in the midst of grief. This Philip now did. He joined in all the fun, though there was no doubt to onlookers that grief co-existed with bonhomie.

The end of shore leave, which coincided with the new year, saw Philip on board the *Whelp*, which resumed its function as a part of the destroyer fleet providing screen for the aircraft carriers *Indefatigible, Indomitable, Illustrious*, and *Victoria* and the cruisers *Suffolk, Ceylon, Argonaut* and *Black Prince*. Their first operation, Lentil, mounted air attacks against the Japanese oil refineries at Pangkalan Brandan, and later that month Operations Meridian I and II protected the air attacks against the oil refineries at Pladjoe and Soengi Gerong in Sumatra respectively.

It was during one of the second set of raids that a Japanese fighter plane downed an Allied bomber, which ditched near its fleet in the hope of being rescued by its own men. Philip once more displayed the presence of mind which was one of his winning attributes. Directing a textbook search and rescue mission, he ordered the *Whelp* to steam to the location where the aircraft had ditched. This was a race against time that required precision, as the Java Sea was full of sharks. There was the additional risk of the airmen being picked up by the Japanese, as would indeed happen to several of their colleagues, who were rescued by the enemy, only to be beheaded by them in Singapore four days after the end of the war. Fortunately for the two man crew of the bomber from the aircraft carrier *Victorious*, gunner Norman Richardson and pilot, later Admiral Sir Roy Halliday, the *Whelp* arrived after they had only been in the open sea for about a quarter of an hour.

A week later, the *Whelp* sailed into Freemantle in Australia, where Philip and the men he had helped to rescue celebrated their good fortune with a pub crawl. Afterwards, Philip re-joined his ship for the journey to Sydney. The following months saw further forays between Australia and places such as Manus Island in Papua New Guinea, where she arrived on 7th March having been allocated for service with the US 5th Fleet. While awaiting the approval of Admiral Ernest King, Commander in Chief, United States Fleet and Chief of Naval Operations, the *Whelp* sailed with the British Pacific Fleet as Task Force 57 for Joint Operations with US aircraft carriers against airfields in the Sakishima group of Japanese islands. No longer could Philip complain, as he had done in the early days of the war, that he was seeing no action. Fighting was fierce, and Philip yet again displayed his mettle when he ordered the lowering of a vessel to rescue a downed pilot and an airman who was clinging to a buoy in an attempt to avoid drowning.

## Chapter III

By the end of March, however, the *Whelp* was ordered to Melbourne for repairs. This proved to be a fortuitous opportunity for Philip to enjoy himself. He had some three months of shore leave, having a riotous time partying first in Melbourne and latterly in Sydney, where Mike Parker 's leave dovetailed with his own. Parker was at pains to insist that though there were, 'always armfuls of girls, nothing happened – nothing serious. What I mean was this: we were young, we had fun, we had a few drinks, we might have gone dancing and that was it.' Parker characterised his friend as being, 'careful', 'self-contained', 'always good company but self-disciplined', 'quite reserved, quite restrained.' According to him, Philip, 'didn't encourage gossip.' Although the rumour mill would say, 'he played the field. I don't believe it. People say we were screwing around like nobody's business. Well, we weren't. You didn't. We didn't.'

Queen Alexandra of Yugoslavia was also at pains to emphasise that Philip was chaste, for all his antics and popularity with the girls. He was indeed matinee idol handsome, as well as tall, fun, entertaining, and a good dancer (this last attribute was extremely important to that generation). He 'hit feminine hearts,' but he 'fought a series of delaying actions all aimed at one objective: non-involvement,' the former Princess Alexandra of Greece said.

The film-maker Robin Dalton, who was there at the time, and would afterwards live with his brother-that-never-was David Milford Haven for five years, told me over dinner some time ago that Philip, for all his charm, was not at all emotionally warm. He did have two girls whom he saw a lot of while he was in Australia, Sue Other-Gee from Melbourne, and a socialite named Sandra Jacques, with whom he remained in touch. No one can categorically say what went on between Philip and either of those girls, except the three of them, but the likelihood is that their relationships were based more on companionship and innocent carousing than on carnality. Sex before marriage in 1945 was simply not the norm between respectable young men and women, irrespective of their class. If men had needs that must be satisfied, to employ the vernacular of the day, there were places to go. These bordellos provided both sexual gratification and anonymity. That, not the nearest rose bush, and certainly not the family sofa, was where young men headed when they needed 'relief'. 'Nice' young men and women simply did not indulge in carnality the way they do nowadays, and the imposition of current standards of behaviour on past generations does not assist in understanding how people behaved in 1945.

Moreover, Philip's character and station in life need to be borne in mind if we wish to tar him with the brush of pre-marital Casanova. His coolly impersonal personality, full of charm and ebullience superficially, but remote personally, was not compatible with the role of Don Juan, nor was the utterly non-tactile method with which he conducted himself. Certainly, his stunning good looks and outgoing personality drew girls to him, but by then there were persistent rumours, in naval as well as social circles, that he and Princess Elizabeth were each other's 'intended'. It was an open secret on the *Whelp* that Philip kept a picture of Princess Elizabeth beside his bed, and that there was a constant stream of letters back and forth between the two of them. Although Philip was careful not to make any declarations or feed any talk, the supposition was quite rightly that they were 'sweet' on each other, and if not exactly 'sweethearts', something akin to that. This provided an additional imperative for him to keep his slate clean. There is little doubt that he was positioning himself to marry her, should he feel so inclined to do. A reputation as a 'cad' or 'swordsman' would certainly have jeopardised his chances as an acceptable spouse. He has always been too intelligent and perspicacious, as well as too astute, to have blotted his copy book in such a way. The fact that no girl has ever come out of the woodwork, suggesting an affair with the bachelor prince, is yet another indication that he was more sexually continent than the rumour-mongers supposed.

Philip was still on shore leave in Australia when Hitler committed suicide in Berlin on 30th April. He was succeeded as President of the Reich by Grand Admiral Karl Doenitz, a World War One hero, who immediately ordered the Chief of Staff of the OKW, the Supreme High Command of the Wehrmacht of Nazi Germany during World War II, Colonel-General Alfred Jodl, to begin negotiations for surrender. He was keen that as many German troops as possible surrender to the western Allies rather than the Soviets, who had already been raping and pillaging their way to victory in the east, in retaliation for the horrors the Nazis had imposed upon the Russian people while occupying their territory. The articles of surrender were signed by Jodl in Rheims on 7th May, to come into force at 2301 hours Central European time the following day. Furious at what he regarded as a slight to the Red Army, Stalin forced Field Marshall Wilhelm Keitel to repeat the signing at Marshal Georgy Zhukov's headquarters in Berlin in the presence of Eisenhower's representative, General Carl Spaatz of the United States Army Air Forces (USAAF).

Despite victory in Europe, the war in the east continued, and after repairs on the *Whelp* were completed, in July Philip and his ship were re-deployed from Sydney with the destroyer HMS *Wager* as escorts for the battleship HMS *Duke of York*. They headed by way of the forward base at Manus in the Admiralty Islands to Guam, and onwards to join the British Pacific Fleet off Japan. On 16th August the *Whelp* was detached from the Duke of York on joining the 3$^{rd}$ US Fleet 200 miles south east of Tokyo, and on 2$^{nd}$ September they were in attendance at the formal surrender of Japan. Thereafter, Philip's ship remained as a part of the British Pacific Fleet based at Hong Kong with the 27$^{th}$ Destroyer Flotilla, assisting in the repatriation of allied personnel from Japanese captivity in the Far East, before returning to Portsmouth on 17$^{th}$ January 1946.

Philip was home. But was Lilibet yet home and dry with him?

# Chapter IV

UP TO THE AGE of eighteen, Lilibet led a sheltered if charmed and charming life. Although her father liked to say that the war had prevented her from having any fun, life at Windsor Castle was actually rather pleasant, even during the war. There were picnics in the park, and an ever-present number of attractive young officers to dance attendance upon the two sisters. Because the royal family was guarded by the Castle Company, as the 300 strong company of the Grenadier Guards was known, and there was a training battalion based there, young officers such as Mark (later Lord) Bonham Carter, grandson of the later 11ᵗʰ Duke of Grafton, would regularly lunch with Lilibet and Margaret and their governess Crawfie. Sometimes their French mistress, Monty, would be in attendance, but less seldom Toinon once she took over. Nevertheless, the girls' way of life was highly sociable and decidedly agreeable.

As the war progressed and Lilibet grew up, her age, and not Margaret's, set the pace, but only to the extent that the younger girl could keep up. A four year age gap is significant in children and teenagers, but the king and queen's way of coping with it meant that the older sister was kept artificially young, while the younger was encouraged to be excessively precocious. By 1943, when Lilibet was seventeen, thirteen year old Margaret was permitted to join the adults for dinner. 'She was allowed to grow up too quickly,' a cousin told me in confidence, but there was nothing anyone could do to remedy the situation. George VI 'used to look at Princess Margaret in sort of amazement that he had produced this object who found everything so easy and was a pretty little thing,' while Elizabeth, oblivious to the dangers inherent in such a situation, went along with it as if it were the most natural thing in the world.

Margaret was undeniably a character, even at that young age. Lilibet, on the other hand, was self-effacing. Words and banter did not come easily to her the way they did to the outrageously entertaining Margaret, and while her face lit up when she smiled, 'it looked rather dead when she didn't', a criticism with which she must agree, as she herself calls it her 'Miss Piggy face'. Crawfie tried as best she could to give Lilibet opportunities to sparkle on her own, encouraging people to ask only her to parties rather than both siblings, but Lilibet herself did not mind being eclipsed by her younger sister. 'Oh, it's so much easier when Margaret's there – everybody laughs at what Margaret says,' she stated, with not an ounce of jealousy or competitiveness.

This was an attitude Lilibet also had towards her mother, who eclipsed her as well. Cecil Beaton; Maureen, Marchioness of Dufferin and Ava; Margaret, Duchess of Argyll and Clare, Duchess of Sutherland would all observe, in the years to come, that Lilibet invariably lapsed into silence when her mother was present. I too noticed it, when I was presented to Queen Elizabeth II and Queen Elizabeth The Queen Mother by the Duke of Atholl at the Ascot Races for the King George VI and Queen Elizabeth Stakes in 1973. It was quite remarkable to observe how the mother dominated proceedings while the daughter happily, and the operative word is *happily*, took a back seat, cheerfully laughing and smiling on the periphery as the Queen Mother sparkled in the limelight. Lilibet was plainly perfectly comfortable on the sidelines, while there was no doubt that her mother regarded centre stage as the only fitting place where she, Elizabeth, should be.

Shy though she was, Lilibet nevertheless was, and has remained, fun loving. Even as a teenager, she enjoyed company. She liked to laugh, and she already had a well-developed love of parties. This was something she had inherited from both her parents, and even during the war, Windsor Castle remained the epicentre of joyful if quiet socialising. This was possible because food, which was produced on the royal estates, was not the wartime problem it was in cities, where people did not have access to agricultural produce the way country folk did. There were also well laid wine cellars, so, even though wines could no longer be imported from France, Italy or Germany, drink was not a problem either. There were small dances, sometimes for up to a hundred, with permanent house guests in attendance such as the handsome, entertaining (Sir) Gerald Kelly, President of the Royal Academy and the man appointed in 1938 to paint the state portraits of King George VI and Queen Elizabeth in their coronation robes. This Old Etonian somehow managed to drag out executing the commission for the duration of the war. George VI would, from time to time, indicate that he wondered when the artist intended to move on, but Elizabeth liked art and artists, Old Etonians and wits, all of which Kelly was. She was also, by this time, an avid collector of the Modern British School, of which Kelly was a leading light. She was remarkably tolerant of people's foibles when she liked them, whether it was a chauffeur who drank too much, a servant who was out of sorts for the same reason, or houseguests like Kelly, who enjoyed the conviviality of this safest of wartime refuges. So he always found something to overpaint or alter, and George VI went along with it because Elizabeth enjoyed having him around.

Certainly, Kelly did a variety of working sketches aside from painting the portraits themselves. He was canny enough to give Elizabeth a sketch of the portrait of George VI, which she kept in pride of place at Clarence House. I say canny because the sketch Kelly gave Elizabeth is not in the pose of the finished portrait. That he kept for himself. I know, because this more valuable and desirable version was sold in the studio sale after his death in 1972, and now hangs in my drawing room.

The war ended just after Lilibet's nineteenth birthday. By her father's own account, she was, 'his pride, Margaret his joy.' Both sisters seem to have been pleased with the roles allotted to them by their father. Mabell, Countess of Airlie, who was Queen Mary's longstanding lady-in-waiting and friend, as well as the Strathmore family's neighbour in Scotland, had known both the king and queen well before they married, in fact from early childhood. Indeed, she had played a crucial part in fostering the union between the obsessed Bertie and the reluctant Elizabeth. She would highlight the crucial role played by Lilibet in her father's life, explaining that she was his, 'constant companion in shooting, walking, riding – in fact in everything.'

This was less an exaggeration than an accurate assessment of the father-daughter relationship. Once Lilibet turned eighteen, her father made her a Counsellor of State. Thereafter, she was obliged to stand in for him whenever he was incapacitated or out of the country. Not all her functions were pleasant. In 1944, when he was in Italy visiting the Eighth Army, she had to sign the reprieve of a murderer's death sentence. Displaying the compassion for which she is still known, she asked, 'What makes people do such terrible things? One ought to know. There should be some way to help them. I have so much to learn about people!'

Mindful of her relative lack of knowledge, and eager to learn, the ever-dutiful Lilibet happily spent hours by her father's side learning the ropes while he was working. He would show her how things should be done; explain to her why he was doing something, or, as the case may be, not doing it. In reality, she was shadowing him, learning the business of monarchy on the ground. It might not have been exciting, and might well have been regarded as boring or onerous by someone less duty-driven than Lilibet, but she was her father's daughter and they, 'loved working together', Princess Alice, Countess of Athlone, who was Queen Mary's sister-in-law and Queen Victoria's granddaughter, said.

# Chapter IV

Learning the ropes this way would prove to be invaluable for Lilibet once she acceded to the throne. She had not expected to inherit the crown for another twenty or twenty-five years, and had much to learn, but, as she explained to friends and family alike, whenever she had a dilemma, she only needed to ask herself, 'What would Papa do?' Whatever the answer, that is what she did.

Although the end of the war saw the end of fighting, it did not see the end of the struggles for the British people and the British crown. In a real sense, prosperity would not return till after the end of a decade. In some ways, life returned to normal, or an approximation of normal, much sooner after the First World War than it did after the Second. This inevitably had an effect upon George VI and Lilibet, who, as sovereign and heiress presumptive, were caught up in the day to day problems, and the solutions required. Although her father was careful not to burden her unduly, Lilibet's place in the line of succession meant that she was already being prepared for the heavy responsibilities she would have to bear in the future as monarch. The fact that she was a serious person, who liked fulfilling her duty, made the task easier, but it also meant that she would never be able to enjoy a life of levity the way her sister Margaret would.

While Lilibet was being introduced to the realities of peacetime, so was Philip. He is on record as stating that he found his peacetime activities in the navy dull in comparison with the excitements of the war: a sentiment shared by many other sailors and soldiers. But one immediate benefit of being posted back in Britain was that he was able to see more of Lilibet. He endured a series of boring postings, firstly overseeing the decommissioning of his ship; then being sent to a naval training base in north Wales; before being transferred to Corsham as a lecturer of petty officers. This lack of excitement might have provided a void professionally, but it did give him the time and space – and one suspects the incentive - to find his excitement elsewhere. Since he drank very little, was not promiscuous, and already had a full social life whose excitements he took for granted, he filled the gap in a way typical for a young person: he fell in love.

By Philip's own account, to his biographer Basil Boothroyd, it was only after he returned to England in 1946 that his relationship with Lilibet intensified beyond that of cousinly affection. At least on his part; her feelings towards him were already anything but merely cousinly.

Crawfie has left accounts of Philip's little MG roaring into Buckingham Palace's courtyard; of Philip jumping out of the car; hurtling down the corridors to Lilibet's suite of rooms; and of the romance being conducted as a three cornered hat. Margaret was inevitably present, but that did not cause problems for either Lilibet or Philip. Sex before marriage was out of the question, not only for the royal couple, but for most of their peers, so there was no need for them to exclude the always present and always entertaining Margaret.

When in town, Philip used to stay in one of two places, either with uncle Dickie in Belgravia, just over the road from the palace, or at his grandmother Victoria's grace and favour flat in Kensington Palace. Robin Dalton confirms that he had to manage on his naval officer's paltry salary plus an allowance of £5 a week from Dickie, who also gave the same amount to her live-in boyfriend, David Milford Haven.

Royal courtships, however, were never conducted in public, so Philip's penury had no impact on the relationship's progress. The end of the war had seen an increase, not a decrease, in the extent of rationing, so in this period of austerity the youngsters would eat fish or the mash and sausages sent up to the princesses' quarters from the palace kitchen, washing it down with something typical like orange squash, before finishing off dinner with a nursery style pudding. It was hardly *haute cuisine*, but this is where the aristocrats' love of nursery food coincided with the propensity to domesticity inherited by the descendants of Europe's Grandfather, the Danish king Christian IX, who was both Lilibet and Philip's ancestor.

When Philip was not roaring up to Buck House to see her, he would stay with his cousin Marina at Coppins. Lilibet would invariably be staying at nearby Windsor with her parents. The young sweethearts would link up, away from the beady eye of her overly-protective father and not entirely approving mother, while surrounding themselves with more sympathetic relations and being properly chaperoned. There was no question of Lilibet's virtue being compromised.

People who have never had access to the country house/castle/palace lifestyle may not realise how ably it fosters budding romances. Firstly, the backdrop of other people means that the wheels of conversation and entertainment are well oiled at all times. The pressure is off the couple to carry the whole occasion on their own shoulders, in a way that they have to do in the artificially engineered environment of dating in restaurants and nightclubs. Without such pressure, everyone is more relaxed, with the result that people usually unfold more naturally and, unless there is a concerted attempt being made to dupe a potential spouse through overt deception, each party to the exchange has a clearer view of what the other party is truly about.

# Chapter IV

Everyone who knows Philip and Lilibet well has always commented on how utterly authentically themselves they both are. Although radically different in some ways, in others they are very similar, and, as the adult Philip and the adult Lilibet got to know each other better and better in 1946, they not only fell deeply in love, but also came to appreciate how complementary their similarities and differences were.

Not all their forays, however, took place behind stately doors. In April Philip joined Lilibet and a group of friends for a visit to the Aldwych Theatre, but this public glimpse of the burgeoning relationship was exceptional.

That August the romance moved to another level altogether when Philip joined the family for a three week stay at Balmoral, to shoot grouse and stalk. George VI was an excellent shot, and the Glorious 12th, the beginning of the grouse shooting season which Hitler had so inconsiderately interrupted in 1939, was one of the most important days in the king's diary. Lilibet herself used to stalk, so that would be another activity the intensely athletic prince and the princess, with whom he was now in love, could share.

Although Philip was not yet a good shot, and did not have the requisite attire, going out into the field in regular trousers rather than plus fours, his aptitude for sport stood him in good stead, and by the end of the stay he was on the way to becoming the superb shot he would end up being.

On one level, the stay was a resounding success. For the first time, Philip acknowledged the depth of his feelings for Lilibet, admitting that it was then, 'that we, that it became, you know, that we began to think about it seriously, and even talk about it.' In his tongue-tied, emotionally suppressed but intensely passionate way, he had raised the subject of marriage to her. Her response was simpler. She said, 'Yes.' The next step was to tell her parents, which they did.

The indications, from those who knew the family well, were that George VI approved of Lilibet's choice – it must be remembered that both he and Queen Mary had been in favour of the match some time before, when it was first mooted - but that Elizabeth, despite masking her opposition behind a cavalcade of smiles, was, if anything, even less enamoured of Philip than she had previously been. According to the Duke of Windsor, Elizabeth's *modus operandi* was to unleash others to do her dirty work for her. Her brother David Bowes Lyon, the closest of her siblings who was also staying up at the castle for Philip's visit, now swung into action, doing all in his power to stir up opposition to Lilibet's intended. Gina Kennard and her first cousin Patricia Mountbatten said what a 'vicious' individual he was. 'He had it in for Philip right from the start,' the former said, while the latter said, 'He did everything he could to ruin things for Philip.'

It is worth examining the dilemma faced by Philip, and why Elizabeth's role in the saga has been underplayed over the years. Lilibet was not only close to her mother; she was in thrall to her. Yet she loved Philip and was not about to give him up. Doubtless, though on a perhaps unconscious level, one of Philip's appeals for Lilibet was that he was strong enough to withstand her powerful mother. In so doing, he would liberate her from Elizabeth's overwhelming influence, at least up to the point that she wanted to be liberated. This, it has to be observed, was not to any great extent. She still wanted, and would continue to want, to bask in her mother's warmth and charm, but only to the extent where she did not have to sacrifice any of the ambitions she had for herself. Lilibet's attitude towards her mother was both complex and simple. She was a dutiful and loving daughter who was intent on maintaining a close and loving relationship with her overpowering mother, and in so doing, remained her mother's child throughout her life; though when necessary, she would take a leaf out of her mother's book and mount opposition behind the façade of lovingness.

In the vernacular, Lilibet was caught been the devil and the deep blue sea. But not so much that she would surrender her most heartfelt wish, which in this instance was to marry Philip. The result was that for the remainder of her mother's life, Lilibet undertook a balancing act between, on the one hand, accommodating her mother in the excessive demands she made, while on the other protecting her own turf against her mother's encroachments. As we will see later, Lilibet was not always effective in keeping her mother at bay. Elizabeth's influence, in years to come, could be detrimental to the smooth running of family life, such as in the way she actively encouraged Prince Charles in habits and tendencies that were geared towards undermining Philip and Lilibet as parents while, at the same time, fostering traits that would tie him more closely to her and, in so doing, perpetuate her influence, at times adversely, into the next generation. As one of Charles's great friends put it, 'Queen Elizabeth encouraged him to whine. She's the reason why he's always been prone to self-pity.'

In royal circles, it was a truism that one must never openly criticise Queen Elizabeth The Queen Mother, because both the present monarch, Lilibet, and the future one, Charles, did not wish to hear a word said against her; the former because she was too conflicted and did not want to have to be reminded of unpleasant truths which she would much rather ignore, the latter because he would never allow fact to interfere with his impression of his beloved Granny. It should therefore come as no surprise that neither

Gina Kennard nor Patricia Mountbatten would ever have laid blame at Elizabeth's door for the opposition which her brother David now embarked upon creating. Yet it was also a truism in royal circles that David Bowes Lyon cut his cloth according to Elizabeth's pattern. The idea that he would, off his own initiative, have been creating trouble for his niece's unofficial fiancé was untenable.

David and Elizabeth had form going way back. They had been child co-conspirators, as they were proud to admit, and while this tendency continued into adulthood, each of them would cause mischief that could, at times, be wildly inappropriate. For instance, Elizabeth tried to block Winston Churchill's appointment of her old adversary, Lord Beaverbrook, as Minister of Air Production in 1940. Unusually for her, she failed to do so, George VI taking the unusual step of backing his prime minister against his wife when Churchill pointed out how imperative the appointment was to the national interest. During the war, her brother David also got up to all sorts of mischief, especially when he was posted to America to assist with the war effort. His machinations and intrigues created such difficulties for Sir Robert Bruce Lockhart, director-general of the Political Welfare Executive which co-ordinated all Allied propaganda against the Axis Powers, and the Minister of Information, Brendan (later 1st Viscount) Bracken (and Churchill's protégé), that they had demanded his recall. Elizabeth, however, thwarted them through the intervention of her friend Lord Halifax, the British Ambassador in Washington, insisting that her brother had to remain in situ. The result was that David remained in his post despite the damage he continued to do.

It is likely that David Bowes Lyon's antipathy towards Philip was inspired, if only in part, by his potential nephew-by-marriage's overt masculinity. Overt masculinity had never been an attribute prized by the British upper classes. In fact, it had always been regarded as somewhat common. The emphasis had to be solidly on status, and the polish necessary to convey it, not on sexuality. This meant that in the days before homosexuality was as acceptable as it now is, it was often impossible to tell whether British gentlemen were gay or straight until they made their move sexually. It also, of course, permitted closet queens such as David Bowes Lyon to hide in full view.

Peculiarly, the under-masculinised gentleman was never a feature of the American male, or indeed of northern Europeans such as the Germans and Scandinavians, or indeed of the Latins. Spaniard, Italian and Portuguese gentlemen were consistently and unmistakably men first and gentlemen second, though for some peculiar reason the French shared the British upper classes' propensity towards submerging their gender beneath a façade of mannerisms dedicated to displaying their social superiority at the expense of their masculinity.

Philip's masculinity, which, I can tell you, was potent in person, set him apart. It was akin to that of Sean Connery at the height of his fame as James Bond. I know this to be a fact for they are two of the most potently masculine men I have met in a lifetime of meeting, and sometimes going out with, some of the most eligible men of my time. This overt masculinity would have antagonised many of the courtiers, who even, as recently as twenty-five years ago, were in the traditional mould and had a distinct patina which set them apart from the rest of their upper class peers. Their manners were so polished that they invariably came across as the nicest of the nice, the grandest of the grand, the most elegant of the elegant. Their charm was legion, their attentiveness to your comfort exquisite. Had you been tempted to believe it, you would have thought that they had spent their whole lives waiting to meet you. They seldom if ever expressed a point of view that jarred with the prevailing atmosphere. They were supremely regal, courtly as well as courteous, oozing clubability through every pore. This made them supremely seductive socially. Their quiet voices and padding footsteps were so practised in the art of unobtrusiveness, that they could insinuate themselves into your regard with almost frightening alacrity. Those who knew the way Courts function, however, also knew that they would jettison anyone whose interests conflicted with their own. It did not matter whether one was the previous Prince of Wales or Frances Roche Burke, who became Viscountess Althorp before being shunned as Mrs Shand Kydd. Everyone who threatened them would be cold shouldered as if he or she had never existed.

No one was more practised in the courtly arts than David Bowes Lyon. Although married at the age of 26 to the Conservative MP Herbert Henry Spender-Clay's younger daughter Rachel, and the father of two children, a daughter named Davina (born 1930) and a son named Simon (born 1932), Sir David, as he later became, was 'rampantly homosexual' as his friend, Burnet Pavitt told me. This wealthy Hoffman La Roche businessman, who was a gifted pianist and sat on the board of the Royal Opera House, used to rent a house on the St. Paul's Walden Bury estate from David, who had been left the magnificent Palladian-style edifice in defiance of the rules of primogeniture. This sixth son of the 14th Earl of Strathmore was, with Elizabeth, one of his father's two favourite children, with the result that that gem of the earldom of Strathmore's patrimony became separated from the title in what was, in aristocratic circles, a shocking display of paternal favouritism over the longer-term interests of the earldom's welfare.

# Chapter IV

David used to host gay weekends at St. Paul's Walden, where the men would dress up as anything and everything that caught their fancy. This was at a time when homosexuality was illegal and punishable by imprisonment. Indeed, two well-known members of the British Establishment would be convicted of the offence of gross indecency, as the crime was known on the statute books, at the very time David Bowes Lyon's parties flourished. One was Alan Turing, the famous code breaker whose work was portrayed by Benedict Cumberbatch in *The Imitation Game* (he opted for chemical castration rather than imprisonment in 1952 before committing suicide), and the other, Edward, 3rd Lord Montagu of Beaulieu, who was imprisoned in 1954.

Burnet spent most weekends at St. Paul's Walden and was often to be found at the big house as a guest. He attended countless social occasions there, and his snapshot of life is worth recounting, because it provides such a vivid portrait of Elizabeth as an individual. He thought her, 'absolutely extraordinary. Even though they were brother and sister and close as could be, you could never forget for one second that you were in the presence of a queen. I have known other queens, and they never behaved like that. With her it was Ma'am this and Ma'am that, even from her brother. He would have to wait at the foot of the stairs when she was due to descend for dinner. She invariably kept him waiting. But he dared not go into an adjoining room. He had to be there, standing, waiting, waiting, waiting, so that when she got to the landing and looked down, she could see him hovering. She would give him a little wave and float down, all smiles, and he would kiss her, and, if you had not been staying for the weekend and were just there for dinner, he would bow and call her Ma'am before leading her in to meet the guests who would be assembled in the drawing room. The whole performance was in case someone had missed his bow in the morning, irrespective of who was and wasn't there. During conversation, he would always address her as Ma'am. That always struck me as extraordinary. Significant. It would be Ma'am, even when it was just the three of us together. Quite extraordinary. And quite unlike the way other queens behaved.'

Burnet Pavitt told me that anyone who did not do exactly as Elizabeth required was cut out of her life. David always took great care to fulfil all her wishes. He was always loyal to her and would never say a word against her, or countenance anyone expressing anything less than fulsome admiration of her. However, he could not resist letting others know that they had maintained their childhood practice of being co-conspirators into the present, and was actually remarkably frank about how much they both loved the intrigues they would share.

Whether Elizabeth set David up, as seems likely, or he displayed his innate tendency to malice without recourse to her encouragement, which seems considerably less likely, the fact is, he now began to cause problems for Philip. Philip, he claimed, was no gentleman. He did not have the proper clothes for shooting. He was too forthcoming and straightforward as a personality. He did not know how to behave. He did not have the right sort of attitude. His personality jarred. His robust masculinity even came in for condemnation as a sign that he would not be able to remain faithful.

Before Philip's visit was over, two other houseguests who were great friends of the king and queen had joined David in giving vent to their feelings of Philip's unsuitability. The first was Bobbety Cranbourne, as Viscount Cranbourne was still known until the following year, when he succeeded his father as the 5th Marquis of Salisbury. He was a close friend of the king and an even closer friend of the queen. Married to Lord Richard Cavendish's daughter Elizabeth, he was a pillar of the Church of England and, as such, someone who spoke the same language as Elizabeth, whose maternal grandfather had been a vicar, and who was a far more committed celebrant of Anglicanism than her husband. Bobbety had also lost a son during the war, another bond with Elizabeth, who had lost a brother during the Great War, and was rabidly anti-German as a result. A High Tory and extremely successful politician, he was summoned to the House of Lords in 1941 via a writ of acceleration as Lord Cecil of Essendon, one of his father's subsidiary titles, after which he became Secretary of State for the Colonies, Lord Privy Seal, Leader of the House of Lords, and Secretary of State for Dominion Affairs. So highly did George VI and Elizabeth regard Bobbety Cranbourne that he was made a Knight of the Garter between that visit to Balmoral and Lilibet's wedding to Philip the following year.

The second of the close friends to pick up the cudgel against Philip was John Scott, 4th Earl of Eldon. His wife Magdalen was called in royal circles a 'girlfriend' of George VI. A fellow Scot like Elizabeth, she was the daughter of the 14th Lord Lovat, Chief of the Clan Fraser. Her sister Veronica, whom I knew somewhat, was married to Brigadier Sir Fitzroy Maclean, 1st baronet, whose sponsorship of Marshal Tito during the Second World War saw the ascendency of the Communists at the expense of the royalists, resulting in the dethronement of Philip and Lilibet's cousin King Peter. Magdalen's brother Brigadier Simon (Shimi) Fraser, 15th (17th) Lord Lovat, was famous during the Second World War for instructing his personal piper, Bill Millin, to pipe his battalion ashore during the Normandy landings in 1944 in defiance of a direct order not to do so. The memorable photographs, which were published worldwide, not only established the Frasers as *stylistes* of the first rank, but provided inspiration for many, demonstrating British pluck at its most indefatigable.

Lord Eldon was also a lord-in-waiting to the king, with 'no ambitions other than to farm, fish, shoot, hunt and take photographs – all of which he did exceptionally well – and to live the life of a good and placid country gentleman.' He and Lord Cranbourne now proceeded to parrot David's objections regarding Philip, in the certain knowledge that doing so would please Elizabeth, while failure to do so would inevitably put a barrier between her and them. They were soon openly declaring that Philip was 'no gentleman', that he was 'unpolished', that he had not been to a suitable school like Eton, that he did not even have suitable attire for shooting. They sneered that he had only one pair of walking shoes, which had had to be sent to the cobblers for refurbishment while he was staying at Balmoral. This particular criticism said more about them than it did about Philip, smacking as it did not only of tastelessness, but also of malicious inquisition of the servants attending upon the young prince. There was no way they could have acquired such knowledge if these self-declared gentlemen had not obtained the information from the servants. In so doing, they exposed themselves as being both uncharitable and badly behaved, for no well-bred person would condescend to cross-examine servants about the possessions of fellow guests in a house party.

While these men were embarked upon their petty skirmishes, a far more momentous event was taking place in Greece. On 1st September there was a plebiscite on the status of the monarchy. According to official figures, 86.6% of the electorate voted, with 68.4% in favour of the continuance of the monarchy. On 26th September Philip's cousin King George II of the Hellenes returned home. The question of Philip's naturalisation as British, which would have to be achieved before he could marry Lilibet (or so everyone erroneously believed), once more had to be put on hold. Previously it had been deemed inappropriate for him to seek to relinquish Greek citizenship while the status of the Greek monarchy was under consideration by the people of Greece. Now it would be equally inappropriate for Philip, who was fourth in line to the throne, to relinquish his Greek citizenship so soon after the restoration. Greece was involved in a civil war, and such a move on Philip's part could be interpreted as being a vote of no confidence in the future of the monarchy. So once more his naturalisation was delayed.

Uncle Dickie used the hiatus wisely. Like Elizabeth, he was a notorious intriguer. Like her, he knew how to use people to achieve his objectives. Unlike her, his political complexion was pink, which did not necessarily play well where she was concerned, but now became useful more generally.

Churchill had been voted out of power at the end of the war, to be replaced by the Labour Prime Minister Clement Attlee. Both Dickie and his wife Edwina were held in high regard by the socialists. To the socialist *nomenklatura*, the one thing more highly prized than a socialist working man was a champagne socialist. If the bubbles fizzed from royal or aristocratic cut glass, as it did on both scores with the Mountbattens, so much the better.

Dickie saw that Philip, if cast in the right light, could also share the appeal he and Edwina had. He had been to Gordonstoun, which had been dismissed by the courtiers as a 'crackpot' school where 'equality' within society was the objective. Although Queen Mary had argued that the school was anything but crackpot, and that its egalitarian approach would prove invaluable for Philip in his new role, the very prejudices that militated so vociferously in courtly corridors could be turned by Dickie to advantage with the socialist politicians. All he needed to do was 'manage' things carefully. This he now proceeded to do through Tom Driberg (later Lord Bradwell), the Labour MP and former Communist Party member who was the most successful gossip columnist of his day.

Driberg was one of those characters whom it would have been impossible to make up. He was a mass of contradictions. Highly intelligent and decidedly colourful, a public school boy who was left-wing, a Communist until expelled from the party during the war, an avid, indeed dedicated, socialite, he was a rapacious homosexual who dealt exclusively in 'rough trade' when he was not swanning around the most elegant salons in the United Kingdom.

Driberg's sexual awakening had come at Lancing College, the prestigious public school on the south coast in West Sussex, where he was befriended by Evelyn Waugh. The two of them would have a lifelong, but sometimes contentious, friendship. They shared a fascination with Catholicism and were deeply religious. Although Waugh would ultimately convert, Driberg remained resolutely High Anglican: a trait he shared with Elizabeth. At Oxford, he became a member of the *avant-garde* Aesthetic movement alongside such later luminaries as the historian A.J.P Taylor, the Labour Party leader Hugh Gaitskell, and the Poet Laureate John Betjeman. He also became friends with Edith Sitwell after he published a poem evoking her style in Oxford Poetry 1926. He was 'the hope of English poetry,' she declared after hearing a selection of his work.

After leaving Oxford, the impecunious Driberg was introduced to the Daily Express by Edith Sitwell. At the time, that publication was the most successful middle-market newspaper in the country. Run by Lord

Beaverbrook, whose attention to detail was second to none, it would enjoy a triumphant position well into the 1970s. Its contents were a mixture of political reportage, opinion forming, and social reportage. Its society pages were read avidly by one and all. Driberg fitted into the slot as if made for it. He wrote an article on London's nightlife which secured him a six-week trial as a reporter, at the end of which it was extended. This appears to have caused problems with Waugh, whose probationary period had not resulted in further employment.

While Waugh would go on to become an extremely successful novelist and one of the pre-eminent satirists of his generation, Driberg's gift was for networking and gossip, which he always recounted with just enough edge to make his stories interesting. Later, he would justify his success as the prime purveyor of frothy society reportage by saying that he always exaggerated the doings of the idle rich with the intention of inflaming working-class opinion against the established order. According to his justification, in so doing he was not writing trivia but purveying invaluable satirical material which would further the cause of socialism.

Such lofty sentiments were very much in the future, however, when the fledgling society columnist filed a story about a Society party at the swimming baths on Buckingham Palace Road featuring eminent author Lytton Strachey and Hollywood star Tallulah Bankhead. Lord Beaverbrook was, according to his granddaughter Lady Jean Campbell, a genius at spotting and nurturing talent. He immediately recognised Driberg's gift as a gossip columnist and offered him a permanent position on the Daily Express as an assistant to Percy Sewell, who wrote a daily column called *The Talk of the Town* under the *nom de plume* 'The Dragoman'. Driberg's contributions to the column proved invaluable. He elevated its tone, introducing such up-and-coming literary figures and socialites as Harold Acton, John Betjeman, and Nancy Mitford, thereby adding ballast to the balloon of duchesses and marquesses who floated over the pages. After four years, Sewell retired, to be replaced by Driberg, who obtained Beaverbrook's agreement to rejig the column into something more substantial. The following year, *These Names Make News* was launched with the by-line *William Hickey* in honour of the 18th century rake.

Driberg had arrived and in a big way. According to the historian David Kynaston, Driberg was the 'founder of the modern gossip column'. For the next forty years, the most popular column in any newspaper in the country was *William Hickey*. It is no exaggeration to say that it was the very first page to which many people turned when they opened up the newspaper in the morning.

For ten heady years, Driberg remained *William Hickey*. He went everywhere; knew everyone; and was received by all. Nor was his writing limited to his gossip column. He went twice to Spain to observe the Spanish Civil War, to Germany following the Munich Agreement, to Rome for Pope Pius XII's coronation, to New York for the 1939 World's Fair, and to Washington following the Japanese attack on Pearl Harbour, to report on President Roosevelt's speech to Congress announcing America's entry into the war. He was openly homosexual, a frank lover of 'rough trade', an avowed socialist, and, following receipt of an inheritance from his mother, the *châtelain* from 1938 of the exquisite Neo-Classical pavilion Bradwell Lodge near Chelmsford.

Despite being a Communist, Driberg had been a fervent supporter of the war against Germany in 1939. He was equally opposed to the Nazi-Soviet Pact. He was eventually expelled from the Communist Party in 1941, though whether for these deviations from party policy, or as a result of the Soviet spy Anthony Blunt denouncing him for passing information about the party to Maxwell Knight of MI5, is open to question. Either way, Driberg's membership of the Communist party was suppressed when he ran for Parliament following the death of Sir Edward Ruggles-Brise, Conservative member for Maldon. Bradwell Lodge was situated in the constituency, and the local boy overturned a previous Conservative majority of 8,000 to end up 6,000 votes ahead of his opponent. Because all the main political parties had agreed not to field candidates for the duration of the war, he was elected as an independent MP.

By 1943, however, Beaverbrook's patience had been exhausted by Driberg's use of the newspaper to agitate. When he wrote a piece intended to damage the government minister and Chairman of the British Iron and Steel Federation, Sir Andrew Rae Duncan (Driberg was in favour of nationalising those industries at the end of the war, while Duncan was not), Beaverbrook withdrew the shield he had previously used to protect his columnist against the consequences of his agitations, and allowed the Express editor, Arthur Christiansen, to dismiss him.

Driberg was not without a platform for long. He wrote a regular parliamentary column for the *New Statesman*, and signed up with *Reynolds News*, a Sunday newspaper owned by the Co-operative Group. He also remained a sitting MP.

Following the end of the war, elections were called which resulted in Churchill's defeat. Driberg, who had joined the Labour party and now stood as the Labour candidate, increased his majority to 7,727. Within days, he had left for the Far East, to report on the appalling condition of the Allied troops in Burma. Dickie, who shared some, though not all, of his political sympathies, and knew him socially, as indeed did everyone else who was a part of what was then known as Society, was the Supreme Allied Commander in the Far East. He paved Driberg's way in the Far East by making him an unofficial temporary special advisor. In so doing, he not only made life easier for Driberg at a time when transportation was a severe problem, but he also got him access that he might never otherwise have achieved.

Driberg would repay the favour fulsomely when Dickie called him in the following year to pave Philip's way in his quest to circumvent potential opposition to the union with Lilibet.

The timing of Driberg's first intervention shows the complications and conflicts surrounding Philip's courtship of the heiress presumptive. As we have already seen, Dickie and the Greek royal family had been laying the ground for a possible marriage for some years before Philip himself switched from cousinliness to ardent swain. Early in August 1946, before Philip had even gone up to Balmoral for what would become the crucial visit during which he actually committed himself to marriage, Dickie had got Driberg to host a luncheon in the House of Commons at which several of the younger Labour MPs met their future queen's possible consort. Dickie shrewdly saw that once the politicians in question met his attractive and progressive nephew, they would appreciate how desirable a consort he would be. This would head off any criticism before it had a chance to materialise, which proved to be the case. When the time came, such opposition as existed – and there was some – came mostly from cranks and dyed-in-the-wool reactionaries rather than the left-leaning politicians, who otherwise might well have formed a solid phalanx of opposition in the mistaken belief that Prince Philip of Greece was the personification of outmoded and irrelevant prejudices.

Dickie, however, cautioned Driberg against acting upon his offer to influence public opinion by writing newspaper articles supportive of Philip's change of nationality from Greek to British. He stated that 'any form of pre-publicity' might well be 'fatal'.

By this time, rumours of a possible engagement were rife. This caused a certain amount of embarrassment for Lilibet. Wherever she went, the crowds would want to know where Philip was. Princess Margaret felt compelled to sympathise with her sister, bemoaning how she was not even allowed her own romance without all and sundry poking their noses into it.

The bizarre situation, of the two central figures in the proposed union being the only two people in the country who seemed unresolved as to its outcome, did not remain for long. Once Philip proposed and Lilibet accepted, Dickie and Driberg swung into overdrive to smooth all obstacles behind the scenes.

There were two main hurdles to surmount. The first was de-foreignising (if such a word exists) Philip. The second was influencing the powers-that-be of his suitability, with the objective of establishing his desirability amongst the populace as well as the Establishment.

Philip's de-foreignising would prove to be relatively easy to accomplish. His mother and grandmother had both been born at Windsor Castle, and his great-grandmother was Queen Victoria's daughter Alice, facts which could be emphasised to demonstrate his Britishness. He sounded utterly British, and if you did not know that he was a Greek prince, you would have thought him more likely to be British than Greek.

Although he had been born a Prince of the United Kingdom as a result of being a descendant of the Electress Sophia, shearing him of his Greek citizenship via naturalisation as a Briton would have the positive effect of stripping him of his patina of foreignness. Only then would the Britishness that lurked beneath come into play, permitting his presentation to the public as essentially British rather than fundamentally foreign. Although there were reports in the British press indicating that there was opposition, 'to a marriage with a foreign prince', Driberg pointed out in *Reynolds News* that he was, 'intelligent and broadminded, fair [notice the adjective: He was really saying blond and pale like an Anglo-Saxon rather than swarthy like a Greek] and good-looking' and his desire to surrender his Greek citizenship was a, 'desire to be disentangled from (Greek politics) permanently.'

In November, Dickie went to see Clement (later 1st Earl) Attlee, the prime minister, who was in the process of offering him the post of Viceroy of India. The purpose of the meeting was to discuss Philip's naturalisation application with him and the longest serving home secretary of the 20th century, James Chuter Ede (later Lord Chuter-Ede). Dickie got them to agree that Philip would retain his royal rank and style and remain His Royal Highness Prince Philip even after he became a British subject.

The subject of a surname now arose. All British citizens have surnames. This was not true of Danish or Greek princes, all of whom had no surname, but were members of the House of Schleswig-Holstein-Sonderburg-Glücks-burg. Indeed, no British prince or princess had actually had an acknowledged surname between the death of Queen Anne (a Stuart by surname as well as by royal house) and the creation of the royal house (and surname) of Windsor by George V in 1917. Upon that queen's death in 1714, the Elector of Hanover, as the ruler was known until the electorate was upgraded into a kingdom a century later, became King George I of the United Kingdom of Britain and Ireland. The royal house of Hanover thereafter reigned in Britain until Queen Victoria married Prince Albert of Saxe-Coburg-Gotha, at which point the dynasty switched from Hanover to Saxe-Coburg-Gotha. This could not have been clearer when King Edward VII succeeded his mother to the throne in 1901, reigning as the first Saxe-Coburg-Gotha king of Britain.

But Hanover and Saxe-Coburg-Gotha were not surnames. They were the royal families of the kingdom of Hanover and duchy of Coburg. Indeed, the royal house of Saxe-Coburg-Gotha was actually a very minor branch of the senior line of the kingdom of Saxony (yet another German territory), Saxe being the French version of that state (Sachsen in German). Gotha was also another place name, signifying yet another minor branch of an already minor branch of the royal house of Saxony. And the ruler of the state of Coburg was known, not as the Duke of Saxe-Coburg-Gotha, as so many modern historians seem to think, but as the Duke of Coburg, Saxe-Coburg-Gotha being the dynasty, not the duchy.

The first surname suggested for Philip was Oldcastle. This emanated from the Royal College of Heralds and was a variation of the name of the previous Danish royal house of Oldenburg, which Philip and Lilibet's great-grandfather King Christian IX had supplanted when his wife's uncle died without a legitimate heir.

Oldcastle, however, found approval with no one, least of all Philip himself, whose links to that dynasty were tenuous to say the least. He could, of course – and possibly even should – have simply invented a British surname the way George V did when he adopted Windsor. But he did not. He allowed himself to be persuaded to adopt the Anglicised version of his mother's maiden name. Although the idea was mooted as having been James Chuter Ede's, in fact it was Dickie Mountbatten's. There is little doubt that this most ambitious of par-royals saw this as an opportunity to restore the royal status of his family, which had been, in his mind's eye, so cruelly stripped from them in 1917. It was also a way of paying back all those who had so unfairly hounded his father from office at the start of the First World War, for once Lilibet ascended the throne, the dynasty of Mountbatten would reign, in keeping with the tradition of a wife's identity being subsumed into her husband's.

Over the years, I have spoken to members of the family about the unforeseen issues that arose as a result of Philip adopting his mother's family name as his surname. All agreed that Philip might well have made a different choice, had he been able to see into the future. Philip himself is on record saying that he, 'wasn't madly in favour' of adopting the name but, 'in the end

I was persuaded, and anyway I couldn't think of a reasonable alternative.' All were also in agreement that he went along with his uncle's recommendation, not only because it was his sole family link to a surname, and he needed one, but also because he is actually a decent and compassionate individual who appreciated his uncle's tireless, and at that time effective, efforts to promote his cause. He also understood Dickie's foibles. He knew his bearing the name Mountbatten would mean the world to his uncle. Everyone who knew Dickie knew he was almost pathetically obsessed with his royal ancestry and his loss of royal status. He had never recovered from being demoted from a prince and serene highness to a mere courtesy lord, and though by the time Philip's surname became an issue he had been made a viscount in his own right on 12th August 1946, the middling aristocratic rank of Viscount Mountbatten of Burma was scant compensation for what had been stripped from him.

On 5th December 1946, the home secretary confirmed in the House of Commons that Prince Philip's application had been submitted by his commanding officer, in keeping with the practice of giving priority to the naturalisation of foreigners who had served in the armed forces during the war. One peculiarity which would later emerge was that Philip opted to be shorn of his royal status. Rather than become HRH Prince Philip Mountbatten, he had opted to be merely Lieutenant Philip Mountbatten, RN. And so he would remain until just before his wedding.

At the beginning of February 1947, King George VI, Queen Elizabeth and both daughters were due to depart for South Africa. Philip was evidently nervous about the separation, and at a dinner party which Edwina Mountbatten hosted (married women always were the sole hosts of parties, never jointly with their husbands) Elizabeth was so 'heartening' about his worries that he wrote to thank her. This calls into question whether she was still spearheading the campaign of denigration which continued to flourish in royal circles – and would do so for at least another decade – or whether she was being disingenuous while indulging in the ploy of hiding her machinations behind sweetness. Certainly, when the royal family returned to the United Kingdom at the end of a very successful tour of southern Africa in May, Lords Salisbury, Eldon and David Bowes Lyon were, if anything, even more vociferous in their complaints about the 'rough' former prince. It seems there was the hope that voicing sufficient criticism of Lilibet's choice might result in weakening the ties that bound her to him while they were separated. Or that he might become so discomfited by the atmosphere of hostility and criticism that he would slink away.

If those were their objectives, they were doomed to failure. Lilibet was sufficiently her mother's daughter to ignore anything untoward that she found uncomfortable, including from her mother. And in this matter, especially from her mother. What made it easier for her to do so was that such criticisms as were being made were never to her face, but always behind her back, though Philip had to put up with a good deal of condescension and more petty stabs at humiliation than anyone should have to endure.

Six weeks after the royal family's departure for South Africa, Philip's demotion to commoner was gazetted on 18th March 1947. This coincided with a large reception Edwina was hosting that evening for seven hundred guests at the Royal Automobile Club in Pall Mall to mark her and Dickie's departure for the sub-continent, where they would oversee the transition from British rule to partition and the creation of the dual states of India and Pakistan. There, she would fall in love with Jawaharlal Nehru, independent India's first Prime Minister, while her husband would oversee the creation of the Muslim state of Pakistan under its first Governor-General, Muhammad Ali Jinnah.

Although Dickie would receive a mixed press for his efforts, his biggest fear regarding the press was not for himself, but for Philip. His main worry was Lord Beaverbrook. This most powerful of press barons heartily disliked Dickie, who was terrified that Beaverbrook's loathing of him would induce him to disparage Philip's suitability as consort and, in the process, unleash torrents of opposition which would scupper the marriage.

Dickie had good reason to fear Beaverbrook. He knew only too well that the likely cause of the press baron's antipathy towards him was personal. Dickie had had an affair with Beaverbrook's *maîtresse-en-titre*, the very-married Lady Grantley, wife of the well-known film-maker Richard Henry Brindsley Norton, 6th Lord Grantley, whose daughter Sarah had introduced Philip to Osla Benning. Jean Norton, as she was known before her husband succeeded to the barony in 1943, reigned in grand style as the *châtelaine* of Cherkley, the widowed Beaverbrook's sumptuous estate in Surrey. When she died in 1945, and Beaverbrook was going through her effects, the suspicions he had harboured about her and Dickie were finally confirmed, sealing his hatred of Dickie.

In the event, the Express stable of papers did not oppose the match. There is the supposition that Dickie neutralised the editors of the Express newspapers when he invited them to his house and asked their opinion of Philip's suitability for British citizenship in his presence. Good manners alone would have prevented them from voicing any objections in Philip's presence, though it has to be said, I have never known a newspaperman who allowed good manners to stand in his way of getting a good story. In the event, they did not voice any objections to Philip's assumption of British nationality. This is meant to have constrained them from publishing any objections when the news of Philip's naturalisation was announced a few weeks later.

My own experience of the press, allied to my many discussions over time with my sister-in-law Jeanie, who was Beaverbrook's granddaughter and worked for him for years, leads me to an altogether less rosy conclusion. Newspaper editors have always turned on a sixpence when it suits them. Silence today does not mean, and has never meant, assent tomorrow. I suspect that what motivated Beaverbrook rather more than any fanciful notion of his editors being honour-bound not to criticise in print today whom they had failed to criticise in person yesterday, was his even greater loathing of Elizabeth. He regarded her as a veritable viper and would never forgive her for trying to block his appointment to the wartime Cabinet. By the time Philip was naturalised, Beaverbrook, who had superb contacts and knew pretty much what was going on in every portal of power, would have known that Elizabeth was antipathetic to the match. That alone would have provided him with powerful incentive not to ruin Philip's chances, for, by failing to stir up opposition to the match, he was scuppering Elizabeth. And that, from all Jeanie said about her grandfather, would have been all the encouragement he needed to lay off criticising Philip.

While she had been away in Africa, Lilibet had turned twenty one. On that occasion, she had broadcast the moving speech dedicating her life, whether it be short or long, to the service of the people of Britain and its Commonwealth and Empire. She had demonstrated that she was an exemplary daughter as well as exemplarily determined to wed Philip. As the *Vanguard* steamed into harbour, the prospect of seeing him so gripped the princess that she, 'danced a little jig of sheer delight at being home again,' according to one of the ladies-in- waiting.

Because Philip wasn't present to meet her, the press naively speculated that the romance might be at an end. Far from it. Lilibet made it clear to her parents that she still wished to marry Philip, and the sooner the better. He even wrote to Elizabeth, diplomatically stating that he was sure the imposed wait had been the right course of action for her parents to adopt, but now that that period was at an end, both he and Lilibet wanted to start their life together as soon as possible. Faced with such obduracy, Elizabeth gave way graciously, evincing delight, even going so far as to write to her sister May (Lady Elphinstone) on 7th July that her daughter had 'made up her mind' to marry Philip. Always one to highlight the drama of every occasion, which was one of her most winning qualities, Elizabeth confided that she was writing 'very secretly' though two days later the news was announced at Buckingham Palace: 'It is with great pleasure that the King and Queen announce the betrothal of their dearly beloved daughter The Princess Elizabeth to Lieutenant Philip Mountbatten,R.N., son of the late Prince Andrew of Greece and Princess Andrew (Princess Alice of Battenberg), to which union the King has gladly given his consent.'

Lilibet had won.

# Chapter V

THE UPCOMING MARRIAGE of Lilibet and Philip would take place against a backdrop of austerity, national penury, and an empire in flux. Britain was broke. At the end of the First World War, which had drained away much of the nation's wealth, it had been predicted that another war would bankrupt the country and finish off the empire. This was now the actual predicament in which Britain found itself, with the predicted consequence about to materialise.

The Second World War had been even more ruinous than the First in financial terms. First time around, Britain had had rich and powerful allies like the French and the Russians to relieve some of the load. But the second time around, Britain had single-handedly fought the victorious Nazis for two years while France and the Soviet Union had each, in its own way, made a contribution to the Axis cause to the detriment of the Allied.

To fund the fight, Britain had sold off most of its overseas investments during the war. This deprived the country of the income it would otherwise had had, once the war was over. With regards to the rest of the economy, Britain after the war was in the process of restructuring itself into a welfare state. It was establishing a national health service, providing subsidies to those who were unemployed or unemployable, creating free education, and generally redistributing the wealth that remained in private hands. Railways, industries such as coal mining, water and electricity were being nationalised. Such industries as escaped nationalisation were taxed to such an extent that productivity sank rather than increased, resulting in less income for the government.

The winter of 1946/47 had been one of the harshest on record. This created a fuel crisis which saw a fall in productivity generally, and in agriculture in particular. This was unrelated to the financial crisis that was being created by the government's redistribution-of-wealth policies, but the one exacerbated the other, creating greater hardship than would otherwise have been attendant upon the effects of a harsh winter.

During the Great War, American President Woodrow Wilson had issued his Fourteen Points, which had effectively been a declaration for the dismantlement of the European empires. Gore Vidal, the famous American author who was the scion of one of that country's leading political dynasties, with links to the Kennedys (he and Jacqueline Bouvier Kennedy shared a step-father), would later argue that America had an imperialist objective. In simple terms, it wanted the destruction of the European empires so that it could benefit from the vacuum created as it became the ascendant world power. Irrespective of whether one agrees with that point of view, the fact remains, at the end of the Second World War Wilson's objective of destroying the great European empires had finally been realised.

Lend-Lease, the arrangement by which the United States had lent Britain money to fund the war, was unexpectedly terminated in September 1945 by the Americans, who would forgive the USSR its Lend-Lease repayments after initial repayments of $2 million, but nevertheless required full repayment from Britain. This debt would not be acquitted in full until 29th December 2006, and was such a glaring double standard that one can well see why Gore Vidal came to the conclusions he did as regards America's desire to bring the British empire to an end.

By 1946, Britain was in such poor financial shape that John Maynard Keynes had to negotiate a $3.75 billion 50-year loan from the US, together with a further $1.19 billion loan from Canada, at a rate of 2% per annum. Within a year, however, much of this money had been gobbled up. There was such a severe financial crisis in the summer of 1947 that the Chancellor of the Exchequer, Hugh Dalton, had to suspend the convertibility of the pound on 20th August. This was a severe blow to Britain's prestige, tantamount to a declaration that the once mighty British Empire was so busted that it couldn't even cover its financial commitments. This led to a rapid loss of dollar reserves while highlighting the weakness of sterling, until finally, in 1949, the pound was devalued from $4.02 to $2.80.

As if the financial humiliation of the British Empire were not enough, while this financial crisis was unfolding in England during the summer of 1947, in India Dickie Mountbatten was overseeing the prying of the Jewel out of the Empire's Crown. On 3rd June India's last Viceroy formulated what has gone down in history as the *3rd June Plan* (also known as the *Mountbatten Plan*), in which the Indian National Congress, the Muslim League, and the Sikhs agreed to the partition of British India into two independent dominions, India and Pakistan. This was duly passed by Parliament as the *Indian Independence Act 1947*, and George VI gave it the royal assent on 18th July 1947. On 14th August Pakistan came into being, India a day later, and it was five days later that Dalton suspended the convertibility of the pound.

It was against this backdrop that the royal wedding arrangements were being made. The government had tried to hoe a path that would render unto Caesar that which was Caesar's, and unto God that which was God's. George VI had requested that the heiress to the throne's wedding day be a national holiday, but the government declined, citing low productivity, strikes, and the general financial crisis allied to rationing, which had actually had to be increased throughout the year.

Funding for the princess and her husband, as well as for their wedding, now became an issue. Tom Driberg once more busied himself behind the scenes, taking soundings and warning Dickie that the feeling on the Labour benches was that a lavish wedding would be unpopular, and so too would a large allowance for Philip. Dickie, now released from the traumas and dramas of the negotiations for the partition of India, and not yet caught up in the bloodbath that would result once independence was declared, took time in July to respond on Philip's behalf to Driberg in a long letter. 'You can rest assured that he thoroughly understands this problem and indeed he spoke to me about it when I was home in May. I am sure he is entirely on the side of cutting down the display of the wedding, and his own personal feelings are against receiving any civil list for the very reasons which you give.'

The editor of the *Sunday Express*, John Rutherford Gordon, put the issue of funding for the couple succinctly when he told his boss, Lord Beaverbrook, that the 'Princess Elizabeth money debate has caused a lot of talk.' He felt that 'the King made a mistake in asking for so much at such a time.' People were of the opinion that, until she came to the throne, 'the Royal Family is very well looked after & that they can afford the heir out of Duchy funds.'

Traditionally, the Duchy of Cornwall was the estate that funded the Prince of Wales, who is also always the Duke of Cornwall. (The son and heir of a British monarch automatically becomes Duke of Cornwall upon his parent's accession. The title of Prince of Wales, however, has to be bestowed by the monarch.)

Although George VI resisted making Elizabeth Princess of Wales on the grounds that that title is customarily held by the wife of the heir to the throne, there was nothing but a lack of precedent, and imagination on his part, preventing him from making her Duchess of Cornwall and Princess of Wales in her own right. After all, queens regnant hold the same title as queens consort, and as long as Lilibet lived as Duchess of Cornwall and Princess of Wales, no son of hers could be created Prince of Wales or become Duke of Cornwall, and therefore no wife of his could become Princess of Wales and, by extension, Duchess of Cornwall. Ever punctilious, however,

Chapter V

George VI took the view that Lilibet was not the Prince of Wales and Duke of Cornwall, so it would be quite improper to 'raid' Duchy funds. They therefore remained untouched.

Nevertheless, it was accepted that Lilibet would have to be funded out of the public purse in keeping with the principle that all public servants must be compensated for their endeavours, whether they be royals, politicians, civil servants, or social workers. Once more Tom Driberg proved to be an invaluable conduit between Dickie and the Labour government. When the subject of an annuity for Philip arose, the government had an accurate view of Philip's finances through Driberg, whose information came directly from Dickie. In one letter, he wrote, 'As you know, the present dynasty in Greece was founded by King George I, brother of Queen Alexandra and younger son of the King of Denmark. The Danish Royal Family was by no means rich enough to endow a younger son with personal riches and wealth on taking up the Crown of Greece. Any small property the family were able to acquire in Greece from personal means was largely destroyed and swallowed up in the many revolutions and periods of exile. The Civil List salary of a Prince of Greece was never very big, and any rights that Philip may have had to a Greek Civil List, he renounced together with his rights of succession in 1944. To my certain knowledge his private means are very small and he is almost entirely dependent on his Naval pay which is slightly under £1 a day and after tax is paid I do not suppose amounts to as much as £300 a year.'

Faced with a prince consort with an annual income less than many workers, whose lot the government was championing as needing betterment, they recommended an annuity of £10,000 for Philip. Out of this he would have to fund his office, buy his clothing, and provide whatever was necessary to maintain the dignity of his position. This sum, however, was taxable, as was 10% of the £50,000 per annum they suggested for the heiress presumptive. In the end, the House of Commons reduced Lilibet's annuity by a fifth, a move that could never have come about had George VI simply created her Princess of Wales and Duchess of Cornwall, thereby providing her with access to the income generated by the highly successful Duchy of Cornwall, which had been created in 1337 by Edward III for his son and heir, Edward, the Black Prince, and had thereafter provided for the household of the heir to the throne.

Although the financial wrangling attracted unfavourable comment in the press, once the engagement had been announced, the marriage itself became increasingly popular. Mountbatten's characterisation to Driberg of Philip as being 'something of a socialist himself,' had hit its mark. Philip enjoyed the support of a large proportion of the backbenchers of the ruling party as well as the Conservatives, and the newspapers followed the politicians' lead and promoted him more as the undoubtedly British war hero Lord Mountbatten's nephew than as a foreign prince. His strong sexual appeal, which might have caused problems amongst the Salisburys, Eldons and Bowes Lyonses at Court, was much appreciated by the general public, and not only by the women. The men themselves understood how a pretty young lady like their future queen could fall in love with such a paradigm specimen of masculinity.

The British people have always been amongst the most compassionate in the world, and they responded on an atavistic level to the innate romanticism of a young and attractive couple in love. Amongst the populace, therefore, there was genuine delight, and, as the day of the wedding neared, people across the land responded with spontaneous and unexpected generosity. For instance, rationing was more than ever a feature of the day. Lilibet's wedding dress would have to be made out of her quota of clothing rations. When this was reported in the press, women from every quarter of the land sent in their own clothing coupons. However, it was strictly against regulations for one individual to use another's clothing rations, so all these many acts of generosity had to be returned.

In such ways, though, did the people make their feelings felt, with the result that soundings were taken within the government and the palace to upgrade the wedding from a drab celebration, which would have had limited appeal, into something akin to a national celebration. No one, of course, did ceremonial better than the British, and once the decision was taken to provide as good a show as possible with the limited resources that were available, the British people were in for a dash of colour in an otherwise grey world, as Winston Churchill so succinctly put it.

Much of the upscaling did not actually cost any more money. For instance, the ceremonial uniforms of the soldiers, who would form a part of the procession between Buckingham Palace and Westminster Abbey, and which would do so much to add splendour to the occasion, already existed, though they had not been used since the beginning of the last war. The coaches that would be used were already in the Royal Mews, as indeed were the horses. The soldiers who would accompany the carriages or stand guard on the route were already in the Army. It really was a case of utilising existing resources in such a way that a splendid show would be created on a very limited budget.

As the wedding approached, Lilibet's dress became the story of the day. Designed by (later Sir) Norman Hartnell, it was a closely guarded secret which would excite much comment on the day itself for its simplicity of line and magnificence of detail. It was embroidered with seed pearls in the shape of the white roses of York, entwined with ears of corn out of crystals. These had had to be imported from abroad, and were very nearly impounded until the customs officer realised they were for Princess Elizabeth's wedding dress. The government having allocated sufficient clothing coupons (300) to permit a generously flaring skirt, the dress itself was made from silk, the antecedents of which became something of a *cause célèbre* in the run-up to the wedding, when the ever-inventive journalists realised that they could create a drama out of whether the worms had been Japanese or Chinese in origin. After a storm in a teacup, the matter was resolved to the satisfaction of all when it emerged that the silk worms in question were from Allied China rather than from Axis Japan.

Wedding presents poured in from all over the world, from the rich and the poor, the invited and the uninvited. One New Yorker sent a turkey, having read all about the privations being suffered by the British. Lilibet received a plethora of nylon stockings, that other luxury of war-torn Britain, and more tea cosies than she would ever be able to use in a lifetime. There were a Singer sewing machine; a refrigerator; china; crystal; a set of cut glasses from President Beneš of Czechoslovakia; a vase from President Truman of America; a necklace of 96 superb Burmese rubies set in gold from the people of Burma; the Greville Bucheron diamond and ruby necklace and the Queen Anne and Queen Caroline pearl necklaces (always worn as one necklace, which Lilibet wore on the day) as well as the Greville diamond chandelier earrings, from her parents; the 1893 Garrard's 'Girls of Great Britain and Ireland' tiara, the Dorset Bow brooch, and the County of Cornwall diamond and ruby brooch and bracelet from Queen Mary; a tiara from the Nizam of Hyderabad; the City of London diamond fringe necklace; even a picnic basket from Princess Margaret; and Astrakhan, the chestnut filly given by the Aga Khan which would go on to win Lilibet her first flat race in 1950, among many other presents.

One thousand five hundred of the presents went on display at St James's Palace, where the public were invited to come and see them. Viewing the wedding presents, and the four tier, nine foot, five hundred pound wedding cake, became the must-do event of the day. Intermingling with the public were the plethora of visiting royals and the senior politicians who arrived from all over the world as guests a few days before the wedding.

Wedding expenses being the traditional responsibility of the bride's parents, the king and queen put up all their royal guests at Claridge's, with the exception of Philip's mother Alice and the bride and groom's cousin Queen Frederika of the Hellenes, who stayed at Buckingham Palace. Leading the list of the guests housed at that most venerable of Brook Street institutions were the head of the house of Schleswig-Holstein-Sonderburg-Glücksburg, King Frederick IX , with Queen Ingrid of Denmark; King Haakon VII of Norway, widower of Princess Maud of Wales and their sole child; the Harrovian King Faisal II of Iraq, who would be murdered eleven years later when his country became a Ba'athist state; the Count of Flanders (Prince Charles of Belgium), regent from 1944 to 1950 while his brother King Leopold III remained in exile following the German occupation of their country during the war; Princess Juliana, a more temporary regent of the Netherlands while her mother Queen Wilhelmina was ill, together with her husband Prince Bernhardt, who would become a great friend of Philip's and be a big influence, especially where the World Wildlife Fund for Nature was concerned; Queen Helen the Queen Mother of Roumania, Philip's first cousin and mother of his childhood friend Michael, with whom he used to holiday at Constanza and in Venice; Philip's Mountbatten aunt, Crown Princess Louise of Sweden, and her husband, who would become King Gustaf VI Adolf in 1950; the Hereditary Grand Duke Jean of Luxembourg, who would subsequently marry King Leopold III's daughter Josephine-Charlotte, and his sister Princess Elisabeth, who would marry Archduke Franz Ferdinand's grandson Franz, Duke of Hohenberg. Also present were other royals unknown to the general public, such as Prince René of Bourbon-Parma, his wife Princess Margaret of Denmark, their three sons and beautiful daughter Anne, who would agree to marry King Michael of Roumania within weeks of meeting him at the wedding celebrations; and Michael's aunt, the former  Princess Irene of Greece, now Duchess of Aosta, whose son was the only male member of the Savoy family allowed to live in Italy following the abolition of the Italian monarchy in 1946.

Philip's cousin Alexandra of Greece, by now the exiled Queen of Yugoslavia, recounted what great fun the whole thing was.  From the moment the guests received their wedding invitations, which also contained subsidiary ones to a pre-wedding dinner and ball at Buckingham Palace, with specific instructions as to which boat train each guest should take from Paris to London, it was obvious that this was going to be an event to relish. The  boat train companions of King Peter and Queen Alexandra included Frederika, whose country was being torn apart by civil war; another Greek cousin, King Michael of Roumania, whose country was now behind the Iron Curtain and whose government was disappointed when he and his mother, Queen Helen The Queen Mother (formerly a Greek princess), failed to take the opportunity of fleeing the country, causing them to force him to abdicate at gunpoint when he returned from the wedding; the English-born, Swiss-resident widow of King Alfonso XIII, Queen Victoria Eugenia (Ena) of Spain, nee Battenberg and as such yet another double cousin of Philip, who was travelling with her son and daughter-in-law, the Count and Countess of

Barcelona, whose son would subsequently reign as King Juan Carlos I; and the Count and Countess of Paris, who would have been king and queen of France had the restoration mooted by General Charles de Gaulle during the Second World War come about.

If the pre-wedding dinner dance at Buckingham Palace was a splendid affair, it was also a private one. Once more, it cost less than might have been apparent. All the staff were already *in situ*, all their livery already existent. The wines and champagne came from the palace cellars, most of the food from the royal estates. The ladies sparkled brightly in their diamonds, tiaras requisite, while their husbands were in Court dress. By common consent, it was a magical evening.

Philip had actually had the first of his stag celebrations a few days before, at the Belfry Club in Belgravia. Organised by the fashionable photographer Stirling Henry 'Baron' Nahum, it was attended by twenty four interesting men, almost all members of the Thursday Club. This was a luncheon club founded by Baron, whose later assistant, Tony Armstrong-Jones, would meet Princess Margaret while on assignment with him. The courtiers would doubtless have dismissed the dinner-jacketed assemblage as *louche*, but they were all vital and accomplished men in their own right. Indeed, the least accomplished was Philip's cousin and future best man, David Milford Haven. Aside from him, there was Arthur Christiansen, the *Daily Express* editor who had done so much to foster a good press for Philip; Bernard Walsh, the proprietor of Wheeler's famous fish restaurant; Michael Eddowes, lawyer, restaurateur who ran the Bistro Vino restaurant chain, and author of *The Man On Your Conscience* about the hanging of Timothy Evans when the real culprit was John Christie of 10 Rillington Place; Sean Fielding, creator of *Soldier* magazine which still remains the Army's official monthly publication and was, at the time of the wedding, the editor of *Tatler*, the prestigious society magazine; and Feliks Topolski, the Polish-born artist, who was an official war artist for Britain, becoming, as a result of his friendship with Philip, an accomplished Court painter who would in the future execute such works as the immense 200 foot mural of the coronation which hangs in Buckingham Palace, as well as a massive portfolio of Princess Margaret's wedding. He also encouraged Philip to utilise his undoubted talent as a painter, and in the process became one of his closest friends.

Another friend who was there was Larry Adler, the Oscar nominee and harmonica- player, who was forced to leave America to settle in England after being blacklisted during the McCarthy years. He remembered the atmosphere of the event as being particularly ribald. 'There were maybe thirty guys there. All cracking jokes at Philip's expense. Ward-room stuff.

Dirty jokes. I could tell that he was uncomfortable.' Philip was as pale as a ghost, and, though Larry Adler thought this was because the reality of what he had let himself in for was impinging itself upon his consciousness with ever-increasing discomfort as the great day approached, I have another interpretation. Philip had always been personally reserved. He has never been someone who would wear his heart on his sleeve, nor did he have a sense of humour that hovered near the gutter. Everything I have ever heard about him, and witnessed on the occasions when I have seen him, leads me to conclude that he is not the sort of man who finds smut attractive. Certainly, he can swear like the naval officer he once was, but in the aristocracy and royal circles, it is perfectly permissible to use foul language when you are upset. The same does not apply to smut, especially when it involves a potential spouse, royal or otherwise.

Baron, who organised the occasion, was an even closer friend of Philip's than Larry Adler, and would remain so for the remainder of his short life. He would die during a hip operation in 1956 at the age of 49. But for that, he would have joined Philip's world cruise as the official photographer.

Philip's friendship with Baron is fundamental to understanding the prince as a person, while also gaining insight into how he handled the role of consort in the early days of his marriage. The two men first met at Broadlands, the magnificent Palladian-style historic house that Edwina Mountbatten had inherited in Hampshire, when Baron was there photographing her and Dickie. Dickie and Baron had been fast friends since the early 1930s, when they had both been in love with the same woman: Yola Letellier, the Frenchwoman who inspired the 1944 novella by Colette upon which the movie *Gigi* was based. Robin Dalton was good friends with Baron, whom she met when Philip introduced him to her and her lover, his brother-who-never-was David Milford Haven. She remembered Baron as being a lovable person of talent and energy. He was great fun and wanted everyone to have a good time. He liked interesting people and was open to all comers as long as they had something to offer. The result was that his luncheon club, which met every Thursday in an upstairs room at Wheeler's Restaurant on Old Compton Street, Soho, was full of fascinating men. (It was an all-male affair.) Some of the members were well-born, others not. What they had in common was intelligence, wit, vitality, and accomplishment. Regulars included Philip, David Milford Haven, Mike Parker, Arthur Christiansen (editor of the *Daily Express*), (Humphrey) Frank Owen (editor of the *Daily Mail* and author of such books as *The Three Dictators: Mussolini, Stalin, Hitler* [1941] and *The Fall of Singapore, The Campaign in Burma* [1946]); the osteopath and artist Stephen Ward, who would sketch Philip and other members of the royal family before becoming embroiled in the Profumo scandal; Larry Adler; actors Peter Ustinov and David Niven; Baron's brother Jack; the columnist Patrick Campbell (Lord Glenavy), and Vasco Lazzolo, whose loyalty was such that, despite being threatened by Chief Inspector Samuel Herbert, that the police would 'discover' pornographic material in his studio, and he might then face prosecution, if he gave evidence on behalf of Stephen Ward during his trial, did so nevertheless. The Chief Inspector was as good as his word, and Lazzolo sought refuge in Malta, where he died at the age of 69 in 1984.

The Thursday Club has gone down in history as a cover for all sorts of *louche* antics. It is meant to have been a scene for womanising on a grand scale. Orgies are meant to have taken place. I knew Larry Adler and Feliks Topolski, and met Patrick Campbell on several occasions. I will recount what they said, though not at this juncture, otherwise the story will get away with itself.

The day before the wedding, George VI bestowed the Order of the Garter on Philip. He had made Lilibet a Lady of the Garter the week before, so that she would always take precedence over her future husband. He also created Philip a British royal highness and a peer thrice over in each state of Great Britain. The dukedom of Edinburgh, earldom of Merioneth, and barony of Greenwich were duly gazetted on 20th November. In royal circles it has always been said that the king did not create Philip a British prince because he assumed that he would automatically become one if he was a royal duke. In fact that turned out to be a false assumption which Lilibet would later put right, when she came to the throne, at which time she went one better and Philip was not created a mere British prince, but one whose rank and style were as if he had been the son of a reigning monarch. Hence why Philip is now styled His Royal Highness The (notice the all-important The, which conveys the message that one is the child of a sovereign) Prince Philip, Duke of Edinburgh.

After the Belfry evening, Philip had a second stag night, this time organised by Mike Parker. It was held at the Dorchester the night before the wedding. Dickie, who had returned from India for the wedding, was the senior guest. All the men were in naval evening dress. David Milford Haven was in attendance, along with all the captains and first lieutenants of the 27th Destroyer Flotilla. Mike Parker said, 'It was a very happy occasion. It was an evening of comrades. Philip was an orphan of sorts and we were family. Philip was happy and we were happy for him.'

After the party, Philip and David Milford Haven went back to their grandmother Victoria's apartment at Kensington Palace. The following morning, the Mountbatten's butler John Dean, who would go on to become Philip's valet, brought the cousins a cup of tea at seven o'clock. He was surprised to find Philip awake and abuzz, displaying not an iota of nerves. This, despite the fact that he was in the process of fulfilling a promise he had made to his fiancée that he would give up smoking that very day.

His cousin Patricia Mountbatten, however, felt that he was more apprehensive than he was letting on. Just after breakfast she saw him and he asked, 'Am I being very brave or very foolish?' She felt he 'was uncertain – not about marrying Princess Elizabeth, but about what the marriage would mean for him. He was giving up a great deal. In many ways, nothing was going to change for her. Everything was going to change for him.'

Across town at Buckingham Palace, the basic structure of Lilibet's life continued in much the same was as it had been and would continue to be. Bobo, who had been and would remain an ever-constant presence, to such an extent that she was sometimes a thorn in Philip's side, brought her childhood charge her early-morning cup of tea. It was still dark so she did not draw the curtains. 'I don't think any of us had very much sleep,' Crawfie said. 'I went along to Lilibet's room very early, and found her in her dressing gown, peeping excitedly out of the windows at the crowds.'

Lilibet was in high spirits now that her dream was being realised. She told Crawfie, 'I can't believe it's really happening. I have to keep pinching myself.'

At nine o'clock, Norman Hartnell and his assistants arrived to dress the bride and make any last-minute adjustments to the wedding dress, which he had personally delivered the previous evening. He had also made the dresses for the eight bridesmaids, who were her sister Margaret; her maternal first cousin the Hon. Margaret Elphinstone (later Rhodes); Lady Pamela Mountbatten (later Hicks), Dickie's younger daughter; Lady Mary Cambridge (later Whitley), only child of Queen Mary's nephew Prince George of Teck who was demoted in 1917 like the Mountbattens but in 1947 was the 2nd Marquis of Cambridge; Princess Alexandra of Kent, Lilibet's first cousin through her father the late Duke of Kent, and daughter of Philip's first cousin Princess Marina, Duchess of Kent; Lady Caroline Montagu Douglas Scott (later Gilmour), daughter of the 8th Duke of Buccleuch, whose sister Alice was married to Lilibet's uncle Harry, the Duke of Gloucester; and Lady Elizabeth Lambart (later Longman), daughter of the 10th Earl of Cavan, goddaughter of Queen Mary, and first cousin of Lady Edith Foxwell (nee Lambart), one of Britain's great characters and married to the film producer Ivan Foxwell, whose works included *The Colditz Story*.

The ascendancy of Lilibet and Philip's mutual ancestors, Prince and Princess Christian of Glücksburg, was truly remarkable. The great royal success story of the nineteenth century, Christian IX and the former Princess Louise of Hesse-Cassel went from being impecunious princelings of an obscure ducal house to King and Queen of Denmark following his nomination to the Danish throne when the last Oldenburg king left no legitimate heirs. Even more impressively, five of their six children ended up being styled king, queen or empress, with the sixth turning down the offer of two thrones, fully justifying King Christian's monikers as Father-in-Law, then Grandfather, of Europe.

Another rags-to-riches story was that of Lilibet's paternal grandmother Queen Mary. By the time of Lilibet's birth in 1926, she was the most venerable queen on earth, but her antecedents were anything but impressive. The sole daughter of King George III's granddaughter, Princess Mary Adelaide of Cambridge (known as Fat Mary for obvious reasons), and the morganatic Count of Hohenstein, who was later elevated to princely status, Mary is seen here with her mother and brothers, the ramshackle Prince Adolphus of Teck (later 1st Marquis of Cambridge); Prince Francis, a gambling addict and putative great-grandfather of the actress Sarah Miles; and the eminently respectable Prince Alexander, later 1st Earl of Athlone and husband of Queen Victoria's granddaughter Princess Alice of Albany.

I

The Greek throne would prove to be a mixed blessing to Prince Philip's family, who were also princes and princesses of Denmark following the nomination to the Greek throne of Philip's grandfather Prince William of Denmark in 1863. King George I of the Hellenes proved to be a popular and stabilising force, but his assassination foreshadowed decades of instability. Here his surviving children are photographed in the 1920s, during a period of restoration, with his widow Queen Olga. L – R front row are their second son George, whose wife was the fabulously rich Princess Marie Bonaparte, and King Constantine I. L – R back row are Prince Andrew, father of the Duke of Edinburgh, Grand Duchess George of Russia (Princess Marie of Greece), Prince Christopher, whose wife was a rich American widow, and Prince Nicholas, whose daughter Marina would marry the Duke of Kent..

Cowes Week has never meant anything to the Queen, but it always did to other members of the royal family, including Prince Philip. Photographed in 1922 are L-R his maternal uncle, Prince George Louis Victor Henry of Battenberg, 2nd Marquis of Milford Haven, with his exotic wife Nada, morganatic daughter of Grand Duke Michael of Russia; Philip's eldest sister Princess Margarita of Greece, and Nada's brother, Count Michael Torby.

Lilibet's dashing Uncle George on the steps of the Belgrave Square House he shared with his wife, Philip's first cousin, the stylish Princess Marina of Greece. Royal to her core, Marina was not enamoured of her sister-in-law Queen Elizabeth, and helped Philip and Lilibet during their courtship, undermining Elizabeth's efforts to deflect her daughter's interest away from Philip onto one of the 'chinless (and non-royal) wonders' she had hoped her daughter would marry.

The Abdication of King Edward VIII in 1936 threw the monarchy into turmoil and turned Lilibet into the heiress presumptive. Here the immediate royal family is photographed at Buckingham Palace following the coronation. L-R, The Princess Royal (Princess Mary, Countess of Harewood), the Duchess of Gloucester, the Duke of Gloucester, Queen Mary, King George VI, Princess Margaret, Princess Elizabeth, Queen Elizabeth, the Duke of Kent, the Duchess of Kent, and Queen Maud of Norway (nee Princess Maud of Wales).

Philip's sophisticated family was a study in the unexpected. Here his Aunt Marie (Princess George), one of the most eminent psychoanalysts of the age, is photographed disembarking from the Orient Express in Paris on 5th June, 1938, with her mentor Dr Sigmund Freud, whose freedom she had to buy before the Nazis would release him following the Anschluss. Meeting them is the American Ambassador in Paris, William Bullitt, a former patient of Freud's whose President, Franklin Delano Roosevelt, also applied pressure on the Nazis for Freud's release.

The road to the altar for the young Prince Philip of Greece and Princess Elizabeth was not as straightforward as either of them would have liked. There was much jockeying behind the scenes, both for and against the union, but the 'sweethearts' dug their own furrow and refused to be distracted or deflected. This early deployment of focus proved to be characteristic of the way they would thereafter conduct their lives, both personally and publicly.

Princess Elizabeth and the newly created Duke of Edinburgh in the Throne Room of
Buckingham Palace on 20th November, 1947, following their marriage with L-R the Hon.
Margaret Elphinstone, Lady Pamela Mountbatten, Queen Mary, Lady Mary Cambridge,
Princess Andrew of Greece, Princess Alexandra of Kent, Prince William of Gloucester,
the Marquis of Milford Haven, Prince Michael of Kent, Princess Margaret, Lady Caroline
Montagu Douglas Scott, King George VI, Lady Elizabeth Lambart, Queen Elizabeth, Miss
Diana Bowes Lyon and Princess Alice, Countess of Athlone. Note the lack of a bouquet: it
had been misplaced and all photographs with one were taken after the event.

Lilibet's first Prime Minister was Sir Winston Churchill. Unfortunately for the royal couple, he loathed Philip's uncle, Lord Mountbatten, and was determined to counter any influence he had over the young couple. This was a policy he shared with Sir Alan Lascelles, the Private Secretary Lilibet inherited from her father, who 'made Philip's life hell,' according to his cousin Patricia Mountbatten.

Lilibet and Philip were 'ardently' and 'passionately' in love, and quickly fulfilled their royal duty by producing the heir and the spare. Here they are at Buckingham Palace following the christening of Princess Anne on 21st October, 1950, with Queen Mary, King George VI, Queen Elizabeth and Prince Charles. Already the affinity between Elizabeth and her favourite grandchild Charles, which would undermine his relationship with his parents, was obvious, even if its consequence would take decades to become apparent.

Kurt Hahn would prove to be one of the greatest influences in Prince Philip's life. A German Jew, whose gifts as an educationalist were nurtured by Philip's progressive, socialising relations, they saved him from imprisonment under the Nazis and encouraged him in the founding of the British arm of the experimental Salem School at Gordonstoun in Scotland.

After the Coronation, Lilibet and Philip were glad to embark upon a tour of the Commonwealth, leaving behind some of the problems which dogged the beginning of the reign, as they developed their idea of a willing union of nations into the force it has become over the decades. Here they are in Ceylon with Sir Michael Adeane, the Private Secretary who replaced the anti-Philip Sir Alan Lascelles; Lady Pamela Mountbatten; Lady Alice Egerton, the lady-in-waiting who would be unfairly accused of informing the Queen about her husband's reputation as a philanderer, and Colonel Martin Charteris, her former and future Private Secretary and my London neighbour.

Broadlands is the magnificent Palladian house which Edwina Mountbatten inherited along with a vast fortune from her German-Jewish grandfather, Sir Ernest Cassel. Here Lilibet's beloved Uncle Dickie, who never got over being demoted from a prince, stands in regal splendiferousness beside his adored niece Lilibet, with his more testy nephew Philip beside the generous, left-wing, but sexually incontinent Edwina three years before her death in 1960. Philip would later damn one of his daughters-in-law by accusing her of being 'no better than Edwina'.

Although Lilibet and Philip were both duty-driven, their family was important to them. Her accession to the throne delayed their plans for more children for a decade, but once the pressure eased up, they had Prince Andrew (named for Philip's father) in 1960 and Prince Edward in 1964. Here they are at Buckingham Palace with L-R Prince Charles, Princess Anne, Prince Andrew, and sitting with his mother on the sofa, Prince Edward. The three youngest children all agree that the Queen and the Duke of Edinburgh were good and loving parents who did the best they could within the constraints imposed by the considerable demands of their extraordinary positions.

The succession was assured into the next generation by 1985, when Charles and Diana, holding Prince Harry, appeared on the balcony at Buckingham Palace for the Queen's official birthday celebrations along with Prince Philip, the Queen, Princess Anne, and Prince William.

No one is more aware of the changes that have taken place during her reign than the Queen, whose family is now representative of the inclusiveness of British society in a way that would have been unthinkable a quarter century ago. She is pictured here at Sandringham on Christmas Day 2017, leaving church with Prince Philip, and L-R Prince Charles, the Duchess of Cornwall, and behind them Princess Beatrice of York, the Duchess and Duke of Cambridge, and Meghan Markle and Prince Harry.

## Chapter V

The two Lambart cousins' roles in Lilibet's life and in Society more generally are noteworthy, because they cast light on the way life was conducted in royal circles. Elizabeth Lambart would remain one of Lilibet's closest friends until her death in 2016 at the age of 92. Hers was a resolutely discreet and conventional lifestyle. She married the publisher Mark Longman of the famous eponymous publishing house and Lilibet stood as godmother to her eldest daughter Caroline. The friendships would continue into the second generation, with Caroline acting as a date for the young Prince Charles, not that they were ever anything but friends. Edith, meanwhile, became increasingly unconventional, conducting open affairs with such pop stars as Marvin Gaye and becoming known, in the process, as The Disco Dowager because of her affiliation with the Embassy Club. Edith was also known as The Queen of London Café Society, not an altogether complimentary title, but she remained on cordial terms with the royals, a fact I witnessed on more than one occasion. Larry Adler was also a friend of hers, and when he eulogised her at the Brompton Oratory, he brought the house down with the classic observation, 'Edith was known never to have a good word to say about anyone.'

All these antics were very much in the future as Lilibet was being dressed on her wedding day, that cold, rainy November morning in 1947. Even in palaces, life never runs entirely smoothly. When the bride wanted her bouquet, it could not be located anywhere. The footman who had taken delivery of it recalled bringing it upstairs, but had no recollection of it beyond that. After a frantic search (which would result thereafter in all royal brides having two identical bridal bouquets, so what happened then could never happen again), he finally recalled putting it out of harm's way in a cupboard, whence it was retrieved. Meanwhile, the tiara Queen Mary had given Lilibet snapped just as it was being put on her head. That necessitated emergency repairs, but was by no means the end of the dramas, for when Lilibet reached for the pearl necklace she wanted to wear, it was realised that it was still on view at St. James's Palace. She asked (Sir) John Rupert 'Jock' Colville, who had been Assistant Private Secretary to the three wartime Prime Ministers, Neville Chamberlain, Winston Churchill, and Clement Attlee, before his recent appointment as Lilibet's Private Secretary, to rush over to nearby St. James's Palace in her car to retrieve it. This was not as easy as it sounds. The crowds had already begun to gather, and there was also the question of whether it would be released into Colville's care by its custodians. Fortunately, they realised he wasn't trying to steal it, and he rushed back to Buckingham Palace just before Lilibet and George VI were due to depart for the Abbey in the Irish State Coach.

All Anglican weddings, even royal ones, follow the same course. Lilibet's was no exception, even if hers was officiated by the Archbishop of Canterbury, Geoffrey Fisher, and the Archbishop of York, Cyril Garbett. Everything went like clockwork from the moment the two kilted pages, Prince William of Gloucester and Prince Michael of Kent, entered Westminster Abbey, until Lilibet and Philip left it as man and wife.

There were one or two marked differences between this wedding and others, however. Aside from the calibre of the guests, there were notable absences. Lilibet's one-time favourite Uncle David had not been asked, nor had his wife Wallis. In protest at this omission, which she regarded as outrageous and indefensible, his sister Mary, the Princess Royal and Countess of Harewood, declined to attend. None of Philip's three surviving siblings was in attendance either. They too had not been asked, a snub which they also thought outrageous, and which they would bemoan for years to come. Though there were sound political reasons for it, at least from the British perspective, they felt that they had been singled out for punishment when they had committed no crime. Certainly, their husbands had all been in the German armed forces, and the war had ended only two years before, but since when were soldiers condemned for fighting on the side of their country? And since when had the despicable German practice of *Sippenhaft* (kith and kin reprisals) crossed the North Sea and become a valid reason for excluding sisters who simply were their innocent wives? How was it, the sisters wanted to know, that King Michael and Queen Helen the Queen Mother of Roumania had been asked, when King Michael's country had been an ally of Nazi Germany throughout much of the war? And what about Helen's sister Irene, wife of the Duke of Aosta, whose son Amadeo had been heir to the Italian throne before Queen Marie Jose produced Crown Prince Umberto? Had not Italy also been an Axis ally? 'It is not very easy, I assure you,' Tiny wrote to their uncle Dickie, 'to make the press (who interview us continually) understand & they keep insisting that we must be estranged, which only makes a difficult & humiliating position even more unpleasant.'

There is no doubt that Philip would have liked his sisters to witness this most joyous of days. The year before, he had borrowed an army vehicle and driven half way across war-ravaged Europe to attend the second marriage of Tiny, when she wed Prince George of Hanover, brother of Queen Frederika of the Hellenes and headmaster of Salem once the school was revived. On that occasion, in April 1946, Philip had come laden with 'care' packages containing food and other essentials which were in short supply in Germany. Philip and his sisters were close and loving, but he was in no position to quibble, especially as how word had already got back to him that there were elements at Court who referred to him as 'The Hun'. It appeared to be in everyone's interest to play down the Germanic aspects of his antecedents, but it was nevertheless hurtful to the three Greek princesses, and hurtful to their brother as well.

By this time, Philip had become painfully aware that he was surrounded at Court by a wealth of detractors who were hostile to his very existence. As his cousin Patricia Mountbatten would subsequently observe, it was 'deeply hurtful,' and 'very uncomfortable,' for him to have to contend with such unwarranted hostility, much of which, it must be said, can be seen with hindsight to have had nothing to do with his German links. Philip was, if anything, less German than King George VI or Queen Mary, whose antecedents the courtiers had no difficulty in overlooking. Had he been as malleable as one of the chinless wonders Elizabeth would have liked Lilibet to marry, they would have had no problem with him. It was their knowledge that his world-view was different from theirs, and this would most likely result in a diminution of their influence at some point in the future, which led them to hide their fear of him behind anti-German xenophobia – a sentiment that still had traction shortly after the end of the Second World War.

Philip, however, did have some close relations at the wedding sitting in the family pews supporting him. His mother Alice was very much in attendance, looking smart in an elegant long dress and matching hat. His grandmother Victoria was also there, as was his uncle Dickie with Edwina. So too were his aunt Louise with her Swedish crown prince husband, as was Aunt Nada, along with Philip's father's only surviving brother, Big George. He appeared with his wife Marie Bonaparte and their daughter Eugenie, who had divorced her husband, Prince Dominic Radziwill, the year before, proving that being a divorcee was no bar to being received by the King and Queen of England when it was in their interest to look the other way. But Philip's other first cousin, Eugenie's brother Peter, was not invited. He had forfeited his right of succession and been cut out of his father's life having made an 'unsuitable' marriage to the commoner Irina Ovtchinnikova in 1941, and was living in exile in the United States. However, there were many other Mountbatten relations present, such as Grand Duke Michael's other daughter, Lady Zia Wernher, and her family. So while his sisters' presence was missed, the wedding was still, as Noel Coward observed, 'most moving and beautifully done. English tradition at its best.'

After the ceremony, a hundred and fifty of the most select guests, all personal friends, relations or courtiers, decamped from Westminster Abbey and headed for Buckingham Palace, where they were treated to a 'modest' wedding breakfast. This consisted of three courses, instead of the ten that had been the order of the day when the late Duke of Kent had married Princess Marina in 1934. The tables were decorated with smilax and white carnations, laid with the 'famous gold plate and the scarlet-coated footmen gave a fairy-tale atmosphere to it all,' according to Crawfie, who was a guest. If the 'swirl of the bagpipes warmed the hearts of those' who were from 'north of the Tweed', the cacophony left many a continental unmoved. 'There were no long speeches. The King (whose stutter would remain a lifelong issue, though it had improved under the ministrations of Lionel Logue) hates them and has always dreaded having to make one. He was brevity itself. The bridegroom, another sailor, had just as little to say. It was a very large room and there were no microphones, so few people even heard the little that *was* said.'

Crawfie was not amongst those who heard, though she was on hand to join the throng who saw Lilibet off after she changed into another Hartnell creation, this time a love-in-the-mist crepe dress with blue velvet travelling coat, offset with a blue felt hat trimmed with ostrich feathers and pompom. The king and queen joined their guests in chasing after the open landau that took the bride and groom, and her favourite corgi Susan, from Buckingham Palace to Waterloo Station, where they were due to board the royal carriage which would take them to Broadlands, Edwina's magnificent Palladian stately home which would house them for the first week of their honeymoon, before they headed up north to Birkhall on the Balmoral Estate for the second. Fortunately for her, Lilibet had a hot-water bottle concealed beneath the blanket that covered her legs, and Susan also provided invaluable warmth against the bitter chill of a cold November evening as the landau clattered out of the gates of Buckingham Palace to roars from the crowd assembled outside. Witnesses observed that George VI, Elizabeth, and Alice all had tears in their eyes.

All three parents were indeed moved. The king told the Archbishop of York, 'It is a far more moving thing to give your daughter away than to be married yourself.' This, from a man who was obsessed with marrying Lady Elizabeth Bowes Lyon, is eloquent testimony indeed to strength of his feelings for his daughter. Alice would write to Philip from Athens, to which she returned right after the wedding, to continue doing her charity work and the setting up her order of nuns, 'How wonderfully everything went off & I was so comforted to see the truly happy expression on your face and to feel your decision was right from every point of view.' And George VI wrote Lilibet a letter which articulated both his and Elizabeth's anxiety: 'Our family, us four, the 'Royal Family' must remain together with additions of course at suitable moments!!'

Chapter V

In those days, marriage was an institution which changed people's lives far more than is the case today. Young people could not have sex freely, the way we do, nor could they co-habit. Brides and grooms had far less time alone then. No matter how well they knew each other on one level, on another there was a degree of ignorance that is virtually unimaginable to the present generation. The result was that, for all willing brides and grooms, there was real anticipation of the pleasures the bridal night would hold. There was also the freedom of being together without chaperones to police your every move, so that you could really get to know each other in the most intimate ways. Honeymoons were therefore far more exciting and magical experiences than they are today; at least in theory, for if you were mismatched and did not know it before the wedding ring encased your finger, you might get a very rude awakening, as some people did. Fortunately, Lilibet and Philip were not among that number.

Proof of Philip and Lilibet's sexual passion came from a variety of sources, some more expected and reliable than others. I know more than one person who has reported being told, as they were being shown around Broadlands by guides, in particular being shown the bridal chamber where Philip and Lilibet spent their bridal night, that the servants were full of talk the following morning about how patently Lilibet had enjoyed her introduction to the pleasures of the flesh. While it is not always a good idea to take what servants say as gospel, I am actually old enough, and from a traditional enough background, to have experience of servants commenting on the honeymoon activities of friends and relations. One didn't enquire too deeply as to how they came to the conclusions they did. It would have been 'unseemly' to 'fraternise' to that extent, as my grandfather would have put it. But when I remember what the servants said, and how the various marriages that were commented upon developed, I realise that they actually had their fingers on the pulse of what was happening in the marital bed far more accurately than we, the relations, did. Possibly it had something to do with the sheets. Or with the expressions on the faces of the bride and groom. Maybe it was the degree of intimacy they detected as they served the couple. Did they touch each other the way people, who enjoy intimacy, do? Did they not? What about the looks of love that are a fool-proof way of detecting when recent lovers truly enjoy each other? People were far more unguarded in certain ways with staff than they would have been with their peers, and this was particularly true with displays of affection and intimacy. Amongst social equals, such displays were regarded as vulgar, exhibitionistic, unseemly.

Servants aside, the couple themselves declared themselves to be ecstatic with their choice of each other. They both wrote letters to that effect. While they were not quite as forthcoming as Queen Victoria, whose written words on the subject of the pleasures of the  marital bed were a veritable paean to sex within marriage, the indications were that Philip and Lilibet were very pleased with each other.  Any doubts that existed were removed when Philip confided in his brother-who-never-was, David Milford Haven, that Lilibet had a very healthy, indeed Hanoverian, appetite sexually.  Inevitably, David told those closest to him, and the secret, which I have heard over the years from more than one person to whom he repeated that fact, was out.  He also let slip, to his other Mountbatten cousin Patricia, that Lilibet had the most beautiful skin all-over, and there has never been any doubt amongst people who knew the couple well that they had a torrid time between the sheets.  If further proof were needed, Colin (3rd Lord) Glenconner also told me that Princess Margaret, who shared Lilibet's Hanoverian genes and propensities, had made it clear to him on many an occasion that Lilibet was as physically besotted with Philip as she was with Lord Snowdon.

'They were both passionate by nature, and you could just *tell*, the way you can with couples, who enjoy each other both in bed and out of it,' Colin said, backing up Princess Margaret's comments with his own observations.

Although Philip was not the most tactile or affectionate of spouses, and would never be – Mike Parker actually suggested to him that he could be more forthcoming with Lilibet, a suggestion he met with withering and silent contempt – she was so plainly adoring of him, that there was never any doubt, amongst those who knew them well, that they were fundamentally compatible and truly in love with each other.

For all his alpha male traits, Philip was personally reserved.  This could come across to onlookers, Parker included, as if he were not affectionate.  Lilibet, however, appears to have seen beyond the reserve to the fact that her husband shared the crippling trait of shyness which was such a feature of her personality.  While her shyness manifested itself socially, with the result that she was always happy to take a back seat in gatherings and let her more outgoing mother, sister, and now spouse, take the floor, his manifested itself intimately.  Robin Dalton would once tell me that she thought Philip was a 'cold fish', but if you knew Robin, who is amazingly robust emotionally and warm to a tropical degree, and if you had met Philip and Lilibet, you could well see what she meant, and how easy it was to misinterpret the emotional reserve of the damaged child for coldness.  What came across to Australians like Parker and Robin as coldness, was in fact reserve that the adult man hid behind, to protect the sensitive and loving child who still reposed within, nervous of letting his emotional guard down lest his feelings be trampled upon yet again, the way they had been before he had had to raise his guard as a little boy.

Time and again, in the years to come, Philip would be described as not wearing his heart on his sleeve. Harold MacMillan would even describe him as being 'brutal' to Elizabeth, but the fact remains, those who knew them well, including her sister Margaret, Princess Margaret of Hesse and the Rhine, his cousins Patricia and Pamela Mountbatten, and Gina Wernher all commented on how happy he and Lilibet were. Witnessing them together confirmed that there was genuine ease between them. In crowded rooms they would search each other out and give each other reassuring glances. In informal situations, the bond between them was visibly tangible. Yes, Lilibet was always the one who would make the first move in terms of physical affection, but the mere fact that she did so without embarrassment or anxiety, meant that the dynamic between them was good, and she was confident that he welcomed her affections.

There is also another dimension which comes into play, and it has nothing to do with Philip being self-protective emotionally. He is actually a very dignified man. I suspect that one of the reasons why he always hung back in demonstratively affectionate terms, was that he was levelling the playing field in terms of the worldly disparities between him and Lilibet. All historians understand the principle of the balance of power, whether it be between nations or political institutions. All students of psychology also understand the balance of power that plays out in personal relationships, and it would have been very surprising if these principles had not come into play with Philip and Lilibet. There is no way around the awkward fact that she was the greatest living catch in worldly terms, while his attributes were virtually all personal. There was therefore never going to be a way of avoiding dealing with the dynamic of the poor but self-respecting man who marries a rich and desirable woman. How he would maintain his personal integrity, while avoiding slipping into a servile role, and in the process coming across as an emasculated supplicant, would say much about his character. Also, about his ability to balance and manage pitfalls in such a way that he would maintain his masculinity and retain the respect of his wife, two things that could easily be lost if he mishandled his role. Had Philip been as openly affectionate towards Lilibet as Parker would have liked, there is every possibility that the ebb and flow between them, which worked so well, might well have ground to a halt. As things stood from the early days of their marriage, and would continue throughout, Philip retained his dignity, while Lilibet did not compromise hers. He remained resolutely masculine, she decidedly feminine. Indeed, because she was the heiress presumptive, then later the monarch, but also a woman, and he was in the inferior worldly position but a man, their relationship could only flourish as it did if she was the feminine initiator and he the masculine recipient of her devotion and love. Any other variation would have resulted in his appearing to lapse into the role of emasculated puppet, or worse, gigolo, neither of which would have had appeal for so proud and heartfelt an alpha male as Philip, nor for so traditional loving but principled a woman as Lilibet.

Despite the absence of overt displays of affection, there is much evidence from a variety of sources to support the fact that Philip is actually emotionally warm. Brusque he might be, unfeeling he is not, nor has he ever been, except when he is antagonised and therefore deliberately callous. Throughout his life, he has been a devoted and affectionate friend to many people, all of whom have sung his praises privately. Feliks Topolski told me that he found him to be warm and kind as well as fun-loving and great company. Princess Margaret of Hesse and the Rhine thought the world of him, as did his former Private Secretaries Mike Parker and Sir Brian McGrath. It is said, 'no man is a hero to his valet,' but Philip in fact literally was a hero to his valet John Dean, as well as to both those private secretaries. Ironically, the most surprising source which confirms the tender heart and compassionate nature which existed beneath the crusty exterior was Diana, Princess of Wales. Many letters exist between them where there is genuine affection and real emotional support, and she herself used to say, at least for many years, that 'Pa was the most wonderful father-in-law a girl could have.'

If the honeymoon at Broadlands was a success in personal terms, the press and public were so intrusive that it blighted the couple's time there. People even hung from trees to get a good look at them. This meant that Lilibet and Philip had to spend more time inside than they would otherwise have done. Also, the Broadlands household was not up to scratch. With Dickie and Edwina still posted to India, where he was now the first Governor-General of post-independence India (the last one had been the nineteenth century Earl of Mayo), things were more lax than they would otherwise have been.

Of course, reigning royalty never travels alone, and Lilibet and Philip were no exception. Bobo and Cyril the footman had accompanied Lilibet, while John Dean was fulfilling his new role as Philip's valet. Bobo still brought her mistress her morning cup of tea and worse, thought nothing of barging in on Lilibet while she was having a bath. This limited Philip's scope for romantic activity, which Patricia Mountbatten claimed Philip never complained about because he knew how much his wife loved Bobo. He did not want to be the cause of a reprimand for the possessive former nursemaid, who continued taking care of her little girl, as Bobo regarded Lilibet. Therefore, from then until 1993, when Bobo died aged 89, she virtually ruled the roost. Mike Parker told the royal biographer Gyles Brandreth, 'Let's face it, he had a hell of a time with her. Miss MacDonald was *always* there. And in charge. Princess Elizabeth was Bobo's baby and that was that.'

People have questioned whether Philip's stoical acceptance of certain customs was a weakness or a strength. His attitude suggests that he was mature enough to realise that his wife had other loyalties from her past, with which interference would be detrimental to her long-term well-being as an individual, and to their long-term happiness as a couple. He therefore accepted Lilibet's support system, realising that by doing so he would help her to remain happy and secure. His approach says much about his maturity and consideration, and was remarkable for a young man still in his twenties.

It is interesting to note that when their son Charles married Diana Spencer, one of the very first things she did was set about getting rid of every friend and member of staff who pre-dated her. This would result in driving him away from her in the long run, though in the short term Diana herself thought she had succeeded in setting up the sort of marriage she wanted.

After five days at Broadlands, Lilibet and Philip stopped off in London for lunch with her parents, where they all enthused about how well things had gone and were going. The Edinburghs, as they would hereafter be known socially, then boarded the train for Birkhall at Balmoral, where they spent the next two weeks. It was cold, with deep snow, but they had quiet and intimate times reading and writing letters before roaring fires, and being attended upon by Bobo, Cyril, Dean, the detective and of course Susan, Lilibet's beloved corgi. According to George VI's Private Secretary Tommy Lascelles, Lilibet had 'a most extraordinary unselfish solicitude for the comfort of others, which is outstanding in anyone, but even more so in her family.' She would therefore tell the staff, 'As soon as we've finished dinner, off you all go,' so that they could visit their friends. John Dean would also recount how considerate Philip was. It was qualities such as these that earned them the respect of each other as well as of their employees.

The honeymoon over, Philip and Lilibet returned to London. Like all newlyweds, they wanted their own home. George VI came to the rescue, giving them two grace and favour residences. Clarence House, which adjoins St. James's Palace on the Mall, would serve as their London home. Built between 1825 and 1827 for King George III's third son the Duke of Clarence (King William IV between 1830 and 1837), the elegant four-storey (excluding basement and attic floors) house had been built to the designs of John Nash, Clarence's eldest brother King George IV's favourite architect. It suffered bomb damage during the war, but had a history which appealed to Lilibet. It had served as the headquarters for the Red Cross and St. John's Ambulance following the death in 1942 of its last royal occupant, Queen Victoria's third and favourite son, Prince Arthur, Duke of Connaught, who occupied it between 1900 and his death. Prior to that, it had been the London residence of Queen Victoria's mother, Princess Victoria of Saxe-Coburg-Saalfeld, Duchess of Kent, between 1840 and her death, following which it passed to Victoria and Albert's second son, Prince Alfred, Duke of Edinburgh (and after 1893 Duke of Coburg), until his own death in 1900.

Clarence House was in such a bad state that it was uninhabitable. The government could only muster £50,000 for the repairs of what was state, as opposed to private, property. After complaining to the Prime Minister, who was impotent to improve upon the grant, George VI dug deep into the savings he had made during the war out of his Civil List payments, and handed over £100,000, so that the property could be brought up to an appropriate standard. Philip was put in charge of the refurbishments. This was an inspired choice. Philip had always been fascinated by gadgets, so he ensured that the house had every modern convenience they could afford. He had also not had a home he could call his own since the age of nine, and the commitment he brought to the project betrayed the depth of feeling he had concerning his own home.

Sunninghill Park had been intended as the Edinburghs' country house. Located near Windsor Castle, this late Georgian two storey stucco house, with later additions, had served as the headquarters of the American Ninth Air Force from 1943 to 1944. It was purchased by the Crown Estate Commissioners in 1945 from Philip Hill, who had renovated it, but it burnt down on 30th August 1947. Although arson was suspected, nothing was ever conclusively proven, so George VI rented another property owned and renovated by Hill. Although not as elegant as Sunninghill, Windlesham Moor was a comfortable Victorian house which had been lived in by Mr Hill's widow. She rented it fully furnished to the king for his daughter and son-in-law. It had four 'good' reception rooms: a reception hall, a fifty foot drawing room, a dining room, and the Chinese room. It also had several lesser rooms including a study, games room, loggia, and five main bedrooms. There was a nursery consisting of two guest rooms joined together, as well as staff quarters, and was surrounded by fifty-eight acres of grounds and light woodland.

Philip revelled in having his own country home, even if it was only rented. He and Lilibet spent every weekend they could at Windlesham Moor. Sometimes, he would pop down on his own if he had time during the week.

He was highly domesticated and, according to Dean, an avid homemaker. He enjoyed hanging pictures, moving furniture about, buying household gadgets to make life easier for the staff of six. The combination of being a descendant of the home-loving Grandfather of Europe while also being the relic of a homeless existence after the age of nine, had obviously had an effect. He would remain ardently home-loving all his life, and was fortunate in having a wife who was also, if not equally, home-loving.

Although Windlesham Moor was habitable, Clarence House was not. Until it was, the Edinburghs' main London base was Buckingham Palace. Philip was assigned a bedroom and sitting room adjoining Lilibet's established quarters, but this was hardly ideal. Elizabeth might have liked living in the palace, but it had limited appeal for Lilibet, and even less for Philip. They wanted their own home. They therefore accepted the offer of the use of Clock House in Kensington Palace, the London home of her great-uncle and aunt, Lord Athlone and Princess Alice, when they went away to South Africa for three months.

The main advantage of staying at Buckingham Palace appears to have been how proximate it was to the Admiralty. There, Philip had been posted, 'shuffling ships around', as he witheringly described the posting that bored him rigid. He used to walk from his temporary residence at one end of the Mall to his office at the other, and was mightily relieved between March and September to be posted to Royal Naval College, Greenwich, where the staff course he attended was at least more challenging and interesting. He was determined that his marriage would not cause him to deviate from the rigor and routine of a naval officer's life, so lived on site during the week unless he had official engagements to fulfil with Lilibet.

As Patricia Mountbatten had rightly observed, marriage would change Philip's life out of all recognition, while barely affecting the structure of Lilibet's. She continued serenely on her way, pretty much doing as she had done before, with only minor and largely positive adjustments to her former existence, while Philip's life had changed profoundly. He had to accompany her on many of her engagements, and now had a royal office to add to the requirements of his naval career.

It was almost inevitable that Philip would be given a rough ride once the honeymoon was over and he and Lilibet returned to start their real life together. The opposition to the union, which Elizabeth's brother and friends had spearheaded, was by no means at an end. The word had spread in Court circles that Philip had to be beaten down before he had a chance to make his mark. He must be made to know his place, his insignificance. There was a deliberate policy of patronisation, of sneering, of belittlement. He was to be made aware from the outset that he was not being given a chance to assert himself. He was to be browbeaten. According to his cousin Patricia Mountbatten's husband, the film producer John, Lord Brabourne, the courtiers, 'were absolutely bloody to him. They patronised him. They treated him as an outsider. It wasn't much fun.' Lascelles especially, 'was impossible.' Philip found things, 'very, very frustrating,' but he had one friend: his new Private Secretary and old naval buddy, Mike Parker.

Larry Adler told me that Philip and Parker reminded him of two schoolboys who were always getting into trouble with a wicked headmaster through no fault of their own. There was a real air of harassment about the way Lascelles and some of the other courtiers, and Elizabeth's cronies, dogged them. They were picked on for everything and nothing. Their very existence antagonised these critics. You could tell, just by looking at them, that Philip and Parker made their skin crawl.

In fact, by selecting Parker as his private Secretary, Philip had not only provided back-up for himself, but had issued a declaration of intent to his tormentors. This added to the antipathy they had already developed towards him. His message, that he and his brash Australian friend would not be altering their straightforward and modern demeanour to accommodate the detractors, was one which antagonised them further.

Ultimately, the courtiers could carp all they wanted, but Philip was not about to alter his identity to facilitate them, especially when he deplored their pompous and old-fashioned attitudes. Just when it looked as if an improvement in Philip's invidious position would be a long time in coming, it improved, if not dramatically, at least meaningfully. Once more, Uncle Dickie was the catalyst. Lieutenant General Sir Frederick Browning had been Dickie's chief of staff when Philip visited him in Ceylon over the Christmas season in 1944. Whether the older man took a shine to the younger one, whose father had just died, or whether the bonds were based on glamour and shared characteristics such as intelligence, energy, perspicacity and a reluctance to suffer fools gladly, they would prove to be surprisingly compatible when 'Boy' Browning was appointed Comptroller and Treasurer to the Household of the Duke and Duchess of Edinburgh.

Philip sorely needed someone who could support him against the palace crew who so patently had it in for him. 'Frankly, Philip, I do not think you can do better,' Dickie told him. 'Boy has drive, energy, enthusiasm, and invokes the highest sense of loyalty and affection in his subordinates. His judgement in all matters that he understands is absolutely sound, and he would rather die than let his boss down.' More important, he 'is not a 'yes man' or even a courtier and never will be.'

Boy Browning was just the person Philip needed. A genuine war hero in both wars, as well as being the husband of the celebrated authoress Daphne du Maurier, he was strikingly good-looking and well known, in his capacity as commander of the British 1$^{st}$ Airborne Division, to have warned Field Marshal Montgomery against landing at Arnhem on the grounds that they 'might be going a bridge too far.' Being a former Guards officer, he was someone whose antecedents were respected by the courtiers, to whom such things as the 'right' regiment or school were all-important. He also had a reputation for irascibility when pushed too far, which was no bad thing in a world where oleaginous hypocrisy frequently blurred boundaries. His unique combination of qualities meant that he was not only a force to be reckoned with, but also someone whom the powers-that-be could respect. Though his appointment did not actually result in the elimination of the courtiers' hostility towards Philip, it meant that the duke had an invaluable ally to help him withstand the pressure.

Before too long, Philip and Browning had developed a fast friendship, bonding over their in common, no-nonsense approach to life and their love of the sea. Both men were avid sailors, and during their first summer together, Browning introduced Philip to the delights of the Regatta at Cowes in his yacht, *Fanny Rosa*. Since then, Philip has been a regular at Cowes Week.

Moreover, Browning was also extremely fond of Lilibet. Her simple, straightforward fastidiousness allied to the natural reserve and sweetness which were often commented upon by people who knew her, meant that he found her a pleasure to serve. He would remain with her for as long as she remained a princess, though he was unable to do so when she acceded to the throne and inherited her father's functionaries. He did remain with Philip, however, until he suffered a severe nervous breakdown in 1959, at which time he retired.

Six months after the wedding, Lilibet and Philip made their first official visit overseas. They went to Paris for four days. Unlike the last official visit, when George VI and Elizabeth had visited France in 1939 in an attempt to give Hitler the message that the Allies would stand together, there was no threat of war this time. It was therefore more of a courtesy call than a drumming up of support exercise, and it would have made Lilibet and Philip global superstars if they had not already achieved that status as a result of their marriage. Like all royal visits, the programme was crammed from beginning to end. They were taken to see the glories of France at Versailles and Fontainebleau. They went to the opera, travelled down the Seine, sat through luncheons and banquets speaking excellent French, he because French was one of his first languages, she *gratis* Toinon de Bellaigue. Their glamour and good looks, as well as their command of the language and their charm, captivated the French. Women swooned before the handsome prince, while Jack Colville noted that 'Princess Elizabeth had conquered Paris.' He also observed rather shrewdly that, 'a visit by a young princess with beautiful blue eyes and a superb natural complexion brought gleams of radiant sunshine into the dingiest streets of the dirtiest cities. Princes who do their duty are respected, beautiful Princesses have an in-built advantage over their male counterparts.'

The true purpose of all royal marriages is the perpetuation of the line. This is truer the higher up the line of succession its participants are. From the Greek royal family's point of view, with or without children, Philip's marriage enhanced their status and elevated him to the first rank of royalty, but from the British royal family's perspective, the main consideration was the creation of an heir and a spare. Both Philip and Lilibet were duty-driven above and beyond the norm. They were also practical and down-to-earth. They knew the score and were more than happy to fulfil the primary purpose of their union. At the time of her Paris visit, Lilibet was three months pregnant. This was cause for celebration indeed, and after she returned to London in triumph, and the announcement of the impending birth was made, she gradually retreated from public life.

On 14th November 1948, six days short of her first wedding anniversary, everyone, republicans excepted, could not have been more delighted, when Lilibet produced a son and heir, Charles Philip Arthur George.

Although no one could have foreseen it at the time, Charles's birth would complicate Lilibet and Philip's life in a wholly unexpected way. According to Colin Glenconner, at first everything was sweetness and light. However, as the baby grew up, his character and personality became a tussling ground between his father and his grandmother. This, however, was still in the future, as the baby and his parents finally moved from Buckingham Palace, where he had been born, into the newly-renovated Clarence House, across the road and a five minute walk down the Mall.

Philip, by all accounts, could not have been happier in what was, in reality, the first home he could properly call his own since the age of nine. Lilibet was also happy to be in her own establishment. She had swapped the regimen of one household, in which her mother was the boss, for another, in which her husband was. This suited her fine. She is on record as having stated that she wanted a husband who was the master of his own household, and this Philip certainly was, and has remained throughout the seventy years of their union.

Feminists and psychologists might consider Lilibet's assumption of the traditional role as demeaning, but she did not, and that is the important factor. Indeed, having been brought up in a household where her mother ruled the roost, it is arguable that she already had a comparable disinclination for the hegemony of feminine assertiveness. This is something she was plainly keen to avoid exercising. It does not matter whether this was because she lacked the need to control her environment the way her mother did, or whether she was reluctant to put her head above the marital parapet and run the risk of having pot shots taken at it by her assertive husband. What matters is that she consciously and definitely made the choice to assume the role of the traditional female who is subservient to her more potent and personally powerful husband.

When the course of the royal marriage is examined, and the sources of strife and conflict emerge, trouble only ever arose when Lilibet felt the need, usually for monarchic reasons, to go against the traditional grain. She therefore made a wise decision to let Philip lead, for it is doubtful the marriage could have succeeded had she been as dominating as her mother was. But then, Philip was a confident, capable, gifted alpha male, while her father was a deeply flawed but decent man who, as Mabell Airlie said, would be made or marred by his wife.

One day over a year and nine months after Charles's birth, Lilibet produced the spare. Anne Elizabeth Alice Louise was born on 15th August 1950 at Clarence House.

The intervening period had not been particularly settled owing to the state of George VI's health. The first sign of a problem arose in the summer of 1948, when the sportive and athletic king, who had been an ace tennis player with the legs to match, and a keen gun to boot, was in residence at Holyroodhouse Palace in Edinburgh. He was walking towards Arthur's Seat with his equerry, Group Captain Peter Townsend, when he suddenly exclaimed, 'What's the matter with my legs? They won't work properly.' For the remainder of the summer, he tried to take a measured approach to the problem, but it worsened until he was in constant pain and his left leg permanently numb.

The specialists were called in. They diagnosed Buerger's Disease, otherwise known as *thromboangiitis obliterans*, a form of arteriosclerosis brought on by smoking. The arteries throughout the king's body had constricted, and the blood, which would have circulated with wider, healthier arteries, had ceased to reach his extremities. The danger was that lack of circulation would ultimately result in gangrene, which would mean that the left leg would have to be amputated. This would have been an absolute disaster for the physically active king, whose greatest pleasure in life was tramping the grouse moors. The decision was taken to maximise his chances by ordering bed rest and giving him exercises to increase the circulation to the affected areas. Bertie did not take kindly to the inactivity, especially as it coincided with the shooting season, but in the run-up to Charles's birth, he had no option but to do as his doctors ordered.

By spring, however, it was clear that more radical measures would have to be resorted to. Professor James Learmonth, the chairman of surgery at Edinburgh University, who was in charge of the case, advised a lumbar sympathectomy, the surgical procedure in which sympathetic nerves in the lumbar region are severed with a view to increasing the flow of blood to the starved area. This was duly done in March 1949, and worked, for though George VI's recovery was slow, it was sure. For the remainder of his life, he retained the use of his affected limb.

Bertie's immediate family had a history of pulmonary problems caused by heavy smoking. Both his parents had always been heavy smokers. While Queen Mary's health and lifespan were not affected by the habit (she would die at nearly 86), King George V's was, as indeed was his grandfather Edward VII's. Both kings suffered from chronic bronchial problems in the latter part of their lives, the former nearly dying aged 63 of a pulmonary abscess in 1928, then dying eight years later of pulmonary problems, and the latter also dying of lung disease, aged 69.

So grateful was George VI to his savour that he knighted James Learmonth in his bedroom, creating him a Knight Commander of the Royal Victorian Order after the surgery was proven to be successful. The honour was not lost on either giver or recipient. The Royal Victorian Order is a dynastic order of knighthood which is in the so-called 'gift of the monarch'. Created by Queen Victoria in 1896, it allows the monarch to circumvent the politicians who might otherwise demand a say in whomever the monarch wishes to honour personally. It is therefore one of the most prestigious of all the orders, specifically excluding as it does all political influences. Ironically, Professor Sir James Learmonth was also a heavy smoker. He would die of lung cancer in 1967.

Between the births of the two children, following his surgery, George VI's health stabilised. Chips Channon did note in his diary that the king had taken to wearing heavy make-up to conceal his pallor, but for the next two years there was a tentative sort of stability that settled over Buckingham Palace. Stabilisation and full recovery were two different things, however, and, as the king struggled to regain his strength and energy, he handed over some of his duties to his heiress. This meant that both Edinburghs now had a heavier rota of royal engagements than they would otherwise have had, for Philip often had to accompany Lilibet to events that her father and mother would have undertaken had his health been better. Ironically, George VI appreciated that Philip loved the sea in a way he never had, despite also being a sailor, so he encouraged his son-in-law to develop his naval career to the full extent he could. Philip soon became the youngest member of the Admiralty's Operations Division.

George VI appears to have recognised parallels between Philip's position and his own anomalous one as the young Duke of York. He shrewdly advised his son-in-law to develop his own spheres of influence, and kick-started Philip's royal career by having him appointed President of the National Playing Fields Association in 1949. This was a cause dear to the king's heart. In 1925, when the association had been founded, he had been struggling to find his own footing. Set up by Brigadier-General Reginald Kentish, the then Duke of York became its first president. The association provided and protected playing fields in areas, disadvantaged ones especially, which either didn't have them or would otherwise have lost them. For the next sixty-four years, Philip would throw himself into his role with the same degree of commitment which his father-in-law had previously shown. It says much about George VI's view of Philip that he entrusted this 'baby' to him, for there is little doubt that the National Playing Fields Association was a cause dear to the heart of the king. Indeed, it had been one of the earliest sources of self-respect for a prince whose existence had been lived in the shadow of his more gifted and glamorous brother, and would continue to do so until the abdication.

As with George VI, the National Playing Fields Association would prove an invaluable template for Philip. He threw himself into the project with all the enthusiasm, commitment and energy that Prince Berthold of Baden and Kurt Hahn had inculcated into him as a young man at Salem and Gordonstoun. Some of his detractors at the palace thought him excessive, but he dedicated himself to ignoring them and mounting appeals, contacting captains of industry, and, in his own words, 'squeezing all the rich people I know for all the juice I can get out of them.' Frank Sinatra helped him to raise £16,000 by coming to London to sing at the Royal Albert Hall, while he co-starred in a movie with Bob Hope about the poor children of London whose only playgrounds were the streets of London, raising another £84,000.

What Dickie Mountbatten had characterised as Philip's socialist tendencies soon paid dividends for the charity. His sense of commitment motivated others within the cause to feats of previously unimaginable accomplishment, and, as the association opened more and more playing fields and provided recreational space for more and more underprivileged youths, the work grew proportionately until Philip was travelling several thousand miles a year. 'I will go anywhere to open a new playing field,' he declared, as those who benefitted from his endeavours grew to have genuine respect for his dedication.

By mid-1949, George VI's health had improved sufficiently for the family to be lulled into the false belief that he had achieved a full recovery. The pressure was off the Edinburghs. With the king better, he and the queen could resume a full schedule of official duties. At that time, the roster of royals who could carry out official engagements was not exactly full to bursting. There was the Duke and Duchess of Gloucester, and the Duchess of Kent, but lesser royals such as Princess Arthur of Connaught, 2nd Duchess of Fife in her own right, did not fulfil official duties, so that left only the budding Princess Margaret to share the workload.

Although Lilibet would actually never relinquish official engagements entirely, her royal duties took a back seat when George VI encouraged Philip to accept the posting of First Lieutenant of HMS *Chequers*, the leader of the flotilla based in Malta. On 17th October 1949 they moved there to begin what Lilibet would characterise as 'one of the happiest periods of my life.' Also there were Edwina and Dickie, who had relinquished being Governor-General of India and returned to the navy as a Vice-Admiral. He had been posted to Malta as commander of the 1st Cruiser Squadron in the Mediterranean Fleet.

Earl and Countess Mountbatten of Burma, as they became on 28th October 1947, lived in splendour in Villa Guardamangia, a sandstone townhouse outside Valletta which had been built at the turn of the century by Sir Augusto Bartolo. Leased by Dickie in 1929, then subsequently bought by him, it was a sumptuous townhouse which the Mountbattens had restored to a palatial standard. It would be home to Lilibet and Philip from 1949 to 1951, and is regarded as where Princess Anne's conception took place. Certainly, it was the site of the most normal period of Lilibet's life. There, she could come and go in relative obscurity. She could shop in town, visit the hairdresser's, which was something she had never done before, sail in the warmth and sunshine, go for swims and picnics as if she were just another society lady married to a well-to-do naval officer, generally leading the life of an ordinary person.

Ordinariness might seem ordinary to the ordinary person, but to someone whose whole life has been extraordinary, who has been cocooned in a royal chrysalis, it was delicious, exotic, intoxicating. All the things the average person takes for granted, Lilibet not only enjoyed, but actually savoured. Philip was also happy, especially when he was promoted in 1950 to command the frigate, HMS *Magpie*. His ambition was to become First Sea Lord like his grandfather Prince Louis of Battenberg, 1st Marquis of Milford Haven, and for this narrow window of opportunity, it looked as if he might have the career that would make such an eventuality achievable. If his and Lilibet's luck held, along with the king's health, they just might have the twenty years of 'ordinary' life which would allow him to realise his ambitions before he had to shelve them to support her in the role to which she would inevitably accede.

While Lilibet and Philip were in Malta, their son Charles remained in England. After his birth, until his parents moved into Clarence House, he spent most of his time down at Windlesham Moor, on the grounds that the air there was better for him than in London, where the smog was so bad that there were frequent peasoupers. In those days there was nothing remarkable about upper-class mothers handing their children over to the care of nurses. It was the 'done thing', even for mothers who were more maternal than Lilibet was. She therefore saw him only on weekends. She nevertheless had the assurance that he was being taken care of ably, indeed far more ably than she herself could have done, by the two Scots women who ran the nursery. They were Helen Lightbody, who had the honorific of Mrs., in keeping with tradition, despite being unmarried – and Mabel Anderson, the nursery maid whose relative humility resulted in her being known to the staff simply as Miss Anderson.

Charles would form an attachment with Mabel Anderson to rival that which Lilibet had formed with Bobo and Margaret with Ruby. Significantly, his attachment to Mrs Lightbody was no greater than Lilibet's had been to Mrs Knight. The reason appears to have been the same. Both women ruled the roost with a rod of iron. Mrs Lightbody regulated the baby's every waking minute, and continued to do so as he grew up and the household moved from Windlesham Moor into Clarence House. According to John Gibson, a Belfast boy who worked his way up to being a footman in the Edinburghs' household, 'There was never any doubt who was head of the nursery department. Things were done the way Nanny Lightbody wanted them regardless of what anyone else might think. Prince Charles was kept in line too – breakfast at 8.45 a.m., a morning walk and then a sleep.'

While nannies in grand households were frequently imperious, Mrs Lightbody went beyond that, displaying serious symptoms of red carpet fever, that peculiar condition from which staff are inclined to suffer when they are catapulted from humbler origins to a very grand lifestyle, in the process becoming even grander than the people they are serving. Nanny Lightbody insisted that Gibson bring up Charles's meal trays and pompously announce, 'I have brought His Royal Highness's breakfast,' before handing it over to her. She would then hand it on to Mabel Anderson, who would transfer it onto Charles's china before laying it before him on the table. This was hardly the way to earth any child, especially one whose food was still being pureed at eighteen months, and while such behaviour might have impressed Nanny Lightbody with her own importance, it also had the paradoxical effect of creating a barrier between Charles and herself. Like his mother before him, he would develop a far stronger and more affectionate relationship with his simple nursery maid, whose carapace was not so monumentally snobbish that it precluded genuine human affection from flourishing.

According to Gibson, before the move to Clarence House, Lilibet and Philip would rush up to the nursery as soon as they arrived on a Friday afternoon to share bath time with their son. And after the move there, they saw far more of the baby than they had while living at Buckingham Palace, for they now lived under the same roof during the week as well as on weekends.

However, once Philip was posted to Malta and Lilibet travelled back and forth, spending months at a time there, Charles saw virtually nothing of his father, and his mother only intermittently, when she returned to the United Kingdom. While she was abroad, he stayed with his grandparents. This seems to have been when the close bond with his grandmother was established, along with what his father would come to view as his 'wet' tendencies.

At first, there was no indication that trouble would loom. Both King George VI and Queen Elizabeth wrote fond letters to their daughter about how 'sweet' and 'adorable' their grandson was. History seemed to be repeating itself, with Charles replicating, with Lilibet's parents, the relationship she had enjoyed with King George V and Queen Mary. The former Elizabeth Bowes Lyon, however, was no Queen Mary, who might have had a real reverence for royalty but nevertheless went right to the heart of the matter regarding the responsibilities and realities of royal life. Queen Mary would never have undermined the authority of her son and daughter-in-law the way Elizabeth gradually did, nor would she have encouraged Lilibet in extravagant tendencies the way Elizabeth, who was herself extravagant, did with Charles. One royal relation told me, 'Queen Elizabeth molly-coddled Prince Charles in the most detrimental way. She reinforced his whinging and encouraged him to be soft when it was really in his interest to be toughened up. Everyone agrees that he has a streak of self-pity as wide as a mile. He can thank his grandmother for that. She is the one who encouraged it from a very early age. It is fair to say that, but for her, he would have been an altogether different character. She undermined his parents at every turn, largely, I think, for two reasons. The first was: she enjoyed being loved, and would say and do anything to anyone that would encourage them to love her, even when it was contrary to their interest. And secondly, she did it because she wanted to establish a special bond with Charles, who was heir to the throne. Tellingly, she didn't undermine the authority of their parents with any of her other grandchildren. You have to ask yourself: why, except for vanity, would she do something that would turn out to be so destructive?'

All of this was very much in the future, however, while Charles remained with the king and queen, and, after Anne's arrival, she too stayed with her grandparents while her parents were in Malta. This allowed the Edinburghs to enjoy a normal and happy life overseas, unfettered by the extraordinary responsibilities they would soon have.

In spring 1951, the king developed a hacking cough which refused to go away. He had a high temperature and was barely well enough to invest his brother Harry, the Duke of Gloucester, as Great Master of the Order of the Bath. Afterwards, he took to his bed with what he thought was influenza, but the doctors diagnosed pneumonitis, a less severe form of pneumonia, on the left lung. They prescribed bed rest and daily doses of penicillin, but were sufficiently concerned about the king's health to suggest that Lilibet and Philip replace George VI and Elizabeth on the tour of Canada and America which was scheduled for September 1951.

Elizabeth loved royal tours, and had been looking forward to returning to North America, where her and Bertie's stock was particularly high as the Warrior King and Queen who had stopped Hitler in his tracks. She knew their return would be a triumph for them, as the tour of 1939 had been, 'the making of us', to quote her. However, she appreciated the reasons for the substitution, and stepped aside with good grace.

Philip was recalled to England on 'indefinite leave' with Lilibet, to resume royal duties. As he said goodbye to his crew in July 1951, he told them, 'The past eleven months have been the happiest of my sailor life.' Privately, he fought against being devastated as he faced the fact that the naval career he loved, and had hoped to dedicate himself to, for the next two or so decades, was at an end. 'There was no choice. It just happened. You have to make compromises. That's life. I accepted it. I tried to make the best of it,' he told his friend and biographer, Gyles Brandreth.

Philip's stoicism, which was already a highly developed feature of his personality, and had been since the age of ten, did not alter the fact that he was sad to lose the career he loved. However, he threw himself into the plans for the tour. Bertie then caught a chill on Princess Margaret's birthday on 21ˢᵗ August while shooting up at Balmoral. By 1ˢᵗ September his condition had deteriorated to such an extent that his doctors convened a meeting at which they were, ominously, joined by the eminent Royal Brompton Hospital, London, thoracic surgeon (later Sir) Clement Price Thomas, whose specialty was cancers of the chest. He joined the other doctors, Sir Daniel Davies, Sir Horace Evans, Geoffrey Marshal and Sir John Weir, in recommending that Bertie return to London for further investigations, which he did on 7ᵗʰ September. Nine days later Elizabeth and the family learnt that he had an obstruction, which was a euphemism for cancer. On the 23ʳᵈ, the affected left lung was removed, as well as some of the nerves of the larynx, to which the disease had spread. This was a cruel irony, for Bertie had always had a beautiful, deep voice, and he had worked so hard over the years to overcome his stammer. There was the very real possibility that he might lose the ability to speak at anything above a whisper, but in the event, Price Thomas managed to save his voice following an operation in a specially-constructed operating theatre at Buckingham Palace. Considering it an honour to have performed the operation on his king, the surgeon waived his fee, and was rewarded with a knighthood of the Royal Victorian Order.

Lilibet and Philip had been due to depart for Canada on the 25th aboard the liner *Empress of Britain*. The decision was taken to delay their departure but not to cancel or postpone the tour. This meant that the only way they could reach Canada and adhere as closely as possible to the original schedule was to fly across the Atlantic; something the courtiers were dead against. So too was Winston Churchill, leader of the opposition, who only climbed down after Philip pointed out to him that he had flown across the Atlantic while prime minister during the war. They took off from London on the evening of 7ᵗʰ October, accompanied by Lilibet's private secretary, Martin Charteris, who had had been serving since the beginning of 1950. The royal party arrived in Newfoundland before progressing to Montreal, where they were met by the governor-general, the war hero Field Marshal Viscount (later Earl) Alexander of Tunis, and the prime minister, Louis St Laurent.

Philip and Lilibet were great hits, the former even more so than the latter. The newspapers complained that she did not smile as much as her mother, while conceding that she was pretty and sweet, while men and women alike enthused about him. Lilibet wrote to tell her mother how delighted she was by her husband's '*succès fou*'. Whenever he waved, the women screamed excitedly at the prince with matinee idol good looks and the 'natural – yet somehow unorthodox – action.' He endeared himself to all onlookers when he wore a ten-gallon Stetson hat to watch a rodeo in Calgary, and acquired the beginnings of his reputation as an action man by taking the co-pilot's seat in the Royal Canadian Air Force plane which transported them, as well as driving the royal train, taking the wheel of the royal barge, and taking to the bridge of the Canadian destroyer *Crusader*.

Having spent a month criss-crossing the vast terrain of Canada as they visited all seven provinces by way of the governor-general's train, they departed for the United States, where Lilibet scored her own *coup*. The president, Harry Truman, was captivated by her, stating, 'When I was a little boy, I read about a fairy princess, and here she is.' The press and public were equally enraptured, the *Washington Star* reporting that 'she had charmed and captivated this city to such an extent that our oldest inhabitants, searching around among their memories, are hard put to recall the name of any past visitor quite comparable to her in terms of good looks and sweetness of personality.'

If America had proven to be the 'making' of her mother and father, it consolidated Lilibet and Philip's status as the mostly glamorous and desirable young couple on earth, eclipsing by far the greatest enthusiasm ever shown to either of her parents. Philip has recounted how the 'adulation' during these early years was 'unbelievable' but that they didn't take it too seriously. They certainly didn't allow it to go to their heads. Certainly, it was pleasant, but both of them understood that approbation was not an objective to be sought after, but a by-product of a job well done, which should be taken in their stride.

Arriving back in England on board the liner, the *Empress of India*, shortly after Charles's third birthday, the Edinburghs were greeted with another dose of fulsome praise, this time by the newly re-elected prime minister, Winston Churchill, who declared that, 'the whole nation is grateful for what you have done for us.'

Originally, George VI and Elizabeth had been scheduled to tour Australia, but the doctors were aware that he was living on borrowed time. Although it appeared as if they had got rid of all the cancer following his successful surgery, in those days one could not be sure. Churchill's doctor, Lord Moran, thought the king had a year at the most to live, and his own doctors felt he was susceptible to a pulmonary thrombosis, which meant he could die at any time. Despite this gloomy prognosis, the family had not been made aware of the severity of his condition. Elizabeth, whom Martin Charteris would subsequently describe as 'a bit of an ostrich', preferred to believe that all was good in the land of the living. Princess Margaret would, years later in my presence, say that her father died 'just as he was getting better', and though Philip and Lilibet were aware that his health was precarious, they too do not seem to have been aware that he could die at any moment.

What was obvious, though, was that George VI was in no condition to undertake any state visits. No sooner did Philip and Lilibet return to England than they therefore had to begin preparing for yet another overseas trip, in two months' time, to Australia and New Zealand, where they would be deputising for her parents.

Nevertheless, the king and queen were also due to travel, on 10th March 1952, to South Africa, where he would be convalescing at the invitation of the Prime Minister Daniel Francois (more commonly known as D.F.) Malans, at his country residence, Botha House.

At this time, there was such concern about the state of the king's health that Lascelles had actually sent a warning telegram to Churchill, who was visiting Washington, to be prepared for any eventuality. Yet the royal family itself remained blithely oblivious. Possibly this was because George VI continued the rigorous pursuit of shooting, as if he were completely healthy. Indeed, the day before he died, he joined the Keeper's Day shoot at Sandringham. According to James Macdonald, who had been on his staff for twenty years, he shot 'superbly' and was 'as gay and happy' as he had ever known him to be. He was still his usual, cheerful self as the two men said good-bye, his parting words being, 'Well Macdonald, we'll go after the hares again tomorrow.'

If the family itself preferred to believe that all was well, and that the king was getting better, he was nevertheless under medical supervision. On 29th January, he was examined in London, after which his team declared itself 'very well satisfied' with his progress. The following evening, he attended a performance of the hit musical *South Pacific* at the Drury Lane Theatre with his wife, two daughters, son-in-law, equerry Group Captain Peter Townsend and some friends.

The next morning, the king went to Heathrow Airport to bid farewell to Lilibet and Philip, who were departing for Kenya, on the first leg of the trip that would take them to Australia and New Zealand. There is a famous photograph of the hatless monarch staring fixedly at his departing daughter, a haunted expression on his face, as if he knew he would never see her again. He looked as if he was 'walking with death', to use Churchill's descriptive turn of phrase, yet, according to the prime minister, who was also at the airport with him, he was actually 'gay and even jaunty' and he 'drank a glass of champagne.' Churchill also said, 'I think he knew he had not long to live', but this observation might well have benefitted from hindsight. It seems more likely that George VI, who was actually feeling better than he had for some time, was enjoying his new lease of life, though Bobo also shared the prime minister's fanciful harbinger of doom. After the fact, she said that the king was more upset saying good bye to Lilibet than she had ever known him to be, and that he also said to her, 'Look after the princess for me, Bobo.' These, however, are words that he would doubtless have used even if he had known he was going to survive till the end of the millennium, so one takes these tragic overtones with the pinch of salt they deserve.

If the king had a presentiment, neither his wife nor younger daughter, who was the apple of her father's eye and loved him unreservedly, did, nor did he share it with them. It is also very likely that, had he had any inkling of his coming death, he would have ensured that he made adequate provision financially for Princess Margaret. He died making none, which would impact severely upon Margaret for the remainder of her life. After the Edinburghs' departure, the king, queen and Margaret returned to Sandringham, where he continued to enjoy the last days of the shooting season.

The day before he died, Elizabeth and Margaret spent the day with the acclaimed Modern British painter Edward Seago. He took them for a spin in his cabin cruiser, after which they departed with a selection of his landscapes. Upon returning to Sandringham, Elizabeth showed them to George VI, who was 'in tremendous form & looking so well & happy'. The three of them had a quiet and enjoyable supper, after which the king retired to his bedroom on the ground floor.

At midnight, the watchman noticed George VI open the window to let in some air.

At 7.30 the following morning, Macdonald brought in a cup of tea. He opened the curtains, drew the king's bath, and, realising that he had not stirred as he normally would have done, shook his shoulder gently. Although George VI looked as if he was asleep, Macdonald realised something was amiss, and feeling his forehead, noticed it was cold. This meant only one thing, so he sent a message to Elizabeth's dresser, then went to inform the king's equerry, Sir Harold Campbell. Elizabeth 'flew to his room, & thought that he was in a deep sleep, he looked so peaceful – and then I realised what had happened,' she wrote to Queen Mary later that day.

King George VI was dead, aged 56.

Lilibet was now the queen at 25.

# Chapter VI

NO ONE KNOWS EXACTLY when Lilibet became queen, because no one actually knows precisely when George VI died. What is certain is that the new queen and Philip were at Treetops, the four-roomed 'hotel' and observation post built in a huge tree above a watering hole in Kenya, looking at the buffaloes, rhinoceroses and elephants, at the moment of her accession.

Up to that point, the royal trip had been ideal. When the royal couple was not on duty fulfilling a packed round of engagements that included presiding over a reception for two thousand five hundred at Government House, as well as visiting a 'brand new maternity hospital for African mothers and their babies,' they filled their time with pleasurable activities such as 'riding at dawn, when the rising sun coloured snowy mountain peaks with pink and gold and there was still sufficient nip in the air to make exercise pleasant.' John Dean, who accompanied the royal couple along with Bobo, recounted, 'This close contact with the wild, and the trout fishing and the riding, made a wonderful holiday which gave immense pleasure to us all.'

The night at Treetops was supposed to be the highlight of the entire trip. It 'had been specially decorated for the Royal visit,' though baboons had broken in and they, 'ate some of the new lampshades', which actually only added colour to the occasion. Because everyone in the royal party remained blissfully ignorant of what had occurred at Sandringham, the new queen left Treetops and continued the itinerary, returning to Sagana Lodge, the hunting lodge which the people of Kenya had given her and Philip as a wedding present. (The lease was given back to Kenya in 1963 when it became independent and is now used by the president when he is on official tours.)

It is easy to forget how very different things were in those days. White visitors were so rare that the natives shied away from their cameras, thinking that a photograph could 'seal their soul', and what then passed for modern communications were so woefully inadequate that the royal party remained ignorant of the king's death long after people all over the world knew of it.

London had sent an encrypted message to Government House, which would ordinarily have unscrambled the message and conveyed the news to

Lilibet's staff. However, the governor and his staff had all left Government House to meet the royal party at Mombasa, where they were due to join the liner the *Gothic* the following day, to depart for Ceylon and the Cocos Islands en route to Australia. So a pile of cyphers lay unread and unanswered, and just about the last people to learn of the king's death were his daughter, son-in-law, their staff and the colonial government. Meanwhile, the news was broadcast far and wide via Reuters News Agency.

The royal couple had had a wonderful night, and were in high spirits. Originally, when King George VI, Queen Elizabeth and Princess Margaret had been scheduled to undertake the Antipodean tour, Kenya had not even been on the itinerary. It was only after Lilibet and Philip replaced her parents and sister that it was added, at her request, so that she and Philip could express their gratitude to the people of Kenya by visiting the hunting lodge that they had been given as a wedding present.

It was by pure chance that Martin Charteris was stopped and told the news of the king's death by a reporter from the *East Africa Standard*. Lilibet's private secretary then tried to get official confirmation, but was unable to obtain it as no one of any seniority remained on duty at Government House. So he telephoned Sagana Lodge and informed Philip's best friend and private secretary, Mike Parker, of what he had been told. Parker managed to catch Philip's eye. Signalling him through the bay window of the sitting room, that looks onto Mount Kenya, to come outside, he dropped the bombshell on Philip. 'He's not the sort of person to show his emotions. But you can tell from a man's face. How he sets his features. I'll never forget it. He looked as if half the world had dropped on him.'

Philip appreciated the implications of the news immediately. His life had changed for all time. The treasured twenty or twenty-five years he and Lilibet had hoped to have, so that he could build his naval career and they could lead a relatively normal life, would now never materialise. He went back inside to fetch his wife, who had loved her father dearly. According to Dean, who was an eye-witness, he broke the news to her in her room. Afterwards, while 'we were busy packing, the Queen and the Duke climbed down the steep path to the river, where they had fished so light-heartedly only a short time before. Together they paced slowly along the bank, and then came back to tea. By five o'clock we were ready to leave.' There were no histrionics. Neither Philip nor Lilibet has ever been inclined to much emotional expressiveness, but that does not mean that she did not feel the death of her father acutely. Dean noticed that, on the way back to England, 'she got up once or twice during the journey, and when she returned to her seat she looked as if she might have been crying.'

What was' truly extraordinary', however, was the new 'queen's reaction' to her changed status. This is best recounted by Martin Charteris, who told me, and many other people as well, how, 'the personally diffident,' Lilibet, 'embraced her new role,' in the, 'most surprising and unexpected way.' 'Gone was all uncertainty. It was the most extraordinary transformation. She rose to the role, all personal diffidence and hesitation disappearing, with a certainty and serenity which were truly astonishing. It was the most amazing transformation.' Where previously Lilibet had been 'tenuous', Queen Elizabeth II was 'sure-footed'. Willing as she was in her personal life to stay on the periphery, allowing more outgoing personalities like her mother, sister and husband to shine while she sheltered away from the limelight, as monarch she embraced the centrality of her role, displaying an immediate certainty of purpose which showed a degree of the mettle which Eleanor Roosevelt had noticed in the young girl who had asked serious questions when the American president's wife had visited England during the war.

According to Bobo, before Lilibet had a 'chance to recover from the first stunning shock of the news, her private secretary, Lieutenant Colonel the Honourable Martin Charteris, had to ask her a question which brought home, forcefully, the heavy responsibility that was now hers and would be on her shoulders for the rest of her life. The question he had to ask her was what name she wished to be known by, as Queen. It seemed awful that affairs of state should be pressed on her so soon. But London wanted to know urgently. The young Queen quietly gave him the answer - Elizabeth.'

'On the forty mile journey by road to the nearest airport I was in the car immediately behind the Queen and the Duke, who travelled with Colonel Charteris and Lady Pamela Mountbatten,' John Dean recalled. 'How the news got around I don't know, but it must have spread by some kind of bush telegraph, for all along the dusty route natives stood with bowed heads, not grinning and clapping as they had done on the outward journey, but offering a silent tribute to the Queen's grief,' which was most moving.

The royal party took a small East African Airways plane to Entebbe in Uganda, where they boarded the BOAC Argonaut carrier, the *Atalanta*, at eleven pm after a wait of several hours owing to bad weather. They stopped at Tobruk the following morning to refuel before continuing on over the Alps. Philip 'joined us in the main cabin quite often and chatted about the flight as we crossed the snow-covered Alps. The Queen came through to the cabin as well, but she only said, "Good morning," as she passed,' Dean recounted.

As soon as the flight landed and 'the engines died the door of the plane was pushed open and the Duke of Gloucester and Lord and Lady Mountbatten came aboard and went into the rear compartment, where the Queen received them. Then they all stepped out of the plane.'

The newly re-elected Prime Minister Winston Churchill was the first to greet them. However, he was so overcome with emotion that 'he seemed unable to speak, as if the words would not come. The Queen acknowledged the reception with her usual composure and then made, in the moment of her return as ruler, a gesture which was typical, and proof, if any proof was needed, that she followed closely her late father's example. After she had spoken to the members of the Cabinet she shook hands with all the crew of the aircraft,' thanking them for the care they had taken of her.

The change in status was immediately evident in another way. Instead of her own car from Clarence House, Lilibet was obliged to enter one of the royal Daimlers from Buckingham Palace. These had been sent to bring her there, where her grandmother, Queen Mary, awaited her. It has often been recounted how the old dowager queen paid obeisance to her granddaughter, curtsying to her in keeping with the tradition that a queen consort curtsies to a queen regnant, but what is less well known is that, prior to this, as Lilibet hove into view, Queen Mary tartly observed, 'Lilibet, your skirts are much too short for mourning!' Only after that reprimand did Queen Mary curtsy.

Upon returning to Clarence House, 'there was great activity, with state officials calling to see the Queen on all the urgent business which could not be delayed.' For the remainder of the day, both Lilibet and Philip were inundated with all the requirements of their new situations.

Elizabeth and Margaret were still at Sandringham, but before Lilibet could join them there, she had one of the most important functions of her reign to perform. It also became a cause for conflict and showed how officialdom intended to whip the young couple into line. The first official ceremony of any reign is the Accession Council. This was scheduled for 10 am on the morning of 8th February 1952. Clarence House adjoins St James's Palace, and there are interconnecting doors which mean that the occupants can move between the two buildings without having to do so externally. As Lilibet and Philip made their way from Clarence House to the entrance to the Levee and Throne Rooms at St James's Palace, they found their way barred. The rules of precedence prevented Philip from accompanying his wife into either the Levee Room, where most of the Privy Councillors were assembled, or the Throne Room, the holy of holies where the select few would actually witness the declaration of her accession. Despite being the Queen Regnant's husband, Philip had no special status because, in the United Kingdom, a husband does not share the rank of his wife, though a wife invariably acquires that of her husband. This meant that the officials were well within their rights to bar him from accompanying his wife. That honour was reserved for the most senior ranking male in the kingdom, her Uncle Harry, the Duke of Gloucester. While there is little doubt that accommodating officials could well have found a way to permit him to enter through the same door as his wife, even if not by her side, Philip was nevertheless forced to gain admittance to his own wife's accession through a back door, accompanied by his private secretary, Mike Parker. The old antipathy towards the new queen's consort was plainly alive and kicking.

This became even more evident when Philip finally gained admittance to the palace. He was firmly excluded from the Throne Room, the main scene of the action, his relative unimportance affirmed by having to remain in the Council Chamber along with all the less important privy councillors.

Both Philip and Lilibet were humiliated and perplexed by what they regarded as callous and uncalled for behaviour, but both of them bided their time before doing anything. There were sound reasons for this cautious approach. Philip and Lilibet, having been born royal, knew the way courts work. They both knew that the British monarchy had by that time become an 'institution' where much of the power reposed in those who run it. Indeed, Philip is on record as having stated that the monarchy was nothing like it had been in the days when the Prince Consort was married to Queen Victoria and was able to influence events. By the nineteen fifties the powers-that-be did things in the name of the monarch, but they were the ones calling the shots. Both he and Lilibet knew, as insiders, how dangerous it would be for either of them to figuratively 'rock the boat'. The last boat rocker had been her uncle David, whose refusal to bow to the demands of the powers-that-be had resulted in his being manoeuvred off the throne. His presence across the water was an ever-present reminder, and threat, as to what happens to those who buck too firmly against the system.

Loyal though Lilibet was to Philip, neither she nor her consort was a match for the wily courtiers who now bombarded her with work. Acceding to the throne was always going to see an increase in her workload – something both she and Philip expected – but what neither of them suspected was that overloading her with work was a ploy to drive a wedge between them so that his influence upon her could be neutralised before he had an opportunity to wield it. Philip recounted how Lascelles, who had helped to ease King Edward VIII off the throne and was now Lilibet's private secretary, ran Lilibet off her feet from early in the morning till late at night as soon as they returned from Kenya. Hindsight would show how Lascelles got Sir Piers Legh, the Master of the Household, and Sir Ulick Alexander, the Keeper of the Privy Purse, to increase her workload so that she was buried in a wholly unnecessary way.

For instance, as soon as Lilibet arrived in London, Lascelles presented her with the red boxes which contain the government papers of the day and informed her that she had to get through them then and there. He knew that Lilibet was like her late father: punctilious to a fault. And when she did not resist and assert who the boss was, he used her workload to turn himself into the man who really called the shots. Ostensibly Lascelles, Sir Piers and Sir Ulick were teaching Lilibet the ropes. But they were actually isolating her from her husband and the influence they, Churchill and Elizabeth feared Philip, and through him Dickie Mountbatten, had over her.

Up to that point Philip had been Lilibet's protector, not as a Svengali but as a loving and traditional husband. They were a close and loving couple and it was this strong, healthy marital bond that the palace clique and Churchill now set about loosening. They were paranoid about Dickie Mountbatten becoming the power behind the throne, but this was a genuine irony, for as Philip himself has often said, 'I was never as close to my Uncle Dickie as everyone thought. Lilibet in fact was closer to him.'

Ironically, the assaults waged against the couple had the paradoxical effect of bringing Lilibet even closer to Uncle Dickie than she might otherwise have been. Another relationship which actually flourished paradoxically under all this heat and dust was Lilibet's with her mother-in-law. To the chagrin of Elizabeth and the palace clique, she developed a genuine and ever-increasing closeness with Alice. This went way beyond the formally correct, albeit loving, relationship Lilibet had with her own mother. The reasons for it were sound. She could relax with Alice in a way she could not with Elizabeth. Though Alice was a true 'character' – her own mother said of her, 'What do you make of a nun who smokes Woodbines and plays canasta?' - she had no 'side'. She was 'simple, and straightforward.' What you saw was what you got. This was not the case with Elizabeth. You seldom got what you saw. She was so adroit at the stealthy and undetectable manoeuvre that it was virtually impossible to pin anything on her, even as you knew that she was working the angles behind the scenes. Admittedly, Lilibet spoke to her mother most days. Admittedly, she was punctilious about being the dutiful daughter. But when she wanted to let her hair down to relax and be unguarded, she did not turn to her mother, but to her saintly mother-in- law. Alice had by this time forsworn the secular world and retreated into the religious life, heading up the nursing order of nuns who tended to the sick and poor in Athens.

Unlike Elizabeth, Alice was beyond the machinations that Lilibet had seen her smiling mother perpetrate upon her many victims. Colin Glenconner told me that he was sure that Lilibet had a true awareness of her mother's manipulative skills, but that she was reluctant to face the enormity of Elizabeth's capabilities. This was unlike Princess Margaret, who had had to face her mother's deviousness head-on as a result of the Townsend crisis. He said Margaret never forgave her mother for the part she played then, and thereafter had a healthy scepticism of her. He believed, however, Lilibet always had a more rose-tinted view, partly because she had never actually had to confront the extent of her mother's manipulativeness, but also because she was an 'ostrich' who didn't like facing unpleasant truths about people. This led her to minimise her mother's failings, but Colin felt both sisters knew their mother to be the 'conniving creature she was.'

What one must not forget is that Lilibet was not only a queen but also a human being. It would have been difficult for any twenty-five year old to reassess her vision of her mother, while maintaining a positive and loving relationship with her, and at the same time having to adjust to the new and demanding role of monarch, while she was also having to adjust to the fractures being placed upon her marriage and her family life. Anyone, no matter how old, mature, well-adjusted and prepared, would have found such profound life changes difficult to cope with, but for a young, innocent, shy and somewhat naïve twenty-five year old, who had been brought up in a very protected environment, and to an extent would always remain in one, the changes were impossible to incorporate quickly or easily.

There is some doubt that Lilibet ever fully appreciated the role her mother played at that time. Throughout her life, she maintained a tolerance of her mother's foibles that suggests that she ultimately accepted only as much of her mother's darker side as she had to. Yet who can condemn her, when one considers that she was caught between conflicting duties: on the one hand, the duty of being a loving and dutiful daughter, on the other, the obligation of being a loving wife, and on yet another hand, the duty of being a good sovereign. If she resolved such conflicts by rendering unto Caesar that which was Caesar's, and unto God that which was God's – and rendered only as much as she had to on each occasion – her choices are surely indicative of a spiritual largesse that does not sink into condemnation when the temptation arises, but rather restricts itself to the acceptance of that which it would much rather not have to deal with, but does so to maintain positive bonds.

Nevertheless, Lilibet's tact and diplomacy with Philip's denigrators had an adverse effect upon her husband. He knew that Lascelles had been Queen Elizabeth the Queen Mother's man from the days of the abdication crisis.

He also knew that his mother-in-law had not approved of him. Being neither stupid nor blind, Philip sensed Elizabeth's unseen hand behind many of these difficulties. Though he understood the exigencies of Lilibet's softly softly approach, he was not blind to the consequences, which hereafter would impact adversely upon her relationship with their two children as well. This was another regrettable effect of the turmoil and overwork Lilibet was subjected to in the early days of her accession, for she soon found herself alienated from her children.

Of course, in those days upper class parents saw children far less than they do nowadays. Most children saw their parents twice a day, for measured periods only, and hers were no exception. She had always tried to see them for at least half an hour each morning and an hour each evening, but that basic schedule had had to accommodate day trips as well as trips abroad. Between the tours she had to undertake for her father and mother, ordinary state business, and the worldwide tour which was now scheduled to celebrate her ascension to the throne and timed to take place after the coronation, she saw so little of the children that there were times when they treated her more like a visiting godmother then a dearly beloved mother. Prince Charles would later bemoan this fact to his biographer Jonathan Dimbleby, but Princess Anne has always taken the view that her mother was the best mother she could be within the parameters which were open to her. Certainly by the time Prince Andrew and Prince Edward were born, things had changed so dramatically that neither of them has ever felt that their mother's role as queen encroached upon that of mother.

Although the Dimbleby biography opened up the question of whether Lilibet was a loving mother, everyone who knows her well has always said that she is a good and loving mother. If anything, the criticism made against her isn't that she is harsh and cold, but that she is too malleable. Three of her four children are on the record stating that she was a good and loving mother to them, and eyewitnesses state that shortly after her accession, when she was being run ragged, it concerned her when she was unable to partake of activities with the children such as bath time.

In the early days of the reign, however, she was so caught up in the demands of majesty, some of which we have seen were enlarged unnecessarily to swamp her with work, that she simply did not have time for family life. The strain to which she was subjected at this time was tremendous. Though she did not appreciate it at the time, she was being tossed to and fro to such an extent that her family ties were disintegrating under her very nose.

In the first weeks of the new reign, which drove home the point to both Lilibet and Philip as to where real power reposed, the Accession Council debacle was only the first of four separate situations which demonstrated how carefully she had to tread in the minefield that she found herself in.

The second situation centred on her and Philip's choice of residence. Both the new queen and her husband wished to continue living at Clarence House. Her mother, moreover, was eager to continue living at Buckingham Palace. Churchill, however, demanded that Lilibet move into Buckingham Palace, on the grounds that Buckingham Palace was the established hub of the monarchy in London. According to the Prime Minister's reasoning, it was not only the London residence of the monarch, but it also housed offices which were fundamental to the running of the monarchy. He made it clear to them that Buckingham Palace was the only fitting residence for the new queen and her family. This demonstrated how limited was the power of the crown when its choices came up against the elected government, driving home the point that neither sovereign nor consort had a choice as to where they could live, if such a choice came into conflict with the opinion of the government.

This was Lilibet's first taste of the sour draught underlying her role as monarch. Under the British constitution, a king or queen might have the power to advise and warn, but once the government recommends, he or she is more or less obliged to accept the recommendation. I say 'more or less' because there is no hard and fast rule as to when and where the monarch can ignore the advice of the prime minister with regard to his or her own conduct, but with the passage of time successive monarchs have seen the sense in being pliable. With time, a successful monarch learns to play the long game, exercising patience until he or she gets a prime minister who will accommodate them in their wishes. But in 1952 Lilibet had no experience, though she had enough wisdom to appreciate that it was in the interest of the monarchy to put to one side her and Philip's wishes as to where their home should be, so she buckled and agreed to sacrifice Clarence House, the place she and Philip regarded as home, and move into the 'office block that is Buck House,' as one of the royals put it.

Although Churchill and the newly widowed Elizabeth, thereafter known universally as Queen Elizabeth the Queen Mother, would function as allies during the third and fourth situations which confronted Lilibet, with regard to this second one, they were in opposition to each other. Once Lilibet and Philip accepted Churchill's dictat and reluctantly agreed to vacate Clarence House and move into Buckingham Palace, Elizabeth remained determined to continue living at Buckingham Palace. She went to the extreme of pointing out to her daughter how easily both of them could live at the palace, with Philip and Lilibet occupying the Belgian Suite on the ground floor, while she remained in her own rooms on the first floor. 'I could be quite self-contained upstairs, meals etc., and you would hardly know I was there,' she argued.

However, neither Lilibet nor Philip wished to share a residence with her mother, and she was made to understand that she would have to swap residences with them. This did not altogether please Elizabeth, who felt that Marlborough House would make a more fitting residence for her than Clarence House. In the reign of Queen Victoria, the former residence had been the London residence of the Prince of Wales, while Clarence House had merely been the residence of the youngest-but-one son. The only problem was, Queen Mary was still alive and resident there. Princess Marina told Margaret, Duchess of Argyll that Elizabeth evidently hoped that if she spun out the decision-making process long enough, the old queen would die and she would be able to move into the more splendid residence. However, the decision to move was made while Queen Mary was still alive, and when she died, Lilibet ensured that her mother could not backtrack by ultimately giving it to the Commonwealth as their Secretariat.

The third situation demonstrated how alliances shift at palace level, with opponents in one conflict joining forces to defeat an adversary in another conflict, with no care to loyalty. Indeed, so acceptable are shifting alliances that the elegant double-cross can be achieved without anyone's integrity being impugned. The third situation began, peaked and concluded while the matter of the royal residences was still being contested, yet the cabal which joined forces to wage a bitter war of attrition that nearly destroyed Lilibet's marriage, consisted of Churchill, his housing adversary Elizabeth, her husband's senior courtiers, Lascelles, who was still in harness in keeping with the custom of the private secretaries remaining in situ during the transition from one reign to another, and Queen Mary. The cause of the conflict was the name of the dynasty which reigned once Elizabeth Mountbatten ascended the throne.

Up to this point, it had been accepted practice in all royal families that each dynasty took the name of a queen regnant's husband. There were ample precedents that established this custom. Some were closer to home than others. Queen Victoria, for instance, had been born into the house of Hanover, but when she married Prince Albert of Saxe-Coburg-Gotha, the name of the dynasty changed to Saxe-Coburg-Gotha. Both King Edward VII and King George V ascended the throne as kings of that dynasty, which is what caused so many problems for George V when Gotha bombers strafed London during the First World War and it became necessary to get rid of the name Gotha before the Gotha dynasty's popularity was affected by the namesake bombers. George V's tactical name-change took place following the downfall of the Romanoff dynasty, which itself had been partially brought down by untrue stories accusing the German-born Tsarina of being disloyal to her adopted country.

The name change of the dynasty from Saxe-Coburg-Gotha to Windsor did not alter the principle, which is that the name of a dynasty is allied to the name of the husband and not the wife. There was a plethora of other royal dynasties whose names had changed when a queen regnant married; it then being standard practice for a wife to assume her husband's name, irrespective of his or her rank. One notable upgrade was when Grand Duchess Charlotte of Luxembourg, a mere Grand Ducal Highness, married His Royal Highness Prince Felix of Bourbon-Parma. Not only did the house of Nassau have Bourbon-Parma added to it, while retaining their ranks and styles as princes and princesses of Luxembourg and Nassau, but all their descendants became royal highnesses.

Upgrades also worked in reverse. A case in point was when Queen Maria II of Portugal married Prince Ferdinand of Saxe-Coburg- Gotha. In keeping with Portuguese custom, not only did he become a King by title when she produced the first of many heirs to the throne, but thereafter the house of Braganza became the house of Saxe-Coburg-Gotha as well.

Some dynasties, of course, retained their original name while incorporating that of the female monarch's spouse. This was a resourceful and elegant way of acknowledging both the past and the present. The most obvious precedent was the Austrian house of Hapsburg, following the marriage of the eighteenth century Hapsburg sovereign Maria Theresa to Francis, Duke of Lorraine. Thereafter, the Austrian royal house was known as Hapsburg-Lorraine, which it still is to this day.

The conflict over the name of the dynasty reigning in Britain in 1952 began simply enough. Dickie Mountbatten was 'thrilled beyond compare', to quote Barbara Cartland, that the royal house of the United Kingdom was now the house of Mountbatten. Never having been one to hide his light under a bushel, Dickie waxed enthusiastic on the subject at every turn. He made the mistake of doing so with such enthusiasm that word immediately got back to Lascelles, and through him, to the newly widowed Queen Elizabeth, both notoriously anti-Mountbatten.

The Duke of Brunswick also played his part. Two nights after Lilibet's accession, he was at dinner at the Mountbattens'. As he listened to Dickie brag about how the British ruling house was now Mountbatten, this royal descendant of George III, whose application to George VI for approval of the marriage of his son George William to Philip's widowed sister Sophie (Tiny) in 1946 had had to be ignored on governmental advice, owing to a state of war that still existed at the time he made the application in 1945, with the result that the fruit of that union would never be in line of succession to the British throne, Ernst August resolved to enlighten Queen Mary of Mountbatten's boast. Martin Charteris agreed in the 1990s that the Head of the House of Hanover might well have been motivated by envy, and knowingly fomented trouble. Had Britain abided by Salic Law the way Germany used to, Prince Ernst August of Hanover, Duke of Brunswick-Luneburg, not Lilibet, would have been sitting on the British throne. Proud of his daughter's accession to the Greek throne, he could never 'quite get over' the 'many reversals of fortune' his family had suffered. They had been stripped of their British dukedoms of Cumberland and Teviotdale, of the throne of Hanover, and here was that morganatic upstart Dickie Mountbatten crowing about the Mountbattens now being Britain's ruling dynasty. Queen Mary promptly contacted Jock Colville, who had left Lilibet's service to return as private secretary to Winston Churchill following his re-election as prime minister, to make him aware that the issue of the name of the dynasty had already arisen.

Each of the main protagonists, in what was effectively the conspiracy to prevent the dynasty from being known as the house of Mountbatten, had their own reasons for opposing a change in the name. Churchill 'deplored' Mountbatten for 'giving away' India and Pakistan in 1947. He strongly suspected Mountbatten of being 'pink' – a charge Mountbatten's daughter Patricia conceded was accurate – and was worried that the overbearing Dickie would try to influence his nephew politically. The Duke of Windsor confirmed that these suspicions were widespread, summarising the prevailing mood in palace circles by stating, 'All are suspicious & watching his influence on Philip.' Mountbatten himself would later state that 'Beaverbrook's hatred of me coupled with Winston's disenchantment with what I did in India' was in part responsible for the campaign that now took shape against the Mountbattens.

Elizabeth was also fearful of the influence Mountbatten might be allowed to yield, not through Philip, who she already knew kept a certain distance from his uncle, but through Lilibet. The better the new queen had got to know this uncle by marriage, the fonder she had grown of him. The time they had spent together in Malta had strengthened Lilibet's ties with the Mountbattens. Elizabeth was evidently fearful that the affection her compliant daughter felt for Dickie might result not only in Mountbatten's increased political influence, but also in a lessening of her own. Elizabeth was only too aware that, traditional and conservative though her daughter was, both her husband and his uncle were modernists who wanted to update the system. According to the Duke of Windsor, Elizabeth was 'pathologically jealous,' and painfully aware that her daughter shared many of the pink instincts which he, Mountbatten and Philip espoused, and which were antipathetic to her mother, her courtiers, and her prime minister.

Although Elizabeth had an even stronger motive than these already strong motives to join the *coterie* which was intent on using the name of the dynasty as a reason for blocking the Mountbattens – more of which later – she also saw how useful this issue could be, and made her antipathy to a name change known to both Lascelles and Churchill. It is interesting to note that it was at this time, rather than earlier, that she began referring to Philip as 'The Hun'. She would continue doing so for some time to come, and never missed an opportunity to snipe at the Germans, meaning Philip and his family, quite forgetting that her own husband was rather more German than Philip had ever been. Unless, of course, the Danes now qualified as German.

Of all the participants, Queen Mary's views were more layered than might first appear to be the case. Her strongest point, that her husband had changed the name in perpetuity in 1917, was legal nonsense. Just as how George V had had the right to change the name of the dynasty at his own discretion, so too did each successive monarch, his granddaughter Lilibet included. His rights in 1917 in no way superseded those of any of his successors, nor did those rights neutralise theirs, so to contend that the ruling of one monarch prevented another from exercising an equal right made no legal sense, even if George V's supposed intentions resonated with the other participants in the plot to disallow the name change. That spurious reason, however, was the straw that broke the camel's back and was trumpeted by all the other participants as the reason for the exclusion of the name Mountbatten and the retention of the name Windsor.

Getting behind Queen Mary's thinking was not difficult. She provided insight into what her real motives were when she stated that 'no Battenberg marriage,' no matter how lawful, could change the name that her husband had decreed for the royal house. In that one sneer, the dowager queen betrayed the prejudice for which she was well known in royal circles, and which seems to have been a strong motivating force for her blocking the Mountbatten name. This, it should also be noted, was a prejudice she shared with the Duke of Brunswick. Mountbatten, it must be remembered, was the anglicised version of Battenberg. The house of Battenberg was not a royal house, but what was then known as par-royal. Par-royal, like par-boiled, meant partly, not entirely, whether it be royal or cooked.

Queen Mary had a massive complex about being par-royal. Try as she had done to live down the ignominy being the product of a morganatic union had signified, this bugbear always hovered close to the surface where she was concerned. She never forgave any of the cousins of her youth who used to mock her, while they were all children sharing family holidays at places like Darmstadt, for her lack of royal status, and it was said within the royal families of Europe, that it was she who had encouraged King George V to rescind the invitation of refuge given by the British government to the Tsar and Tsarina in 1917, not out of fear of what the consequences would be for her husband's dynasty, but because she had always hated 'Alix' for needling her about not being properly royal during family holidays when they were both youngsters at Darmstadt.

Because Queen Mary's antecedents played such an important part in the naming of the new dynasty, it is worth seeing why she felt the way she did. Her mother had been properly royal. A granddaughter of King George III, who was also King of Hanover and Duke of Brunswick-Luneburg, Princess Mary Adelaide of Cambridge shared, with her cousin Victoria, the distinction of also a princess of Hanover and of Brunswick-Luneburg. Commonly known as 'Fat Mary' because of her immense girth, she had a reasonably pretty face, but she was so enormous that she was unmarriageable. That is, until she met Prince Francis of Teck, when she was already past thirty and regarded as permanently on the shelf. The pair hit it off and he proposed marriage. In the ordinary course of life, such a union would have been unthinkable. He had not even been a prince at birth, his title being granted three years before the marriage by his cousin the King of Wurttemberg in an attempt to make him more appealing on the marriage market. He had been born Count Francis von Hohenstein, the son of Duke Alexander of Wurttemberg, a second son of the second son of the Duke of Wurttemberg, and Countess Claudine Rhedey von Kis-Rhede, a minor aristocrat who was created Countess of Hohenstein in her own right by Emperor Ferdinand I of Austria, in keeping with the custom of foreign sovereigns endowing morganatic wives with titles in their own right, so that the products of such unions would have aristocratic titles. Queen Victoria was much more open-minded than her German counterparts, and, realising that this handsome but penniless princeling was her cousin's only hope of avoiding a lifetime of spinsterhood (then regarded as akin to living death), she allowed the marriage in 1866, even though she was only too aware that most of European royalty disapproved.

Five years into the marriage, which had resulted in the kingdom of Wurttemberg having some reflected glory through its connection with the British royal family, Prince Francis of Teck's cousin King Charles I of Wurttemberg, further elevated him, creating him Duke of Teck.

Four children were born to the couple, three sons and a daughter: Princess Victoria Mary the year after her parent's marriage – note the Victoria, in honour of Mary Adelaide's cousin the queen, though it was never used, May being the name by which she was known; followed by Prince Adolphus (1868-1927 - later Marquis of Cambridge); Prince Francis (1870-1910 – according to the actress Sarah Miles, he was the natural father of her grandfather Francis Remnant); and Prince Alexander (1874-1957 – later Earl of Athlone). All of them, their father included, were mere Serene Highnesses. Although Princess Mary Adelaide consistently applied to her first cousin to raise her husband to the rank of Royal Highness, it was not until 1887, to coincide with her Golden Jubilee, that Victoria elevated the Duke of Teck to the dignity of His Highness. She would never make him a Royal Highness.

The Tecks were a somewhat rackety and tremendously extravagant couple. They were resolutely minor members of the then-large British royal family. It was as if the duchess felt that she had to maintain the most sumptuous way of life to compensate for the lack of regal status her husband's inferior rank suggested. They entertained lavishly, dressed magnificently, and travelled luxuriously and frequently. Mary Adelaide had a state annuity of £5,000 (some £500,000 per annum today), but her mother, the widowed Duchess of Cambridge, nevertheless often had to bail them out at a time when debtors customarily went to prison. The doors of Marshalsea did not open for either of the Tecks, though they did suffer the ignominy of having to put up the most valuable effects of their grace-and-favour apartment at Kensington Palace, as well as those of White Lodge, their out-of-town grace-and-favour residence in Richmond, for auction in 1883. Afterwards, they left for the continent for two years to try to live down the disgrace and recover financially. There, they resorted to the then-common practice of travelling under incognitos. In Europe, Victoria often travelled as the Countess of Balmoral, but the Count and Countess of Hohenstein discarded this pretence when they realised that they got better service as HSH the Duke of Teck and HRH the Duchess of Teck.

Their financial misfortune was their daughter May's educational good fortune. The two years she spent living on the continent broadened her horizons in a way that nothing had done before. By the time the family returned to Britain in 1885, she was one of the most refined, well-educated and well-rounded princesses of her time. She was also pretty, amenable and level-headed. Above all, she was dutiful, with a reverence for the monarchy that few shared, not even in those days when monarchs were semi-deities.

Misfortune had a way of turning into May's good fortune. When Queen Victoria was thrashing around, trying to find a stable, sensible princess, who would make an ideal wife for her popular but wayward grandson Eddy, the eldest son of her eldest son and heir Bertie, Prince of Wales, her gaze settled on May.

May's character and good looks were the deciding factors. Prince Albert Victor, Duke of Clarence and Avondale would not only be king one day, but he was also another of the rackety characters who proliferated in the Hanoverian royal family. Like all of Victoria's uncles and many of her aunts, one of whom had even given birth to an illegitimate baby – and like his father the Prince of Wales, who had recently played a prominent role in the Tranby Croft Royal Baccarat Scandal, receiving wide publicity that made him unpopular for some time to come, to add to the many romantic entanglements he was always getting implicated in – Eddy had already been involved in several romantic scrapes. He has gone down in history as a possible Jack the Ripper, which is unfair, as he was in Scotland when some of the murders were committed and there is no evidence to link him to any of the deaths, nor any suggestion of his having ever been violent or knowledgeable about the medical procedures which Jack the Ripper used. But a grand name is often an irresistible spur to scandal, and this absence of evidence has not stood in the way of the sensationalist claims made against him.

Not that Eddy needed any fabrications to blacken his name. Queen Victoria would write to her daughter Vickie about his 'dissolute' lifestyle, but even when he was not being dissolute, he was careless and louche enough to become involved in scandals in which he played no real part. In 1889, for instance, his name was dragged into the Cleveland Street scandal, when the Police raided a homosexual brothel at that address and the pimps and rent boys yielded up the name of Lord Arthur Somerset, an extra Equerry to Eddy's father the Prince of Wales. Further investigations saw Eddy's name raised, and while there is little doubt that the 'ardently heterosexual' heir to the throne's name was raised to still further investigation (the ploy succeeded), the affair received wide publicity abroad, albeit not in the United Kingdom, with the *New York Times* ridiculing Eddy as a 'dullard' and a 'stupid, perverse boy' who should 'never be allowed to ascend the British throne.'

To add insult to injury, a year later Eddy fell in love with the Roman Catholic Princess Helene of Orleans, daughter of the Count of Paris, royalist Pretender to the French throne. The family was then living in exile in England.

At first, Queen Victoria opposed the match, for the Act of Succession specifically forbade an heir to the throne from marrying a Catholic, but when Eddy offered to relinquish his rights to the throne, and Helene agreed to make the sacrifice of joining the Church of England to spare his place in the succession, his grandmother, always a romantic, was moved to support the union. In the end, Helene's father refused to countenance the marriage, and when she appealed to the Pope, Clement XIII also refused to allow her to give up her religion, so the couple accepted defeat.

Seemingly incapable of keeping out of trouble, Eddy's next romantic foray ended when his inamorata, the Gaiety Theatre chorus girl Lydia Miller (stage name Lydia Manton) committed suicide by the grotesquely painful method of drinking carbolic acid. At the inquest, Lord Charles Montagu, as her nominal lover, gave evidence, but no one was fooled. The overseas press named Eddy as her real lover, stating that he had wanted her to give up the stage, while the London newspaper *The Star* was widely quoted by the regional press when it stated, 'It is a fact so well known that the blind denials of it given in some quarters are childishly futile. Lydia Manton was the *petite amie* of a certain young prince, and that, too, quite recently.' *The Manchester Courier and Lancashire General Advertiser* asserted, quite accurately, that the death was 'a scandal of the first magnitude,' and was 'on the lips of every clubman.'

Determined to rescue Eddy from further waywardness, Queen Victoria swung into action. She was filled with admiration for the way May had coped with her own parents' waywardness, and she orchestrated the match between her twenty-seven year old grandson and her equally wayward cousin's twenty-four year old daughter over the objections of his parents. Arthur Balfour (later 1st earl, foreign secretary and prime minister) wrote to Lord Salisbury in 1890 that the 'Teck girl they won't have because they hate Teck and because the vision of Princess Mary haunting Marlborough House makes the Prince of Wales ill.'

Queen Victoria was nothing if not determined, however. The better she got to know May, the more she appreciated what a gem the young woman would be as a queen consort. By this time, she was also relatively mature in marriageable terms. This was both a weakness and a strength which Victoria could, and did, exploit. The anomaly of her semi-royal status mattered not at all to the practical but romantic queen, whose main concern was that her grandson marry someone who would be a good influence upon him. Since May was both sensible and good looking, there was every reason for Eddy to be attracted to her both in and out of bed. Such things mattered to Victoria, and they plainly mattered to her grandson as well. He gradually became captivated by May, writing to tell Lady Sybil St. Clair Erskine that he was in love once again, and on 3rd December 1891, he proposed to May to her 'great surprise,' at Luton Hoo, then the Danish Ambassador's country residence but later the seat of Sir Harold and Lady Zia Wernher, where Philip would spend so many happy times with his Russian grand ducal cousins.

Queen Victoria was exultant. She wrote to her daughter Vickie, describing May in glowing terms as 'ideal – charming, sensible and pretty.' She immediately gave her consent to the union, despite her son Bertie and daughter-in-law Alexandra's reservations, and the wedding was set for 27th February 1892.

After a happy Christmas, while plans were being made for the wedding and for Eddy's appointment as Viceroy of Ireland, he fell ill. The influenza pandemic of 1889-1892 had the country in its grip, and Eddy became but one of the many casualties, dying of pneumonia on 14th January 1892, six days after his twenty eighth birthday. His whole family was disconsolate, but his grandmother kept her head. She recognised that May, who had been so eminently suitable for Eddy, would be just the consort needed by the new heir to the throne, his younger brother George. Georgie, as he was known in the family, had not been trained to be king. He was nowhere as intelligent or personable as his elder brother, of whom he wrote, 'how dearly I did love him; & I remember with pain nearly every hard word & little quarrel I ever had with him & I long to ask his forgiveness, but, alas, it is too late now.' Georgie would need a strong, intelligent, capable and obliging wife every bit as much as his more wayward brother had needed such a gem, albeit for different reasons. Where Eddy would have needed distracting and reining in, Georgie would need stimulating and bringing out. His childish handwriting demonstrated the extent to which he would need supplementing, and Victoria encouraged May and Georgie to comfort each other in their joint loss, in the hope that it would bring them together.

The system of monarchy meant that Georgie immediately filled the shoes vacated by Eddy. Whether he wanted to be or not, he was the new heir presumptive. As he took over his late brother's role, his grandmother made it plain that nothing would give her greater pleasure than seeing him fill Eddy's shoes in a personal sense as well. This was not as unthinkable to royalty in the nineteenth century as it might be to the average person in the twenty first. Georgie's Aunt Dagmar, sister of his mother Alexandra, Princess of Wales, had been engaged to the Tsarevitch Nicholas of Russia, but had married his younger brother Alexander following Nicholas's death. Suitable queens consort were entities to be relished, not commodities to be lightly discarded, and both Georgie and May were sufficiently dutiful to actually want to please the old queen. May also had got a glimpse of how differently people treated her once she had moved up the royal ladder, and she would not have been human had she not regretted the prospect of being relegated to the lower rungs once more. Switching allegiance from one royal brother to another was something she was willing to do, and not only because she was fulfilling all her ambitions in a worldly sense. She would after all one day occupy one of the greatest thrones on earth, and that, to someone as enchanted with monarchy as she was, was like being promised heaven on earth. She also was genuinely drawn to Georgie. Though duller than Eddy, he was more masculine, less effete, and there appears to have been a genuinely strong sexual attraction between them. This would be borne out by their practice, highly unusual in royal and aristocratic circles, of sharing a marital bed throughout their marriage.

Moreover, they were well suited, or, to be more accurate, May tailored her personality so that they appeared to be well suited. She suppressed a lot of the fire, imagination and interests she had, to create a snug fit with Georgie, who might have been decent, but was utterly unimaginative and every bit the dullard the New York Times had inaccurately described his more colourful brother as being.

May proved to be a good wife who prioritised the needs of her husband over those of her children. She was so in awe of being the wife of a future, then actual, king, that she allowed George, who was a tremendous bully with his children, an untrammelled reign of terror within the family circle. Although he could be an affectionate father when the mood took him, he was more frequently a martinet who proudly stated that he had been terrified of his father and he expected his children to be terrified of him. They were. David, the eldest, who became the revered Prince of Wales before progressing to King Edward VIII and Duke of Windsor, was an obedient child who finally got fed up with never being able to obtain his father's approval, and in adulthood became a rebel. He despised his father and, tellingly, never had one photograph or portrait of George V in his own houses, though his mother's proliferated everywhere. As the world now knows, Bertie was so scarred from his childhood that he was handicapped all his life with a severe stammer and stomach problems, all of which stemmed from nervousness. Mary, the sole daughter, was a sweet, plain woman who married the much older Earl of Harewood and embraced the pleasures of relative anonymity in Yorkshire, where she could escape from the crippling shyness which was a residue of her father's strictness. Her son George Harewood would later say that it was a tragedy that his mother's family was unable to unfold or express any human emotion: the ability had been beaten out of the children by their bullying father. Harry was fortunate in that he was a dimwit, but even his limited intelligence did not protect him against the scars of his childhood, and he never broke free of the mould, seeking refuge in the bottle. George, the brightest and most attractive of the children, even more so that the stylish and stunningly attractive David, became a bisexual drug addict before turning his life around with the help of David and his exotic and strong-minded wife Marina, with whom he shared as normal and happy a life as any child of George V could. The last son, John, was in some ways the most tragic, yet fortunate, of all the children, at least where discipline was concerned.

Prince John of Wales was born a normal baby, but by the age of four he was showing signs of being 'painfully slow'. He then had his first epileptic fit, and as he grew older, the fits became more frequent. He also displayed behavioural problems which suggest he suffered from the then unknown condition of autism. He was boisterous, unmanageable, and liable to say whatever popped into his head. The king once told the American president Theodore Roosevelt that 'all my children are obedient, except John.' He has often been portrayed as having been banished from the bosom of his family. In fact, he was an integral part of it until he turned eleven in 1916. He was then moved to Wood Farm with his nanny, Charlotte 'Lala' Bill. There, he had his own mini-establishment, with a full complement of staff to take care of all his needs. Since this is the same house that Prince Philip elected to move into in 2017 following his retirement, and which the Queen shares with him when they are together at Sandringham, and the Great War was at its height when John moved, it suggests that the choice was made on grounds of practicality and security, rather than as a form of banishment.

John's parents also had to consider the effect of his illness on the rest of the family. Lala wrote that they dared not 'let him be with his brothers and sister, because it upsets them so much, with his attacks getting so bad and coming so often.' A further indication of John's deterioration was that his tutors were disbanded, as he no longer had the ability to concentrate on his lessons. He was not, however, abandoned by his family, as later television programmes have suggested. His siblings and mother, and to a lesser extent his father (who was busy with the war) used to go to see him, and he was also on visiting terms with them when they were in residence on the estate. Moreover, Queen Mary deliberately contravened the code of conduct whereby royal children never mixed with anyone but their peers, and allowed John to play with such local children as Winifred Thomas and Leslie Seaward Heath. According to the British Epilepsy Association, 'There was nothing unusual in what King George V and Queen Mary did. At that time, people with epilepsy were put apart from the rest of the community'. John died at the age of thirteen, two months after the end of the Great War, in his sleep following a particularly bad seizure. In her diary, his mother wrote that the news was, 'a great shock, tho' for the little boy's restless soul, death came as a great relief. I broke the news to George and we motored down to Wood Farm. Found poor Lala very resigned but heartbroken. Little Johnnie looked very peaceful lying there.'

For all Queen Mary's insufficiencies as a mother, her children never doubted that she loved them. She simply loved the crown more. Yet, over the matter of the name of the dynasty, she broke faith with her own beliefs.

Mary had always been close to Lilibet. She had helped to shape and educate her granddaughter. She had influenced her and given her the level-headed perspective that countered Elizabeth's more sentimental, and in Mary's opinion, dangerous approach to the crown. Had she been consistent in her reasoning over the issue of the dynasty's name, Mary would have taken the view that Lilibet, as the sovereign, should be deferred to in much the same way that she had always deferred to George. However, for the first and last time in her life, she put her personal preferences before her obligations to the crown. The idea that the Battenbergs could become the dynasty of the British crown was intolerable to her, not when the Battenbergs were not even the morganatic branch of a kingdom such as the Tecks had been, but were the relicts of a mere grand duchy. She, who had suffered so much at the hands of the Hesse family, notwithstanding her father's uncle having been a king, simply could not countenance such a progression. 'What the devil does that damned fool Edinburgh think that the family name has to do with him,' she demanded, ignoring the fact that it had everything to do with him, and nothing to do with her any longer.

Churchill, who had exploded with a vengeance when the subject had first been broached with him, referred the matter to his cabinet, making his own views known. It was therefore hardly surprising when the cabinet recommended unequivocally that the dynasty retain the name of Windsor, and moreover suggested that the prime minister impart their advice to the new queen at the earliest opportunity.

Within days of ascending the throne, Lilibet therefore found herself caught up in the first crisis of her reign. Feeling obliged to listen to the advice of her prime minister and his government, she found herself torn between the crown and her husband, who was adamant that the name of the dynasty should include his own. Paradoxically, however, he did not want it changed to Mountbatten. He wanted the altogether more accommodating and, in fact politically clever, Windsor and Edinburgh. This would have spelt out the links between Scotland and England in a way that reflected the Scottish origins of the royal family, while also acknowledging his children's paternity.

However, the government of the day was determined to stymie Philip and, through him, his uncle Dickie. Harold Macmillan is on record as stating that he thought it 'a very good thing that the influence of the Consort and his family have had an early rebuff.'

Common usage and justice had nothing to do with the decision, nor did consideration of the problems the decision would cause within the marriage. In fact, one of the reasons why the politicians and courtiers were so eager to pursue the matter to the conclusion they sought was to create problems within the marriage. By driving a wedge between husband and wife, they would be lessening the influence of the Mountbattens. An isolated queen, shorn of the support of her ultra-masculine and socialistic husband, would be more amenable to their prompting.

Sir Martin Gilliatt, Queen Elizabeth the Queen Mother's Private Secretary, asserted that 'the manoeuvring of a few well-placed courtiers and members of the government, who were jockeying for positions of influence over the new monarch,' placed Lilibet and Philip's marriage under great strain as soon as she succeeded to the throne. Mike Parker stated that Philip was 'deeply wounded,' and Colin Glenconner would later agree, saying that the issue of the name caused problems within the marriage. Even Patricia Mountbatten stated that Prince Philip was furious as well as hurt, and that it took him a long time to recover. She also said that she believed that the outcome would have been different had Lilibet been ten years older: 'She would have told them to stop being so silly, and that would've been the end of the matter.' Philip himself was quoted as saying, 'I'm just a bloody amoeba, that's all,' though he also stated privately,' All they wanted was my sperm. I'm nothing but a fucking sperm factory to them.'

On 9th April, the *London Gazette* announced, 'Today the Queen declared in Council Her Will and Pleasure that She and Her Children shall be styled and known as the House and Family of Windsor, and that Her descendants other than female descendants who marry, and their descendants, shall bear the name Windsor.'

What is interesting to note is that the advice from the government would most likely have been very different had the Labour politician Clement Attlee still been prime minister. Unlike Churchill, who was anti all things Mountbatten, Attlee had no prejudices against Mountbatten, whose political viewpoint accorded more closely with his own.

By cynically manipulating the marriage onto shakier ground that it had been on at the start of the saga, the powers-that-be ensured that they would retain their influence over the sovereign. Queen Elizabeth The Queen Mother's official biographer, William Shawcross, asserted in his official biography, 'The Private Secretary, the Lord Chamberlain, the Keeper of the Privy Purse, the Master of the Horse, the Surveyor of the Queen's Pictures – all of these and many more wanted to serve their new monarch and wanted her to see them do so. They wanted access to the Queen, not to her husband.' They also wanted the new monarch to continue in the same vein as her predecessor. This, however, would not be possible unless they created a breach between husband and wife. They did create difficulties, but not to the extent that they had intended, for they did not create quite as severe a rupture as they intended. Although it was most, 'decidedly an issue,' as Colin Glenconner confirmed, and though it did, 'create problems between them,' even at the worst of times Philip and Lilibet's marriage remained on a, 'solid if less untroubled footing.'

That is not to minimise the first trauma of their marriage. Philip was deeply hurt and remained so for the remainder of the decade. He, 'kept the issue alive,' and articulated his displeasure in no, 'uncertain terms on many an occasion,' about, 'feeling let down by his wife'.

For her part, Lilibet, 'could not help but be torn,' caught as she was between her duty as a wife and as a constitutional monarch. 'What made it worse for her was that she herself felt she had failed her husband. Given the choice, she would have opted for his option. But both she and the Duke of Edinburgh understood that she had really had no choice. She simply could not have ignored the advice of her prime minister and his cabinet within days of succeeding to the throne. That (reason) helped a bit. But only a bit. Undeniably, the name thing remained a real issue,' according to Colin Glenconner.

At the time that this problem arose, Lilibet was deeply in love with her husband, and as happily married to him as any woman can be. She reeled from the shock of her marriage being compromised the way it had been, according to Colin Glenconner. This personal destabilisation took place at the same time that she was having to adjust to her new and demanding role as monarch. This entailed the impersonal, as well as now personal, conflicts inevitable when an heir to a throne accedes, and made the transition far more difficult than it would otherwise have been.

What Lilibet did not yet realise was that her mother, whom she loved and trusted, was taking full advantage of the conflict to retain as much power and influence for herself as she could engineer. Elizabeth was not motivated by malice. She simply wanted to avoid the diminution necessitated by her role changing from queen consort to dowager queen. Between 1936 and 1952, Elizabeth had actually been the *de facto* monarch in everything but name. She loved power and was superb at wielding it. This was well known in political circles, hence Beaverbrook's antipathy towards her and Hitler's comment about her being the most dangerous woman in Europe. Even Lascelles, who was a great admirer of hers, felt compelled to complain to his diary about the control she exerted over the king, 'who could never tell,' him, 'what he thought about anything until after he had consulted,' Elizabeth.

Prior to George VI's death, all dowager queens had stepped back from the central role of consort as soon as they were widowed. It was an accepted feature of royal life. Queen Mary had done it; Queen Alexandra before her; Queen Adelaide before her, and so on, back into the sands of time. Elizabeth, however, was determined that she would be the first, and possibly the only, dowager queen in Britain who would continue to maintain a high and visible profile, retaining as central a role as she could create for herself. For that, she needed Winston Churchill's assistance as well as Lascelles'. The Duke of Windsor used to say that Elizabeth was an extremely skilled game player. She now proved right both her admirers and detractors, who were in accord about her effectiveness as she exploited the conflict surrounding her daughter to her own advantage.

Three days after Bertie's funeral, Elizabeth made the first of many skilful moves to avoid relegation to the royal shadows. Through Tommy Lascelles, who remained the monarch's private secretary despite the change of sovereign, and who was also an old and trusted friend as well as ally of hers, she issued a statement which was masterful in laying the ground for keeping herself in the limelight. 'I want to send this message of thanks to a great multitude of people – to you who, from all parts of the world, have been giving me your affection and sympathy throughout these dark days. I want you to know how your concern for me has upheld me in my sorrow, and how proud you have made me by your wonderful tributes to my dear husband, a great and noble King.

'No man had a deeper sense than he of duty and of service, and no one was more full of compassion for his fellow men. He loved you all, every one of you, most truly. That, you know, was what he always tried to tell you in his yearly message at Christmas; that was the pledge he took at the most sacred moment at his Coronation fifteen years ago.

'Now I am left alone, to do what I can to honour that pledge without him. Throughout our married life we have tried, the King and I, to fulfil with all our hearts and all our strength the great task of service that was laid upon us. My own wish is that I may be allowed to continue the work we sought to do together.'

The Duke of Windsor said that as soon as he saw Elizabeth's message, he knew that she would do everything she could to remain centre stage. There might be one monarch, but there would now be two consorts. Elizabeth, he believed, would capitalise upon the trust her daughter had in her, and the distrust that had been created surrounding Philip, to 'advise' and 'steer' her daughter in the 'path' and 'ways' of the monarchy that were so precious to her and the senior courtiers, but so antipathetic to Philip.

The message also revealed how completely the constitutional boundaries had become blurred during the previous reign. It was as frank an admission as any consort had ever made, that she, with her husband's assent, had failed to differentiate between his role as sovereign and hers as consort. It showed how they had both consolidated their roles, with her absorbing his kingliness and incorporating it into her apolitical role as consort. Now she was making a play to continue doing so even after his death on the spurious grounds that his coronation pledge extended to her. However, the pledge had been his, and his alone. His pledge had died with him. She had not shared it in life, nor could she do so in death. And the influence of consort was meant to die with the monarch, hence why dowagers took a back seat.

The Duke of Windsor believed that the 'ambitious' Elizabeth intended to make a 'stab' at 'grabbing as many of the goodies for herself' as she could, and in so doing was failing to respect her daughter's rights as monarch, as well as those of her son-in-law as consort. After all, if Philip, the true consort, could have his wings clipped before he had even had a chance to lay down his marker, surely Elizabeth's should be prevented from soaring over territory to which she no longer had a right. Did not logic dictate that the rules of conduct applied equally to all consorts? If they could be applied to limit the role of the present consort, surely those limitations should also be applied equally to the role of the previous one? All the high-sounding talk about principles, precedent, tradition, and ethics were really only so much cant, a cover with which to effect what the Duke of Windsor viewed as a power grab.

The week after George VI's funeral at St. George's Chapel, Windsor Castle, on 15th February 1952, Elizabeth made another move. She informed Lascelles that she wished to continue to act as a Counsellor of State.

'Naturally I would like this, as it would give me an interest, & having been one, it seems so dull to be relegated to the "no earthly use" class.' Under the Regency Act of 1937 (amended 1943), her right to be a Counsellor of State had been vested in her role as queen consort. It had died with her husband.

Together with the four most senior adult heirs-in-line to the throne, Philip, as sovereign's consort and parent of the immediate heir to the throne and the heiress presumptive after him, now possessed the right that Elizabeth no longer had. If she remained a Councillor of State, it meant that she did have a say politically. Every time Lilibet was out of the country, or sick, or if she became incapacitated, Elizabeth would be one of the Counsellors of State who acted in her stead. By remaining a Counsellor of State, Elizabeth would therefore not only retain a degree of power to which she was no longer entitled, but she would also be acknowledged by her daughter to possess a degree of influence and power which she would retain in the event of her daughter's absence or incapacitation. And should Lilibet die, and Charles succeed to the throne while a minor, Elizabeth could very well end up wielding as much power as, if not more than, she had exercised while Bertie was king.

My father-in-law, the Hereditary Master of the Queen's Household in Scotland, was only one of many well-placed personages who were nobbled with alarmist stories about how regrettably necessary it was to build up Elizabeth as a counter-weight to the dangers posed by Philip and his uncle Dickie. According to his daughter Lady Jean Campbell, her grandfather Lord Beaverbrook felt that there were sufficient parallels between the position the new monarch found herself in, and the position Edward VIII had been in during his reign, for the situation to be potentially dangerous for Queen Elizabeth II. He also felt that both the new queen and her husband, and indeed Mountbatten as well, were sufficiently naïve not to appreciate the games that were really being played. No one will ever know to what extent that analysis was accurate, but what is evident is that Lilibet, Philip and indeed Dickie, had the good sense to save the fight for another day. Whether intentionally or unintentionally, this was a shrewd move, and one which would preserve their positions from the dangers to which Beaverbrook saw them exposed. None of them objected to the Regency Act being amended in 1953 so that Elizabeth became a Counsellor of State along with Philip, who would act as Regent in the event that Lilibet died. Of course, the Queen always travelled with the Duke of Edinburgh, so the likelihood of both of them perishing in an accident at the same time rendered it likely that the regent would not be Philip, but even if he should become the regent, Elizabeth would remain a Counsellor of State until Charles's majority.

Elizabeth's next move was to involve Churchill in recommending that her role of dowager queen be expanded so that she could continue performing a full schedule of public duties, as if she were still a consort. After the recommendation had been made, at the end of her period of mourning, Queen Elizabeth the Queen Mother duly returned to public life. There she successfully flourished as the nation's favourite granny, in all but name the second consort in the land. It is to Philip's credit that, rather than clip his mother-in-law's wings, he accepted the situation and simply worked his way around her the way he did around Bobo.

In the interim, Elizabeth showed how resourceful she was at playing both sides off against the centre. As soon as a monarch dies, the coronation of the new monarch becomes one of the first objectives of the new reign. All state ceremonial occasions are organised by the Earl Marshal, a hereditary office in the possession of the Dukes of Norfolk since 1672. The 16th duke, Bernard Marmaduke Fitzalan-Howard, was a man who did not mince his words and had great organisational abilities. He had organised the coronation of George VI as well as his state funeral, both of which had gone off seamlessly. He was equally determined that Lilibet's coronation would run like clockwork. He determined when the crown would be placed on the young queen's head to within a few seconds, and when the bishops were proving to be unacceptably ill-disciplined during a rehearsal, he remonstrated with them, pointing out that they would be here all night if they didn't improve their performance.

Knowing that whoever chaired the coronation committee would have their power limited by the presence of Bernard Norfolk, Elizabeth shrewdly suggested to her daughter that she appoint Philip to chair it. Norfolk would be the Vice-Chairman. As she explained, Philip was not the sort of person who could be left idle; he would become impossible. This was a shrewd way of distracting him, of making him feel that he was involved, while in fact restricting his scope for action. Of course, Philip himself would not realise that he was being offered a sop, for he had no means of knowing how unlikely it was that he would be able to influence the process. If Elizabeth expected Philip's appointment as Chairman of the Coronation Committee to be nothing but an empty distraction, she had reckoned without her son-in-law's ability to encourage and persuade. Moreover, the appointment publicly boosted Philip's already considerable popularity, the public viewing it as a testament of faith by the new monarch in her young husband.

Lilibet also took another important step to counter the denigration of her husband by the cabal of traditionalists. On 30th September 1952, the *London Gazette* announced an Order she had made:

# Chapter VI

'The Queen has been graciously pleased by warrant bearing the 18th instant to declare and ordain that His Royal Highness Philip, Duke of Edinburgh.....shall henceforth upon all occasions.....except where otherwise provided by Act of Parliament have, hold and enjoy Place, Pre-eminence and Precedence next to her Majesty.'

If Lilibet hoped that this would prevent Lascelles and the other intriguers from further antics, she would be disappointed. A few weeks later, her first State Opening of Parliament was blighted by yet another petty and unnecessary slight. This time they removed the consort's throne from beneath the canopy where it ordinarily reposed beside the sovereign's throne, replacing it beyond the canopy with a mere chair. In so doing, they were reminding not only the consort but also the queen, and the whole governing body of the nation as well as the nation itself, that Philip did not enjoy any official standing despite being the consort. The message was loud and clear.

Philip was reputedly and justifiably infuriated by this latest and unjust humiliation, and not only for himself, but also for Lilibet. She was equally upset, though less expressively so. Both of them could see that these potshots reflected adversely on the two of them. The dilemma, however, was whether it would be possible to bring such behaviour to a quick halt. The answer, disappointingly, was no. Partly, this was because Elizabeth and Lascelles were functioning as a unit. Quite when Lilibet and Philip realised what was going on is not something anyone can any longer determine with accuracy, but Princess Margaret would later tell friends that they gradually became aware that her mother had been 'up to her tricks' with Lascelles. While the Mountbatten family was more circumspect in their comments, and failed to link Elizabeth with Lascelles, they are on record attesting to how 'monstrous' Lascelles was to Philip, and how it was 'one thing after another'. This meant that there was precious little Lilibet and Philip could do to neutralise Elizabeth as long as Lascelles was private secretary. And he would remain in his post until the coronation, which was scheduled for Tuesday, 2nd June 1953. The date was chosen by the weather forecasters in the belief that it was the most likely day of the year to be warm and sunny.

The young couple's positions were delicate where Elizabeth was concerned. Lilibet loved her mother and did not wish to have a rift with her. Nor did she wish to marginalise her. Meanwhile, Philip made no attempt to undermine his mother-in-law's position, which was due to undergo a massive increase in stature as soon as she came out of mourning. Churchill had already been nobbling Lilibet on Elizabeth's behalf, and, being a good and dutiful daughter who wanted to give her mother the purpose in life she claimed she needed if her continued existence were to have meaning, Lilibet and Churchill had already agreed that Elizabeth could re-emerge with a fuller agenda than any dowager queen had hitherto enjoyed.

The complications inherent in such a conflicted predicament were obvious. It is to Philip's credit as well as to Lilibet's, that they both displayed a degree of understanding of and acceptance for Elizabeth's needs. This showed how mature they were despite their relative youthfulness. Their attitude said much about the young couple's spiritually enlightened approach to the needs of loved ones. There can be few men in their early thirties who would have taken such a benevolent view of a mischievous mother-in-law, but if there was one lesson the young Prince Philip of Greece had learnt, it was that love involves sacrifice. The lessons of his youth had taught him that life is not perfect. You have to accept inconvenience and try to work around it if you are going to be a truly decent person. Life is not always easy, nor is doing the right thing, irrespective of the baser instincts to which emotions make all of us prey. Truly moral individuals do the right thing, then find ways of minimising the inconvenience. They do not duck and avoid the hard options, because it is the very embracing of the hard option that shows that they put their principles before their comfort. This is how principled people behave. This is what inspires trust in others, and demonstrates, throughout a lifetime of small and large choices, whether you are someone of principle or not. This is what forges truly unbreakable bonds between a likeminded husband and wife, hence the great trust and respect Lilibet and Philip now have for each other.

As 1952 gave way to 1953, Philip and Lilibet dedicated themselves to preparing for the coming coronation, having resigned themselves to coping with the realities of their new existences. As mentioned, the date for this most sacred of royal ceremonies had been chosen because the weather forecasters believed it to have the best chance of being a dry and sunny day. Though the government struggled to find the £3 million needed to celebrate the event, the nation itself was vociferous in its enthusiasm. Philip's friends in the press had also gone to work to counteract some of the behind-the-scenes denigration by boosting his profile publicly. This was as easily done as said, because Philip himself was so personable. He was refreshingly unpretentious to meet. He treated everyone as an individual, a tactic which might have caused raised eyebrows at the palace but went down very well with the average Briton.

Knowing about the backroom antics of some of the courtiers through such well-placed informants as Tom Driberg, the left-leaning *Daily Mirror* ran a poll asking whether Philip should be at his wife's side at the coronation. Of the forty-something thousand people polled, a hundred to one were in favour.

The *Sunday Dispatch* also sang Philip's praises, asserting that though he was at the beginning of his career as consort, he had as much 'prestige (apart from his great popularity)' as the revered Prince Albert the Prince Consort had had, 'at the end of his life.' They attributed his success to being 'a man of character and ability, proven in war and in peace'. Even Lord Beaverbrook came to the conclusion that Philip was something of a good egg, 'infinitely preferable' to his uncle Dickie, whom, of course, Beaverbrook loathed.

The one sadness came on 24th March 1953, when Queen Mary died at the age of eighty five. She had been failing gradually for some time, so much so that her son David (the Duke of Windsor) and daughter Mary were able to sail, upon the advice of her doctors, on the *Queen Elizabeth* from New York, arriving on 11th March. Like her husband and many of her sons, Mary had been a heavy smoker, but old age rather than pulmonary disease was responsible for her demise. She left instructions that, should she die before the coronation, her death must not be allowed to interfere with it. Her wishes were respected. She lay in state at Westminster Hall, where a vast multitude of public mourners queued for hours to pay their respects, and was buried beside her husband in the nave of St. George's Chapel, Windsor. Lilibet, who loved her grandmother, felt the loss acutely, but Princess Margaret, who always felt that Queen Mary had no time for her because she was never going to be queen, evinced indifference. The Duke of Windsor came over for the funeral, but was not among the twenty-eight royal guests for dinner at Windsor Castle after the funeral. Chips Channon wrote that a 'wave of emotion has swept over the land, and there has not been a word of criticism of the grand old lady.' He found her to have been 'magnificent, humorous, worldly, in fact nearly sublime, though cold and hard. But what a grand Queen.'

Once Queen Mary was buried, 'Coronation Thrombosis', as Chips Channon described the public obsession with the coming event, returned with a vengeance. So too did Lascelles' vituperation. When the issue of Lilibet's entry into the abbey arose, he insisted that she must proceed on her own. Philip must not be permitted to accompany her. Martin Charteris stated, 'That was very much the advice of Tommy Lascelles. It looked *awful*.' He also thought, 'it was not calculated to make him feel cheerful,' and was indeed calculated to make him look awful. While Lascelles schemed behind the scenes to denigrate Philip, the public remained blissfully unaware of the machinations, or of the stresses and strains which the scheming was having on the couple and their marriage. Philip himself has said that the adulation both he and Lilibet received was so extraordinary that they had to take the decision to keep it in its proper place by not focussing too firmly upon it, lest it turn their heads. Seating for millions of viewers was erected on the eight mile route the procession would take. At Westminster Abbey, where every monarch since William the Conqueror has been crowned (with the exception of the boy-king Edward V, who was killed in the Tower of London, and Edward VIII, who abdicated before his coronation), seating was erected for eight thousand where normally only two thousand can be accommodated. On the day itself, two million braved the rain that, of course, poured down, contrary to the forecasters' predictions. Many had spent the night before camped out on the scheduled route, impervious to the weather. When the day itself dawned grey and chilly, the crowds did not allow the typical London summer's day, with drizzle giving way to heavier showers, to ruin the joyousness of the occasion. The immense Queen Sālote of Tonga proved a particular favourite with them as she sat in her open carriage, undeterred by the weather. Philip's sisters and their husbands were in attendance this time, and while they sat behind the British royal family in the royal box, and actually formed an integral part of the procession into the abbey, they did not take part in the carriage procession, but made their way by car. Alice was particularly impressive, garbed in a spanking new grey habit, akin to the habits worn by her nursing sisters, now that she headed up the order of nuns she had finally managed to get off the ground in Athens. According to Colville: 'Never has there been such excitement. Never has a monarch received such adulation.'

Coronation day would emerge as the perfect coming-together of hope, expectation, national pride, and jubilation. That morning's papers had been full of the news of Britain's conquest of Mount Everest. Edmund Hillary, the New Zealand-born mountaineer, had climbed to the top of the world's highest mountain with his Nepalese Sherpa, TenzingNorgay, and though in years to come people would make the distinction between his land of origin and Britain, pointing out that Hillary and Tenzing's accomplishment had nothing whatever to do with Britain, in 1953 the perceptions were different. Hillary, by virtue of being a New Zealander, was as British as anyone born in Yorkshire or Sussex, and the country went wild with joy, viewing the accomplishment as being a further harbinger of a second Elizabethan Age which, it was hoped, would be as glorious as the first one had been.

In reality, Elizabeth II would be called upon to oversee an age that was every bit as mixed and progressive as Elizabeth I's had been. There would, however, prove to be important differences. Elizabeth II would reign over a country whose wealth and power diminished as its people enjoyed a standard of living infinitely better than anything known throughout their history. Her predecessor had reigned over a country whose power and riches increased without improving the standard of living of the masses. In its own way, the Second Elizabethan Age would therefore prove to be every bit as glorious as the first, albeit for different reasons. And both Lilibet and Philip would play integral parts in bringing this new age to fruition.

Thanks also to Philip's input, the largest television audience up to that point in time was able to see the ceremony in all its magnificence. He had been in favour of televising the event from the outset, and he fought off all resistance, seeing, quite rightly, that the event was one of national as well as international significance. The monarchy could not be fairly judged to be relevant to the tens and hundreds of millions of people all over Britain and its Empire and Commonwealth, unless they were given a chance to partake in it. The result was that all over the world, those who could, saw it on television, and those who could not, were afforded the opportunity of hearing it instead broadcast over the radio. It is now accepted that this one event, more than any other, boosted television in the United Kingdom in a way that nothing had before, or has since. It also boosted the monarchy.

# Chapter VII

IF LILIBET AND PHILIP were mindful of the limitations placed upon the monarch's power, they were also acutely aware of the considerable responsibilities that went along with the crown. While some of these were political, others were not. She was now the titular owner of a vast portfolio of property, for which she was ultimately responsible. If she failed to execute her obligations adequately, she would endanger her position as monarch. This portfolio included Buckingham Palace, Kensington Palace, Hampton Court Palace, Windsor Castle, Holyroodhouse Palace in Scotland, the duchies of Lancaster and Cornwall as well as the Crown Estate, with its 1,900,000 acres of land and significant real estate holdings in places such as central London. Personally, she now also owned the Balmoral and Sandringham Estates, and these too would have to be administered.

Philip had already been recognised by his naval superiors as having superb administrative skills. These dovetailed perfectly with Lilibet's personal vision of matrimony, in which the man took charge as the head of the family. As she and Philip were still very much a family unit, even if one that was under siege, as soon as she succeeded to the throne, Lilibet put Philip in charge of a range of the properties. He was appointed Ranger of Windsor Great Park, a position he still holds, and became responsible for overhauling the way the palaces, Buckingham Palace in particular, were run.

Executing the brief with his usual aptitude and enthusiasm, Philip undertook a detailed examination of Buckingham Palace. No member of the family appears to have ever before inspected all, or indeed most, of the hundreds of rooms, but Philip did. In doing so, he discovered that some of the palace was dilapidated, while there were unthought of treasures which everyone had forgotten about. He also discovered that there was tremendous waste in the way the place was run. The antiquated system, which had been in place for centuries, had come about when *noblesse oblige* was the order of the day and a plethora of people was employed to little or no useful purpose save to provide work for the needy. Although such social considerations were no longer required, the system remained intact. For instance, if the royal family or the ladies and gentlemen of the Household wanted some mundane item, the Page of the This was required to fetch it and hand it over to the Page of the That for the Page of the Other, who would take it next door to the Page of the Yet-Something-Else for onward transmission to yet another two or three pages before it could be delivered to the interested party. Sometimes six or eight people were called upon to fulfil the simplest of tasks. As all the workers were fed at the palace, this meant that the wages bill was not only far in excess of what it should have been, but so too was the food bill. This drove up costs exponentially, for staff had to be hired to feed and serve the excess of staff already employed. Edward VIII, of course, had tried to update the very same system in 1936, and had fallen foul of Elizabeth, Lascelles, and a host of critics who were eager to use whatever they could to denigrate his every attempt at modernization, with the objective of creating the very atmosphere of opposition which had driven him off the throne. Now Lilibet was on the throne, and there was every reason to keep her on the throne, but money needed to be saved, so her mother and private secretary did a volte face and willingly accepted the necessity of the money-saving improvements. Moreover, they had a useful tool to use against Philip should they ever need to. If it suited them sometime in the future, they could always criticize his cost-cutting initiatives in the way they had done with Edward VIII. Fortunately for Philip, this eventuality never arose.

Lilibet and Philip hoped that a semblance of manageability would return to their way of life once the coronation was over. Notwithstanding the great success the event itself was, it became the forum for a wholly unexpected constitutional crisis when Princess Margaret flicked a bit of fluff off the uniform of the tall, devastatingly handsome Comptroller of her mother's Household, Group Captain Peter Townsend (1914-1995). An eagle-eyed photographer recorded her doing so, and the profound intimacy of the action declaimed the nature of the relationship between the twenty-two year old princess and the thirty-eight year old divorce. Within days, the royal family found itself embroiled in a worldwide media sensation, with newspapers everywhere openly speculating upon the nature of the relationship and asking whether the princess should be allowed to marry her divorced swain.

The romance was the big news story of the time. It had only been sixteen years since Margaret's uncle Edward VIII had been forced off the throne because of his love of a divorcee. Would history repeat itself? Would Princess Margaret be forced by a hard-hearted Establishment to relinquish her right to love, or would she be allowed to marry the man of her dreams? What made the story so appealing was that Margaret was a beautiful young woman while Townsend was a handsome war hero. Moreover, he had been the innocent party in a divorce from his wife Rosemary the year before. She had gone on to marry the famous portrait painter Sir Philip de Lazlo's son John, and there was tremendous public support for the marriage.

In fact, the newspapers were simply catching up with the back story. Mark Sykes, a grandson of Sir Mark Sykes, Bt, of Sykes-Picot fame, provided me with background information that has hitherto never been revealed. 'My mother had a very close relationship with King George VI. She used to dine frequently at Buckingham Palace *à deux* with the king. What the public did not know was that the Townsends were having relationships with both father and daughter at the same time – George VI with Rosemary Townsend, Princess Margaret with Peter Townsend. Queen Elizabeth liked Peter and neither George VI nor Queen Elizabeth could ever deny Princess Margaret anything. The relationship between Margaret and Townsend was already well underway by the time the family returned from that South African trip. Everyone knew about it. It was an open secret.' There is a famous photograph, which supports Mark Sykes's contention, of King George VI looking down benevolently and smiling approvingly on Margaret as she adoringly watches her beloved sleeping on a picnic blanket. Colin Glenconner also told me that both George VI and Elizabeth 'had known about the romance for some time.'

The question of whether George VI would have allowed the marriage between his adored younger daughter and favoured equerry is one that is often asked, but seldom answered. Colin Glenconner told me that Princess Margaret used to say, 'Papa viewed Peter as the son he had never had,' and she herself told him, 'Papa would have arranged things so we could have married, had he lived.' She believed at worst she would have had to wait until she was twenty-five, the age at which she no longer needed the sovereign's consent under the Royal Marriages Act of 1772 once she had served notice of her intention to marry.

The death of George VI derailed Margaret's life entirely. Not only had she worshipped her father, as he had worshipped her, but she took his death, which was completely unexpected as far as she was concerned, harder than either her mother or her sister. Her marital prospects were affected, as were her financial. Because George VI himself had not expected to die, he had made none of the provisions previous kings had made for their children. Margaret was left, in royal terms, penniless. Unusually for the child of a king, she would never own her own country house. Even George V's spinster sister Princess Victoria had owned her own house, Coppins, which she left to her nephew Prince George, Duke of Kent, when she died in 1935. But Margaret was left so badly off that she could not even afford to buy one of her own, and, most tellingly, her mother, who could easily have afforded to buy one for her, never did.

By Margaret's own admission, she would have unravelled when her father died, had it not been for Peter Townsend. Elizabeth also found Peter a congenial presence. Although he was not a particularly capable courtier – Sir Martin Gilliatt found him incompetent, and his reputation for affability did not extend to capability – his personability was such a feature of life at Court that he became almost as indispensable to Elizabeth as to Margaret. This meant that when Elizabeth came to set up her widow's household at Clarence House, she looked no further than her late husband's personable equerry and promoted Townsend to Comptroller of her Household, notwith-standing his divorced status.

This, more than anything, demonstrated the exceptional place he had in her life. Ever since the Abdication, Elizabeth had espoused the highest moral standards where divorce was concerned. Divorce(e)s were invariably *persona non grata* – unless, of course, she wished them to be *grata*, in which case she overlooked their divorced status. Lilibet, Philip and Margaret had formed a trio during the years of their courtship, and now Peter, Margaret and Elizabeth formed another one, sharing happy lunches, teas, suppers, dinners, weekends, and picnics *à trois*. They lived in ostensible harmony, but, as Colin Glenconner would later observe, the agreeable atmosphere concealed fissures which would surface once news of the Townsend/Margaret romance got out.

By the time Townsend obtained his divorce from Rosemary in November 1952, on the grounds of her adultery with John de Laszlo, whom she would then marry and have two further children with, Lilibet and Philip knew of Margaret's desire to marry. There is corroboration of this fact in the archives, because Townsend went to see Lascelles as soon as he was divorced and informed him that he and Princess Margaret wished to marry. Lascelles asked him who else knew of their intentions. He replied, 'only the Queen and Prince Philip.' The private secretary suggested he also inform Elizabeth as soon as possible, and later stated that they did not do so until February 1953.

This claim of Lascelles was one of the many details which alerted Margaret to the fact that her mother, whom she thought was neither encouraging nor discouraging the union, was playing a double game, for both Elizabeth and George VI had known of the lovers' intentions from before his death. Elizabeth had never once actively opposed the union, though it has to be said that she had never once espoused it either. She had, up to that point, been resolutely sympathetic and understanding, encouraging almost in terms of the personal difficulties faced by her daughter and favoured courtier, without actually coming out one way or another for or against the marriage. This led both Margaret and Townsend to conclude that they had her support. They also appreciated the delicacy of her position. She could hardly be called upon to actively campaign for the marriage of her daughter to a divorced man when she had fought so hard to prevent the marriage of Edward VIII and Wallis Simpson.

Elizabeth's anodyne exterior, however, concealed rather more than benevolence, as Margaret would subsequently discover. Unfortunately for the wellbeing of all concerned, as Margaret learnt more and more about Elizabeth's double dealing, Philip and Lilibet also got sucked into the maelstrom. The outcome would impact adversely not only upon the tenor of their marriage, and damage the sisters' relationship, but would have such a devastating effect upon Lilibet that she would have to seek psychiatric help to cope.

Lascelles believed that, once Margaret had discussed her proposed marriage with her mother in February 1953, Elizabeth had discussed the matter with Lilibet. Little realizing that this version of the facts was fabricated by Elizabeth to create an opening enabling him to intervene in his capacity of private secretary, and thereby making a constitutional issue out of what had hitherto been a purely private matter, he wrote to her asking if as the 'Queen, Head of Church & State, & high priestess, so to speak, of the ideal of family life – whether she should or should not be advised to allow her sister to marry a divorced man in a registry office.' He also stated that the question of Margaret's marriage was, 'after all (and especially since 1936) fundamentally a State matter,' which was the line both he and Elizabeth had taken at the time of the Abdication Crisis. This, however, was not a line Margaret, Lilibet, Philip or George VI had taken.

Elizabeth responded to Lascelles on 12th June 1953. 'I would like to talk to you, soon please. I have nobody I can talk to about such dreadful things.'

Not surprisingly, Margaret was outraged when she discovered that her mother, who was pretending to her and Townsend that she possessed 'characteristic understanding', and was 'never anything but considerate in her attitude' to them, was now going behind their backs and telling Lascelles that she was 'quite shattered by the whole thing.' Margaret told Colin Glenconner that that was when she realized that her mother was an 'arch hypocrite.' She believed that Elizabeth could easily, and should willingly, have supported her union, or remained above the fray, a posture she had been careful to assume with Margaret and Townsend. However, by acting as she did, she was conveying the message to Lascelles that she was against the marriage, and thereby giving him tacit permission, indeed encouragement, to oppose it.

This Lascelles now did. Having decided that the marriage was an affair of state, in his capacity of private secretary to the monarch, Lascelles requested a meeting with the prime minister. This was an exact replication of the tactic used by his superior Hardinge in 1936 with the then-prime minister, Stanley Baldwin, which had turned the purely private matter of the king's marriage into a constitutional issue requiring the involvement of the politicians, and had resulted in the abdication of Edward VIII.

Churchill was at Chartwell, his country house in Kent, so Lascelles drove down there to see him. At first, Lascelles's deadpan courtliness created confusion for the romantic prime minister, who had also been in favour of King Edward VIII marrying Mrs Simpson. He misunderstood what his response was supposed to be, and enthused, 'What a delightful match! A lovely young royal lady married to a gallant young airman, safe from the perils and horrors of war!'

Lascelles's stony silence conveyed the message that this was not the response he, and by extension, Queen Elizabeth The Queen Mother, required. Clementine Churchill, however, was more attuned to what the sovereign's private secretary required of the prime minister. 'Winston,' she remonstrated, 'if you are going to begin the Abdication all over again, I am going to leave! I shall take a flat and go and live in Brighton.'

Both Churchills knew Elizabeth well. They knew that, without her backing, the venture would be all but impossible to execute. However, the prime minister's conscience would not allow him to stand in the way of the happiness of a young couple in love, so, rather than oppose the match, he recommended that the marriage proceed once Margaret was of age, as long as she renounced her rights of succession to the throne. This was a compassionate and practical approach to take, and was one which would be followed later by Prince Michael of Kent, the Earl of St. Andrews, and Lord Nicholas Windsor, when they wished to contract problematic marriages.

It has been said that Churchill did not want Elizabeth II's reign to be overshadowed by a constitutional crisis caused by her sister's marriage so soon after her coronation. While there is some merit to that interpretation, it is by no means the whole story. Lascelles was determined to 'foment as much trouble' as he could, to quote Princess Margaret. Churchill had provided him with a painless and practical solution which could easily have been implemented. Lascelles, however, proceeded to twist Churchill's solution, going so far as to report back that the prime minister required Margaret to surrender her status as a royal highness and to be excluded from the civil list. These claims were untrue, as Churchill's private secretary Colville was at pains to point out two years later, when matters came to a head and he stated in writing that Churchill 'was in reality opposed to any attempt to prevent their marrying.'

Lascelles returned from his meeting with Churchill with the clear intention of creating sufficient obstacles to avert the popular choice of an early marriage. Lilibet's position as Supreme Governor of the Church of England was used to steer her away from agreeing to her sister's marriage on the grounds that such agreement would be incompatible with the teachings of the church. This meant that she could not give her permission to the union under the Royal Marriages Act of 1772, so Margaret would have to wait two more years, until her twenty-fifth birthday, before she could marry without her sister's specific permission. Philip, who had himself been a victim of Lascelles and Elizabeth's machinations, counselled caution, not because he was against the marriage, but because he felt it was his duty to protect his wife's interests. While this was understandable, when it got back to Margaret, which it would not do for another two years, she was livid. Up to that point, Philip and Margaret had been as close as it was possible for a brother and sister-in-law to be. However, when she discovered that his recommendation had been less fulsome than she had expected it to be, she chose to regard it as a betrayal of her interests at the expense of his and her sister's expediency. She also alighted upon the fact that Townsend had always been a great favourite of both her father and mother, while Philip's rather rougher edges had at times rubbed both of them up the wrong way, her mother especially. She detected an element of jealousy and competitiveness where there was likely none, for Philip, unlike Townsend, had admirers far and wide. The last thing he needed was the adulation of parents-in-law, especially a mother-in-law who had proven herself over the years to be full of guile and mischief beneath the fabled charm.

That particular conflict, however, was still in the future as Lascelles returned from his meeting with Churchill and proceeded to influence events. He and Elizabeth both knew that Churchill was yesterday's man. His health was failing, support for him was draining away in the Conservative party, and there was every likelihood that he would not be in power in two years' time, when Margaret came of age. A new prime minister, less romantic than Churchill, might well prove to be a welcome preventative to the marriage.

Taking both the short and the long view, Lascelles returned from Chartwell to spearhead the campaign to 'destroy my happiness,' as Margaret put it later. She developed a loathing of the man that was truly remarkable. Every time she saw him walking on the road in the Kensington Palace compound, where he lived in a grace-and-favour cottage nearby her apartment No. 1A, until his death in 1981, she would tell her chauffeur to run him over.

With Lascelles in charge, acting as 'Mummy's mouthpiece,' according to Margaret, matters now built to a quick head. Lascelles advised that Townsend should be moved out of England to a foreign posting. Elizabeth and Margaret were due to depart on a tour of Southern Rhodesia on 30th June. Townsend had been scheduled to travel with them. Elizabeth, however, no longer wished him to accompany them. She wanted him replaced with Patrick (7th Lord) Plunket, the son of her great friends Dorothé Lewis Barnato and Terence, 6th Lord Plunket, who had died in a 'plane crash in 1938, after which she and the king often had Patrick and his two younger brothers to stay. The three Plunket boys were effectively foster brothers of Lilibet and Margaret, and would remain lifelong friends, a fact I can personally attest to, as Patrick's youngest brother Shaun was a friend of mine for over thirty years, and he went to just about every private party of any consequence Lilibet had, until his death in 2012.

Elizabeth's decision to jettison Townsend from the tour had a degree of merit, for she accurately discerned that his presence would deflect attention away from the purpose of the trip. The lovers would become the focal point. His presence would also be a silent announcement of Elizabeth's support of the marriage, a position she was not prepared to adopt though she did not have the courage or decency to say so to her daughter.

According to Colin Glenconner, Elizabeth was 'the most self-centred person,' he had ever encountered in his life, and the one thing she could never tolerate was anyone snatching attention away from her. He felt that this tendency created problems between her and Margaret, who, while young and beautiful, was the cynosure of all eyes, much to the annoyance of her competitive mother. Whether that is fair or not, Elizabeth and Lascelles were in agreement that Townsend should not only withdraw from the tour, but he should resign his post as Comptroller of her Household as well. His continued presence in that post would also convey Elizabeth's unspoken support for the marriage, and since this was actually contrary to her true position, he needed to be terminated.

The man chosen to wield the axe was Sir Arthur Penn, Elizabeth's Treasurer. He had also, in their youths, been her suitor. He took Townsend to dinner on 16th June and advised him that his best option would be to retire gracefully from the scene for a while. The implication was that this was a tactical withdrawal, to facilitate the marriage, when in fact it had the opposite purpose. Both Townsend and Margaret knew that Penn was acting on Elizabeth's behalf, and the letter Townsend wrote her the following day, informing her that he would accept any post he was offered, was fulsome in his appreciation for all the supposed help he and Margaret were receiving. 'Your Majesty is going through so much for us and I can never thank you enough for your kindness and your help, and for the way you have stood by Princess Margaret. We will never forget how much you are thinking of the Queen too, and will always do everything we can to consider her,' he wrote.

Townsend then accepted a posting as Air Attaché at the British Embassy in Brussels. Both he and Margaret were led to believe that he would not depart until after the end of the African tour, thereby giving them time to say goodbye. Neither of them yet realized to what extent Elizabeth had colluded with Lascelles, and as the lovers prepared for their future together, neither imagined that the confidence they had placed in Elizabeth was misguided.

Margaret left for Africa with hope that all would be well. She truly believed that her mother was acting on her behalf, and confidently expected that, at the end of the two years' wait, when she was twenty-five, she and Townsend would be able to marry without any further obstacles being placed in their way. Admittedly, things had moved on from the year before, when she and Townsend had confided in Lilibet and Philip, and her sister had expressed happiness for them and asked only that they wait until after the coronation to announce their forthcoming marriage. Margaret would also say that her mother had also seemed happy for Peter and herself. Certainly Elizabeth gave her no indication of being against the marriage. She was fond of Peter and she had always gone along with whatever Margaret wanted, in keeping with the regimen of indulgence established by George VI, who was never known to say no to his younger daughter. Margaret knew that her mother's opposition would have scuppered any chance she had of being allowed to marry, but, accepting Elizabeth's conduct at face value, she felt fortunate to have such an understanding mother. The feelings of betrayal that she experienced when she finally realized the part Elizabeth had played in ruining the possibility of the marriage can be easily imagined.

While in Africa, Margaret discovered that Townsend would be leaving for Brussels before her return. She was so distraught that she was unable to function for days, taking to her bed and wailing with anguish. When she had recovered sufficiently to resume her part in the tour, she was still unaware that those opposing the marriage were taking succour from her mother's stated 'distress' at this 'terrible thing'. But Margaret was intelligent, and it was now only a matter of time before she added up the dots.

Still confident in her family's support when she returned to England, Margaret was happy to go up to Balmoral with her mother to stay with Lilibet and the rest of the family. Afterwards, Elizabeth moved to Birkhall, where she entertained her good friends Bobbety and Elizabeth Salisbury. She used the occasion to confide her 'distress' about Margaret's forthcoming marriage, laying the ground for him to oppose it in Cabinet when the time came.

On 24th November, Lilibet and Philip left on the coronation tour of the Commonwealth that would last until 10th May 1954. Lilibet was the first British monarch who was specifically the queen of several Commonwealth nations, where her predecessors had been sovereigns of imperial possessions. The Commonwealth was a new concept that was intended to replace the Empire. She believed in it, and already displayed an appreciation of and commitment towards it that would last for the remainder of her life. This would enable what was essentially a free collection of states, all of whom would become independent in the next decade or so, to flourish in a willing community of nations, their ties to the Crown and each other matters of choice rather than force.

The break from the United Kingdom had other dimensions as well. Both Lilibet and Philip were still finding their sea legs on the ship of state, and they welcomed the time away, not only to strengthen ties with the Commonwealth countries, but also to escape some of the pressures back home. The tour took them to Bermuda, Jamaica, Fiji, Tonga, New Zealand, Australia, Ceylon, Aden, Uganda, Malta and Gibraltar. It gave them an opportunity to regain some of the levity that had left their personal lives since her accession, to lessen the strains that Lilibet's failure to incorporate Philip's name in the identity of their descendants had caused. It worked, but only up to a point, for Philip remained bitter about his erasure dynastically. According to Lord Brabourne, 'He remained angry about it for a very long time.' In fact, his rage would not be appeased until the end of the decade, when Lilibet reversed her decision. In the meantime, it was the elephant in the room that sucked a lot of the oxygen out of their happiness.

While Lilibet was away, Elizabeth and Margaret acted as Counsellors of State along with the Duke of Gloucester, the Princess Royal and her son George, who had succeeded his father as the 7th Earl of Harewood on 24th May 1947. Elizabeth was having the time of her life as chief Counsellor, while Margaret was trying to lead the semblance of a normal life. She would later reveal that her life revolved around writing to, and receiving from, Townsend 'long, long letters'. The rest of her time she filled by going out clubbing most nights with her friends, and spending as many weekends with them as she could. These friends formed what became known in the press as the 'Margaret Set'. They included Sharman Douglas, daughter of the American Ambassador, Lewis W. Douglas; the Earl of Dalkeith (whom Elizabeth had wanted for Lilibet); the Hon. Dominic Elliot-Murray-Kynynmound, a younger son of the 5th Earl of Minto; Billy Wallace, who would remain a lifelong friend; and the then Hon. Colin Tennant, another lifelong friend who would become the 3rd Lord Glenconner and features in this work as Colin Glenconner.

Margaret and Colin became such cosy friends that he fancied he had a chance with her if she did not marry Townsend, and claimed that she accepted the proposal he ultimately made. She, however, always denied doing so.

There is a back story of why Margaret and Colin could both have been speaking the truth, and why each clung to their version of events throughout the years, even as the other was contradicting it. The Tennants are a Scottish family and a former Scottish Tai Pan of one of the great Far Eastern trading companies, a cousin of another Scot whom I nearly married, told us in the 1970s, at a dinner party at my West Eaton Place flat, the real reason Margaret was not permitted to marry Colin. Her mother fiercely objected to a marriage because Elizabeth had been told that the Tennants, who had once had sugar estates in the West Indies, had, 'coloured blood'. She was adamant that there was no way she would ever agree to such a marriage, and, since Margaret was not actually in love with Colin, and would only have been marrying him because she had not been allowed to marry her, 'one true love,' she declined his proposal after having first accepted it. This smacks of the truth, not only because the source of the story was an impeccably placed Scot of the highest reputation, integrity, and lineage, who was way beyond the cheap gossip that wannabees indulge in, but also because Colin and Margaret remained the closest of friends all her life, notwithstanding the fact that each was effectively calling the other a liar. The supreme irony of this saga is that Colin's father had once wooed Elizabeth. She had been an eager recipient of his attentions, and there was sufficient encouragement (the Strathmores were infinitely grander but nowhere near as rich as the nouveau Glenconners, whose barony predated the proposal by only a decade) for Christopher Glenconner to have even purchased a ring. However, when push came to shove, he declined to pop the question, and the ring remained firmly in his pocket.

Scotland is a small country. The aristocracy know each other, and have always done. Because everyone is effectively inter-connected with everyone else, there is a cosiness and a warmth that are lacking in England. The flip side to this coin is that it's virtually impossible to keep anything private there.

This would work to Margaret's advantage and Elizabeth's disadvantage as the two-year waiting period came to a close.

Margaret turned twenty-five in August 1955. Traditionally, the royal family decamped to Scotland from August to October. This year was no exception. They were at Balmoral, along with over three hundred reporters who were camped outside the gates in the unrealistic hope that an announcement would be made regarding a forthcoming marriage now that the liberating milestone had been passed. Nothing happened, which is hardly surprising, because, within the castle walls, the subject was being strictly ignored. Elizabeth had taken to refusing to countenance Margaret making even the most opaque of allusions to it. Whenever Margaret tried to broach the subject, Elizabeth would become so distressed that she would have to abandon its discussion. Such discussions as she had were invariably behind her daughter's back, at which time she would convey her disapproval, by expressing her tremendous distress at the very subject being raised

This left Margaret out on a limb, which is where Colin Glenconner felt Elizabeth intended her to be. Margaret, hoping against hope that she would somehow be able to gain her mother's approval if she played along with her, also had to cope with a brick wall of silence from her sister. Lilibet had decided that she must not engage with Margaret at all on the subject. According to her line of reasoning, anything she said, or did not say, might influence her sister, and she wanted the decision to be hers, and hers alone. Too much was at stake, and she hoped that by adopting this posture, she would avoid damaging the relationship with the individual who had been her closest friend from childhood. It was an earnest attempt to separate her responsibilities as Margaret's sovereign from those of sister and friend. Her tactic would shortly backfire in the most massive way, for Margaret was now isolated, surrounded by a sea of silence, when what she needed was open, concerned discussion. It was inevitable that she would end up feeling that her mother and sister had abandoned her, which, in a way, they had.

What can be said in favour of Lilibet is that her motives were as pure as her position was conflicted, for the role of sister was not compatible with that of Supreme Head of the Church of England, and she now had to contend with a new prime minister, Anthony Eden, whose attitude towards the marriage was far less supportive than Churchill's had been. This was largely the fault of Bobbety Salisbury, who threatened to resign from the Cabinet if the government agreed to the marriage. In truth, Salisbury's resignation would not have brought down the government, but the threat was there, and Eden, who had only recently replaced Churchill, having spent an arduous time trying to do so, was not prepared to chance an election over Margaret's marriage, or indeed, over anything else at all. Having waited so long for power, he intended to cling to it for as long as he could. The fact that he himself was a divorce – his second wife was Churchill's niece Clarissa – did not prevent him from taking the view that while it was now perfectly alright for a Prime Minister of the United Kingdom to be a divorce, it was still not acceptable for a member of the royal family to marry someone who was the innocent party in a divorce. However, he was relieved, after his first visit to Balmoral on 1st October, that Lilibet had not raised the subject in their weekly audience.

The marriage remained popular with the public at large. In September, Townsend returned to England to attend the Farnborough Air Show in his capacity as Air Attaché in Brussels. He made no attempt to hide away. He went to and fro, chauffeured around in a Daimler limousine with the press in hot pursuit. He and Margaret both believed that public support for their marriage would make it more likely, and, as he was snapped getting into or out of the limousine, Margaret's reaction was to wave his picture in newspapers to friends and state how handsome he was.

Martin Charteris said he was not sure about the wisdom of 'courting publicity' the way Townsend did, and wondered whether it assisted Margaret, but there is every reason to suppose that she supported the tactic. The only doubt is whether she believed that the publicity would exert pressure upon her family to finally provide her with the support that she knew she needed, and which she felt she had been promised initially.

If Margaret had hoped that having the topic of her prospective marriage on the front pages of the newspapers would encourage her mother and sister to discuss the subject, by the time Townsend returned to Belgium, she understood how completely on her own she was. Yet Lilibet was supportive in her own way, even if their mother was not. Townsend was returning to England for three weeks on 12th October, and she encouraged her sister to see as much of him as she could. She suggested they stay with friends and relations, and generally see as much of each other in familial and friendly setting in an attempt to 'test drive' the relationship. Martin Charteris thought that Lilibet was in her own, quiet way, doing all she could to prevent her sister from making a mistake. Although she knew how much in love Margaret was, she was also afraid that Margaret might make a sacrifice she would later regret. This she wanted to avert without spelling it out in so many words.

Margaret took the night train down from Scotland on 11th October. Townsend arrived in London on the 12th, staying with Lord and Lady Abergavenny at their maisonette in Lowndes Square. Elizabeth arrived back

at Clarence House on the 13<sup>th</sup>, stepping onto a merry-go-round of social
activities which she seems to have hoped would keep her out of her daughter's
way. Margaret also had free rein socially, hosting a series of dinner parties at
Clarence House which were 'surreal' in that the atmosphere inside was one of
tremendous 'peace and calm', with no one ever raising the one subject which
was on everyone's lips everywhere except at Clarence House.

As a precursor to what happened when Diana, Princess of Wales died,
Lilibet remained at Balmoral while the greatest news story of the day was
unfolding in London. Bobbety Salisbury stepped into the fray – Colin
Glenconner said Margaret always believed at Elizabeth's instigation – and
recommended that Clarence House issue a statement before the frenzied
speculation began to damage the monarchy. Elizabeth and her private
secretary Oliver Dawnay consulted with Buckingham Palace over the wording,
which was duly issued by the Press Secretary. This was a limp appeal asking
the press to leave Margaret alone as 'no announcement concerning Princess
Margaret's personal future was at present contemplated.' Unsurprisingly,
it had the effect of increasing rather than decreasing speculation upon the
subject, which, unbelievably, Elizabeth was still refusing to discuss with
Margaret.

That weekend, while her mother went down to Royal Lodge, Margaret
and Townsend went to stay with her goddaughter Marilyn's parents, Major
John Willis of the tobacco family, and the former Hon. Jean Elphinstone,
daughter of Elizabeth's sister Mary, and therefore Margaret's first cousin and
good friend, at nearby Allanbay in Berkshire. The press were camped outside
and police protection did little to prevent them snatching photographs.

The following Tuesday, while the lovers were enjoying their moment in the
limelight and hoping for a positive outcome, Lilibet was in Scotland listening
to the advice of her prime minister. Eden spelt out the alternatives. Salisbury
was threatening to resign, which prevented the Cabinet from approving the
marriage. Should Margaret insist on going ahead with the marriage, he would
have to introduce a bill in Parliament. Lord Kilmuir, the Lord Chancellor,
was looking into the legalities of altering the Royal Marriages Act of 1772
while allowing Margaret to remain a princess on the Civil List. Nevertheless,
she would have to surrender her right of succession to the throne along with
the rights of any children she might have. Soundings were being taken from
the Dominions and Commonwealth. More ominously, she would have to
cease being a Counsellor of State, a right she enjoyed only because of her
place in the line of succession, and might well be obliged to forego her
income from the Civil List. As neither she nor Townsend had any money,
this meant that they would be obliged to lead a life of real penury. There was

also the possibility that, if none of the above materialized, she might have to live abroad, if only for the first few years. This resonated with the fate of their Uncle David, whose 'deal', to return a year after the abdication, had turned out to be a monumental mirage. Unlike him, though, they would not have the cushioning of a crown which would allow them to lead a sumptuous, elegant life such as his in Paris.

This was not good news. Eden did not have Churchill's stature nor inclination to help beyond what was politically expedient. Lilibet and Philip returned south that week, to meet up with Margaret and Elizabeth over the weekend. According to Colin Glenconner, who learnt what happened from Margaret herself, at the meeting the four of them had on Sunday, 23rd October, this was the first occasion upon which Margaret appreciated the full extent of the opposition that had arisen in government circles. A biographer of Elizabeth states that, by 'this time mother and daughter were scarcely on speaking terms and on one occasion Princess Margaret had even thrown a book at her mother's head.' The antipathy was, in fact, even worse than that. Once Margaret was informed that Salisbury had threatened to resign from the government, she immediately realized that he would never have done so had he not had her mother's blessing. She condemned her mother as an 'arch hypocrite' and 'spat bricks' about Elizabeth having facilitated the marriage of her brother the Hon. John Bowes Lyon's divorced daughter Anne, Viscountess Anson, to Prince George of Denmark at Glamis Castle on 16th September 1950, while she, Elizabeth, was now allowing her 'mouthpiece' to prevent her, Margaret's, marriage. When the Queen Mother tried to imply that Margaret was being rash and unrealistic and had not even considered where she and Townsend would live, Philip waded in on Margaret's behalf and cuttingly told his mother-in-law that it was still possible to buy a house. Elizabeth was so infuriated at what she perceived to be impertinence that she stormed out of the room, slamming the door after her. Lilibet tried to play the peacemaker, but Margaret rounded on her, accusing her of failing to give her the support she had initially promised, and when Philip stepped in to protect his wife, she tore into him as well.

Up to that point, Lilibet had been shielded from the rumours surrounding Philip's purported extra-marital activities. No longer. Margaret provided chapter and verse on every rumour she had ever heard, in particular how Baron's Park Lane studio was little better than a 'knocking shop' at which his friends met obliging girls, some models, others hopefuls, but all young and beautiful and many up for any fun that was to be had. These rumours, which deserve examination in greater detail, will be addressed at a more appropriate time. Suffice it to say that, by the end of the meeting, Margaret had well

# Chapter VII

and truly lobbed a grenade into the still pond of the three people closest to her. In so doing, she had blown them, and a lot of the flora supporting their decorous lives, out of the water.

Three days later, Margaret picked up *The Times* to see an excoriating editorial demanding that she be made to give up her royal status if she went ahead and married Townsend. She knew only too well that the Palace worked hand in glove with *The Times*. She was convinced that the story was a plant. She knew her sister and brother-in-law would never have had a hand in it, but saw her mother's fingerprints all over it. Her cousin Lady Patricia Ramsay, the former Princess Patricia of Connaught, who had surrendered her royal status in 1919 to marry the Hon. Alexander Ramsay, warned her, in no uncertain terms, that she must not, on any account, make the same mistake she had made. She spelt out chapter and verse how different life was when one was no longer royal, pointing out that, while a happy marriage was some compensation for the loss of status, at the end of the day, nothing could eradicate the loss. Margaret should either retain her royal status and marry Townsend, or she must give him up.

In his autobiography *Time and Chance*, Townsend reveals that he thought he and Margaret faced a starker choice than they did in fact face. On page 231 he asserts that the choice was between renunciation of the marriage or renunciation of her royal status: 'conditions which, frankly, would have ruined her.' Yet the official documents, and the subsequent comments of the participants, including Colville and Kilmuir, show that this was not so. As the government was briefing the Palace, the withholding of pertinent information to Margaret can only have come from the Palace's failure to convey to her what they knew.

Now that the matter had become openly constitutional, Lilibet was being fully briefed by her private secretary. Since 1953, this was the Right Hon. Sir Michael (later Lord) Adeane, who was not Machiavellian like Lascelles, nor was he one of Elizabeth's cohorts. There were two methods through which Lilibet was being informed: Adeane's direct briefings and through the Red Box papers. The Assistant Private Secretary, Martin Charteris, was also being kept fully up to speed with what was going on at governmental level. Colin Glenconner said, however, that Margaret was never made fully aware of what her real options were. She blamed her mother rather than her sister, and if the sequence of events is traced, it becomes apparent that Lilibet herself was only put fully in the picture by Eden just before the confrontation with Margaret at Windsor. Thereafter, the channels of personal communication between the two sisters were disrupted, and since no one else was as supportive of

Margaret's right to make her own choices, the one benevolent source of information as to the real consequences of the marriage had been silenced.

By this time, Margaret knew that her mother was no ally. She therefore did not expect her to provide her with information that might actually allow the marriage to take place. What she did not expect was that her mother would starve her of accurate information by ensuring that she, rather than Margaret, received accurate briefings which the courtiers doubtless assumed was being conveyed by mother to daughter, and Elizabeth was failing to hand it on. According to Margaret, none of the courtiers actually provided her with any information at all. She blamed her mother for this, and felt that Elizabeth had positioned herself in such a way that she was being actively obstructive when she could either have remained neutral, or been more supportive. The result was that Margaret had no knowledge of what her true options were, at the very moment when it was absolutely crucial that she know them.

Ignorant of the important fact that she would actually have been able to keep her royal status, though not her place in the line of succession, following the meeting at Windsor Margaret and Townsend had spoken over the telephone about it. He said that she was 'in great distress' throughout the conversation. Knowing that their call might be monitored, she did not tell him, 'what had passed between herself and her sister and brother-in-law, but doubtless the stern truth was dawning upon her,' he said. But he knew Margaret well enough to read between the lines and understand that her mother's antipathy, allied to the loss of her royal status, would indeed ruin her. He would also have realized that a marriage without Elizabeth's active support would end up isolating them. He only needed to remember how Elizabeth had frozen Crawfie out of court circles, following the publication of her book *The Little Princesses* in 1950, when Elizabeth had actually initially encouraged Crawfie in the project, before changing her mind, then labelling the anodyne and admiring work a betrayal. Thereafter, she called all betrayals 'doing a Crawfie' and ensured that the loyal governess, who had sacrificed getting married for over a decade to stay with the girls, was completely isolated. Elizabeth had been so implacable beneath her smiling and serene exterior, that even Queen Mary and Lilibet, who at first had not frozen out Crawfie, ended up doing so. As Crawfie lived at Kensington Palace, and all support for her drained away once Elizabeth made it known that everyone had to choose between her and the retired governess, no one dared speak to Crawfie, much less entertain her or mix with her socially. Elizabeth had organised her exclusion as completely as she had organised the Windsors'.

Townsend was not foolhardy. It was now clear they were being set up to become the new Windsors: isolated, spurned, admired by the public but reviled in royal circles, only penniless as well. Their choice was between great pain and greater pain.

After that conversation, both Margaret and Townsend had a troubled night. In the morning he telephoned her to suggest that they loved each other so much that possibly the best way of showing that love was to sacrifice getting married.

In the 2012 biography entitled *The Untold Life of Queen Elizabeth The Queen Mother*, this author wrote, 'Margaret would later claim publicly that she and Townsend came to the joint decision not to proceed with the marriage at this stage of the proceedings. However, she confided in Colin Glenconner and other friends that it was actually he who pulled out. Whether his motivation was because he believed she would lose her royal status, or realized that Elizabeth's lack of support would always be a drag on their marriage, he would undoubtedly have been influenced by the fate.... that had befallen Lilibet and Margaret's governess Crawfie when she dared to hoe a different furrow from that which Elizabeth desired. Making an adversary of the Queen Mother was not something any but the very brave did, and while he was a courageous, decorated war hero, an enemy in the sky was one thing, but one on the ground – and a palatial ground at that – was another. He might also have understood that, by marrying a degraded princess, much of the glamour which had attached to her position of sister to the Queen would have disappeared, and along with it, her desirability. That left just Margaret the woman.'

Had Margaret the woman not been enticing enough for Townsend? Or had he decided to throw himself, suttee-like, on the funeral pyre for love? It is impossible for anyone to answer that question. Only Townsend could have done so. However, Margaret now found herself confronted by a lover who was recommending that they loved each other so much that they should sacrifice a life together. She fell into line and they agreed to renounce each other, though she also made it clear to Colin Glenconner that the outcome might well have been different if Townsend had not made the suggestion that he did. In short, she was prepared to make the sacrifice, but he was not. The evening after she returned from Windsor, they drafted a statement of renunciation together. It highlighted the religious aspect, which Eden, himself a divorce, would try to have removed, but which she insisted remain. She had had quite enough of hypocrites, and though she had not been able to prevail against her mother, she was determined that she was not going to spare the feelings of that 'other arch hypocrite, the Prime Minister.'

Margaret had an appointment to see the Archbishop of Canterbury on Thursday, 27th October. Neither she nor Townsend had yet told anyone of their decision to part. Decidedly not her mother, with whom she was still living but avoiding 'like the plague', nor her sister and brother-in-law. She was enough her mother's daughter to want to stand on her dignity and salvage as much of her pride as she could. She therefore sailed into Geoffrey Fisher's book-strewn office and informed him, 'You can put away your books, Archbishop, I am not going to marry Peter Townsend.' She gave Christian grounds as the reason for her decision, then left the following day with Townsend for one last time together as a couple. They spent the weekend in Uckfield, Sussex with Lord Rupert Nevill, younger brother of Lord Abergavenny, Townsend's host in London, and his wife Mickie, who were good friends of Lilibet as well. Margaret would later recount to Colin Glenconner and other friends that this was the best weekend of her life. She and Peter were completely content in each other's company, and not even the bittersweet element could lessen the absolute joy she felt in his presence

That Monday morning, 31st October 1955, Margaret was driven back to Clarence House and Townsend to London. He dropped in early that evening *en route* to Brussels via Uckfield, for a last goodbye. They drank to what had been and now would never be, and after a poignant farewell, he drove off into the night and out of her life.

Hugo Vickers, in his biography of Elizabeth, captures the underlying heartlessness that allowed Elizabeth to collude in ruining her daughter's greatest chance at happiness, when he describes the aftermath of Townsend's departure. 'That night Princess Margaret was at Clarence House, while Elizabeth was due to keep an evening engagement at the University of London. The Queen Mother set off for this, unaware or unconcerned that her daughter would be having dinner alone on a tray.'

There are two corollaries to this sorry saga. In November 2017, one of Townsend's greatest friends, a retired British ambassador, told me that 'Peter said that he never regretted marrying Marie-Luce (Jamagne, the Belgian Princess Margaret look-alike he married in 1959). He was too much of a gentleman to say that he didn't regret not marrying Princess Margaret, but the implication was clear. He didn't. He didn't entirely approve of the way she turned out.'

From Margaret's point of view, the old magic remained even into old age. Anne Glenconner has told how he came to visit towards the end of his life. Margaret enthused about him as if he were still young, dashing and handsome, when in fact all Lady Glenconner could see was a wizened old man.

There is little doubt that Margaret was damaged by the loss. Townsend was her first love. They were well suited. And she would undoubtedly have had a happier marriage with him than she subsequently had with Antony Armstrong-Jones. Although the latter was utterly charming and a great 'swordsman', and their union was originally torrid, it is arguable that Lord Snowdon, as he became, could ever have been happily married to any woman. He had a very difficult and conflicted relationship with his mother. He knew that she had never really loved him. She had been exceedingly cruel to him while he was growing up. She used to send him travelling in the third class carriage with his sister Susan while her two sons with the Earl of Rosse travelled with her in first class. She was so cold and unfeeling that she never once visited him the whole time he was in hospital with polio, and while he naturally yearned for her love, he also, justifiably, hated her. Experience has taught me that it is not possible for a man who hates his mother, even if he also loves her, to love the woman in his life without transferring that hatred of the mother figure onto the woman with whom he shares a bed. Townsend, on the other hand, had none of these psychological problems.

With Townsend out of the way, Margaret picked up the pieces of her life as best she could. She continued living with her mother, whose treatment of her, according to Colin Glenconner, 'was a disgrace. You wouldn't treat a dog so badly.' However, she was still a maiden princess, and maiden princesses lived under their parent's roof until they married. So Margaret and Elizabeth lived like two ships passing in the night – 'preferably far enough apart to not have to dip their lights at each other.'

Down the bottom of the road, at Buckingham Palace, the fallout from the Margaret/Townsend debacle was also considerable. Dr Michael Davies, a fashionable psychiatrist who was very much a part of the smart set as well as being professionally eminent, told me, 'I know as a fact the Queen had psychiatric treatment. In the vernacular, she cracked up under the strain of her sister's revelations about Prince Philip's activities.' Lilibet, it must be remembered, was desperately in love with Philip. The rocks they had had to negotiate since her accession had had an effect upon her, the way they would on any other sentient human being in love with her husband. She was only too aware that Philip had been badly bruised by his treatment. While they had coped with the difficulties these issues had created, no human being with feelings could be blind to the underlying pressure created in their relationship.

Margaret had always been Lilibet's closest friend as well as sister. To have the spotlight of rumour, which might or might not be true, shone so decidedly on Philip's fidelity, would have been painful for anyone. However, not only had Lilibet been jolted into having to deal with the gossip about her husband's activities, and to work through whether they were true or not, and if they were true what the consequences would be, and if not, how to repair the fractures, but Margaret had done far more than merely raise the question of Philip's fidelity. She had angrily struck back at her best friend and loving sister, so Lilibet was confronted with having to cope with the damage wrought to her two closest relationships, by one of those two people. In psychological terms, this was a perfect storm.

Lilibet was far too intelligent and sophisticated to ignore the ramifications of the rumours. If they were true, she would have to make adjustments. There was no question of a divorce, nor did she want one. She was still in love with Philip. If the rumours were not true, she would still have to make adjustments.

There was also the question of her relationship with her sister. While Lilibet the sister had tried, in her own way, to be supportive, she had patently failed, and this fact cannot have escaped her. Off everything I have heard from people who knew both sisters well, Lilibet's behaviour and attitude towards Margaret for the remainder of her life betrayed a certain amount of guilt. She spent the rest of Margaret's life compensating for the loss she knew deep down she had done nothing to avert, and doubtless she was con- temporaneously conflicted as well. She cannot have failed to appreciate that Margaret felt justifiably let down. It was as if Margaret had decided that since she couldn't have happiness with the man she loved, she failed to see why she should continue protecting the sister who had failed to protect her.

Such enquiries as Lilibet made, as to what went on at Baron's studio, would have fed, rather than lessened, any initial doubts. In Robin Dalton's memoirs, she hints that some of the practices at Baron's studio could be interpreted as 'louche'. These, it must be said, were nothing out of the ordinary. Even though the Sexual Revolution of the sixties had not yet erupted the way it would a decade later, what is now commonplace in terms of sexual activity within the general population, was already commonplace within fashionable circles by the mid-1950s. In fact, the Sexual Revolution had already taken place in those particular circles, and was in the process of trickling down into more general ones. Undeniably, there were still pockets of prudery within the Establishment, with old fashioned values such as those which Lascelles and others of his ilk espoused, but by the mid-50s, bachelors' establishments often had revolving doors through which a host of attractive girls came and went. Of course, 'nice' girls still didn't 'do it' as a rule, but other girls did. Moreover, the rule was in the process of changing at that very moment, for contraception was becoming increasingly effective, and once the fear of pregnancy disappeared, so too did the constraints that had led to virginity being prized as a virtue.

Baron was a bachelor. He was also a man about town. He was one of the young, attractive, successful photographers who made photography sexy. He and his assistants, who included a young Antony Armstrong-Jones, made no pretence about chasing skirt with relish. Sex was in the air, so to speak, and if one of his friends liked a girl he knew, Baron had no compunction about making introductions. What people chose to get up to, once they had been introduced, was their own business.

The Thursday Club, by comparison, was tame. Although Philip was a dedicated member, the luncheons held there were restricted to male banter. Yes, some of it was ribald, but by and large, it was just a group of men getting together to let their hair down and have fun. It was as innocent as any all-male establishment, which wants to enjoy itself, can be. Larry Adler told me that there was no possibility of any man bedding a girl there, or even meeting one. The Thursday Club had an all-male membership, which precluded women being in attendance, and moreover, there simply wasn't the space to do anything, even if women had been present.

Nevertheless, the Thursday Club had, by this time, developed a richly undeserved reputation for louche activities. No one knows whether Lilibet was fed the true, or the invented version of what her husband and his friends got up to, but Philip's continuing friendship with Baron suggests that she either came to believe that he was not an adverse influence, or then Philip pursued the friendship against her wishes. Nevertheless, Margaret's revelations evidently did trigger a crisis for Lilibet. 'She definitely received psychiatric treatment,' Michael Davies said.

The logistics medically were less straightforward for Lilibet than they would have been for anyone else. Being the head of state, she could not simply leave Buckingham Palace and drive herself to Harley Street or to a clinic the way she could drive herself to Windsor Castle on the weekend, with her dogs in the back, one of them usually lying on the shelf, behind the back seat. She couldn't hit the bottle, nor could she be given drugs. She needed to have her wits about her to carry out her functions as sovereign. Yet she now found herself in such a painful place that she needed help to deal with the pain. Of course, Philip himself was from a family which had availed itself of therapy as and when it was needed. Although such medical help was then viewed with suspicion by the British general public, for people as sophisticated as Lilibet such prejudices were not a consideration. They called in therapists when there was mental, emotional, or psychic pain, just as readily as they went to a dentist when they had a toothache or a doctor when they had a sprained ankle. The question wasn't whether to avail oneself of the help of a therapist, but which form of therapy was appropriate to the present circumstances. A long, drawn out course of therapy on the couch simply wasn't possible. Lilibet needed to be functional, to be kept functional, and to remain functional. She could not afford the luxury of time and space. For neither the first nor the last time in her life, her special status as sovereign dictated that she would not and could not be treated the way any other person in her shoes would have been. 'Uneasy lies the head that wears the crown' had an entirely different meaning in this context, for the interests of the state had to be considered as well as her own personal ones. A course of treatment had to be devised that would be compatible with her responsibilities while, at the same time, hopefully answering the medical needs of the human being who was also the monarch. According to one of the country's leading psychiatrists, whose information came from another colleague who was involved with the case, she was given shock treatment.

Shock treatment was then a fashionable and speedy remedy which circumvented the need for lengthy therapy sessions. It also had the merit of having fewer side effects than drugs, another course of treatment which would have been incompatible with her station in life. Drugs and monarchy simply don't go together, for the monarch needs to be clear headed. He or she also needs to be able to function without the aid of substances. Drugs invariably have side effects, and managing any monarch's drug intake, so that it would not impede his or her performance and abilities, would be well-nigh impossible. That left shock treatment. Although it fell out of favour towards the end of the last century, and came to be regarded as barbaric, it has recently been recognized as being particularly effective in resolving certain forms of depression. It literally shocks the patient into mental recalibration, like a computer being rebooted. In its more natural forms, shock can also recalibrate the psyche of a sufferer, as is evidenced by the way Philip's sister Cecile's death shocked Princess Alice back into good mental health.

A few sessions of shock treatment followed by cognitive therapy can be a particularly effective way of treating someone who is going through an emotional crisis. The shock treatment takes the edge off the pain just enough for the subject to work through his or her difficulties – difficulties which, without shock treatment, overwhelm the individual.

As 1955 drew to its close, there were discreet comings and goings at Buckingham Palace as Lilibet set about recalibrating her life with psychiatric help. It is to her credit that she would work through the issues in such a way that her marriage remained intact and the relationship with her sister, once so precious and now damaged, would be restored. Her life wasn't simple, and the demands made upon her were seldom straightforward, but she would find ways and means to cope and, in so doing, move on in such a way that she would end up with the respect of the world and the love of both her husband and her sister.

On the other hand, the relationship between Philip and Margaret would never recover its earlier intimacy. Nor would Margaret's relationship with her mother ever recover from what she saw as her mother's betrayal. Prue, Lady Penn, has recounted how she used to sympathise with Elizabeth for the appalling way in which Margaret spoke to her mother. Elizabeth would always indicate that she was not to worry; she was used to it. Colin Glenconner would say that she deserved it; Margaret was the wronged party.

If Margaret's relationship with Elizabeth never recovered, Lilibet's relationship with her mother would continue to flourish. As Lilibet matured, she continued to hone two attributes she had always had since youth: acceptance and tolerance. She would therefore emerge from this period stronger, wiser, and richer, not by hardening herself, nor by escaping from unpleasantness by the judicious use of wilful blindness the way her mother did , nor by dulling the pain with pleasure-seeking and alcohol the way Margaret did, but by confronting situations and applying sterling spiritual virtues. Whether instinctively or consciously, she understood that being a good monarch coincided with being a good woman. One would not be possible without the other. In some ways, that knowledge made her task as a wife, sister and queen clearer and easier, though it left little room for self-indulgence. Philip would also emerge from this phase of his life having learnt similar lessons, which he too has applied since then.

Princess Margaret did not. She fell prey to self-indulgence, but then she did not have the public role, or the public platform, that they did. It was always my impression that she felt that her life would have been different had she had greater responsibilities to live up to, the way her sister and brother-in-law did. Comforting as that thought might have been to her, it seemed to contain a large element of self-delusion. It is true that Lilibet and Philip had large platforms, and would go on to develop them for the good of mankind. It is also true that Margaret's lesser platform gave her less scope for activity and accomplishment, and less incentive too. She seemed to think a junior role simply wasn't worth the effort. Yet there is no evidence of her possessing the attributes of self-sacrifice and self-abnegation, which both Lilibet and Philip exhibited. I know that when she was young she felt that she could have made as good a queen as her sister did. But the evidence suggests otherwise. Both Lilibet and Philip exhibited qualities of making the best of the hand life dealt them, and of being willing to come to terms with the outcome of their decisions, and of circumstances, irrespective of whether things turned out the way they wished or not. This degree of acceptance was not something Margaret possessed. That, in my opinion, is ultimately why her life turned out to be one of unfulfilled promise, while theirs has been a cornucopia of promise fulfilled.

# Chapter VIII

NINETEEN FIFTY SIX would prove to be a year that was trying for Lilibet, but productive for Philip. While she was coming to terms with the difficulties in her personal life, and was reconstituting her two closest relationships, she found herself involved in Britain's first major political crisis since the end of the Second World War.

This began on 26th July 1956, when Egypt nationalised the Suez Canal. This waterway had been a joint French and British project, constructed between 1859 and 1869 by Count Ferdinand de Lesseps under the aegis of French Emperor Napoleon III and the British. In its conception and execution, the Suez Canal had been created to be the vital link for British and, to a lesser extent French, shipping between Europe and the East, as it significantly shortened the journey between Europe and India and the Far East. Thereafter the two powers jointly owned and operated the canal, under the umbrella of the Universal Maritime Suez Canal Company, being its largest shareholders. They regarded the canal, which had been their creation from beginning to end, as vital to their national interests.

Throughout the nineteenth and twentieth centuries, Egypt's history had been interwoven with Britain's. This followed Nelson's victory over Napoleon's fleet at Aboukir during the Battle of the Nile in 1798, which would ultimately lead to Napoleon abandoning his Egyptian ambitions and returning to France in 1801. The chaos caused by Napoleon's withdrawal left a power vacuum which was ultimately filled by the Ottoman commander of the Albanian regiment, Kavalili Mehmed Ali Pasha, who was afterwards acknowledged by the Ottoman Sultan as the Khedive of the Province of Egypt, which was technically still a part of the Ottoman Empire. Between then and 1882, the Muhammad Ali Dynasty, as Mehmed Ali's family became known, ruled the rich and *de facto* independent country, despite it being officially a province of the Ottoman Empire. In 1882, however, Egypt and its wealth, not to mention its influence because of the Suez Canal, caught Britain's eye. British territorial ambitions in North Africa resulted in a fight between the two countries, resulting in the British defeating Egyptian forces at Tel el-Kebir. Egypt lost its independence and, though still technically an Ottoman province, was in reality a British territory, becoming known to history as a 'veiled' protectorate between 1882 and 1913. In 1914, the Great War prompted the British to rip the veil asunder and declare a formal British protectorate.

The only difficulty was that the British did not have the co-operation of the reigning Khedive, Abbas II Hilmy (1874-1944). So they replaced him with his uncle, Hussein Kamel (1853-1917). Following the example of Napoleon, who had rewarded his ally the Elector of Bavaria by upgrading him into a king when the French Emperor dissolved the Holy Roman Empire, the British elevated the new Egyptian ruler to a sultan. One head which was not turned was that of the new sultan's only son. In his acclaimed novel *Palace Walk*, Naguib Mahfouz has a character saying, 'What a fine man Prince Kamal al-Din Husayn is! Do you know what he did? He refused to ascend the throne of his late father so long as the British are in charge.' Sultan Hassan's brother Fuad, however, had no such compunctions, and following his death at the height of the Great War, ascended the throne as Fuad I. In 1922, after the war had been safely won, and Egypt officially remained a British Protectorate, the British allowed the accommodating Fuad to convert his sultanate into a kingdom. Egypt finally had a king, its first since its days of ancient greatness.

Although the kingdom of Egypt had a parliamentary system, a prime minister and all the trappings of independence, Britain's right to station troops in Egypt following the 1923 constitution became an increasingly sensitive issue in the country. Despite the Second World War dampening disaffection with the British presence, by the early 1950s dissatisfaction was again rife in the country.

In 1952, matters came to a head when the Free Officers of the Egyptian Army, under the leadership of Colonel Gamal Abdel Nasser (1918-1970), staged a coup. Nasser was a nationalist who wished to strip Egypt of British influence. He was also a republican and a totalitarian, whose goal was to turn Egypt, from a constitutional monarchy with political parties and a democratic, parliamentary structure, into a one-party state.

King Farouk (1920-1965), not realising Nasser's aims, mistakenly believed that his abdication in favour of his infant son Fuad II (1952-), would end the unrest which the plotters had been fomenting. He therefore abdicated and left Egypt with his wife, Queen Narriman, and their son, while his cousin, Prince Muhammad Abdel Moneim (1899-1979), was installed as Head of the Regency Council.

By 1953, it was apparent that Farouk's sacrifice had been in vain. All he had done was leave the field clear for Nasser's assumption of total power. This the colonel set about achieving. Firstly, he abolished the monarchy, installing in its stead as republican Egypt's first president, General Mohamed Naguib (1901-1984), the figurehead senior officer who had taken part in the 1952 coup. The general's presence had given the low ranking working class and petit bourgeois officers, who made up the First Officers, a gravitas and respectability they would otherwise have lacked. The following year, however, Nasser placed Naguib, who opposed his plans for a one-party state, under house arrest, where he would remain for the remainder of Nasser's life. Two years after the president's detention, in 1956, Nasser deposed him altogether, installing himself as the second president of Egypt.

By then, Nasser had also officially adopted, as the principal principle of Egyptian foreign policy, 'positive neutralism'. Along with President Josip Broz Tito of Yugoslavia and Indian Prime Minister Jawaharlal Nehru, who were the leaders of the Non-Aligned Nations, he declared himself as aligned to neither the east nor the west. This posture, however, was not quite as neutral as the declarations made it appear. All three leaders aligned themselves with the Soviet Union far more closely than with the west, and one year later, Egypt was given a new constitution. This ratified the one-party state, which confirmed that Nasser's policies were on a collision course with British and French interests.

In response to Nasser's demands that foreign troops leave his country, Britain had agreed in 1954 to withdraw its military from Egypt, and the last British troops departed on 13th June 1956. By his own account, Egypt's second president decided on 23rd July 1956 to nationalise the Suez Canal, and three days later, he did so. This was hardly evidence of positive neutralism, and was viewed in Whitehall and Paris as being an act of aggression.

Not surprisingly, the Israelis, who had been in a state of war with the Egyptians since the First Arab-Israeli War following Israel's creation in 1948, seized the opportunity to ally themselves with Britain and France. The three governments got together and plotted their response. Despite being warned by the American president, Dwight Eisenhower, against taking military action, they decided to do so.

The British, French and Israelis finally responded by triggering what is known in some quarters as the Second Arab-Israeli War, and in others as the Tripartite Aggression or the Sinai War. With the aim of toppling Nasser, they colluded in the Israeli invasion of the Sinai Peninsula. This would permit the British and the French to enter Egyptian territory as 'peacemakers'. Regrettably for them, in early October 1956, before they could invade, the UN adopted a resolution recognising Egypt's right to nationalise the canal as long as it continued to allow the passage of foreign ships through it. This meant that, by the time Israeli troops entered the Sinai Peninsula on 29th October, quickly overrunning Egyptian army posts and achieving their objectives, there was no valid *casus belli*. Two days later the British and French invaded, bombing the Canal Zone and crushing all Egyptian opposition. Nasser responded by sinking or disabling forty nine ships at the entrance of the canal, doing the unthinkable and thereby realising the west's greatest fear by blocking the canal from all traffic.

Despite the three invading armies enjoying outstanding successes against the Egyptians, the war was lost when the invasion was roundly condemned by the United Nations. President Eisenhower, himself a World War Two hero and head of the allied armies in Europe at the time of the invasion of France in 1944, came out firmly in support of the UN resolution calling for the withdrawal of all occupying forces. This meant that British and French objectives could never be realised, making the whole military exercise utterly pointless from their point of view. Faced with universal condemnation – the positions of the Soviet Union and the United States were uniquely almost identical – Britain, France and Israel had no choice but to capitulate and withdraw their forces.

Ironically, the Israelis alone profited from the catastrophe that was Suez. They obtained freedom of navigation through the Straits of Tiran, which Egypt had blocked to Israeli shipping since 1950.

The fall-out from Suez was considerable. The USSR is commonly held to have been encouraged by the developing Suez Crisis to invade its satellite Hungary and crush its nascent independence movement, which it did between 23rd October and 10th November while the world's attention was focussed elsewhere. That success would lengthen by decades the Soviet occupation of central and eastern Europe, which a successful Hungarian uprising might have brought to a much earlier end. Anthony Eden (1st Earl of Avon, 1897-1977) was made to resign as British prime minister, to be succeeded by Harold Macmillan (1st Earl of Stockton, 1894-1986). Sir Anthony Nutting, Bt. (1920-1999), the British diplomat, made the valid point that the invasion 'established Nasser finally and completely' as the leader of Egypt, thereby ruining all chances of reinstating a parliamentary system in that country.

From Britain's perspective, the outcome was equally detrimental, albeit in an entirely different way. Britain was unmasked as a paper tiger, a formerly great power that was no longer of the first rank. Until Suez, the country and its leaders had been able to convince themselves, and the world, that they were still a pre-eminent power. Thereafter, this would no longer be possible. The country's humiliation was complete, the only good to come out of the invasion being the creation of the United Nations Expeditionary Force, established by the General Assembly on 7th November 1956 with Resolution 1001 (ES-1) as a way of ending the war. Lester B. Pearson, the Canadian Minister of External Affairs whose proposal it was, also won the Nobel Peace Prize, but this was more of a slap in the face for Britain than a sop, for the Canadian's victory highlighted the divergence between the eminence of Britain of yesteryear and the Britain at that time.

While Suez was building throughout 1956, implicating Lilibet in the first fully-blown political crisis of her reign, Philip was focussed elsewhere. He had been deprived of the ability to play even the most peripheral of roles politically by Lascelles and Churchill, but with both those men no longer having roles of any real influence, and with their replacements taking less hostile stances, the coast had been gradually clearing for him to eke out a meaningful place in public life. This time he had the support of his wife. She had learnt from bitter experience that keeping an energetic, active and dynamic husband inactive, passive and thwarted would only build up trouble for them as a couple. The maxim of the devil making work for idle hands might not have been completely apt, but it was partially, and uncomfortably, so, for once she had acceded to the throne and Philip had had to give up his naval career, with nothing to replace it, he had turned to pleasurable activities for want of anything better to do. Whether they had been innocent or not was, in some ways, beside the point. No consort of a British monarch in the mid-1950s could be neutralised the way the courtiers had neutralised Philip, without the likelihood of adverse consequences. The fate of Elizabeth's great-grandfather Edward VII, kept idle and powerless by his mother Queen Victoria throughout his long indenture as Prince of Wales, resonated with those who understood that Philip had a more recent example of the destructive effects of idleness even closer to home. His father Andrew had also diverted his energies into the pursuit of pleasure once enforced inactivity had prevented him from meaningful occupation. Kurt Hahn had warned years before that Philip was the sort of person whose best was magnificent but who needed structure and challenge, failing which the alternative hardly needed articulating. If there was one positive outcome of Margaret's explosion, it was that she had brought out of the shadowlands and into the open, the inevitable consequence of continuing to force Philip into a life of inactivity. In plain terms, the choice was stark. Either he would be allowed to develop a meaningful and rewarding role for himself, or he would end up like Edward VII and Andrew. Such an outcome, however, would not only be disastrous for Lilibet personally, but for the monarchy in the longer run. There was already wild chatter and second-hand speculation about his extramarital activities, confined fortunately to fashionable circles, but if this way of life were made to continue, word would inevitably get out, until finally the gossip would be so widespread that it would become general knowledge. And that would damage the monarchy.

Fortunately for Lilibet and Philip, in the four years since her accession to the throne, the old guard had been replaced with newer and more progressive personalities. These men were also alert to the danger of disallowing Philip from having a meaningful role. He was therefore given scope, and came up with the idea of creating two organisations which would profit mankind while providing him with the means to satisfy his need for service.

The first, and more important of these ideas, was The Duke of Edinburgh's Award scheme, which he founded in February 1956. Originally aimed at boys aged 15 to 18 – the upper age limit would later be changed upwards as the scheme took off – it was intended to give opportunities to those who might not have them, as well as to those who did but wished to improve themselves. Philip being Philip, the programme was both fun and challenging, a series of self-improvement exercises intended to counteract Kurt Hahn's 'Six Declines of Modern Youth'. With the assistance of adult Leaders, the youngsters selected objectives in four areas:

1) They volunteered to undertake useful service to other individuals or to the community;

2) They improved themselves physically in an area of sport, dance or through fitness activities;

3) They developed social and practical skills as well as personal interests;

4) They planned, trained for and completed an expedition: a journey of adventure either in the UK or abroad.

Having successfully completed those four categories, the participants were awarded either bronze or silver awards, depending on how well they had executed them. If they chose to participate in the Residential level, which required them to work and stay away from home for five days while taking part in a shared activity, they received a gold award.

In the first twelve months, 7,000 boys enrolled in the scheme. Like all good ideas, it was simple. Pleasure, self-respect, self-awareness, and fun were all built into it. It was accessible to all irrespective of class, creed or background. In a day and age when class and colour barriers existed, it aimed to circumvent them and attract teenagers who wanted to improve themselves.

It was uniquely individualistic for its time. Unlike other youth programmes, such as the Cubs or Scouts, which required participants to join an organisation, including wearing a uniform, it was remarkably informal. It did not require the participants to join any organisation, nor did it have a uniform. This harkened back to Philip's days of penury. As a young man, he had had no changes of clothes, and Dean had chosen to wash his dirty socks and shirts in the full knowledge that, if he did not do so, Philip would have no change of clean clothes. Unlike just about everyone else in Establishment circles, he had experienced deprivation and therefore calculated for it in such a way that lack of funds would not put anyone off The Duke of Edinburgh Award scheme.

Prince Edward, who has gradually over the years taken over most of his father's duties with the scheme, told a friend of mine that it was 'a cause very close to (Philip's) heart'. He saw a gap in the market, so to speak, and resolved to fill it. It was basically providing teenage boys who wanted or needed an opportunity, to come together and learn how to improve themselves while having fun doing so with other boys. In so doing, they would not only learn to develop skills within and outside of themselves, but would also learn how to better appreciate themselves, their surroundings and the other participants. In short, it was character and community building wrapped up in fun and useful activity.

In November 1957, the scheme was expanded to include girls, the first of whom joined in September 1958. Since then, year by year, participation in the DofE scheme has grown. The age limits have also been both lowered and raised, to allow youngsters between the ages of 14 and 24 to participate. In 2017, some 420,000 young people of both sexes throughout the UK took part in nearly 11,000 designated DofE centres. These include schools, youth clubs and businesses. Over 6 million people have taken part in the UK from the time of founding till 2017, 8 million worldwide. Abroad, the awards are modelled on the scheme and presented by sponsoring organisations affiliated with The Duke of Edinburgh's International Award Association in 144 countries: 29 in the Americas; 36 in Africa; 32 in Asian Pacific countries; and 47 in Europe and the Arab countries and Mediterranean basin.

The scheme was, and remains, completely voluntary. Its strength is that it makes learning fun. It 'empowers the young,' giving them a sense of awareness that is both individual and communal. Philip's painful childhood as well as the saving graces of Kurt Hahn's philosophy have been integral to the founding and continuing success of the scheme. Philip himself wanted to embrace the young, to encourage them the way Kurt Hahn had encouraged him. He set about giving disadvantaged youths the opportunity to grow beyond their narrow and possibly painful circumstances, by showing them that there is always another way and another life outside of their own. Restricted and restrictive circumstances can be surmounted. All you need are the tools and a desire to do so. Many a participant over the years has said that the DofE award gave them their first inkling that they had the ability to improve themselves. It gave them not only hope but a glimpse of future possibilities, by putting them in touch with their potential. Since this was the first scheme which sought to invigorate youths, not for political or nationalistic advantage, but for their own advantage and that of society generally, and since it has had an impact upon millions of lives over the decades, it is fair to say that Philip made an incalculable contribution to society, one which is not yet recognised fully, but which, with time, might well be. Even if it is not, however, lack of recognition does not take away from the accomplishment, nor from the gift the scheme gave to the millions of participants who benefitted from it.

The other original, altruistic enterprise upon which Philip embarked in 1956 was the founding of the Commonwealth Study Conference. One of the challenges faced by Lilibet and Philip was to update the old imperial system into something more relevant to the modern age. They were both aware that the British Empire was in the process of being dismantled. Britain could no longer afford its empire, nor could it service it any longer as it had when it ruled the waves. They appreciated the economic and political realities long before most politicians did, and understood the importance of revamping the empire into a Commonwealth of willing nations. This was a vision they shared, and the mere fact that Philip was, at this particular time, founding something related to the Commonwealth demonstrates that they were still functioning as a couple. The Study Conference was conceived as a bridge-building exercise, but this time the objective was not between people and themselves as well as between people and each other, the way the DofE Award scheme was, but between industry and the community.

In 2006, Philip described how the first conference came about, saying, 'The purpose of the conference was to look into the tensions, problems and opportunities created by this dichotomy between industrial enterprise and community development.' The first conference was held in Oxford to study the human aspects of industrial issues throughout the Commonwealth countries. Philip agreed that it was 'an extraordinary experiment' that provided people in all walks of life from all over the Commonwealth the opportunity to break out of their usual roles and, by joining a diverse group, to expand their horizons and knowledge as they examined the relationship between industry and the communities surrounding it. Participants were from all sectors of society and included such diverse groupings as trades unionists, governmental representatives, businessmen, non-governmental organisations, and health workers. Since its inception, there have been ten separate conferences. These have taken place in such diverse locations as the United Kingdom, Canada, Australia, New Zealand, India, and Malaysia. There have also been a number of related regional conferences which have been offshoots of the major conferences, and these have examined areas of concern that are particular to one region but not necessarily shared by others.

There is a third project which was being worked on in 1956, which also demonstrated that the marriage was in better shape than the press believed, for by this time there were rumours that Philip and Lilibet were estranged, though, typically for that more deferential age, most of the stories were published abroad and not in the United Kingdom. This other project would end up coinciding with the Suez Crisis, and would actually be misrepresented and used as evidence of trouble within the marriage, when in fact its conception and execution proved that there was less conflict between Philip and Lilibet than was being supposed.

Philip had been asked to open the 1956 Summer Olympics in Melbourne, Australia. These were due to take place in November and December, and were only the second Olympics which were split between two countries. The first had been the 1920 Olympics, which took place in Belgium and the Netherlands. The 1956 Olympics were split between the Antipodes and Stockholm in Sweden, because Australian law prevented the importation of horses for the equestrian events. At Buckingham Palace, the new and younger courtiers took the decision with Lilibet and Philip to accept Australia's invitation and to send out the newly-commissioned royal yacht *Britannia*, and to take advantage of the proximity of Australia to visit other far-flung British territories in the Southern Hemisphere, as well as Antarctica. This initiative was conceived to strengthen links between the Mother Country and its far-flung possessions, whose status, as stated above, Lilibet and Philip, and their Household, were concerned to convert from imperial allegiance to Commonwealth co-operatives.

The *Britannia* left Portsmouth on 28th August and, avoiding the Suez Canal because of the deteriorating relations between Britain and Egypt, took the long haul down the west coast of Africa via Freetown, Luanda, and Cape Town before arriving in Mombasa in Kenya on the east coast. Margaret was already there, having flown out from England to begin yet another of the tours calculated to strengthen ties between Britain and its East African possessions. Her standard was hoisted and she boarded the yacht, which conveyed her on the first legs of her five week tour, stopping off at Aldabra Island, Assumption, the Farquhar Islands and Zanzibar, before depositing her at Dar-es-Salaam. The *Britannia* then headed back to Mombasa, where Philip boarded her for the main part of his four-month tour.

Philip was accompanied by Mike Parker as well as his good friend and artistic mentor, Edward Seago, with whom he sketched and painted many a scene over the coming months. Baron had been expected to go along as well, as the official photographer, but he went into hospital for routine surgery on his hip shortly before and died unexpectedly at the age of forty-nine. Philip , Robin Dalton and all his other friends were naturally saddened by this unexpected turn of events, but the expedition, which was intended to study plant life and other scientific matters, required another photographer, so Mike Parker duly went to Baron's studio to see whether Baron's assistant, Antony Armstrong-Jones, would be suitable. He returned firmly vetoing the idea: the young man was simply too bohemian. Three years later, when Margaret was marrying him, Philip, who was going to be giving her away, had a good laugh with Parker about how this latest addition to the royal family hadn't been suitable for employment as a photographer, but was now suitable for inclusion in the family.

From Mombasa, Philip and the royal party steamed to the Seychelle Islands, Ceylon, Malaya, New Guinea, before heading to Australia, where he opened the Olympic Games. Afterwards, they continued the tour, taking in New Zealand, the Falkland Islands, South Georgia, Gough Island, Tristan da Cunha, St. Helena (where Napoleon died), Ascension and The Gambia. The purpose of the tour was serious. Philip was already interested in the budding ecological movement, which he would do so much within a decade to put on the map, and the plan was that he and a group of scientists would board the research ship, the *John Biscoe,* and journey to twelve separate research stations in Antarctica, when the royal yacht reached the southernmost point. The remainder of the tour would be the typical meet-and-greet, hand-pumping, drumming up support that characterised royal tours. While some of the activities were light-hearted, others were typical, with lunches, receiving lines, receptions, and dinners: the standard fare for such occasions. There were serious explorations, formal functions, and less serious swimming expeditions in bays and at picnics, with bare-breasted native girls dancing at the occasional official reception, which would later be portrayed as exceptional and lascivious when, in fact, they were neither, such ceremonies being common practice on royal tours, representative as they were of the traditions of the people being visited.

Some of the tour was actually arduous, but the British press were not interested in reporting the discomforts or the underlying seriousness of it, whether it was scientific or political. Intent on coming up with a good story, irrespective of the facts, they undermined its true purpose, which was primarily the strengthening of bonds between the Mother Country and the remaining colonies and Dominions, and secondarily the scientific work which was being undertaken. Both Philip and Mike Parker would later complain that 'the media was only interested in exploiting it in a salacious way.' With nothing more exciting than serious issues to report, the press took to ever-increasing reports about Philip and Lilibet's marriage being in trouble. There was a short leap from that to the trip being characterised as being a cover for a lascivious, boys' own adventure: a massive waste of public funds. Visions of pretty girls being smuggled aboard the *Britannia* for nights of pleasure were evoked, along with hints that Philip and his suite were nothing but typical sailors who had a girl in every port and one or two in their cabins between ports. Alternatively and contradictorily, some of the stories also implied that Philip was being punished for having been a naughty boy back home. In that rendering of the tale, the trip was an updated version of banishment to the colonies, to teach him how much better off he would be if he returned to England and behaved himself like a proper consort, instead of like Jack The Lad.

Of course, the press have never needed to know the facts before embarking upon a sea of speculation. All they need is the hint of a rumour to run with it in print. Speculation is inflated into headlines and, before you know it, a few whispers in the corridors of power are turned into stories that might, or might not, be true, but which have a life of their own and are read as if speculation is fact. Yet one cannot blame the press entirely. Philip's demeanour since the accession had not helped. It was apparent to all onlookers that there was a problem, and a major one at that. King Peter of Yugoslavia, who had married his first cousin Princess Alexandra of Greece, hit the nail on the head when he said, 'It was as if a volcano had been stoppered up. You could feel it all underneath.' Like many others, he wondered, 'how long he can last…bottled up like that?' Because Philip confided in no one, and never spoke about his feelings, which always remained severely guarded with everyone, including those closest to him, and because those feelings were so patently disaffected, onlookers cannot really be blamed for registering the fact that something was seriously amiss. It was a short leap from noting his simmering rage to leaping to the wrong conclusions. Add to that the tendency of the press to leap to conclusions and make twenty two of two and two, instead of four, and their need to sell newspapers, and it is easy to see why they now purveyed rumour and speculation as fact.

By this time, rumours of trouble within the marriage were rife. This was hardly surprising. Newspaper magnates like Lords Beaverbrook and

Rothermere, owners of the Express and Mail newspapers respectively, had impeccable connections. There had indeed been gossip not only about Philip's dissatisfaction with his lot, but about the underlying reasons for his demeanour. In fashionable circles, the word was that Philip and Lilibet's marriage was in trouble because of his infidelities.

To an extent, the press cannot be blamed for leaping to the wrong conclusions. Society was awash with rumours about Philip's conduct and the Buckingham Palace policy of always keeping them in the dark, and the Queen's Press Secretary's reputation for intentionally starving them of all information, whether accurate or not, did not help the press in their search for the truth.

It also didn't help that Philip was a devastatingly handsome man who liked women. He treated them with an ease of manner that few upper class Englishmen of the time possessed. Being patently unhappy with his lot, it was almost inevitable that molehills would be mistaken for mountains from the perspective of the press. What also fed the rumours about Philip's interest in women was that he was fun-loving and gregarious. Despite being guarded on an emotional level, he was always up for a good laugh, and for a good time, and his forthrightness meant that he did so openly.

Philip himself would say that he sought to hide nothing because he had nothing to hide. But to those of less frank disposition, his behaviour was deemed to be an illustration of his contemptuous for their more discreet ways. They criticised him for flaunting his indiscretions in their faces with a brazenness that was typical of The Hun, and decided that he was not only indiscreet, but also arrogant.

Bearing in mind that one of the earliest objections to Philip had been his frank and rampant masculinity, and the belief that no one as potently masculine as he could ever be faithful, the tendency of women to swoon in his presence did not help. What he regarded as perfectly innocent behaviour, however, was easily misinterpreted by others, not all of whom were his detractors, though the latter leapt upon all misinterpretations to further their denigration of him.

It is difficult, once a reputation in public life has been established, to live down early misconceptions. This is the dynamic that now came into play where Philip was concerned. The Lascelleses, Salisburys, Eldons and Bowes Lyonses had laid the ground so well that thereafter everyone would be looking for infidelity whether any existed or not. A case in point is how his behaviour with Pat Kirkwood became twisted into something sordid and adulterous. She was an extremely sexy and striking blue-eyed brunette, the highest paid musical star throughout the forties and fifties. Billed as Britain's answer to Betty Grable because of her magnificent legs, which in turn were billed as the eighth wonder of the world, she met Philip in 1948 when she was starring at the London Hippodrome in the Starlight Roof revue. This show was one of the hits of the day; it also introduced a twenty year old soprano called Julie Andrews to the West End stage. Baron was having an affair with her at the time (her previous boyfriends had been the movie star Peter Lawford, later married to John F. Kennedy's sister Patricia, and Danny Kaye), and after a long and boozy lunch at the Thursday Club, he suggested that he, Philip and his naval equerry, Captain 'Basher' Watkin, 'take in' the show. Lilibet was incapacitated, being heavily pregnant with Charles. There was nothing untoward about Philip going on from the Thursday Club to a show. In those days, wives did not expect their husbands to dance attendance upon them while infirm, the way they now do, but expected them to entertain themselves without additional consultation.

After the show, Baron took Philip and Watkins backstage to meet his girlfriend in her dressing room. The four of them then went for a late supper to *Les Ambassadeurs*, the private club in Mayfair at the opposite end of Piccadilly from Leicester Square. Philip drove Pat Kirkwood in his MG sports car, while Baron and Watkins made their way separately. Philip, still relatively gauche and still showing the effects of his former penury, asked her if she wished to share his choice of drink, beer, to which she snorted derisively, 'Beer?! I'd like some champagne, please.' After supper, the four of them adjourned to the Milroy nightclub upstairs, where Philip spent the remainder of the evening dancing exclusively with her. This, of course, was hardly surprising, as she was the only female member of the group. Afterwards, the party adjourned to Baron's flat, where they ate scrambled eggs, or, as the royals called them, buttered eggs.

Pat Kirkwood explained her appeal. 'He was so full of life and energy. I suspect he felt trapped and rarely got a chance to be himself. I think I got off on the right foot because I made him laugh.'

Within days, London was ablaze with stories about the evening. *White's Club*, that bastion of the Establishment whose membership included virtually every senior courtier, past and present, as well as such political figures as Winston Churchill's son Randolph and his protégé Brendan Bracken, was abuzz with talk of an affair. As the rumour mills ground on, the story got better and better, until they were claiming that Philip had given Pat Kirkwood a white Rolls Royce. This, of course, should have been a red flag to any knowledgeable bull at the palace, for Philip simply did not have the means to buy himself such an expensive trinket, much less a putative girlfriend who was actually the girlfriend of his good friend, Baron. But the rumours suited Philip's detractors, who at the time were intent on 'keeping him in his box', and it was only a matter of time before word got back to George VI. He was furious on Lilibet's behalf, and according to one of Clarence House household, 'the King sent for Philip and gave him a colossal dressing down, to his great resentment.'

Philip was resentful for two reasons. Firstly, his and Pat Kirkwood's conduct had been entirely innocent, and was being twisted into something it was not. Secondly, he was furious that he was being treated as if he were a little boy who had been misbehaving, when he was an adult male who had not. If he expected greater loyalty and trust from his father-in-law, he did not from Lascelles and his ilk, especially as how the rumours were undermining his position, while furnishing them with proof that they had been quite right in expecting Philip to be incapable of marital fidelity.

The power of fiction to flourish as fact is never easily countered. Lilibet certainly believed in the innocence of Philip's encounter, and went with him to see Pat Kirkwood perform as the Principal Boy in a pantomime. Pat Kirkwood would also be invited to partake in four separate Royal Variety Performances. After each one, she was presented to Lilibet and Philip.

By 1954, she was such a huge star that she was the first female to have her own, hour-long show on British TV: *The Pat Kirkwood Show*. That same year, she also broke box-office records with a sold-out, three month cabaret season at the Desert Inn in Las Vegas.

Pat Kirkwood was firmly convinced that the rumours linking her and Philip had an adverse effect upon her career. I am not so sure; at least, not at first. The rumours elevated her profile and kept her at the forefront of the public eye. Philip also appears to have relished the attention at first. According to her third husband, actor, playwright and composer Hubert Gregg, 'The truth is that he was flattered to be linked with a famous and beautiful star.' That might well be so, for Philip is sufficiently vain and unconventional to have enjoyed having his desirability affirmed at the very moment that he was causing discomfort to the 'moustaches', like his *bête noire* Lascelles, at the Palace. Gregg also claimed that Philip actually asked his wife to a Sweethearts and Wives Ball at the Royal Naval College. This might well be so too. It has all the hallmarks of the young Philip: assertive, rebellious, demanding to be allowed to breach the confines, in an overt demonstration of his innocence of the charges laid against him. It might also have silenced the rumourmongers once and for all. Pat Kirkwood, however, declined.

Chapter VIII

The Pat Kirkwood saga, however, was only the first of a long line of stories which were spread about Philip and women. However, the constant reiteration of the rumours of them having had an affair had so adversely affected her well-being and public image that she claimed that they had 'ruined my life.' She wrote to Philip in the hope that he would issue a formal denial.

Philip's response was interesting. 'I am sorry indeed to hear that you have been pestered about that ridiculous rumour,' he replied. 'The trouble is that certain things seem to get into journalist folklore and it is impossible to get it out of the system. Much as I would like to put a stop to this, and many other similar stories about other members of the family, we have found that, short of starting libel proceedings, there is absolutely nothing to be done. Invasion of privacy, invention and false quotations are the bane of our existence.' He recommended, 'your best bet is to put the facts squarely in your book. It may not make a difference to what the evil-minded may think, but I am sure that most reasonable people would accept what you say, and then it would be on record.'

Pat Kirkwood, however, had spent several decades issuing denials. She felt that only a denial from Philip would matter. But the Palace, as a matter of policy, invariably refused to refute rumours, in the belief that refuting some, but not others, would lead to substantiation of those which could not, truthfully, be denied. She therefore wrote to Philip again, stating rather pointedly and somewhat bitterly, 'I think if there had been some support from your direction, the matter would have been squashed years ago instead of having to battle a sea of sharks singlehanded.'

Her fourth and last husband, Peter Knight, a solicitor and former president of the Bradford and Bingley Building Society, agreed that she had been damaged. 'My wife has been a star for 66 years and has given a lifetime's service to the public and to charity. Anyone else with her pre-eminence in the field of pantomime and musicals would have been made a Dame of the British Empire. She does not even hold an MBE.' She concurred, stating, 'It is an episode that has done me an immense amount of harm.'

By this time, Pat Kirkwood had become extremely litigious as she unsuccessfully fought a rear-guard action to bury the rumours and come out from under the silt they had tipped over her. An example is how she responded when she discovered that Tim Heald was writing Philip's authorised biography, *The Duke*, in 1991. His publishers received a letter from Daynes, Hill & Perks, her solicitors, warning them that she would sue for libel if there was any suggestion of a romantic relationship. Philip's private secretary and good friend , Brian McGrath, telephoned her at home in West Bruton on the North Yorkshire Dales, making the extraordinary suggestion that she should write out what she wished to appear in the book. He informed her that Philip, who was checking the proofs of the book himself, would ensure that her account appeared exactly as she wrote it.

Despite this denial, a few years afterwards, the continuing stories were causing her such distress that she and her husband went to see Sir Brian McGrath. When she was informed, in the politest and most considerate of terms, that they would not actually breach Palace policy and overtly deny the rumours, she complained, 'A lady is not normally expected to defend her honour publicly. It is the gentleman who should do so.'

If Pat Kirkwood ended up feeling that Philip had failed in his gentlemanly duty to protect her reputation, the other woman, who featured prominently in the rumourmongers' stories in the first decade of the marriage, took a far more understanding view of the constraints under which he was functioning. This was because Helene Cordet was actually from a far more sophisticated background than Pat Kirkwood. She understood how royalty operates. Born Helene Foufounis on 3rd July 1917, she was from a prominent Greek royalist family, which went into exile when the monarchy was abolished in 1922. 'I've known Prince Philip more or less all my life,' she told me in 1992. 'My family lived in Marseilles and his in Paris when we were children.' They also had a beach house at Berck Plage near Le Touquet in Normandy. Helene had a brother, Iaini, and a sister Ria, who was crippled with a defective hip. Her mother and Philip's were close friends, and the two families spent as much time together as they could. There had been talk in the Greek community when they were both children that they might one day marry, but Philip and Helene were like brother and sister. She told me there never was a glimmer of romantic attraction between them, though they were extremely fond of each other. They also shared the experience of exile, which was an additional bond, but again, not one which triggered romantic feelings.

In 1938, Helene married her first husband, an Oxford undergraduate named William Kirby. Following a civil ceremony in Oxford, Philip was both best man to Kirby and gave her away at the Greek Orthodox ceremony in Bayswater, in a mark of how close the two families were. By 1943 the marriage was over. Helene fell in love with Captain Marcel Boisot of the Free French Air Force and gave birth to his son, Max Henri Boisot, on 11th November 1943, in Maidenhead, Berkshire. Fifteen months later, on 8th February 1945, she gave birth to a daughter, Louise, also in England. Had Philip not married Lilibet, and had Helene Cordet not gone on to become a huge cabaret star following that marriage, a discreet veil could have remained drawn over the births of the two children. The elder was born out of wedlock, before she had a chance to divorce Kirby and marry Boisot, which she did in January 1945. Philip was godfather to both children, something that would never have happened had he and Helene had anything to conceal. Of course, it was virtually unheard of for well-bred young ladies like Helene Boisot to produce children out of wedlock in the 1940s, so the very fact that she had, and that the children were openly acknowledged by Marcel Boisot, should have been enough of a story to keep the gossips happy. Not a bit of it, however.

After Boisot was posted to Egypt, Helene's marriage to him fell apart and she returned to Paris, where she had a hard time making ends meet until she decided to exploit the singing voice she had always been told was beautiful. 'My family did not approve when I went into show business,' she told me. 'They thought my choice of career *infra dig*. I started as a singer.' Being slim, blonde and attractive, with a vibrant personality and 'sex appeal', she soon came to the attention of Henry Caldwell, the producer of the BBC hit series, *Café Continentale*, which ran from 1947 to 1953. It 'was a great success and became the No. 1 show,' Helene said. She became the show's presenter in 1951, so by the time of Lilibet's ascension, Helene, who took the stage name of Cordet, was a household name. Regrettably for all concerned, the irregularity of her children's births had, by this time, captured the imagination of the gossips. Without even bothering to delve into the facts to come up with an explanation as to why one of the Boisot children had been born out of wedlock, the rumourmongers decided that both Max and Louise were Prince Philip's. This caused grave embarrassment, not only for the Foufounis family, which had already had to put a good face upon Helene's unconventional behaviour, but also for the children. So began the tale of Philip's illegitimate children, which to this day is accepted as gospel in uninformed quarters.

Helene Cordet told me, 'The stories bothered us all greatly, my children especially. Max even went to the extreme of announcing that the man named on his birth certificate was his father, not Prince Philip. Of course, the press has paid not a blind bit of notice. It really was a case of not allowing the facts to interfere with a good story.'

Throughout the 1950s and into the 1960s, Helene remained in the public eye. According to her, 'My second husband and I opened up a restaurant at 6 Hamilton Place on the site of the Inn on the Park. It was a success but made no money, what with food going off and pilferage and all the other wastage that restaurants suffer from. I wanted to get out of the restaurant business, I was looking around for something else to do when I went to a club in Paris with good music. That gave me the idea to simplify things with our restaurant, to open up a place with good music that served only simple food like hamburgers. So I opened up the *Saddle Room Club*.' This she did with her lover, a dashing Guards officer named Major Peter Davies, following the end of her marriage. Although they never married, they were solidly a couple. This club was London's first discotheque. 'It opened on 4<sup>th</sup> October 1961. It was also on Hamilton Place off Park Lane, near to the restaurant, which had been at number six. It was a great success.' So successful was it that it survived into the early 1980s, when plans to open similar establishments throughout Europe took her to Switzerland, where she remained for the rest of her life, protesting about the way her friendship with Philip had been misrepresented.

Throughout Philip's Australian and Antarctic tour, there had been speculation in the foreign newspapers to the effect that his marriage was in trouble. Once more, the stories about his philandering were rife. However, the British press was still relatively quiet, so it was easy for the royal family to ignore the rumours. Then Mike Parker's wife Eileen lit a match by seeking to separate from her husband during the tour and, when this became public, the ensuing conflagration not only scorched her husband but also Philip and Lilibet. Divorce was still supposed to be a preventative to a career at Court, Townsend having got away with his because he had been the innocent party. But Parker was no Townsend, and the consequences for him were therefore different.

What happened next has been twisted over the years, with Philip being portrayed as eager to accept his friend and private secretary's resignation while Parker would have preferred to remain in his post. In fact, Parker himself has suggested to the contrary, and Martin Charteris confirmed this years later in a conversation at the Cundy Street Flats in London's Belgravia. When the story broke, Parker immediately offered Philip his resignation. Not only did Philip not accept it, but he also spoke to Lilibet, who herself telephoned Parker and told him not to be precipitate. They did agree, however, with his suggestion that he return to London when the *Britannia* docked in Gibraltar. Not only would such a course of action divert the press's attention away from his private life back to official business – Lilibet was due to fly out to Portugal for a state visit, which had been planned to dovetail with the end of Philip's tour – but there was also every necessity for him to return home to see his wife, who had not yet instituted proceedings.

In the years since Parker and Philip had become friends in 1942, Eileen Allan had gone, from being the actor James Robertson Justice's flame, to Parker's girlfriend and finally his wife in 1943. By 1947, when Philip asked Mike to join his Household, she was an integral part of the Edinburghs' circle. By her own account, she, Mike and their young son Michael often went to lunch with the boss and his wife at Windlesham Moor, the country house in Surrey George VI rented for them. They also made up foursomes for dances at such places as the Dorchester, to the theatre, to restaurants and even to nightclubs. These foursomes continued in Malta, where they also shared picnics, with the two women taking trips to the hairdressers. The Parkers also used to go up to Balmoral, but after the birth of their daughter, Julie, they began drifting apart.

Following the accession, Eileen Parker began to feel like a grass-widow. What cannot have helped was the evident pleasure her husband took in the turn his life had taken since becoming Philip's private secretary. Though he and Philip were now grown men with families and worldly responsibilities, they thoroughly enjoyed each other's company, and both had a propensity to schoolboy pranks, which they indulged in to their delight and her increasing displeasure. She complained that he was on call six days a week, and enjoyed his duties at the Palace more than being with her. Gradually she grew to resent her husband as well as those who she felt had taken him away from her, while Parker is on record stating that he felt that their marriage had been the biggest mistake of his life. Reading between the lines of her 1982 memoir, *Step Aside for Royalty*, one can detect real anger at how he preferred being at the palace to being with her. Even the title of her book betokens the resentment she felt at being supplanted. Mike Parker would later claim that the moves she initiated, while he was on the tour with Philip, to separate, came like a bolt out of the blue. She wanted to cause maximum damage, and she succeeded. She believed that his career had destroyed her marriage, so now she intended to destroy that career.

When the *Britannia* docked in Gibraltar, Parker disembarked, to return home by air on a flight where every seat but his and his lawyer's was occupied by a journalist. At London airport he found himself obliged to give a press conference, and thought how 'splendid' it was of Commander Richard Colville, the Queen's press secretary, with whom he had a strained relationship, to have 'motored down from the Palace, presumably to help out.' Just as he was about to thank him, Colville said, 'Hello, Parker. I've just come to let you know that, from now on, you're on your own.'

Although Colville might have thought he was issuing the *coup de grâce*, in fact Mike Parker knew he still enjoyed the support of his boss and the boss's wife. They knew how preposterous were the rumours surrounding the goings-on on the trip. There was supposed to be a girl in every port, as if either Philip or Parker could have been making assignations ashore when they were followed everywhere by the press and state officials. Equally ludicrous was the idea that they were smuggling girls on board the royal yacht. It had a full complement of crew, officers and ratings. All comings and going were noted by the harbour master as well as the watching press. There was no way anyone could have smuggled anything on board. It simply wasn't possible. Moreover, Edward Seago, the *artiste-en-voyage*, was a good friend ,not only of Philip's, but also of Queen Elizabeth The Queen Mother's. Was Philip likely to philander under the eyes of someone who would take word back to his mother-in-law? In the overheated cauldron of press sensationalism, reason gave way to rumour, which only fanned the flames heating up the bubbling stew further.

When Parker returned to London, he saw that his wife was determined to get a divorce. Supposedly the final straw for her was when he neglected to contact their daughter to wish her a happy birthday while he and Philip were away. According to their son Michael, 'It is no secret our parents had an unhappy marriage.' Eileen would later claim that her husband and Parker used the names Murgatroyd and Winterbottom to leave the palace so they could 'gallivant'. This was taken as confirmation that they were partners in adulterous goings-on, but there was an alternative, and more accurate, interpretation. They were both high-spirited and fun-loving young men who hadn't outgrown the pranks of their youth. They would indeed be out and about 'gallivanting', but the gallivanting they were doing was partying with friends, meeting up for lunch, drinks, or supper, knocking back a few drinks and, in typical naval fashion, enjoying the camaraderie of other men. It was all Boy's Own stuff, tiresome in the eyes of the courtiers, who also resented their pranks, such as skating along corridors when they weren't tearing around town speeding from one all-male gathering to another, but readily understandable when one of the duo had a wife who was always otherwise engaged, while the other had a wife with whom he did not wish to engage. It is easy to understand why Eileen Parker was fed up with her overgrown boy-husband, and even more fed up with his overgrown boy-boss, whom she blamed for leading her husband astray, but equally easy to see Parker's point of view. He said that she blamed Prince Philip for being a bad influence on him, but the truth is, she had settled into middle-aged respectability while her husband, who did not really want to be with her, had not. Angry at what she perceived as his 'abandonment', she wanted out, and there is little doubt that it was gratifying to her that in so doing, she would destroy his career and bring the Boy's Own party of Murgatroyd and Winterbottom to an end.

In those days, there were few grounds for divorce: cruelty, desertion and adultery being the choices. 'Divorce was very difficult in those days and my father did the decent thing and provided grounds for my mother to divorce him. He made an appointment with a photographer who "caught" him in bed with another woman,' his son said.

This was standard practice at the time. Mrs Mary Alexandra Thompson was a plant who came to the Parker house at Smith Street, Chelsea, after which Eileen had grounds for the divorce she wanted. She applied for it, getting it in early 1958. By that time, her husband, 'an honourable man' according to his son and everyone else who knew him, knowing what his wife had in store for him, had fallen on his sword. Although Philip was reluctant to accept his resignation, they both realised that the ensuing publicity would turn the divorce into a '*cause célèbre*', which it did. As the protocol was that members of the Royal Household should not be the story, neither man had much of a choice. His son Michael remembers how his prep school even went to the extreme of removing the newspapers to shield him, a fact which a friend of mine who was at school with him confirms to have been the case. So Parker did the decent thing by both the boss he loved and the wife he did not, and Philip regretfully accepted his resignation.

This could not have come at a more poignant time for both men. Boy Browning was in the throes of a serious nervous breakdown, exacerbated by heavy drinking, and though Philip and Lilibet exercised great patience, giving him two years in which to recover, he finally resigned in 1959.

Meanwhile, both Philip and Lilibet agreed to reward Parker with the overt demonstrations of support they felt he deserved. Philip therefore commissioned him to continue fulfilling various duties on his behalf, and the two men remained friends, keeping in touch for the remainder of Parker's life. For her part, Lilibet demonstrated her support in the most vocal way she could, creating him a Commander of the Royal Victorian Order.

Under any circumstances, there was a pressing need to fill the crucial role of private secretary, but with Boy Browning ill as well, it was necessary to do so as quickly as possible. Parker was therefore replaced by James Bernard Vivian Orr (1917-2008), an Old Harrovian police officer who had also attended Gordonstoun and was a graduate of the military college at Sandhurst. Parker eased his replacement into the role, helping out where he could. Although Orr was capable and efficient, and though he and Philip enjoyed a cordial relationship, they never had the close friendship that the two naval buddies had had. He served until May 1970.

While the saga of the Parker divorce was unfolding over a period of a year, Philip and Lilibet did everything in their power to demonstrate that there was no 'rift' in their own marriage. The first demonstration took place two weeks after Parker's departure for London, when the *Britannia* docked in Lisbon. Philip drove to the airport to meet Lilibet, who was arriving by air to begin the state visit to Lisbon. In typical enthusiastic fashion, he ran up the stairs of the aircraft to greet the wife he had not seen for nearly six months. While on his trip, he and many of the other men had grown beards. Although he had now shaven his off, when he entered the aircraft, everyone on board, his wife included, was sporting a huge ginger beard. This was just the sort of prank he relished, and after much laughter, he and Lilibet emerged from the aircraft wreathed in smiles. Their evident pleasure, in seeing each other after such a long time apart, went some way towards countering the rumours, though not for long, as events would subsequently prove.

To further get the point across that there was no rift in the marriage, on 22nd February 1957 Lilibet granted Philip the style and title of a Prince of the United Kingdom by Letters Patent. To those who knew about royal rank, style and title, this was exceptional, and to those who didn't, the message was unmistakable when the London Gazette made it clear that Philip had been raised to the stature of a sovereign's son. Thereafter, he would be known as His Royal Highness The Prince Philip, Duke of Edinburgh. The all-important The was what conveyed her Majesty's supreme pleasure in her husband, for only the children of monarchs are Their Royal Highnesses The Prince or Princess of Anywhere, all other royal princes and princesses, Prince Philip of Greece included, having to manage without that all-important definite article.

This was a declaration of intent, which, it was hoped, would silence the Doubting Thomases, for Lilibet had promoted Philip as no other consort had been since Mary Tudor's husband Prince Philip of Spain in the 1550s. Nevertheless, the press remained convinced that the marriage was in trouble. Partly, this was through ignorance: most journalists simply did not understand the minutiae of titles, so the true meaning escaped them. They therefore alighted upon the fact that Philip had not been made Prince Consort as further proof that there was a slight or a con somewhere in the transaction, ignorant yet again that 'the title of Prince Consort is meaningless', to quote Martin Charteris. It was a straightforward honorific with which Victoria had endowed Albert, who had also had to face opposition from the press and politicians.

This, however, was the beginning, not the end, of the doubts expressed by the press. Yet another suspicious viewpoint was propounded in the American papers by *The New York News* and *Chicago Tribune Dispatch*. This was that the elevation had been to prevent Philip from being called as a witness in the Parker divorce. 'Despite his title as duke and first gentleman in the land, Philip could have been subpoenaed to testify for Mrs Parker until his elevation to prince on February 22 lifted him beyond the range of a subpoena,' they declared. They had plainly never heard of Prince Albert Edward, Prince of the United Kingdom of Great Britain and Ireland, Prince of Saxe-Coburg-Gotha, Prince of Wales, Duke of Cornwall and Rothesay, Earl of Chester and Dublin et al, heir to his mother Queen Victoria, the first heir to the throne to be compelled to appear, in June 1891, in an English court of law as a witness since 1411. They plainly also did not understand that the precedence Lilibet had given Philip in 1953 particularly excluded his son Charles when he, as heir to the throne, took precedence by British law, and if a Prince of Wales – any Prince of Wales – could be hauled into court as a witness, anyone else, Philip, included, whether he was a British prince or merely a British duke, could be as well. The sole exception was the sovereign, who could not be forced to testify in British courts, as they were her courts and all criminal cases were brought in her name.

Despite the speculation about the state of their marriage, which Philip has conceded both he and Lilibet found irritating, by 1959, they were privately enjoying a re-structured life. She had come through the difficulties thrown up by Princess Margaret's thwarted love affair and was now back on a firm and loving footing with her sister. Her relationship with her husband had also evolved. Like all marriages, theirs had had its ups and down, but had grown from the first burst of romance into something altogether more substantial. All couples who have been married for a decade need to make adjustments, whether they be prince or pauper. The reality of the beloved is always somewhat at variance with the initial expectation, and the marriages that grow successfully are those that make the transition from hope to reality. Philip still felt bruised by the 'name issue', but he understood Lilibet's predicament and it was not the 'hot potato between them that people seemed to think it was.' Privately, they were mutually supportive. They remained deeply committed to each other. They were no more demonstrative in terms of affection than they had ever been, but that did not mean there was not deep love there. Not only was it evident to people who knew them well, but it was so obvious that several people, from royals to bishops, have told me the same thing to cover various periods of their lives, from the 1950s to four years ago. They never display physical affection, not even the briefest touch, which in itself is nothing remarkable, for few well-bred people of their generation did. Touchy feely was regarded as inelegant. 'No unseemly displays of affection,' my mother used to warn us when we were newly married and inclined to want to touch and kiss *en famille*, but despite this class injunction, it has always been possible to tell who had a good relationship. With Lilibet and Philip, there was, and remains even at this late stage of their lives, a palpable bond of affection between them which everyone who is in their company for any length of time picks up on. They often glance over at each other, checking to see that everything is alright, or just merely catching each other's eye as if to say, 'Everything's fine with me. Hope it is with you.' When it isn't, they swiftly but subtly make their way over to one another, butting in and defusing whatever situation needs to be dealt with. They also have the easy camaraderie of genuine affection. He will tell her to 'shut up, you don't know what you're talking about', while she will encourage people to defend their stance when Philip, always challenging, has someone on the spot. Such conduct is the mark of genuine affection, and, as it is conveyed so subtly, it cannot be faked. Indeed, it is as vivid as the glances with which lovers, who wish to conceal their relationship, reveal themselves.

Publicly, Lilibet and Philip have always been equally supportive, albeit in a less detectable way than privately. They have achieved a *modus vivendi* which has worked for them as a couple and as a team. Like two flanks of the same army closing in on a target, they strike out separately, but always with the plan of action in mind as they seek to achieve their objectives, which has always been whatever is good for the monarchy and its citizens. It might sound precious to those who do not understand such things, but both of them are deeply spiritual people who believe in God and believe that He placed them on this earth, and gave them their positions, so that they could achieve something positive for mankind. Their attitudes are vocational. In a way, they are like a secular priest and nun. This is not a stretch, for Lilibet takes her position as Supreme Governor of the Church of England seriously, and is, in fact, the equivalent to the Pope in Anglican terms, while Philip's mother was the head of a religious order. It would have been surprising if two people, steeped in religious heritages as they were, with well-developed spiritual dimensions to their personalities, would have taken a self-aggrandising approach to their positions. The fact that they did not is what has ultimately allowed them to flourish the way they have done. Or, as Philip's grandmother Victoria put it, 'What will live in history is the good work done by the individual & that has nothing to do with rank or title.'

# Chapter IX

THE LAST YEAR of the old decade was a time of renewal in another way. After Princess Anne's birth in 1950, Lilibet and Philip had briefly enjoyed the respite offered them by George VI's improving health to enjoy themselves before having any more children. This reprieve had turned out to be only too brief, for, before they could take full advantage of it, their whole lives had derailed as a result of the king's ill-health and death. In the nine subsequent years, they had not been in command of their destiny. Only now, as the 1960s loomed, did they feel that they were sufficiently in control of their lives to permit themselves the luxury of adding to their family.

Family and family life mattered greatly to both of them. They were both young and aware that this was the time to have more children, if that is what they wanted. It was.

Early in 1959, Philip flew to India and Pakistan for a tour. He was entertained by Indian and Pakistani royals as well as by the governments of both countries. Twelve short years before, his uncle Dickie had presided over the greatest bloodbath and population upheaval of all time, during the independence of those two countries, so the trip was important, both in terms of healing wounds and building new relationships. The late Rajmata of Jaipur, whom I knew, was at the time of Philip's visit the Maharanee. She used to be very funny describing how she and her husband, the reigning Maharajah, hosted 'a very easygoing' Philip – 'He was such fun' - on a tiger shoot.

The most problematic leg of the tour having been safely dispensed with, Philip flew to Rangoon, where he embarked in the *Britannia* for visits to Singapore, Sarawak, North Borneo, Hong Kong, the Solomon Islands, the Gilbert and Ellice Islands, and Christmas Island. He was back in England in time to give a speech to the NATO Banquet at Guildhall on 14th May 1959, and to impregnate Lilibet.

The date of conception is important, for later on, in the 1990s, the gossip columnist Nigel Dempster (1941-2007) would spread the rumour far and wide that the baby conceived in May 1959 could not be Philip's, claiming that 'the dates don't fit'. He asserted both privately and publicly, on television in the United States as well as in various newspapers, in private conversations and on public occasions, that Prince Andrew, who was born on 19ᵗʰ February 1960, was definitely the son of Lord Porchester, the beau whom George VI had said he'd 'be buggered' if he would allow his daughter to marry.

Porchy Porchester and Lilibet had remained close friends. In 1956, he had married a very pretty American named Jean Margaret Wallop of Big Horn, Wyoming. She was a scion of an eminent but relatively penurious Anglo-American family, whose head was the Earl of Portsmouth. It was, and would remain, a love match. Within three years of marriage she had produced two sons, George (known as Geordie), the 8th and present earl, whose godmother Lilibet became, and Henry 'Harry' Herbert, who would go on be one of Diana, Princess of Wales's closest friends. Their family home, Highclere Castle (now best known as Downton Abbey from the eponymous series) is near to Windsor Castle. The two families had maintained their friendship, and Porchy and Jean Porchester and Philip and Lilibet saw each other as often as their diaries allowed.

Porchy and Lilibet had one overriding passion in common: love of horseflesh. Philip, on the other hand, was bored by the turf. Typical of any healthy, well-adjusted couple, they gave each other the space to pursue independently interests the other did not share. This meant that Lilibet, who by this time was on the way to creating one of Britain's leading stables, had her horsey friends, while Philip occupied himself otherwise. Turfites are a breed apart, as I can attest from personal experience. My father's family was racing mad. They were leading owners and trainers for the first thirty years of my life. They lived and breathed thoroughbred racing. It was more than an interest; it was a passion, as it always is with turfites. They would happily talk about horse flesh and everything related to it for hours on end, while those of us, myself included, who had no interest became Swedes following a conversation in Swahili. As anyone who has had to endure a close relationship with a turfite knows, you either learn to love the turf or you absent yourself. There are, believe me, better things to do at five o'clock in the morning than getting out of your warm bed to watch horses exercise – unless, of course, you are an avid turfite, in which case the activity represents a high watermark in the pool of pleasure. There are also few conversations less stultifyingly dull than listening to an owner, a breeder, a groom and a trainer jabber on about the relative merits of two yearlings. Nembutal is an invigorator compared to hearing about the history of the dams, sires, foals and fillies that fill out the bloodlines going back centuries. All self-respecting turfites possess the most intimate knowledge of the pedigrees of each and every race horse that has ever won a race. They are obsessed with breeding, and even someone as well read as my father found greater pleasure in perusing *The Bloodstock Breeders Review* (which was a genealogical reference work on racehorses going back hundreds of years) than in reading anything else. As Philip and my mother both learnt once married, if you can't summon up that degree of interest naturally, you really are better off leaving them to their own kind. For all its limitations to those of us who have no real interest in it, the racing world has very obvious appeal. It is exciting, thrilling even, filled with fascinating people whose love of the sport shines through their eyes. It is also a world of absolute equality. Whether you are a rich man, a sovereign, a prince or the humblest groom, everyone listens to anything you have to say, and weighs up the content of your contribution, not on your background or worldly standing, but on its merit. It is truly one of the most classless of sports, a genuinely level playing field where nothing counts but improving your knowledge so that you pick, or breed, or ride, or own, or groom, more winners than anyone else. The result is that relationships with the strongest of bonds are formed between turfites. Sex seldom plays a part in it, possibly because the greatest thrill an avid turfite can achieve isn't a climax in bed but a win on the racecourse. The lack of sexual frissons is as outstanding a feature of the racing world as its classlessness.

It was therefore no surprise to anyone that Lilibet and Porchy became as close as they did. She had his confidence, and he hers, because they were evenly matched in knowledge of the track: a rarity, and one to be relished in the racing world. There was nothing ominous, suspicious, or sexual in any of this. But Dempster knew that the word in Palace circles was that Lilibet found Porchy 'attractive', as indeed he was. Many women found him attractive, just as how many women found Philip attractive. Tall, handsome men are attractive: it's as simple as that.

Never one to miss an opportunity to create mischief, especially if he felt someone had not given him his just deserts or indeed needed hauling down a peg or three, Dempster alighted upon this perfectly innocent scenario and set about creating Everest out of a cup of sand on a beach. Because he had written a biography of Princess Margaret in 1981, and had a tenuous association with her, he used those facts to boost the veracity of his claims, implying that the 'truth' of the baby's paternity had come from Margaret herself. This, believe me, was truly outrageous, but proved how right Josef Goebbels was when he pointed out that it's easier to get people to believe a big lie than a little one.

Because the story that Dempster invented and disseminated gained such wide coinage, and to this day is believed in certain quarters, it might be helpful to provide an insight into its source. The scion of a respectable, middle-class Western Australian family, Dempster's father was a mining engineer and his mother an Anglo-Indian nurse at the Calcutta Hospital. He was born in Calcutta, India, but brought up in England. He attended Sherborne School, a minor public school in Dorset, which would have been a huge source of discomfort to him, obsessed as he was with the 'right' school and the 'right' background. The two E's could have been coined to describe him: it was Eton and England, or nothing, where he was concerned.

Although Dempster's parents were perfectly respectable, this was not good enough for him. He was so ambitious, pretentious, and such a social climber that the only things that exceeded his social aspirations were his malice and his self-hatred, the latter being carefully concealed as arrogance. Nevertheless, it was as apparent as the nose on Pinocchio's face, to anyone who had a grain of sense in his or her head.

Regrettably, I had the displeasure of knowing Nigel Dempster rather too well; not that we were ever friends. In fact, I successfully sued him for libel and had the pleasure of walking away with a nice amount of damages as well as my legal fees. These cost his employers dearly, but if you sup with the devil you shouldn't complain when you get indigestion. I also had the pleasure of unmasking him for the fraud he was, in *The Sunday Times*, when he tried to discredit me and I ended up discrediting him, revealing to all and sundry what his background, of which he was deeply ashamed, was. This was after twenty years of him knowingly writing lie after lie about me, each of which had involved his papers' lawyers and mine in extensive and costly correspondence. But Dempster took pride in the number of writs his editor received, regarding them as badges of honour, quite forgetting that he wasn't tilting his sword at windmills but at living, breathing people, who at least deserved being written about truthfully. He was like a sociopathic murderer, who views his murder victims as scalps, and misses the point that accomplishment, to be positive, cannot be based upon a negative, and if it is, it is more akin to a disgrace than a credit.

Despite his amoral approach, Dempster was on cordial terms with many people with whom I was friendly, so I got to learn about both his good and bad side. For instance, his second wife's stepmother Caroline, Lady Hobart, was a friend of mine. She would sooner have drunk arsenic than sipped water from the same reservoir as her step-daughter's husband. But he was undoubtedly clever, and could be charming, witty and entertaining, though you were either someone whom he was cultivating to exploit, or you were an acolyte to whom he would be a good and loyal friend as long as you sucked up to him. There was no in between. When people didn't play ball with him, his fury was either hot and out of control, or cold and contained. His abuse of his staff was legion. His reactions were so bizarre that you couldn't have made them up. For instance, he was once caught up in a traffic jam. His response was to turn off the engine, get out of his car, taking the keys with him, leave it in the middle of the street right where it was stopped, walk a block or two and hail a taxi to get to where he wanted to go. Of course, his irrational and irresponsible action gridlocked traffic for hours, but he was so self-centred, so uncaring of the consequences of his actions, so lacking in proportionality, that he actually took pride in what he had done. The only sensible conclusion to come to was that he possessed a serious personality disorder.

Where Dempster's column was concerned, he didn't so much dip his pen in acid as relish destroying people. He would hack through reputations with crazed delight the way axe murderers gleefully delight in chopping up their victims. One of his friends told me that his problem was that he was ashamed of being mixed race, and was always on the attack in case people should discover his secret and cause him to be mocked by his smart friends. His hit list of targets included the Aga Khan, Queen Noor of Jordan, Sir James Goldsmith, Margaret, Duchess of Argyll, yours truly, and the Queen.

For some years, Dempster used to write a gossip column in the satirical magazine, *Private Eye*, along with an altogether more decent journalist named Peter McKay, who, incidentally, has one of the greatest sense of humour known to man. From Dempster's point of view, this column was a repository for every story he couldn't get past the legal team at the *Daily Mail*, where his main column gradually supplanted *William Hickey* in the *Daily Express* to become the leading gossip column in the country. Truth, however, remained the last of his concerns. A good story was all that mattered, and if it could achieve the dual purpose of dragging down someone who was better placed in the pantheon of life than he was, while boosting him, so much the better. For a while, his craven enviousness actually passed as fearless unmasking, and during this honeymoon period, the editor, Richard Ingrams, nicknamed him *The Greatest Living Englishman*. This was a droll moniker, akin to giants being called Tiny, for Dempster was neither great nor an Englishman, though he wished he could be mistaken for both, and was known on occasion to remind people in all seriousness that he was the greatest living Englishman. Mad. Absolutely mad.

Once, I was lunching in *Drones* on Pont Street, and Dempster was on the adjoining table openly stating that he felt it was time the Queen recognised that he was indeed *The Greatest Living Englishman* by knighting him. He must have been drunk but he wasn't joking. None of his companions was laughing either. He had recently written a biography of Princess Margaret (1981 – *Princess Margaret, A Life Unfulfilled*) and demanded a knighthood as a reward for having rescued her reputation. This, notwithstanding the fact that he had actually been largely responsible for breaking the news of her romance with Roddy Llewellyn to the public, and could more fairly have been accused of helping to bring her into disrepute.

In fairness to Dempster, he could well have had a neurological condition with which he might have been born. He would die of progressive supranuclear palsy, and whether this was brought on by a genetic weakness, or his heavy drinking contributed to it while exacerbating his irrationality, or he was just a born sociopath who had always had a problem, and took to drink to self-medicate, the fact remains that he was expelled from school for being disruptive, and spent the rest of his life being wilfully destructive. He was mischievous in the worst meaning of the word, a sadist who enjoyed causing pain to those he took against. The two journalists who actually wrote his column once it had been established as the leading gossip column, which it was by the mid-1980s, were Helen Minsky and Adam Helliker. I know them both and they are both decent people as well as excellent journalists. Both of them used the same words to describe him to me at different times, saying 'he's not quite right in his head.'

Whatever Dempster's problem, he was a nasty piece of work who dragged everyone whom he targeted into the gutter. The very first time I met him was in 1975 after I had featured, much to my distress, on the front pages of tabloids all over the world. While my family and I found such attention distasteful, many others thought it quite an accomplishment. Dempster was one of those, sailing up to me at a party, introducing himself (I had no idea who he was, even after he gave me his name: I didn't read tabloids in those days), then tried to impress me by saying that his father had been a Governor of Jamaica. When I pointed out that none of the governors had been a Dempster, he said that his father was Lord Caradon, who as Sir Hugh Foot had been governor of Jamaica and latterly Cyprus. This I knew to be untrue, for my parents had known Hugh and Sylvia Foot (known to us as The Feet) and, as Dempster so succinctly and incorrectly observed with regard to another matter, the dates didn't tally. Also, my brother Mickey was, at that very time, a pupil in Hugh's brother, Sir Dingle Foot's chambers at 2 Paper Buildings, Temple, so my knowledge of the Foot family was rather greater than Dempster had reckoned with. This, however, was just the sort of silly but self-aggrandising lie for which Dempster was notorious. Had the Feet not been the leading socialist Establishment dynasty in the country at the time – a third brother, Michael, was a Deputy Leader of the Labour party prior to becoming its leader, and Britain had a socialist government at that time – he would not have been seeking to boost himself via an association, no matter how illegitimate in all meanings of the word, with them. To say that I found him preposterous doesn't even begin to convey how I felt.

Nevertheless, by the time our paths crossed, he was on an upward trajectory as a gossip columnist. He espoused socialist values (a joke if ever there was one) and pretended to possess a contempt for the privileged classes that even then was transparently dishonest, for he was a crashing snob who was flagrant about cultivating only the socially prominent. This hypocritical stance provided valuable cover for him as he ponced his way through Society, cutting a swathe with his pursed lips and mincing little walk that even someone as camp as Noel Coward would have had difficulty emulating, writing the most vicious stories about those who were either grander than he was (very easy) or would not kowtow to him.

One of his favourite targets was my step-mother-in-law, Margaret, Duchess of Argyll. Still a great beauty in her sixties, she supplemented her thinning hair with a hairpiece. Because she had severed relations with him, following his attempt to write a biography of her which was prurient and untrue, he took to referring to her in his column as the 'periwigged' Margaret, Duchess of Argyll. Virtually every week he would have a go at her either in the *Daily Mail* or in *Private Eye*, bitchily using the objectionable description and, I am told by journalists who witnessed it, howling with glee at the humiliation he was heaping on her head every time her solicitor wrote complaining. Then he went too far, inventing an incident in which her hairpiece got stuck in the revolving door of the Grosvenor House, where she lived. The only problem being, wigs, peri or otherwise, cannot get stuck in revolving doors. I recount this because it shows the way he functioned: vicious, spiteful, relentless, and untruthful.

This, then, was the creator and disseminator of the rumour that Prince Andrew was Porchy Porchester's son. There was never any doubt in my mind that his reason for spreading the falsehood was malice, pure and simple, because he had wanted to be knighted, and was punishing the Queen for not knighting him. As if knighthoods are given to purveyors of gossip. His utter lack of attachment to reality, his complete disproportionality where his desires and actions were concerned, was really quite something to behold. In his own way, he was fascinating, in much the same way that one would be transfixed by a snake wrapping itself around a baby separated from one by impenetrable glass. You wouldn't be able to take your eyes off the ghoulish spectacle, nor would you be able to escape from the true horror of what was happening.

Dempster's tawdry interpretation aside, Andrew's birth was a happy time for the royal couple. In the run-up to it, Lilibet also set about righting the wrong that had been done to Philip in the weeks after her accession, when the name of the dynasty had become an issue. The opening shot was fired by Edward Iwi, a Jewish solicitor and constitutional expert, who had been ' on several occasions proved right and on at least one of these occasions could have caused the government grave embarrassment – I refer to the unfortunate mistake by which Princess Arthur of Connaught was named as a Counsellor of State in 1944. Iwi spotted the error but was good enough to keep quiet about it,' Sir George Coldstream, the Lord Chancellor's private secretary, wrote to Lord Kilmuir. My great-grandmother was born into one of the world's great Sephardic families, and the word in the Jewish community has always been that Iwi was happy to join forces with Philip, on a point of principle, and on a further point of solidarity with Dickie Mountbatten, whose wife Edwina was also of Jewish heritage. He was not only intent on righting a wrong but also helping the larger Jewish community by ensuring that the partly-Jewish Mountbatten dynasty would receive its rightful recognition as the reigning dynasty of Britain.

Iwi would turn out to be successful, but not for want of opposition from the government. In September 1959, he wrote to the prime minister, Harold Macmillan as well as to Buckingham Palace, thereby ensuring that any governmental opposition could be thwarted by Lilibet, who felt that the time had come to right the wrong of 1952, 'When the new baby is born,' Iwi wrote, 'as matters now stand it will bear the Badge of Bastardy namely, it's mother's maiden name. As far as I know it will be the first legitimate child to be so born. You will recall that Windsor was the Queen's maiden name and on marriage she took her husband's surname of Mountbatten. Prince Charles and Princess Anne were born with the surname Mountbatten.'

The government's response was immediate and, it hoped, decisive. Lord Kilmuir told Macmillan, 'This is in very bad taste. Iwi must be silenced,' while Macmillan responded to Iwi, asserting, "You are quite wrong in stating that Windsor was the surname of Her Majesty before marriage or that Mountbatten was ever the surname of Prince Charles or Princess Anne. Moreover even if you are right about this, I could not think that the surname Windsor could be other than a distinction or that there is anything ignominious in bearing the name of a great house derived through a female ancestor.'

Iwi, however, was not prepared to be silenced. He was already in touch with Mountbatten, and knew that he had the full support of both Philip and Lilibet. He responded on 17th November, pointing out, 'No one is infallible,' before continuing, 'If the royal family has never possessed a surname or a family name, then the Proclamation of 1917 substituting Windsor for Guelph would never have been necessary....The 1952 Amendment changed the children's name from Mountbatten to Windsor and conferring on children yet unborn what to the man on the Clapham Omnibus [the hypothetical benchmark for the English public in legal terms] is a badge of bastardy, namely the mother's maiden name or family name.' Iwi pointed out that he had 'reason to believe that many right thinking people share my view,' an allusion to the sermon recently preached by Thomas Bloomer, the Bishop of Carlisle, who had come out in support of the name change.

It is doubtful that this was idle coincidence. Nevertheless, Macmillan remained reluctant to go along with the name change. He has written about a visit with the Queen and the Duke of Edinburgh in which she was perilously 'close to tears' while Philip was 'brutal' about the change being effected, but Macmillan had completely misread the desires of his sovereign. It was only in January 1960, the month before the baby was due, that any real progress was made. Macmillan was on an official visit to South Africa and the Home Secretary, Rab (Richard Austen) Butler (later Baron Butler of Saffron Walden) (1902-1982) turned up for his first audience with the Queen in his capacity as acting Prime Minister. He was an altogether more approachable personality than the aloof, inhibited Macmillan (whose wife Dorothy had been conducting a decades-long affair with the Conservative MP Robert 'Bob' Boothby [1900-1986]), and Lilibet seized the opportunity to inform him that she had 'absolutely set her heart' on changing the royal surname. Faced with such opposition, Macmillan relented and on 8th February 1960, she issued a new declaration, this time to the effect that all her descendants who did not enjoy the title of royal highness would be known by the surname Mountbatten-Windsor. The following evening, Edward Iwi joined Dickie Mountbatten and Philip for a celebratory drink at Broadlands.

What made Dempster's invention so objectionable was the accusation of cynical hypocrisy which was redolent throughout. Lilibet and Philip would have had to have been as amoral and sociopathic as he was, to go to the trouble of having the descendants of a bastard, which, in Dempster's interpretation, Andrew was, bearing Philip's surname. Even worse, they would have had to be truly gross to go further and compound such an act of overt dishonesty by naming the child, who Dempster was claiming was Porchester's, after Philip's father. Such cynicism would have been breathtaking indeed, and one is left with Philip's description of 'evil-minded' to explain Dempster's behaviour.

Towards the end of his life, Dempster admitted that he had made the whole thing up. He tried to pass it off as a joke, something which none of those affected by it found funny.

In the run-up to Andrew's birth, another event was taking place in the family which was a cause for celebration. Margaret was due to be married. The announcement of her engagement was delayed until after the impending birth, but Lilibet had given her consent to the marriage, notwithstanding many within the Establishment seeing the groom as unsuitability personified.

Margaret had met Baron's former assistant Tony Armstrong-Jones at a dinner party given by her lady-in-waiting, Lady Elizabeth Cavendish (1926- ), daughter of the 10th Duke of Devonshire, head of one of the most interesting families in the land. One sister-in-law of Elizabeth's had been John F. Kennedy's sister Kathleen 'Kick' Kennedy, Marchioness of Hartington; another was the former Deborah 'Debo' Devonshire, wife of Andrew, then the 11th duke; their aunt Dorothy was married to Harold Macmillan. The 10th duke even figured as a suspected victim of the most profligate serial killer of the age, having been commonly supposed to have been murdered by Dr John Bodkin Adams. He was suspected of the murder of over 160 patients, 132 of whom had left him as a beneficiary in their wills. Unimaginably, he was acquitted of murder in the most sensational trial of the time; a trial which made front page news all over the world. According to P.V. Cullen in *A Stranger in Blood: The Case Files on Dr John Bodkin Adams* (2006: Elliott & Thompson), there is considerable evidence to suggest that an acquittal was engineered at the highest level, for Dr Bodkin Adams was charged during the Suez Crisis, at a time when Harold Macmillan had succeeded Anthony Eden as prime minister. The view of the government was that public confidence in the Establishment would be threatened, and the National Health Service undermined, if an eminent general practitioner like Dr Bodkin Adams were found guilty, especially one who could be accused of killing the prime minister's father-in-law.

How arrangements were made is instructive of the way the British Establishment worked. Lord Goddard, the Lord Chief Justice, dined with the former Attorney General, Sir Hartley Shawcross, and Bodkin Adams's lover, Sir Roland Gwynne, in Lewes during the committal proceedings. The trial lasted seventeen days, at the end of which Sir Patrick (later Lord) Devlin 1905-1992), the trial judge, instructed the jury to acquit in not-so-subtle terms, using the novel premise that 'the word of a professional (namely Dr Bodkin Adams) should be preferred (by the jury) to that of non-professionals (namely the witnesses).' Dr Bodkin Adams, of course, denied murder.

## Chapter IX

The case of *Regina v Bodkin Adams* has entered the history books not only because such a prolific serial killer could have been allowed to evade justice, but because Devlin's instructions to the jury are still used by trial judges to let crooked solicitors off the hook when clients take them to court, notwithstanding the ruling of that great jurist, Lord Denning, in Griffiths –v– Evans (1953) that the word of a client, whether professional or otherwise, should always be preferred to that of a solicitor when here is no written record of an agreement regarding costs.

Despite the best efforts of people such as Lord Devlin to stymie change through such actions, change was nevertheless taking place. Nowhere more so than with Princess Margaret. Although it had been less than three years since she and Townsend had parted, and they were still in close touch, she had 'moved on', so to speak, and was now ripe for another big romance. It was the done thing in those days to introduce people in the hope that something would click, not that Elizabeth Cavendish actually expected Margaret and Tony to hit it off the way they did.

Still alive at the time of writing, she was a childhood friend of both Lilibet and Margaret, and would remain one of the latter's closest friends until her death in 2002. She had what was then known as an artistic circle of friends. In fact, her way of life was what the courtiers would have called 'Bohemian'. The very soul of aristocratic discretion, she did as she pleased, but paid lip service to convention. She was the girlfriend of the famous poet, and later Poet Laureate, (Sir) John Betjeman, an acknowledged bisexual with whom she had been having an 'established relationship' since 1951. His wife Penelope was the daughter of Field Marshal Lord Chetwode, and a Roman Catholic, so divorce was impossible. Nevertheless, the lovers were accepted in civilised circles as a couple, to such an extent that when John Betjeman died, his daughter Candida Lycett Green, a great friend of Prince Charles, described Elizabeth Cavendish as 'my father's other wife.'

Nevertheless, the sparks that flew when Margaret and Tony met were unpredictable. Both were young, good-looking and highly sexed. Both were charming and rebellious. Both were witty and fun-loving. Both commanded a room. There was therefore an instant and overpowering attraction which would manifest itself sexually and remain so even after they loathed each other.

More than merely irreverent, Tony was really a wild, somewhat disturbed, spirit whom no woman could satisfy, much less contain. Margaret, of course, did not realise what trouble he was as she embarked upon a torrid affair with him. When she discovered that Peter Townsend was planning to marry the twenty year old lookalike who had replaced her in his affections, she more or less proposed to Tony. He was actually in love with Jacqui Chan, who was completely in love with him. The West Indian-born actress gave him all the freedom he needed. And he needed a lot. He had had affairs with both men and women, including Susan Grindling's sister Camilla and her brother-in-law Jeremy Fry. The Jamaican playwright Sam Hillary, who moved in that crowd at the time, told me that when word got out that Tony was planning to marry, the question everyone asked wasn't, 'To whom,' but 'To what?' Margaret, Duchess of Argyll, who was an old friend of his mother's, also said that Anne Rosse was instrumental in convincing her son to marry Margaret. She was 'extremely socially ambitious', and he could have been under no illusion that the surest way into her good graces would be to give her the Queen's sister as a daughter-in-law. His strongest motivation, therefore, seems to have been a desire to please the mother whom he had never before been able to please, and please her he did. Only then did he achieve parity with his two half-brothers, Brendan, Lord Oxmantown, and the Hon. Desmond Parsons, his full sister having already risen in Anne's eyes when she had married Viscount de Vesci in 1950.

Also pleased with Margaret's choice was her mother. Elizabeth 'adored Tony', who was charm itself when he wanted to be. Colin Glenconner also felt that Elizabeth was happy that Margaret had not made a spectacular marriage. She was 'very competitive' with her daughter and was happier if she did not achieve her full potential. 'Her worst nightmare would've been PM making a truly grand match,' Colin believed. 'Tony also buttered up Queen Elizabeth shamelessly, and she was vain enough to relish the treatment.'

If Elizabeth and Lilibet were pleased that Margaret had found herself a husband, royalty was dumbfounded and most of the invitations to the wedding on 6th May 1960 were turned down. Although there were two thousand guests present, and it was the first royal wedding to be televised, attracting three hundred million viewers worldwide, the only European royals who attended were those who had a link to Philip. These included his aunt Queen Louise of Sweden and her husband, King Gustaf VI Adolf, as well as his nephews Prince Karl of Hesse, and Princes Ludwig and Maximilian of Baden. The irony of these relations, who had been spurned at Philip and Lilibet's wedding, being the lion's share of the royal presence, was not lost on anyone.

Margaret's happiness mattered greatly to her sister, if not to their mother, and Lilibet was happy to lend her the royal yacht for her honeymoon. After the couple returned to London, they moved into Princess Louise, Duchess of Argyll's, old apartment at Kensington Palace, which was done up to the

Chapter IX

nines, much to the annoyance of some of their neighbours, who complained about the noise the refurbishment caused.

At first, all was well. Lilibet and Philip were happy for her, and Philip and Tony got along as well as chalk and cheese can. At least they had a fascination with gadgets in common, each of them being something of an amateur inventor. But this shared interest was not sufficiently strong to override the basic differences in their personalities. Philip was basically too restrained and considered a personality, too service orientated, to have much in common with so Bohemian and cavalier a personality as Tony. There was also Tony's cruel streak and his rampant promiscuity and pan-sexual approach, which, though kept from his in-laws, nevertheless bubbled beneath the surface.

The different tastes and interests of both couples also ensured that, while they got together for family events, their lives began to diverge in a way they had not when Margaret had been single. The Snowdons became the hot, glamorous couple of the sixties, out and about socially with the international elite like Elizabeth Taylor and Richard Burton, or Peter Sellers and Britt Ekland. Meanwhile, the former Edinburghs had settled down to a less glamorous existence, and seemed to relish the approach of middle age. Nevertheless, Margaret was as family orientated as her brother-in-law and sister, and within a year of the marriage, she was pregnant. On 6$^{th}$ October 1961, Lilibet created Tony Earl of Snowdon and Viscount Linley so that her sister's baby would be titled. On 3$^{rd}$ November 1961, Margaret gave birth to a son, David Albert Charles Armstrong-Jones, Viscount Linley, and two and a half years later she would produce a daughter, Lady Sarah Frances Elizabeth Armstrong-Jones on 1$^{st}$ May 1964. Eight weeks before, on 10$^{th}$ March, Lilibet had also given birth to her fourth and last child, Edward Antony Richard Louis, named in part after her charming brother-in-law.

Edward's birth and paternity passed without question, just as Andrew's did contemporaneously. Yet his too would become the subject of speculation in the early nineties. Before he died, Dempster would admit that he had made up the whole Andrew business. He did not claim to be the source of the Edward story, but then, he wouldn't have done so, because he was thwarted before he could disseminate it as far and as wide as he had done with the Andrew one.

Both stories were based upon resemblances, Andrew to Porchy, and Edward to his putative uncle, Shaun Plunket. Dempster was quoted by Christopher Hitchens in *The New York Times Magazine*, 'Get hold of a picture of Prince Andrew and then one of Lord Porchester at the same age. You'll see that Prince Philip could never have been Andrew's father.' Just as that story was getting traction, all of a sudden the coincidental resemblance between the Hon. Shaun Plunket (1931-2012) and Edward began to be commented upon. Before it could gain traction the way his one with Andrew had done, Shaun Plunket, his wife Andrea, and I knocked heads together and found a way of diffusing it.

It so happened that Shaun was an old friend of mine. I had first met him when he was married to Elizabeth de Sancha, whose daughter Antonia would create a stir when she had an affair with the Conservative politician David Mellor. After Elizabeth's suicide, he used to escort a dear friend of mine, Lorna, the Baronessa Moncada lo Guidice, and we saw a lot of each other; but she too died prematurely, of breast cancer. He then married Andrea Reynolds, the exotic Hungarian whose third husband had been the film producer Sheldon Reynolds. I did not know Andrea until Shaun introduced us, but we became great chums. She was very bright, and had achieved a not-altogether respectable renown when she fell in love and lived with Claus von Bulow between his first and second murder trials. It was actually Andrea who spotted the anomalies and sought out the lawyer Alan Dershowitz, who got him off. Although some people thought her brash, Shaun found her 'entertaining. I married her because she entertains me,' he told me. She was also very salt of the earth, and while not everyone liked her, I did.

To her credit, Lilibet did not take the prudish view either, but embraced Andrea once Shaun had married her, always asking them to all her important private events. To Andrea's credit, she was very discreet about Shaun's friendship with the royal family, for it was not only Lilibet with whom he was friendly. He was also close to Queen Elizabeth The Queen Mother and Princess Margaret, as all the Plunket brothers were. In fact, Patrick was David Linley's godfather.

In the early 1990s, before Shaun and Andrea moved to upstate New York, where they lived for the remainder of their lives, we decided to nip in the bud the rumours that had started to circulate in smart circles about Edward being his eldest brother Patrick's son. Patrick had been the 7th Lord Plunket. He had also been an equerry to King George VI before becoming one to Lilibet from 1948 to 1954, after which he became Deputy Master of the Royal Household. This was a position of some influence and responsibility, but it was no sinecure. He knew how to throw the most amazing parties, the like of which have not been seen at Buckingham Palace since his death at the age of only 43 in 1975.

All three Plunket boys were effectively Lilibet and Margaret's foster brothers, tucked under the wing of Elizabeth when she was queen consort following the death of their parents in a plane crash in 1938 *en route* to stay with William Randolph Hearst at Xanadu. No event of any consequence ever took place without the Plunkets being invited. Shaun loved Lilibet like the sister he had never had, but was always very respectful of her, even though they had known each other since childhood. He always referred to her as The Queen, even to Andrea, and called her Ma'am in person.

Although I didn't know Patrick (he died before Shaun and I became friends), I knew that Lilibet and Patrick had been extremely close friends. They both had good senses of humour and could be cripplingly funny. She has always been a very good mimic, with a very dry sense of humour, and that, added to his irreverence, made for some very funny opportunities as they bounced off each other, especially after events which he had organised on her behalf. Each of them, in their own way, was also something of a conspirator: he in organising events that would be interesting and appealing for her and her guests, which would reflect well upon her and advance her and Philip's agenda of making the monarchy more relevant, less starchy, more up-to-date, and she because she loved nothing better than when something went awry and they could have a good laugh about it. In his own way, Patrick was Lilibet's party Porchy. Social events were, and remain, an important part of the royal, or indeed presidential, way of life, so she and Patrick had a common goal in planning events that might, on the face of it, look just like another reception, or another dinner, but in fact had an unseen momentum and higher purpose. Social life, at royal or aristocratic level, is a far more serious pastime than outsiders might appreciate. It can also be deadly dull, or far more fun than you would otherwise imagine, but what makes it so is the people. For that reason, anyone whose life requires a degree of official engagements relishes being with people who make them laugh. And Lilibet had absolute confidence in Patrick, whose ability, taste, and integrity made him a reliable Master of her Household.

In fact, when Patrick was diagnosed with cancer in his early forties, Lilibet insisted that she be kept abreast of his progress. As the prognosis became more tragic, she insisted on being kept up-to-date with what was going on, and when she knew the end was near, she ordered that she be informed of the end as it was coming. In fact, he died while she was on an official engagement, which was interrupted to give her the news. She burst into tears; one of the few times in her life she has been known to cry.

Reigning royals do not usually attend funerals. There is a good reason for this. Their circle of friends and acquaintances is so wide that they'd end up at gravesides with such frequency that their mental health would be jeopardised – and that is without considering their even wider official and political circles.

Equerries, lords- and ladies-in-waiting and other representatives therefore stand in for them at funerals. Patrick Plunket's, however, was the exception. Lilibet not only attended his funeral at the Chapel Royal, but his memorial service at the Guards Chapel. She also ensured that he was buried in a place of honour, befitting that of her eldest and closet foster-brother, in the royal family's private burial ground at Frogmore in Windsor Park. She then went further and built a memorial to him in Valley Gardens, Windsor Great Park, where a little pavilion with four columns looks out over the valley.

Because of the closeness of the families, Shaun was anything but pleased when the story that Edward was his brother Patrick's son started making the rounds. He, Andrea and I knew that Nigel Dempster was behind it, and we decided to take the wind out of his sails before he could stir up more turbulence. The last thing Shaun wanted was a re-enactment of the Porchy storm, which at that time raged across the Atlantic as actual news. Not only was it unfair to Edward and Lilibet as well as Philip, but it also had the potential to damage his relationship with her. And that meant a great deal to him.

At the time, I was contracted to write a book on the royal marriages, and we decided that the way to beat Dempster at his game was for me to write about the rumours, making it clear that they were only rumours. None of us wanted to say that we knew it wasn't possible because Patrick had been a confirmed bachelor. Nowadays, that might not matter, but twenty five years ago, it did. Of course, we knew that 'everyone' knew where his real interests had lain, and if I wrote about the rumours in a decorous enough manner, Dempster would lay off, for the one thing he would never do was give oxygen to anything I had touched upon. So I did it; Shaun was pleased; Dempster dropped it like a hot potato; and Andrea, in typical Andrea fashion, sent me a Christmas card from Prince Shaun and Princess Andrea, with a host of exclamation marks accentuating the point.

It would not be fair to end this section without allowing Nigel Dempster credit where it is due. When I heard he was dying, and dying horribly, I telephoned him, really to make him feel bad. 'Georgie,' he said in a very shaky and earnest voice. 'You of all people 'phoning. I don't deserve it. I wish I could take it back. All of it.' A lump rose in my throat. I had intended to tell him that I'd heard of his illness, and I hoped he'd use the time left to reflect upon the pain he had caused so many people. I didn't have the heart to say any of it. I told him I would pray for him, and he told me that he was under the care of a priest we both knew. It was then that I realised that he had indeed been reflecting upon the havoc he had wreaked. He thanked me again for 'phoning, and I rang off. I did pray for him. But I refused to go to his memorial service, and to this day struggle to understand how he could have created the amount of mischief he did. Although he affected my life for twenty years, it is nothing compared to the damage he caused to Lilibet, Philip, and Andrew, and would have caused to Edward as well, had Shaun, Andrea and I not knocked heads together and come up with the way to stop him in his tracks.

# Chapter X

IF THE RUMOURS of Lilibet's extra-marital relationships can be traced back to Nigel Dempster, the source of Philip's is not so straightforward. As we have seen, the suspicion of infidelity was present even before the marriage, despite the lack of any proof or indeed overt inclination on Philip's part.

In the early days of the marriage, Philip did something which was perfectly innocent but would be used against him to suggest that he might well be proving his detractors right when they assessed him as incapable of fidelity. Sometimes he would arrive at Windlesham Moor with a female friend, driving her down in his MG sports car. They would go into the house, have tea, and leave, through the front door and by the MG whence they had come. He did not introduce her to the staff, not because he had anything to hide, but because the master of a house does not introduce his visitors to his staff (a nuance which seems to have been lost on those who presumably had never had staff and didn't know the form), although they were both being served. The presence of this strange woman raised eyebrows, leading to speculation of the wildest sort. Only too soon, his detractors at the palace were asking searching and downright silly questions, none of which included the most obvious one: If a married man is going to have sex with a girl, will be bring her back to his marital home, in full view of the staff, before he leads her into a drawing room, whose doors are not locked and whose curtains are not drawn, meaning that anyone can walk past outside and look inside and see what is going on, or barge in on them from the inside while they are *in flagrante delicto*? There are surely more discreet away of beginning a life of infidelity than having your employees bear witness to the fact as they advertently or inadvertently walk in on you? It says much about Philip's detractors, and about the level of suspiciousness they were intent on harbouring from the most innocent of activities, that perfectly straightforward visits with a female friend, who was openly served tea and nothing else, could have been used the way it was.

Yet, at the root of that early story lies a clue as to why Philip's life has been dogged by rumour. In the late 1940s, few upper class men had female friends the way Philip did. British upper class men were even worse than continentals. Having spent their early lives at boarding school, women were an alien species with whom they co-habited. But for companionship, the average gentleman looked to his male pals. In the broadest sense, women served many functions, but friendship was not one of them.

Philip, on the other hand, liked women. He always had and he always would. He had been the golden only boy in a family of girls, adored by both his mother and his father, as well as by his four sisters. As he grew up and his family splintered, he remained close to his four sisters, in a way he might well not have done, had he possessed a home to which he could return. But their homes were the nearest thing he had to his own home, and with that continuing closeness to them came an ease and an appreciation of women that was wholly unusual for the time. Helene Cordet confirmed to me that Philip was utterly at ease with the female sex in a way that few men of his generation were. There was nothing sexual about it, yet there was nothing asexual about it either. He remained the full-blooded alpha male which he had always been, while they remained the feminine beings they were. Without either party to the relationship surrendering any of their sexuality, they managed to forge relationships that did not include sex, but remained close. Philip had that rare gift: a real man who could be friends with a real woman without sex rearing its head.

Off what Robin Dalton has said in the past, I would say that Philip betrayed, even at that early stage of his life, a marked reserve and restraint sexually. He could separate sex from friendship in a way few men of his generation could, because he was motivated more by a desire for companionship than sexual intimacy. In his own way, he was very reserved, and has remained so throughout his life. A bishop who knows him and has observed him *en famille* told me that Philip is the most 'self-contained person' he has ever encountered, yet he 'accepts the adoration of women as if it were his due' but does not respond in kind. Indeed, he does not respond at all. That is possibly why he is sometimes taken for being a 'cold fish', not, in fact, that he is cold. He is 'completely self-contained' in a way that is indicative of a child who has learnt that he is worthy of being loved, and will be loved, but whom life has taught to keep his guard up at all times. He is a complex individual, plainly marked by the pain of his youth, but without the bitterness or dis-trustfulness that would have prevented him from becoming the attractive and life-enhancing man that he is.

Had Philip kept his guard up conversationally, the way he has done sexually, he might well have starved the rumours of the oxygen which they needed to flourish the way they did. However, he did the absolutely opposite, and to that extent, he shares some responsibility for the way his amatory reputation has spread. The film producer Peter Kares, who is married to one of my most longstanding friends for decades, told me of an incident that happened in the mid 1970s which absolutely typifies how Philip's naval tendency to let his hair down in a hail-fellow-well-met way has fed the rumours of infidelity over the years. He and Lilibet attended the premiere of the movie *Aces High* at the Odeon Leicester Square. She, of course, played her part to perfection, meeting all the stars and being perfectly majestic. He was the ideal consort, admirably accompanying her until she left to return to the palace at the end of the film, when Philip and the leading lights adjourned to a nearby club for the after party, at which point he not only fell into the spirit of the evening, entering into banter of the most raunchy kind with several of the men, but brought his competitive streak into play, and managed to exceed them in the most memorable way. Peter went away convinced that Philip was not only one of the raunchiest men he had ever come across, but was actually a major philanderer. 'He is one of the raunchiest men I have ever come across,' Peter said. 'And that's saying something,' for he has come across some major players in Hollywood.

What has also always fed the rumours about Philip is his rank physicality. He imbibed the lessons of Kurt Hahn so fully that even at ninety one he was vaulting over fences. As a younger man, his physicality was also noticed and commented upon. According to Ayesha (Rajmata of) Jaipur, 'he played polo with a gusto that had women going weak at the knees. When he leapt off his horse at the end of a game, many a woman was thrilled to the core by his potent masculinity.' To many an onlooker, the reasoning was: someone who is that sexy just has to be torrid. Torrid he might well have been, but the supposition that he put it about simply because he was torrid, was actually not proof of promiscuity, simply of being sexually appealing. And sexually appealing Philip undoubtedly was.

The Profumo Affair was really the first time Philip's name was dragged, if only peripherally, into a fully blown sex scandal. The scandal began simply enough. In 1961 Jack (John, 5th Baron) Profumo (1916-2006) met a stunningly attractive, nineteen year old sometime model and good-time-girl, named Christine Keeler (1942-2017). This was around the swimming pool of Cliveden, the splendid Italianate stately home owned by William Waldorf Astor II, 3rd Lord Astor (1907-1966). She was staying for the weekend as the guest of Stephen Ward, the society osteopath and Thursday Club member, who had a weekend cottage on the estate. Ward liked the company of pretty young girls, whom he often put up in his Marylebone mews house for months at a time. He seldom if ever slept with them, but occasionally his friends would do so. His conduct raised no eyebrows in those days, at least not in fashionable circles, though it would later be viewed with sanctimonious outrage by the press and the judiciary. It would certainly be regarded as remarkably unremarkable nowadays when promiscuity passes for freedom and sexual licentiousness is confused with the free exercise of choice. He was merely an aging bachelor who enjoyed seeing his friends having a good time, and made no moral judgements if people sometimes enjoyed themselves sexually.

Unfortunately for all concerned, another friend of Ward's was Yevgeny Ivanov (1926-1994), the senior naval attaché at the Soviet Embassy in London. It was no secret in political circles that many a spy was posted under the guise of being a diplomat, whether to London by a foreign power, or by Britain to foreign powers. Ivanov was known by British Intelligence to be a spy, and they hoped to turn him. This was at a time of great tension in the Cold War, with the Berlin Crisis of 1961 leading to the construction of the Berlin Wall, and the Cuban Missile Crisis the following year leading to the possibility of war between the USSR and the USA. MI5 therefore arranged for the managing editor of the Daily Telegraph to introduce Ivanov over lunch at the Garrick Club to Ward, who was happy to befriend him in the hope of encouraging him to defect. Ward introduced Ivanov to Keeler, who happily took him into her bed. Soon they were embarked upon an affair, unbeknownst to his wife Maya, who had accompanied him to London. The daughter of Alexander Gorkin, the chairman of the Supreme Court of the Soviet Union, she and her husband were in, Soviet terms, Red aristocrats, Ivanov was at the pool party at Cliveden when Keeler met Profumo, but any supposition that Keeler was anything less than generosity itself with her sexual favours would be unfounded. She was also the bed companion of several other men, all from the widest cross section of society, ranging from the black jazz promoter Johnny Edgecombe, another black West Indian, the jazz singer and cook Aloysius 'Lucky' Gordon, to the Red spy and the Minister of War in the Macmillan government.

In 1962, Ivanov and his wife were recalled to Russia, just as Keeler's unsavoury sexual antics were setting in motion the events that would bring down the Minister of War and Macmillan himself. On 27 October 1962, Edgecombe accosted Gordon with a knife at a seedy joint called the *Flamingo Club* as a result of Keller complaining to the former that the latter had assaulted her and held her captive when she tried to end their relationship. Gordon required 27 stitches to his face, but when Edgecombe asked Keeler to help him find a solicitor to defend himself, she refused to help the man whom she had incited to defend her welfare. Instead, she fled from her flat on Sheffield Terrace to Ward's place in Marylebone. Holed up there, she refused to come out of hiding when Edgecombe came to confront her on 14th December. So he shot up the door of the mews house, as people of such predilections are apt to do when remonstrating with the tarts whose non-existent virtue they have defended. He was duly arrested, charged and tried. Although acquitted of assaulting Gordon, he was nevertheless jailed for seven years, five of which he served, for possession of a firearm with intent to endanger life.

The trial, and Keeler's propensity to sell stories to the press, led to the greatest sex scandal of the age. Although every sophisticate anywhere in the world would have known how ludicrous a proposition it was that a vacuous neophyte like Keeler would have been capable of inducing Profumo to betray state secrets between the sheets, for her to pass on to Ivanov, the remote possibility was excuse enough for the press to declare that state secrets had potentially been compromised and 'heads must roll'.

It was at this juncture that Profumo made the fatal mistake of denying in Parliament that he had ever had an improper relationship with Keeler. This was an error of judgement, for he had ended their brief affair when the Security Services informed him that Keeler was also sleeping with a Russian spy. Within weeks, he had to tender his resignation, not because he had slept with Keeler, but because he had lied to Parliament, and the Secret Services knew it.

By this time, all sense of proportion had long since ceased. The Labour MP George Wigg stoked the fires in the House of Commons in the hope of bringing down the government or, failing that, making life as uncomfortable for them as possible, while the press increased the conflagration with the most sensationalistic reportage possible. More heads were demanded, and heads the press got in droves. Although Ivanov was safely out of the reach of the British press, his career stalled thereafter and his marriage crumbled under the exposure of his affair with Keeler. She was charged with perjury and sent to prison. Ward was charged with the ridiculous offence of living off the earnings of prostitutes, Keeler and her sidekick Mandy Rice-Davies. Tarts they might have been, professional prostitutes they most certainly were not. They lived off Ward's largesse, as well as the generosity of the many sugar daddies who bought them 'presents' and gave them 'pocket money' or 'cab fare' in appreciation of their practised horizontal skills.

Ward, who had been 'run' by MI5, was abandoned by the Establishment and turned into a sacrificial lamb in the frenzied atmosphere concocted by a sanctimonious and cynically hypocritical press, and the equally hypocritical sanctimony of the Labour party. He was tried in what must be one of the most knowingly flagrant abuses of the judicial process in the history of the United Kingdom, but committed suicide rather than go to prison for an offence he had not committed, the night before the guilty verdict which the kangaroo court intended to deliver was tendered.

There are two small footnotes to the Ward saga. The first was that George (by that time Lord) Wigg was charged with kerb-crawling towards the end of his life, an irony if ever there was one. And the second took place in the 1980s, when I was at an auction at Christie South Kensington. I had attended the viewing the previous day and was hoping to bid on several of the Stephen Ward portraits which were being offered for sale. All were priced from between the cost of an air fritter and a breeze ball. However, they were excellent pictures. He was a fine draughtsman and a portraitist of real talent. He not only captured a likeness superbly, but also conveyed character with subtlety. Each of his pictures was beautiful, which is a recommendation when all the other elements are artistically there as well. As I recall, there was a pastel of Princess Alexandra and another of Prince Philip, amongst several others. Many of the potential bidders were regulars at the auction house, so we knew each other. The protocol was that, if you wanted a picture and started to bid for it, you would look behind you to alert potential bidders as to your identity. There was a courtesy between the regulars which meant that we did not step on each other's toes and drive up the prices unnecessarily unless we really, really wanted an item, at which point competitors would do the decent thing and drop out. As the bidding started, I looked behind me and saw a man in a suit slip into the room and signal to the auctioneer to desist. I could tell it was a Savile Row suit. This was no ordinary art dealer or art lover, who would not have been turning up for a South Ken sale attired in such a manner, nor would the average person have the temerity to instruct an auctioneer to interrupt an auction with the most peremptory of signals. I was astonished to see the auctioneer stop, and seconds later someone else walked up to the podium, whispered something in his ear, after which he announced that all the Stephen Ward lots had been withdrawn from the sale. Later, I was told by a friend at Christie's that the man in the suit had been a courtier from Buckingham Palace. Two decades after the Profumo Scandal, the Palace was still determined to keep the connection between Ward and the royals under wraps.

Yet there is little doubt that the Establishment, which orchestrated the destruction of Stephen Ward's life, would never have bothered, had the royals been the only Establishment figures to protect. A far stronger motive was to protect the politicians. Yet, in throwing Ward to the wolves the way they did, the effect was to distance Philip from him. The two men had been friends, not close personal friends, but social chums. Both of them used to attend the Thursday Club, Philip more frequently than Ward. But the latter was nevertheless a fairly frequent attender, according to Larry Adler. There is no question of Philip himself being party to the miscarriage of justice that resulted in Ward's trial and death, but there is also little doubt the Palace were happy to close ranks with the rest of the Establishment and in so doing, prevent the monarch's husband from being dragged further into the scandal than he already had been. And by this time, word was rife in fashionable circles that Ward and Philip used to attend orgies together: orgies which Ward helped to organise, and which Philip was supposed to have attended. The most lurid of all these stories was that Philip was the naked man in the mask who would serve the other orgiasts at dinner.

Although these rumours were pretty widespread, it would have been virtually impossible for the average person to get verification of their extent. Yet the Master of the Rolls, the judge who presides over the civil division of Court of Appeal and who in 1963 was also in charge of the Public Record Office, was called in by the government and given the brief to create a Report into the Profumo Affair. As he himself would inform my step-mother-in-law, one of his briefs was to enquire into whether Prince Philip was the Man in the Mask. So it was as much to ascertain what, if anything, could be proven against Philip, as to dampen the hysteria in the press by appointing this most senior of judges e to investigate wrongdoing in public life, that the government appointed Alfred Thompson (Tom), Lord Denning (1899-1999).

Lord Denning began his investigations in the spring of 1963, and he published his conclusions that autumn, on 24th October 1963.

The Denning Report had a simple brief. It was to investigate wrongdoing in public life with regard to the Profumo Affair. Concurrent with the Profumo Affair, however, another sex scandal was taking place north of the English border, in Scotland, where my father- and step-mother-in-law, Ian, 11th Duke of Argyll, and Margaret, Duchess of Argyll, were slugging it out in the Edinburgh divorce court as he tried to divorce her citing adultery with multiple lovers. This case had been dragging on for over four years, and, unluckily for Margaret, it concluded two weeks before Jack Profumo resigned on 5th June 1963. Much was made during the trial about the identity of the supposed Headless Man, her lover whose head had been out of shot in the Polaroid pictures he and Margaret had taken of her fellating him. Margaret had declined to identify him to the Court, and the rumour spread, as rumours will, that he was either the Defence Secretary(later Lord) Duncan Sandys (1908-1987), who was married to Sir Winston Churchill's daughter Diana; ; movie star Douglas Fairbanks Jr.; Baron Sigismund von Braun, the diplomat brother of atomic scientist Wernher von Braun; American businessman John Cohane; or Peter Combe, who had been the press officer of the Savoy Hotel and was well known to be a confirmed bachelor (though he would later marry and father three children).   On 20th June, Duncan Sandys informed the Cabinet of the rumour that he might be The Headless Man, which opened up a new avenue of investigation for Denning.  He promptly announced that he wished to interview Her Grace as to the identity of The Headless Man, notwithstanding the fact that my parents'-in-law divorce had absolutely nothing to do with the Profumo Affair in England.  In so doing, he linked the two scandals, inflating each, notwithstanding that neither Ian nor Margaret was in government nor did they have a political position, and the Denning Report was specifically briefed to look into the Profumo Affair alone, not to enquire as to the identity of Margaret's lover.

'I cannot tell you how furious I was,' Margaret recounted to me years later, after I had met Lord Denning and made the mistake of telling her how much I admired him.  'How dare he drag my name into that sordid stink?  When he demanded that I come and see him, I told him in no uncertain terms that there was no way I would be doing any such thing. He told me he had the authority to compel me to attend, and I told him nothing would induce me to leave my house and go and see him.  He **loved** publicity and fully intended making me run the gauntlet.  Can you imagine the circus that would've been, if I'm been dumb enough to see him in his chambers.  The press would've been out in force. So I dug my heels in.  I told him he would have to arrest me, but even then I would still refuse to attend. After much toing and froing, we agreed that I would receive him at no 48 (Upper Grosvenor Street, her then-residence opposite the American Embassy).  I told him I would give him a drink, and that's what I did.'

According to Margaret, 'When he arrived, he didn't even bother to pretend.  He plunged right in.  He wanted to know who the so-called Headless Man was.  I declined to answer on the grounds that his identity had nothing to do with the Profumo Affair. He said he had a right to ask if it was Duncan Sandys. I conceded that right and told him everyone knows Duncan has concertinaed legs, and since the man in the picture did not, it obviously couldn't be him. Then he asked whether it was Prince Philip. **Prince Philip!** I asked him if he was mad.  I said even if it had been, which it wasn't, since Prince Philip had nothing to do with the Profumo Affair, he was exceeding his brief. He assured me in the most decisive terms that he was not.  He said Prince Philip's name had come up in the Profumo Affair and he wanted to know whether Prince Philip was The Man in the Mask. What man in what mask? I asked him.  I truthfully had no idea what he was speaking about.

Then he gave me chapter and verse. I asked him how I could possibly know such a thing? Did I look the sort of woman who would be attending an orgy? Do you know what he had the gall to tell me? He had been reliably informed that Prince Philip and I had had an affair! The inference was that both Prince Philip and I were therefore capable of anything, including attending orgies with him running around naked, serving diners, while wearing a mask, and me witnessing the scene. If I could have slapped his face, I would've. I told him plain and straight that I had most certainly not had an affair with Prince Philip, then went further and informed the impertinent little man that even if I had had an affair with him, I would most certainly not have been attending an orgy with him. I ask you, I said to him, can you be seriously wasting public money on nonsense like this? Can anyone in their right mind believe that Prince Philip would be attending an orgy and with me no less? He thanked me for my time and left, his tail between his legs. I am still furious. The absolute nerve. My parting shot was to inform him that he'd better not drag my name into his muckraking, otherwise I would sue him. Ghastly little man.'

In the end, of course, Lord Denning could not link Margaret Argyll to Philip, nor could he verify the rumours about Philip being either The Headless Man or The Man in the Mask. Of course, it's never possible to prove a negative, as Saddam Hussein discovered when George W. Bush insisted that he prove that he did not have the weapons of mass destruction which he did not have. But the mere fact that the Master of the Rolls felt compelled to cross-examine Margaret about the possibility shows to what extent Philip's reputation as a lothario had taken root.

To her credit, Margaret took the identity of The Headless Man to her grave. In fact, it was none of the six men Denning asked her about. He was her longstanding boyfriend, William H. (Bill) Lyons, a handsome, debonair Pan American executive who lived in London and whom she hoped to marry.

There is a footnote to the Denning episode as well. In the early nineties I met someone who used to run Elizabeth Arden on Bond Street when it was **the** place to which all the ladies went. He gave me an interesting piece of information. Both Princess Margaret and Margaret, Duchess of Argyll were regulars. 'We were under strict instructions that the two of them should never be on the premises at the same time. The Palace said if Princess Margaret should ever cross paths with your Margaret, she would take her custom elsewhere.'

The year after the Profumo Affair, Lilibet gave birth to Edward. It was around the time of his birth that the first of the new crop of women whose names would be linked with Philip's arrived on the royal scene. Nanette Newman was a beautiful actress who enjoyed great success in Britain, though neither she nor her husband, the actor/writer/director/producer Bryan Forbes, ever made the first tier of Hollywood success in the way Sir David Lean or the actress Julie Christie did. Nevertheless, in British terms, they were of the first rank. The actor Peter Sellers had fallen in love with Newman when she was nineteen, despite an age gap of several years, but this was not the reason she failed to respond to him romantically, for she married Forbes, who was thirteen years her senior, when she was twenty one. Theirs was a happy marriage. Forbes had a sensitive side to him which Sellers did not, and it ended only when he died in 2013 after fifty eight years of matrimony.

Despite the rejection, the notoriously tetchy Sellers remained friends with Newman and Forbes. It was while he was married to Britt Ekland that Sellers introduced them to his good friends the Snowdons, who were then the most glamorous royal couple on earth, outstripped only by the Burtons as the most glamorous couple on earth. The Snowdons and the Forbeses clicked, and they became friends. In time, Margaret and Tony introduced them to her sister Lilibet and brother-in-law Philip, who also took them up socially.

By this time, the Snowdon marriage was a febrile nest of infidelity, with Tony bored by his royal wife and she inordinately possessive, but nevertheless indulging in tit-for-tat affairs to match his numerous ones. Sellers claimed to have had an affair with Margaret, which she always denied, but he was so enamoured of his royal friend that he once gave away his daughter Victoria's horse to Margaret's children.

It was against this backdrop that Philip and Lilibet met and befriended Nanette Newman and Bryan Forbes. They were a young, attractive, civilised, entertaining and interesting couple, so there should be no mystery as to why they enjoyed great success socially. All hosts and hostesses prefer attractive and entertaining people to the alternative. Although the rumourmongers soon alighted upon the preference shown by Philip for Newman, noting that they were entertained at Windsor Castle and Buckingham Palace, it would be a mistake to think that the couple was friendly only with Lilibet and Philip. They remained close friends of the Snowdons and were even entertained at Royal Lodge by the Queen Mother. The question one has to ask here is: would Elizabeth have been entertaining her son-in-law's paramour if there was any truth to the rumours which soon began to swirl around about Philip and Newman? The answer is so self-evident that one does not even need to articulate it, especially when one considers that Philip's relationship with his mother-in-law, though superficially cordial, was not steeped in deep trust or high regard.

Next up for the award of Prince's Mistress was Merle Oberon (1911-1979), the Anglo-Indian actress who was formerly married to Sir Alexander Korda (1893-1956), the great Hungarian-born film producer/director who was at the apogee of the film world on both sides of the Atlantic. By the time her name was linked to Philip's, she was the wife of the immensely rich Italian-born but Mexican-based industrialist, Bruno Pagliai, with whom she adopted two children. They lived in great style in Mexico, and when Philip came to visit, the rumourmongers went into a frenzy of speculation. This, despite the fact that Oberon was ten years older than Philip, past her prime, married to a jealous Italian, and about to leave her husband for the handsome Dutch actor Robert Wolders, twenty five years her junior. She would marry him two years after meeting, in 1975, and die of a stroke four years later, following which he became Audrey Hepburn's partner. I met him in the late eighties/early nineties with her at a charity reception, which I had helped to organise, and he was stunningly handsome as well as impeccably mannered. Clearly no toyboy, he was patently a gentleman who simply preferred older women, which was something Philip decidedly did not.

Another lady whose name was linked to Philip's at this time was Susan Ferguson, nee Wright. Better known as Susie Barrantes (1937-1998) since her younger daughter Sarah's marriage in 1986 to Prince Andrew, Susie was a pretty, fun-loving romantic who had married Major (then Lieutenant) Ronald Ferguson at the age of eighteen. Within a year, she had produced one daughter, Jane, followed by another, Sarah, two years later. The sixties were a time of tumult, no more so for society than for the Fergusons, who were a young, fashionable, attractive and well-bred couple. Both were scions of the aristocracy, Susie being a descendant of the Earls of Coventry and Bucking-hamshire as well as Viscount Powerscourt, Ronald of Viscount Hampden and the even grander Duke of Buccleuch. Not only did King Charles II's blood course through his veins, but his first cousin once removed was Her Royal Highness The Duchess of Gloucester. As the decade wore on, their marriage wore out. By Susie's own account, she met Philip 'at polo. Doesn't everyone meet at polo?' Ronald being a highly ranked polo player, it was inevitable that Susie would run across the Duke of Edinburgh, who was himself an avid polo player at that time.

I knew both the Fergusons slightly, though by this time they were divorced. She was charming, gracious, and completely natural. Stunningly attractive, with hair down to the small of her back, she seldom wore make-up, but still managed to be effortlessly elegant. He was a charming, entertaining, naughty man who spent a whole night stroking my back in full view of everyone at a ball he accompanied his daughter to when she was still married to Prince Andrew and which she attended as the guest of honour; I chaired it. One could not take offence; there was an innocence to him that made such attentions funny rather than obnoxious. It was almost as if Major Ron knew he was expected to flirt outrageously, and flirt outrageously he did. In fact, the only time I ever saw him behave with restraint was when he attended an event organised by Prince Alexius Bassey, a rich Nigerian who was then very much sought-after in fashionable circles because of his extreme generosity. Ronald attended with Lesley Player, a young woman with whom he was having an affair. It was interesting to note that that was the only occasion upon which Ronald refrained from flirting with anyone, Miss Player especially. This just goes to show: when there is something to hide, it is hidden. When there is not, it is not.

Nevertheless, Ronald was well known to have problems keeping his zip up. Two years after Sarah's marriage to Andrew, the *News of the World* newspaper revealed that he paid visits to a private massage parlour, the Wigmore Club, 'a health club and massage parlour in London staffed by girls who, dressed in starched white 'medical' gowns, allegedly offered a la carte sexual services to members'. The major claimed that he used the club solely as 'a kind of cocoon where I could shut myself away for an hour and think.' According to him, his massages were just massages, 'and by that I mean a totally straight one'. His denials fell on deaf ears, the main point seemingly eluding virtually all his critics. The fact that he was patronising such establishments indicated that he was not sleeping around, at least not in his circle, and, if his word could be relied upon, he wasn't sleeping with any of the masseuses either.

This was hardly an infraction worthy of the loss of one's professional position, yet when his appointment came up for renewal as deputy chairman of the Guards Polo Club, whose patron is The Queen and whose President, since its formation on 25ᵗʰ January 1955, has been Prince Philip, Ronald was not re-elected. He was incensed and made no secret about it.

One of Ronald's great virtues was his straightforwardness. There was absolutely no side to the man. He issued a statement asserting, 'I have not been sacked. I have not resigned. I was not re-elected chairman for 1988-9 and was not prepared to accept the alternative position.'

He explained, 'Having given a lifetime of devotion and dedication to the Guards Polo Club, I feel very sad and extremely angry at the way the whole matter has been handled.' Issuing the *coup de grace* to his old polo-mate, he said, 'I was deeply wounded by Prince Philip's refusal, as President of the Club, to discuss it with me. I made repeated requests to see him, and appointments were made which were subsequently cancelled.' Privately, he also said that he would 'never have marked Prince Philip down as a hypocrite, yet here he is refusing to see me when far worse has been said about him, including about him and my first wife. I didn't behave like that towards him, and I don't think it's right that he should behave like that towards me. '

Conversely, he was deeply touched that Prince Charles kept him on as his Polo Manager, and praised the younger prince for his 'loyalty'. That position too, however, came to an end in the early nineties when Ronald's escapades with Lesley Player hit the front pages of the newspapers, and his daughter Sarah found herself embroiled in an even more sensational scandal as a result of Johnny Bryan kissing her foot in the South of France. (He did not suck her toes.)

A part of Ronald's distress with Philip's lack of support resulted from how loyal he himself had been in the late sixties, when the polo fields of England were awash with rumours of Philip's affair with Susie Ferguson. The Galloping Major, as the tabloids dubbed him, he had kept his counsel and continued playing polo with him, refuting the rumours with open support.

How much foundation, however, was there to the rumours? There is no doubt that Susie was an attractive woman and Philip an attractive man. They certainly had a flirtatious relationship, but did it go any further? This is one of the questions which needs to be answered, but as all the relationships with women fall into one category, the only sensible approach is to answer all the questions at once.

The next relationship that also raised questions, and caused even more talk, was that of Philip and Lady Westmoreland. In fact, Lilibet and Philip were great friends of the 15th Earl, David Anthony Thomas Fane (1924-1993), and his wife, the former Jane Barbara Findlay (1928-2009), daughter of Lt. Col. Sir Roland Findlay, 3rd baronet. In her day, Jane was quite a head turner. Even when I used to see her, by which time she would've been in her forties, she was still a very attractive woman. Sunny (11th duke of) Marlborough, whose sister Lady Sarah Spencer-Churchill was one of my close friends, had been in love with her, but she had dumped him and married Westmoreland instead in 1950. The Westmorelands had three children, Anthony David Francis Henry Fane, Lord Burghersh (1951-); the Hon Henry (Harry) St Clare Fane (1953-), and Lady Camilla Diana Fane (1957-).

All three of the Westmoreland progeny moved in fashionable circles. It was virtually impossible from the mid-seventies till the early eighties to go anywhere without seeing Burghie, as the heir was known to one and all. He was a tall, handsome, personable, down-to-earth guy whom everyone liked. Camilla used to accompany Prince Charles from time to time to events, the word being that everyone hoped something would 'take', though by then few well-bred girls wanted to marry into the royal family, the restrictions of the role being too onerous. Harry would emerge as a friend of Diana, Princess of Wales, one of the few well-bred girls who did want to become royal.

The sibling whose path crossed the most with mine was Burghie, as the heir was known to one and all. Although we were not close friends, we often ran into each other, especially after he took a job in the mid-seventies as greeter at Wedgie's, the private members' club/discotheque on the King's Road which was launched by Liz Brewer, another friend of mine. Like all the other young people in the then smart set, I frequented the club three, four, five times a week on average, for lunch, dinner and dancing. It is no exaggeration to say that it was virtually impossible to be in Wedgie's and not see at least five seriously famous people and fifteen hyper-well-connected ones at all times. The place was a magnet for gossip columnists and their stringers; it was also a magnet for gossip. One of the many topics was Burghie's parents, his mother in particular, who the rumourmongers asserted, with a certainty they could not have possessed, was Prince Philip's 'girlfriend'. This was taken to mean that Lady Westmoreland, as we all called her (respect was still a feature of the age, and one did not refer to one's elders by their Christian names unless invited by them to do so), was having a fully-blown affair with the prince. I met her once or twice. She was tall, good-looking, charming, with a strong personality and great presence. Lord Westmoreland was more sanguine, attractive in the way that the old aristocracy was; utterly unpretentious and beautifully mannered, cuddlesome almost, so blanketed did you feel by his air of reliability. I used to think how lucky Burghie was to have such nice parents; I was not alone in that.

All of the Westmoreland family were at the pinnacle of what was then known as Society. Although the winds of change were blowing through the corridors of power, the old elite still had a stature with and fascination from the general public which it no longer does. The aristocracy still counted as something desirable and enviable, and aristocrats with royal links carried far more clout socially than even the most famous celebrities. Lord Westmoreland had been a Lord-in-Waiting since 1955, and in 1978, by which time Burghie was at Wedgie's, he was made Master of the Horse. He held that position until 1991, stepping down and returning to being a Lord-in-Waiting until dying at the relatively young age of 69 in 1993.

I don't know how widespread the gossip about Philip and Jane Westmoreland was in the general population, but it certainly was in what was then the smart set. People were fascinated by how Lilibet could be such close friends with Jane and her husband while she and Philip were supposed to be conducting this romance. It seems not to have occurred to anyone that possibly, just possibly, there was less to the relationship than met the eye. Rather than the smoke resulting from fire, it was actually the haze of dry ice creating an illusion of fieriness when the temperature was significantly cooler than onlookers suspected.

Despite the obvious delight that Philip and Jane took in each other's company, the member of the family whose conduct got out of hand with her was Tony Snowdon's. This is hardly surprising, when one considers the personality of the individuals concerned. Philip has always been a continent individual, while Tony Snowdon was the embodiment of incontinence. His tongue, demeanour and penis were all given free rein as he gave full expression to his urges. Despite being excellent company and a gifted artist and inventor, his incontinence would, with the passage of time, detrimentally affect his marriage, his standing, his family, and his friendships. In the early years of his marriage, before this tendency had had a chance to wreak the havoc it did, he was embraced with a willingness that would recede as his lack of control became more visible. It was in the early, halcyon days, that Margaret and Tony asked Lord Westmoreland to become godfather to their daughter Sarah. This is all the testament needed to confirm that the Westmorelands were also friendly with the Snowdons and therefore the friendships were familial rather than sexual. Not, of course, that sex doesn't sometimes rear its head when couples become so close that social intimacy gives way to the biological imperative. So it proved to be with Tony Snowdon. One of the women to whom he took a fancy was Jane Westmoreland. She did not reciprocate his desires, and there was an ugly scene at a party when he tried to cut in while Jane was dancing with Peter Cazalet, Queen Elizabeth the Queen Mother's trainer. When Cazalet declined to vacate the floor, an infuriated Snowdon threw two glasses of wine over him, one red, one white.

Although it is possible that Snowdon would have considered it a feather in his cap to usurp Philip's position in the bed of an inamorata, it is unlikely that he would have made his desire for Jane Westmoreland so apparent if she and Philip had indeed been having an affair. He would have been more discreet, especially as how he was always careful to stay on the good side of Lilibet and Elizabeth, even more so after his marriage to Margaret started to unravel, which it had done by this time. So canny was he at playing Margaret's victim, when in fact she was his, that both her mother and sister sympathised with his predicament, not hers. The timing and mere fact of this incident, attested to by many, suggest that Philip's disclaimer of any impropriety with Jane Westmoreland has merit.

A rather less attractive woman with whom Philip was supposed to have an affair around this time as well was the actress Anna Massey. She denied it, as did he, and their denials are believable, if only because they met only briefly. More crucially, she was not exactly a beauty, and Philip has only ever been drawn to good looking women. As her ex-husband, the actor Jeremy Brett (1933-1995), pithily put it when asked about the rumoured affair, 'I don't believe the consort is into mercy fucking.'

No mercy was extended when rumours of an affair between Princess Alexandra and Philip surfaced. People who knew them were appalled; people who didn't, captivated. It is worth examining the individuals and their background, to see how probable it was, as Philip, Lilibet, Alexandra and the whole family she married into were so interconnected, over several generations, that it is only by shining a light on their interconnectedness that one can determine the believability of the rumours.

Alexandra was born on Christmas Day 1936, two weeks after the abdication of her uncle David, at 3 Belgrave Square, the elegant Belgravia townhouse of her parents Prince George, Duke of Kent, and the former Princess Marina of Greece. Hers was the last royal birth at which the Home Secretary, Sir John Simon, had to attend, the custom being abolished thereafter. It had come into being following the birth of Mary of Modena and King James II's son Prince James in 1688, when the Protestants tried to delegitimise the heir to the throne by spreading the story that the queen's baby had been stillborn and was replaced by another infant in a warming pan.

There was no doubt that Princess Alexandra of Kent was the legitimate child of her father Prince George, Duke of Kent, and his duchess. Paternally, she was Lilibet's first cousin; maternally, Philip's first cousin once removed, her mother being his father's niece. Princess Marina was renowned internationally for her style and beauty, and Alexandra not only looked like her mother, and once grown up, dressed equally stylishly, but had a sweetness her mother lacked.

To this day, Alexandra is known in royal circles as the embodiment of the perfect princess. She is always elegantly turned out, always impeccably mannered, invariably good-natured and gracious. I would not say she has the common touch, for she never ceases being regal. Not that she is stand-offish or stiff, for she is neither. While Queen Elizabeth The Queen Mother and Diana, Princess of Wales had the common touch, and would manage to say the winning thing that made you think how socially skilled they were, Princess Alexandra's charm is both down-to-earth and humane without ever straying beyond regal parameters. You leave her presence knowing that she is both a lovely lady and the archetypically ideal princess.

Two vignettes illustrate the sort of person she is. In about 2001, there was an event at Windsor Castle to which I took a friend: Charles Hanna. He was presented to her, and two nights later they both attended something at the Royal Opera House for the Royal Ballet. Without missing a beat, before the presentation could take place, she said, 'I know you We were together at Windsor the night before last.' Of course, he was flattered, and they had a nice chat about the choir at St George's Chapel and the orchestra at Covent Garden, before she moved on to someone else. The other vignette demonstrates her loyalty to her friends, even as their fortunes decline. For many years, she used to go to the West Indies as the guests of Freddie and Lou Wanklyn. A rich and chic couple, they lived in some style there, but suffered financial reversals and ended up in the south west of France near where I had a chateau. Every year, Alexandra still came to stay with them. The reduction in their scale of living made no difference to her; friends are friends, and if you stayed with them in halcyon days, you still stay with them when they have had to scale back.

Alexandra is regarded by everyone who knows her as having never once, in over eighty years, put a foot wrong. She still performs a schedule of engagements, which have lessened now that arthritis has taken hold, but I saw her at something a few months ago, and she was still the same beautiful charming, impeccably turned out and gracious woman she has always been.

When Alexandra was born, she was sixth in line to the throne. At the time of Lilibet's accession, she was one of only five British princesses by birth, the others being Lilibet's younger sister Margaret, her daughter Anne, their aunt Mary the Princess Royal, and their great-aunt by marriage and cousin by birth Princess Alice of Albany, Countess of Athlone.

There were two other British princesses, the daughters of the previous Princess Royal, but they had been born Lady Alexandra Duff and Lady Maud Duff and raised to the dignity of princesses, with the style of highness rather than royal highness, by order of their grandfather King Edward VII in 1905, when their mother Louise, Duchess of Fife, replaced her aunt Victoria, the late Empress Frederick, as Princess Royal. Five years later, their cousin George V succeeded to the throne and made it known that he did not wish either of his cousins to use their princely titles. Although Alexandra would marry her cousin Prince Arthur of Connaught and therefore retain a princely rank through him, Maud was reduced to being known as the Countess of Southesk until she succeeded to her father's dukedom of Fife following her sister's death. Although known in Scotland as Princess Maud, especially after Bertie's, then Lilibet's, accession, she was nevertheless caught in an anomalous position, being officially a princess but not to be known as one.

Princess Alexandra of Kent had no such contradictions with which to contend. Throughout her whole life, she would be that rarity, a born British princess, and a fully-fledged member of the royal family. In royal circles, she enjoys an eminence which is second only to Princess Anne. All the female additions to the family have to curtsey to her when they are not in the presence of their husbands, each of whom outranks her. At the time of writing, although her place in the line of succession has fallen to below fiftieth, she is nevertheless one of only four born princesses, the others being Anne, now the Princess Royal, and the Duke of York's two daughters, Beatrice and Eugenie. She continues to enjoy a pre-eminence over those two younger princesses by virtue of having performed royal duties all her adult life.

Because Alexandra's father Prince George died when she was a little girl, she grew up in a fatherless household. Her early years were primarily spent at Coppins, the Kent family home in Buckinghamshire, where Marina gave refuge to the young Philip and Lilibet so they could court in peace. She was the first British princess to attend boarding school, Heathfield School near Ascot. Her elder brother Edward succeeded to the dukedom as a minor, and while this prevented him from undertaking royal duties until his majority, it did not curtail their mother's full schedule of royal engagements. 'Princess Marina was always everyone's first choice,' Margaret, Duchess of Argyll, who knew her well, told me, 'because she was so beautiful and stylish. The end in chic and glamour.'

During the war, while her mother was embarked upon a full schedule of royal engagements, Alexandra spent much of her time with her grandmother. Queen Mary was billeted down at Badminton, the magnificent estate of her nephew by marriage, Henry Hugh Arthur FitzRoy Somerset, 10th Duke of Beaufort (1900-1984). Known by one and all as Master for his love of the hunt, he founded the Badminton Horse Trials and was Master of the Horse from 1936 until 1978, when Lord Westmoreland succeeded him. His wife was Lady Victoria Constance Mary Cambridge (1897-1987), nee Princess Mary of Teck, daughter of Queen Mary's elder brother Adolphus, who was born Prince of Teck, became Duke of Teck and, after 1917, Marquis of Cambridge.

Queen Mary had as profound an influence upon Alexandra as she would have upon Lilibet, which somewhat casts doubt upon Princess Margaret's dismissal of their grandmother as having cared for her elder sister only because she was going to be queen. There was never any prospect of Alexandra succeeding to the throne, yet Queen Mary influenced this other granddaughter to ensure that she too would grow up to be the perfect royal princess. Something which both Lilibet and Alexandra succeeded in becoming while the less disciplined and more rebellious Margaret did not.

While still a schoolgirl, Alexandra was a bridesmaid at Lilibet and Philip's wedding, a role she also fulfilled for Dickie Mountbatten's daughter Lady Patricia Mountbatten when she married Lord Brabourne. She was bridesmaid yet again in 1962 when her cousin Princess Sophie of Greece married the heir to the Spanish throne Prince (later King) Juan Carlos.

Alexandra's work life shows much about the respect Lilibet had for this younger cousin. Since her majority, Alexandra has carried out an extensive schedule of royal duties. In 1959, for instance, the twenty two year old toured Australia, where she behaved with a decorum and maturity which commended her to everyone. When Nigeria gained its independence on 1st October 1960, she was the Queen's representative and opened independent Nigeria's first Parliament two days later, once more acquitting herself successfully. Her style, glamour and beauty were much commented upon, as well as her maturity.

At the age of twenty-six, on 24th April 1964, Alexandra married the Hon Angus Ogilvy, second son of the 12th Earl of Airlie. The whole Airlie family was steeped in royal service. The 12th earl had been made Lord Chamberlain to Queen Elizabeth in 1937, partly because the Strathmore and Airlie families were close friends and neighbours in Scotland, and Elizabeth was keen to advance the Scottish aristocracy as long as they had been close to her family. But equally relevant was the fact that the 12th earl's mother Mabell (1866-1956) was one of Queen Mary's closest friends as well as one of her longest-serving ladies-in-waiting. Mabell had distinguished herself because she had been one of the few adults who took an interest in the Prince Bertie when he was a boy and was being dismissed by all and sundry because of his stammer and nervousness. She discerned his kindness and strength of character, and helped Lady Strathmore to progress the courtship between a reluctant Elizabeth Bowes Lyon and an avid Prince Albert. Elizabeth never forgot the favour she owed the family, and when she developed an interest in racing, especially steeplechasing, this solidified an already solid friendship even further, for the 12th earl was a successful owner: his steeplechaser, Master Robert, had won the Grand National in 1924.

The Airlies had two castles near to each other in Angus: Corthachy and Airlie. I've been to both and they are charming, homely places. Indeed, I first met Angus Ogilvy at Corthachy. He went around asking everyone, 'Have you seen **the** wife?' The next time I saw him, he picked up my connection with Jamaica and regaled me with stories about his good friend Sir Robert (Bobby) Kirkwood, who lived in Jamaica and with whom he stayed when he visited the island.

Alexandra's marriage to Angus Ogilvy was welcomed by both the royal family and the Scottish aristocracy. Televised worldwide, with over 200 million viewers, virtually the whole royal family attended, as well as every politician of note. Lords Avon and Attlee were there with their wives, as well as Lady Churchill without the ailing Sir Winston. Foreign royalty attended in force, unlike at Princess Margaret's wedding. Her aunt Olga, Princess Paul of Yugoslavia, King Olav of Norway, Queen Frederica of the Hellenes, Queen Victoria Eugenia of Spain, Queen Helen The Queen Mother of Romania, Queen Louise of Sweden, Queen Ingrid of Denmark, and sundry royal princes, princesses, arch dukes and arch duchesses, were all there.

At the time of his marriage, Angus was offered an earldom but declined it. He also refused a grace-and-favour apartment at St James's Palace, preferring that Alexandra retain her modest dwelling there which they could then use as a *pied à terre* when in London. Instead, he asserted his independence and acquired a sublease on Thatched House Lodge, a Crown Estate property in Richmond Park, for the then considerable sum of £150,000 from Clare, Duchess of Sutherland. In 1994, he extended the lease for 150 years for a premium of £670,000, again at fair market rate. Unlike other Crown Estate properties such as Bagshot Park or Royal Lodge, Thatched House Lodge has been repaired, improved and maintained by its leasee, meaning that Princess Alexandra and her heirs can dispose of it to whomever they please, without the need to offer it back to the Crown Estate for the duration of its lease.

Although Angus would be knighted in 1988, and became a Privy Councillor in 1997, he did not possess a hereditary title, so the couple's two children, James Robert Bruce Ogilvy, born 1964, and Marina Victoria Alexandra Ogilvy, born 1966, were born plain mister and miss.

Angus had to make his way in the world. Unlike his elder brother David, he had neither a rich wife nor prospects. In 1952, David had married Virginia Fortune Ryan (known to one and all as Ginny), an American heiress whose father was New York socialite John Barry Ryan, and whose maternal grandfather was the immensely rich, German-born Jewish American financier Otto Kahn. David, who was also the most handsome man imaginable, had a glittering career in the city. A merchant banker, he started out as a director of Henry Schroder Wagg & Co in 1961, becoming chairman in 1973. When

Schroders went public in 1977 he continued as chairman until he retired, in 1984, to become Lilibet's Lord Chamberlain. By this time, Ginny had been appointed a Lady of the Bedchamber to Lilibet, and remains one of her closest friends.

Following in the wake of his elder brother, Angus also opted for a career in the city. After graduating in 1950 from Trinity College, Oxford, with a BA in Philosophy, Politics, and Economics, Angus got a job with the Drayton company. He then joined its subsidiary, London and Rhodesia Mining and Land Company (Lonrho), which had begun operating in Africa in 1909. In 1961, the fabled entrepreneur Roland 'Tiny' Rowland (1917-1998) joined the company, whose profits were a mere £158,000. Appointed Chief Executive in 1962, he transformed the company into a worldwide conglomerate, dealing in newspapers, hotels, distribution, textiles and many other businesses. By 1989, profits were £272 million.

Unsurprisingly, a company which expands at such a rate under the leadership of someone as thrusting as Rowland will attract attention and enemies. Rowland became a public figure who was both revered and reviled. The ruthless businessman, Sir Edward Matheson, in the film *The Wild Geese*, played by the Hollywood matinee idol Stewart Granger, was commonly supposed to be based on him, and he was profiled yet again as a ruthless businessman in the documentary, *The Mayfair Set*, by Adam Curtis.

By 1973 several members of the board of Lonrho were desperate to get rid of the goose who was laying the golden eggs. Eight of them brought a law suit in the High Court seeking Rowland's dismissal, complaining about his temperament and claiming that he had concealed financial information from them. Although Rowland failed to defeat them in court, they failed to defeat him where it really counted, namely with the shareholders, who backed Rowland. Into this melee waddled the then Prime Minister, Edward Heath, who criticised Lonrho's management conduct in the House of Commons, famously declaring it to be 'an unpleasant and unacceptable face of capitalism'. In fact, Heath had misread his speech, which referred to an 'unacceptable **facet** of capitalism'. Subsequently, the Department of Trade weighed in, publishing a report into the company's activities which criticised Angus in his role of director. This brought his career to a halt, which created something of a hardship for the family, as they were reliant on his income. Although Alexandra remained on the Civil List until it was abolished in 2013, the £225,000 per annum she received was repayment for the expenses she incurred in relation to her royal duties, and the Queen was in any event obliged to repay the sum to the Treasury. This meant that money was always tight within the family, for after his retirement from business, Angus spent the rest of his life devoting himself to unpaid charity work.

It was following the debacle of the Lonrho report that stories began to circulate that there was trouble in the Ogilvys' marriage. It has to be said, when I saw them at Cortachy a year or two later, I could detect no evidence, not even a hint of substantiation, for the rumours. The one thing everyone in the public eye learns, however, is that rumours have a life of their own. It was therefore only a matter of time before they had grown to include Philip, who was now supposed to be having an affair with his cousin.

One of Princess Alexandra's ladies-in-waiting was my good friend Lady Sarah Spencer-Churchill's sister, Lady Caroline Waterhouse. Another of my friends was a cousin whose name must remain unmentioned. Both of them agreed that the stories were preposterous. Alexandra was a close friend of her cousin Lilibet. Her brother-in-law and sister-in-law, David and Ginny Airlie, were also close friends of Lilibet. All the parties concerned would have had to have hearts of stone and carapaces of steel for Philip and Alexandra to be having an affair. Moreover, she had known Philip all her life as a beloved cousin. The dynamics were all wrong for a love affair, and certainly neither she nor Philip was as sexually incontinent as Tony Snowdon, so a purely sexual liaison also seemed impracticable. Despite its unlikeliness, at least to those who knew the participants, the rumours gained traction amongst those who did not, to such an extent that Alexandra's name is still often mentioned as being one of the women with whom Philip had an affair. This, despite the fact that Lilibet has promoted her cousin above and beyond what was necessary, and, in doing so, has shown the high regard she has for her, both as a relation and as a fellow member of the team. Alexandra is not only a Royal Lady of the Garter, but Lilibet has raised her in the order of precedence to reflect her dedication to the royal cause, outranking her in palace terms before even the wives of the two most immediate heirs to the throne, Camilla, Duchess of Cornwall and Catherine, Duchess of Cambridge. It is hardly credible in a world where planes fly and fish swim that such honours would be bestowed upon the paramour of her husband. Only in a parallel universe where lead floats and treachery is commensurate with loyalty would such conduct be rewarded, and it says more about the people who believe such nonsense than it does about Lilibet, Philip or Alexandra and their conduct towards each other.

The next woman whose name was linked romantically with Philip's was certainly attractive. Tall, dark, slender and utterly natural, she was also much younger than he, being the daughter of his old friend and distant cousin Gina Wernher, who had once been mooted as a possible bride for him.   Born

Alexandra Anastasia Phillips in 1946 to Gina and her husband, the late Lt. Col. Harold Pedro Joseph Philips (1909-1980), and always known as Sacha, the wife of the 5th Duke of Abercorn could not have been better connected. Her father had been Edwina Mountbatten's great love before Nehru, and her paternal grandmother was Mary Mercedes Bryce, whose brother Major Francis (Frank) Bryce's daughter Janet married Nada Milford Haven's son David and is the mother of the present head of the Mountbatten family, George, the 4th Marquis. Their uncle Ivar Bryce was not only an immensely rich Bermudian but a well-known homosexual who was also godfather to my ex-husband, after whom he was named by my parents-in-law in the hope that he would leave Colin Ivar his money. He did not.

Through her maternal grandmother Lady Zia Wernher (nee Countess Anastasia Torby), Sacha was in the line of succession to the British throne by virtue of being a descendant of the Electress Sophia, by way of Zia's father, Grand Duke Michael Mikhailovitch of Russia. Philip and Lilibet always spent the nearest weekend to their wedding anniversary with the Wernhers at Luton Hoo, where, it will be remembered, Philip had spent many happy times while growing up.

Sacha's husband was also well connected. Married in 1966 while he was still the Marquis of Hamilton, James (now 5th Duke of) Abercorn's first cousin was Johnnie, Viscount Althorp (later 8th Earl Spencer), whose daughter Diana would become Princess of Wales in 1981. The owner of a splendid 15,000 estate near Newtownstewart in Country Tyrone, Northern Ireland, his seat is magnificent, Grade A-listed Baronscourt Castle. When he and Sacha were married, he was sitting in the House of Commons as the Ulster Unionist MP for Fermanagh and South Tyrone, succeeding Lord Robert Grosvenor, later 5th Duke of Westminster and father of his brother-in-law, Gerald (then Earl) Grosvenor, who would succeed his father as 6th Duke in 1979. Upon losing his seat in1970, James Hamilton was appointed High Sheriff of Tyrone. He succeeded to the dukedom of Abercorn in 1979 and served as Lord Lieutenant of County Tyrone from 1986 to 2009. In 1999 he was appointed by Lilibet to the most prestigious order of chivalry in the world, becoming a Knight of the Garter. In 2001, he was appointed Lord Steward of the Household, making him the first dignitary of the Court. He held that position until 2009, and on 17th October 2012, he became the Chancellor of the Order of the Garter. It is impossible to have a greater honour, and says much of the regard in which he is held by Lilibet, in whose personal gift such appointments are.

Although Sacha Abercorn's parents and grandparents were close friends of Lilibet and Philip, her first memory of meeting them was when she was about eight years old and they came, with Charles and Anne, to stay with her parents at their then home, Thorpe Lubenham in Leicestershire. The Phillips family also stayed at Balmoral on occasion, and she has distinct memories of the times she spent while growing up with the royal family. She remembers them all having 'so much fun'. Everything was very 'jolly' and the royal children got along well with their parents. She distinctly remembers how Philip 'used to help Charles with his Go-Kart.' Philip was inventive at entertaining his children, telling them stories he had made up, and she has no recollection of any harsh words or will-tempered times. As she grew older, she was included more and more in the adult activities, such as Cowes Week. On one occasion, her parents were supposed to attend with her, but her father, who was suffering from cancer at that time, was too ill to attend, so she went on her own. Lilibet practically never went to Cowes. Sailing was no more her forte than racing was Philip's, but Princess Anne was there, along with all the lady clerks (secretaries) from Philip's Household. The men sailed and 'the girls were there to have fun,' Sacha recalled. She and Anne dressed up as serving wenches and had a 'hilarious' time. When she married James Hamilton, all the royals were there, but it was only once she was a married woman with children of her own, and trying to find the true meaning of life, that she moved from the background of Philip's life into being a central figure. She remembered the occasion that the transition took place. Her brother Nicky (Nicholas Harold Phillips, 1947-1991) used to live at *The Gables*, an eleven-bedroomed house on the Luton Hoo Estate where his widow, the Austrian-born former Countess Maria Lucia Czernin von und zu Chudenitz still lives, and from which he ran a shoot. Philip was there for the shooting and they struck up a conversation about the eminent psychiatrist and psychoanalyst, Carl Gustav Jung (1875-1961). She had always been interested in Jung's work, ideas and objectives. 'And Philip is interested in Jung,' she confirmed, which is hardly surprising, considering his family background.

Both Sacha and Philip shared the quest for life's deeper meanings. That, by her own account, is what brought them together. Theirs was a strong bond, a bond of the spirit, of ideas. Their interest was shared by Michael Mann (1924-2011), the former Bishop of Dudley who became Dean of Windsor, and therefore the Queen's personal chaplain, in 1976, a post he held till 1989. Educated at Harrow and the Royal Military College, Sandhurst, before serving in the Colonial Service in Nigeria from 1946 to 1955, Mann was ordained in 1957. He was just the sort of all-rounder with appeal for Philip, who had encouraged his predecessor as Dean, Robin Woods – another all-rounder – to develop a training college and conference centre for clergy at St George's House, Windsor, where both clergy and laity could meet to discuss ideas and consult upon possible solutions to problems. Over a three year period, while these consultations were taking place at Windsor, Philip encouraged Sacha to contribute to the fora by roping in her Jungian associates. As anyone who shares an intellectual or artistic passion will know, the joy of adding to a companion's dossier of knowledge is as valid a form of excitement as lovers sharing more physical intimacies. When she recounts how thrilled she was to discover Anthony Stevens' Archetypes: *A Natural History of the Self*, and how thrilled Philip was to be enlightened as to its existence, the purity of a shared intellectual pursuit is so evident that only those who have never had such experiences can doubt that the relationship had to have so debased a basis as a sexual one.

By Sacha's own account, her relationship with Philip was passionate, founded as it was on a shared spiritual quest. It would be wrong to suppose, however, that her husband was not a part of many of their shared activities. Philip was not only embarked on a quest for spiritual enlightenment, but also at the height of his activities in trying to get the ecological movement off the ground. Those of us who are old enough to remember will recall the scorn with which his ideas were greeted in the 70s and 80s. Nowadays, of course, the contribution he made to the cause is equally unjustly underplayed, largely because in this non-deferential age it is anathema for the proponents of so-called equality to acknowledge that people from privileged backgrounds might be as capable as their less-privileged brethren of having mental powers that haven't been stupefied by their heritage. Yet the recognition of the movement's aims which Philip sought, as being of crucial importance to the future of the planet, is now acknowledged, and even if his own part in it is often overlooked, he would be the first to say that the most important thing has been achieved. It doesn't matter who helped to achieve the recognition, only that that recognition was achieved.

Nevertheless, the 70s and 80s were exciting times for Philip. There are few more stimulating things in life than believing that you are helping the world to continue to exist, and to improve humanity's part within it, in practical, ecological terms, as well as in more esoteric, spiritual terms. The reason why causes of this nature have such appeal is that the participants are embarked upon a much bigger cause than their own puerile, individual existences. The appeal of such worthy causes is undeniable, hence why they attract so many followers.

Undeniably, Philip had many admirers as well as detractors. Those who didn't dismiss him as a crank felt they too were working towards making the world a better place. Sacha was only one of the many people who genuinely admired Philip, not for his rank or position, but for his heart, soul, mind and patent sincerity in trying to improve himself, mankind, and the world itself. She remembers accompanying him with her husband James and another couple, Aubrey and Kay Buxton, as they travelled in the *Britannia* to Borneo, Sarawak, and the Galapagos Islands. She summarises Philip as 'totally a sentient human being', which, in my view, is a very clever and succinct way of describing him. For all his restraint, you would have to have a total absence of empathy to spend even thirty seconds in his company and not appreciate that you are in the presence of that rarest of individuals: a thoroughly alive and feeling individual who does not mask his passions, even though he does try to contain them.

To onlookers, the relationship between the young and attractive duchess and the older and still attractive duke was full of passion, affection, and interest. They therefore concluded it must be sexual, and when they were seen holding hands as they walked on the beach on Eleuthera Island in the Bahamas, that was all the confirmation the rumourmongers needed.

Sacha understands why people might have jumped to the conclusions they did. 'It was a passionate friendship, but the passion was in the ideas.' She denies that it was a 'full relationship' and categorically states, 'I did not go to bed with him.' She does agree, however, that it 'probably looked like that to the world,' and concedes that she 'can understand why people might have thought it,' but confirms that 'it didn't happen.'

One detail that tends to confirm her denial is that she and James often entertained Philip at Baronscourt when they used to host carriage-driving competitions. He would invariably attend with Penny Romsey, another even younger and even prettier but less intellectual relation of his, who, the rumourmongers decreed, was Sacha's successor as his *maîtresse-en-titre*.

The final and most long lasting of Philip's women, Penny Romsey, who is now the present Countess Mountbatten of Burma , has undergone many transformations throughout her life while, at the same time, retaining a clearly defined individuality. She was born Penelope Eastman on 16th April 1953 to Reginald Wray Frank Eastwood (1912-1980) and his wife, the former Marian Elizabeth Hood (1928- ). Her father began his working life at the age of 15 as a butcher, before founding the Angus Steakhouse chain. By the time Penny, as she is called by her friends, was born, her father was a multi-millionaire and she had all the perks of wealth. She was privately schooled and attended Keele University in 1972 before transferring to the London School of Economics in 1973. Sonia Palmer, the first lady clerk of colour in the Prince of Wales's office, remembered Penny well. According to her, they worked together and, while she was pleasant, she was very ambitious.

She also emulated the demeanour of the peer group she wished to become a part of, becoming 'plummier with time' according to Palmer.

In the course of her time at the palace, Penny met the royals as well as their extended family. Sonia Palmer voiced dissatisfaction and envy that Penny, who was tall, blonde and beautiful, had greater success with the men than she did. She believed her colour might have been a bar to the ambitions the two women shared, and while that might well have been so in those more racially prejudiced days, Palmer's awkward and chippy personality would have put off even men who preferred their maidens dusky. Penny's personality, on the other hand, was all rounded corners and no edges.

While Sonia Palmer seethed, Penny Eastman began the ascent that would end up with her being embraced by the royal family as if she had been born one of their own. She started by befriending everyone at the palace and ended up going out with the Hon. Norton Knatchbull (1947- ), son and heir of John (Lord) Brabourne and Dickie Mountbatten's elder daughter, Patricia. I remember Norton from that period. We sometimes attended the same parties. He was tall, good-looking and pleasant, but he was no babe magnet, to employ the vernacular. He was too stolid, self-conscious and simply not beddable enough. Those of us who were looking for hot men gave him a wide berth.

Norton and Penny's courtship was not rushed. He took his time making up his mind. Then, on 27th August 1979, his grandfather Lord Mountbatten was killed by IRA bombers, on board the family fishing boat, *Shadow V*, at Mullaghmore in County Sligo, Ireland, along with his grandmother Doreen, the Dowager Lady Brabourne, one of his younger twin brothers, Nicholas, and the 14 year old boatman, Paul Maxwell from County Fermanagh. His mother and father were seriously injured in the explosion, the other twin brother Timothy less so. Two months later, on 20th October, the new Lord Romsey, whose mother had succeeded to her father's title and was therefore now Lady Mountbatten of Burma in her own right, married Penny Eastman at Romsey Abbey, where his parents had married in 1946 when Lilibet and Margaret had been bridesmaids. The royals attended the wedding in force.

Coming as the wedding did following a monumental tragedy, Penny Romsey's inclusion in the family took place at a poignant time. In some ways, that made her adjustment to a new world easier but more difficult in others. One of my oldest friends in one of her best friends, and her conduct from the outset was as exemplary as it would remain. Although not to the manner born, there was nothing pushy, arriviste or untoward about her. She fitted right in as if she had always been a minor royal, which is what she now became, for the Mountbattens regard themselves as royal as a result of being princes and princesses of Battenberg. India Hicks is on record as referring to her mother Pamela, who is Norton's aunt, as 'a German princess', which in fact she is, contrary to the assumption of those who believe the Mountbattens are merely aristocratic. When George V made the Battenbergs surrender their German titles and princely rank in 1917, their demotion did not extend to Germany, which recognises them to this day as princes and princesses of Battenberg. They are therefore like the dukes of Wellington, who are also princes of Waterloo in the peerage of the Netherlands, a title they do not use ordinarily.

In the early days of their marriage, the Romseys were a happy couple. They produced three children, a son, Nicholas Louis Charles Norton Knatchbull (1981 -) and two daughters, Alexandra Victoria Edwina Diana Knatchbull (1982) and Leonora Louise Marie Elizabeth Knatchbull (1986-1991). Tragedy struck again when their younger daughter was four. She was diagnosed with kidney cancer. Like anyone else who finds himself or herself facing a child's struggle for life, Norton and Penny Romsey were tossed around on a roller coaster of hope and despair. When little Leonora died one year after her diagnosis, both parents took her death badly, as any parents with feelings would.

According to people who know the couple well, this other tragedy marked the whole family. Norton coped with greater difficulty than Penny, even though she was the more grief stricken of the two. She, however, has mettle, a backbone of steel, the ability to weather life's storms in a way that he does not. It is fair to say in some ways neither of them fully recovered from their loss. It is also fair to say that this loss highlighted a character trait she and Prince Philip share, for neither of them shies away from their feelings, though neither of them allows loss to lessen their ability to appreciate life and its pleasures to the full.

Any psychologist will tell you that when a child is dying, the other children in the family are also affected. Not only do they have to cope with the loss of their sibling, and with this early reflection of their own mortality, but they also have issues of abandonment, for no matter how well the parents try to counteract the phenomenon, the reality is that much of their focus, both emotionally and practically, shifts to the dying child. This causes problems for the remaining children, who might also feel the guilt that survivors often feel. In such a predicament, the older a child is, the more likely it is to be affected profoundly. It was therefore no surprise when the son and heir, who is Prince Charles's godson, began manifesting problems, which escalated into fully blown drug addiction. Fortunately for the family, the surviving daughter remained on a more even keel.

Although the family remained united, the strains of living with so much tragedy began to show in other ways as well. Prince Charles was 'a great support' to Penny as well as Norton, and gradually, as they dealt with one problem after another, they did so in their own ways. At first, the divergence was subtle, but it was there nevertheless. Norton floundered, while Penny did not. She and Philip gradually developed a close friendship, based partly upon a shared spiritual quest, then upon shared pleasurable activities such as carriage-driving. Sacha Abercorn puts it very well when she says that Philip 'needs a playmate.' Penny became Philip's new playmate, especially after Sacha's activities started to diverge from his, and they saw less of each other. He had replaced one much younger and distant relation with another as his primary playmate. It was as simple as that.

In 2005, John Brabourne died and Norton succeeded him as the 8th Lord Brabourne. He and Penny moved up from being Lord and Lady Romsey to Lord and Lady Brabourne. Their son Nicholas became Lord Romsey, though their daughter Alexandra remained an honourable. Norton now had a reputation for being 'taciturn', weighed down by the travails of his life and by his responsibilities. Penny, on the other hand, was made of more robust stuff, like her playful companion Philip, and she enjoyed the regard of all for her capabilities in running the estate in Hampshire and Broadlands. Her hardier background was plainly paying dividends generally if not maritally, for Norton left her in 2010 to start a new life in the Bahamas with the widowed Lady Nuttall.

I remember well the day Penny's and my mutual friend telephoned to ask if I knew anything about baronet Sir Nicholas Nuttall's widow. I had to point out that Jamaica is hundreds of miles from the Bahamas, but, after being told that, 'everyone knows that everyone in the West Indies knows or at least knows of everyone else, and you'll definitely know people who know her if you put on your thinking cap,' I agreed to make a 'phone call or two. I discovered that she had been born Jeannie McWeeny, and had been widowed three years beforehand. Sir Nicholas's previous wife had been Miranda Quarry, once the wife of Peter Sellers and by this time married to Alexander (Earl of) Stockton, Harold Macmillan's grandson. She had also been in business with an old friend of mine, the designer Michael Fish. Of particular concern in England was whether the Dowager Lady Nuttall was 'black'. I was able to report back that she might 'be café au lait' but that she was definitely not black. She was also, by all accounts, beautiful, great fun, as well as the premiere beneficiary of her late husband's considerable estate, and was genuinely in love with Norton. I was told, 'If you knew her, you'd love her. She's fabulous.' She was also a successful businesswoman in her own right, the owner of a fashion label, Jeannie McQueeny, which was stocked in Harrods and other well-known shops on both sides of the Atlantic. She had warmth and a 'lovely West Indian sense of humour' and 'could put a smile on anyone's face, including Norton's.' She had no interest in moving to England and playing the role of a Mountbatten ladyship. She was already a Nuttall ladyship and had no ambitions to swap a good and luxurious life in the Bahamas for a more onerous and difficult one in England. In other words, Penny had nothing to worry about. Her position was safe.

Unfortunately for Norton, the relationship petered out after several years living together in the Bahamas, and he returned home to Hampshire. He and Penny both reside on the estate, and while they both remain close to the royals, she is actually closer than he to them now.

Abandoned as she was to a solitary life when Norton left her, Penny found that not only her friends, but both Lilibet and Philip, came to her rescue. Her widowed mother-in-law also maintained a stoical loyalty to both her daughter-in-law and son, until her death on 13th June 2017, at which time he became the 3rd Earl Mountbatten of Burma and Penny his countess. By then, they were both residing on the estate, though not entirely together as a couple.

In the years while she was on her own, Penny was often to be found staying with Lilibet and Philip at places like Sandringham, and he would often come and stay with her at Broadlands, which she ran, very capably too, on her own. One weekend, while Philip was staying there, Lilibet came over from Windsor for lunch. The whole house party was transfixed by how warm and relaxed the three of them were with one another. 'It was all sweetness and light. You'd never have known that people thought she and Philip had been lovers for years. The Queen treated her like a daughter, and seemed so happy to be there. So relaxed. The Queen acted as if it is the most normal thing in the world for her to be dropping in on them.'

By this time, the gossips were convinced that Philip and Penny were having an affair. The arithmetical phenomenon of a man of over ninety hopping into and out of bed with a woman younger than some of his children, who are even more on the wrong side of middle age than she is, seems to have eluded them.

Yet the belief betrays something about Philip. Even at this great age, his vitality and force of personality are as strong as the potent masculinity he still exudes. This is no mean feat. It also feeds the conviction that Philip and Penny are having an affair because they so openly have an easy, cosy, affectionate relationship.

It would be a mistake to think, however, that Philip has not invited other younger and attractive women to keep him company while he was driving carriages. He used to be on the lookout always for younger, attractive, well-situated playmates who would share fun times with him. He would ask them to join him as he carriage-drove, the way he would ask Penny. I know this to be a fact because sometimes he asked the daughter of a friend of mine, but she and Penny are different personalities and the fundamentals were simply not there on a personal level for them to enjoy as companionable a relationship as he has with Penny. She was also grander than Penny, with far more responsibilities, and far less time to spare, so she didn't have either the time or the ability to be haring about here, there and everywhere with Philip while he kept himself active, occupied and pleasurably engaged.

The point nevertheless is that Philip likes the company of women. He always has. From childhood until the present time, he has surrounded himself with attractive, preferably adoring, women. It must be remembered that he had close, non-sexual female friends during his adolescence and in his twenties. Princess Margaret was one of them, the perpetual third wheel on the tricycle of his relationship with Lilibet until they set up their own home away from her. No one thought he was having a *ménage a trois* with both sisters, so why the supposition now that every close female companion is his mistress, especially when all the women with whom he has been connected are also close to Lilibet? The fact that these women have got younger as he has got older is not such a mystery either. How many ninety-something year old women exist who have the means, ability and inclination to join him on his carriage-driving forays? I doubt even one.

This brings us to the fundamental question: Has Philip cheated? Have his playmates been like, love or lust?

In royal circles as much as outside of them, the supposition has always been that any man who is potently masculine must have trouble keeping his flies buttoned up. It must be remembered that Philip is from an ancient line of continental royals. His always was a more sophisticated and open world than Lilibet's. Rather than chipping away at their horizons, he has expanded hers without restricting his. His attitude has always been: If it is not morally wrong, and I want to do it, I will. If people have dirty minds, that's their problem. I will not allow their narrow-mindedness to prevent me from doing anything that's not wrong.

Chapter X

To an extent, he never stood a chance of ever being regarded as a beacon of fidelity. Before Lilibet had even accepted his proposal Lascelles and Elizabeth's other cronies were casting aspersions upon his ability to remain faithful. They started the ball a-rolling; it should have come as no surprise to them that it would gather muck as it hurtled down the hill. And muck it did acquire.

There is, however, another dimension to the matter of Philips' reputation. Coming as he did from a background of continental royals, the courtly tradition of the *cavaliere servante* was something he was used to. He would have thought nothing of openly befriending women, nor of flirting with them. His was a world where gallants fulfilled a valid role. Gallants were gentlemen who were the swains of queens, empresses, princesses, and great ladies. Courtly love was an art form practised by them, and much admired since medieval times, whence the custom originated. Gentlemen traditionally outdid one another in singing the praises of well-placed women. Sometimes they did it through poetry, sometimes through music, sometimes through simple declamation. *Cavalieri servanti* not only professed undying love to the objects of their desire, but danced attendance upon them. For instance, at tournaments they stood behind the chair of the lady in question. They would bend down and whisper sweet nothings in her ear, and, after a successful joust, they would lay their reward at the feet of the lady in question in full view of the public. It was a game, a courtly game, a game of flirtation where the ladies were openly admired, but the parameters were straightforward: public admiration, private abstinence. Sexual congress played no part, even as sexual desirability was being trumpeted. It is from the conduct of these *cavalieri servanti* that the expression of couples 'courting' derives. Even today, the flirtatiousness that is the characteristic of the old order is evident in all the European courts, the English included, and there are few stately homes, castles or palaces where frank flirtation doesn't flourish. Of course, some chancers do try to take things further, and there is little doubt that some women allow them to do so, but, by and large, flirtation ends in the drawing room, not in the bedroom.

Of course, things being taken further, or misfiring from time to time, have always been a feature of flirtatiousness, courtly or otherwise. Sometimes the consequences could be spectacular, none more so than with Anne Boleyn, who signed her fate and that of her husband Henry VIII's good friend Henry Norris when she flirtatiously observed in April 1536 that he was aiming to fill her husband's shoes after the king's death. That one comment set in train a series of events which would result, in a matter of weeks, in the execution of the queen, Norris, and several other men.

Inevitably, the boundaries delineating any mode of behaviour will blur. Use encourages abuse, especially when something as fundamental as sexual appreciation is being openly trumpeted. It was only a matter of time before the occasional lady took advantage of the practice of courtly love to permit more private forms of satisfaction. What is surprising isn't how often the abuses were present, so much as how little. Possibly this is because adultery with the wife of sovereign was a capital offence and adultery remained a questionable activity until the advent of the pill in the 1960s.

Of course, today we enjoy an unprecedented level of liberty in Western society. Even so, hundreds of years ago, notwithstanding how different things were, civilised people understood that the demands of an active social life would place an inordinate burden on husbands and wives. Therefore, as society grew more sophisticated, and there was greater tolerance of the need for married couples to function independently of each other, the tradition of the *cavaliere servante* was used not only to free busy spouses from the social obligations their less busy counterparts wished to partake of, but also as a cover for extra-marital affairs. King George V's first cousin Queen Marie of Romania, for instance, openly conducted an affair with the Romanian Prime Minister, Prince Barbu Stirbey, who was undoubtedly the father of her youngest son, Prince Mircea, and most likely of her youngest daughter, Ileana, in an update of the tradition which meant that the *cavaliere servante* was now the prime minister of her husband's country. This sort of conduct added a whole new layer of confusion which did little good to the custom of the *cavalieri servanti*, whose absence of carnality had been the defining feature of the tradition.

Confusion or none, social life could not function with only married couples, and too many couples wished to indulge in separate interests without actually breaking up their marriages or taking lovers, so the system was updated. By the mid-twentieth century, the accepted norm in fashionable circles was therefore for married couples, who wished to stay together but sometimes lead separate social lives, to have established escorts. These were often referred to as 'boyfriends' and 'girlfriends' but, nine times out of ten, the relationship was sexless. All that was needed was a spark to be present between a spouse and a friend. For instance, one of my closest friends in Scotland, now sadly deceased, used to refer to me as her husband's girlfriend. The degree of innocence is revealed by the fact that he and I have never exchanged so much as anything but a kiss of the cheek, not even after her untimely death in the early nineties.

Now that homosexuality is viewed as a normal and acceptable part of life in the twenty first century, the role of the gusband has been incorporated into the old *cavaliere servante* tradition. Many a socialite could not function without one, myself included. Yet the origin of the gusband lies in the eighteenth century. No one has ever put the attraction of a gusband for a heterosexual woman better than the famous eighteenth century *saloniste* Mme (Louise Florence Petronille Tradieu d'Esclavelles) d'Epinay, mistress of Jean-Jacques Rousseau, Frederich Melchior and Baron von Grimm, who described the virtues of her gusband , the Venetian ambassador, Marchese Alvise Mocenigo, to the Enlightenment figure Ferdinando Galiani in the following terms: 'nothing equals the friendly companionship afforded to a woman by men of those persuasions. To the rest of you, so full of yourselves, one can't say a word that you don't take as a provocation.....Whereas with those gentlemen one knows quite well they want no more of us than we of them – one feels no danger and deliciously free.'

Because social life in the upper reaches of society has always had greater importance than social life at more pedestrian levels, providing much-needed relief and entertainment while also furnishing cover for networking and other worldly or professional activities under the guise of pleasure while being anything but, the means have had to be found to make socialising palatable or at least bearable, to those who have to partake of it. Nowadays, it no longer matters whether one is royal, aristocratic, merely rich, grand, political, corporate or from the world of fashion or entertainment; all that matters is that the demands of social life must be met. Half the social events that the magazines portray as the end in glamour are nowhere near as pleasurable as the public believes. Duty demands that one attends, so one does. Such demands are most effectively met by couples, if only because you need a sidekick to be able to keep boredom or uneasiness at bay. But the couple is question doesn't have to be married, and certainly doesn't have to be sleeping together. Nowadays, the couple doesn't even have to be male and female. The phenomenon of couples being pairs of people who do not sleep together has greater coinage today than at any other time in the history of civilisation. There is a reason for this evolution. It is practical. The passion of sex will wax and wane, creating jealousy and conflict, whereas an absence of sex creates more predictable long-term harmoniousness. Hence why, ever since homosexuality was legalised in the second half of the twentieth century, the gay escort for the straight woman has become a feature of contemporary social life. It took an avid socialite like Nancy Reagan to bring the custom out of the closet and start a fashionable trend when she was seen out and about as First Lady with Jerry Zipkin, an openly gay man who was called her 'walker' – a term no civilised person would deign to use. Now that Western society has become so sophisticated that there is general acceptance of the practice of husbands and wives having established social partners, who are not their spouses, but who often function, so to speak, in *loco coniugi*, what started centuries ago as gallants stroking the egos of their leaders and their leaders' wives by paying court to them, has ended up being a practical feature of everyday life. While it remains more common for women to have what used to be known as 'dancing partners' than for men, largely because the husbands of socialites are still often richer and more frequently otherwise engaged professionally than their wives, the reality has always been that there are a handful of women whose time is more occupied by worldly responsibilities than their husbands. This is particularly true of female sovereigns, hence why Philip has always, to a certain extent, had to endure, and been able to enjoy, a total role reversal socially, and has had the need of female playmates.

Does he have sex with them? Sarah Bradford baldly asserted in her biography *Elizabeth: A Biography of Her Majesty The Queen*, that Philip does. One of the women, with whom she was certain he had had a sexual relationship, was Sacha Abercorn. The duchess, however, is even more certain that they never did have sex. Since she is one of the two people who would indisputably know whether she and Philip had actually slept together, and he has also denied sleeping with her (or indeed with any other woman since his marriage except for his wife) I find myself tempted to believe Sacha Abercorn over Ms Bradford, especially as how that author's assertions were backed up not by detail or fact but by the assumption that her authority was great enough to render it beyond question.

Penny's friends also have no doubt that the relationship, though passionate and loving, does not, and never did, include sex. My friend the bishop, who has stayed at Sandringham with Penny and Philip, as well as other couples such as the Vesteys and the Tollemaches, is equally certain that Philip is speaking the truth when he denies ever having had a sexual relationship with her. The dynamics are simply not there, when you see the playmates together, and together with Lilibet. The giveaway is that no one changes their demeanour. Philip does not become less accepting of the adulation his playmate directs towards him; the playmate does not monitor her conduct; and Lilibet accepts it all as completely natural and totally acceptable. Which no woman who loves her husband, as Lilibet undoubtedly loves Philip, would tolerate if there was something untoward going on.

The circumstantial evidence of Philip having an affair with Penny while having Lord and Lady Tollemache to stay is also overwhelming, if you realise that Philip's name was also linked with Xar Tollemache's in the eighties. Married to Timothy John Edward, 5th Lord Tollemache since 1970, the former Alexandra Dorothy Jean Maynell is a successful garden designer and has been another of Philip's (lesser known and established) playmates for decades. She is also friendly with friends of mine going back nearly five decades, as well as being a friend of Penny Mountbatten. The idea of Philip surrounding himself with women with whom he has been or remains sexually involved, and entertaining them in family homes such as Sandringham, and even worse, getting his wife to play hostess to them, is so outlandish as to be believable only to people who think that pigs fly. Not only would such conduct be callous in the extreme, but it would also show disrespect for the Queen. And the one thing both admirers and detractors of Philip will jointly concede is that he has a great deal of respect for Her Majesty.

Lilibet also has a great deal of respect for Philip. According to her, he has been her 'stay and strength'. He is her unsung hero, the man who has been by her side, sometimes tetchily, often amusingly, always interestingly, sometimes maddeningly, but loyally through thick and thin. She would be the first to concede that the contributions he has made to her reign have been incalculable. She knows that he is an extraordinary man. She, on the other hand, is a very ordinary woman whom destiny required to fulfil an extraordinary role. She has done so with a constancy, dedication, and consistency that are truly remarkable. She would doubtless have made an excellent monarch irrespective of whom she married, but she knows that the choice she made has not only added to the world in which we all live, but has raised her reign above and beyond what it would otherwise have been, had she been married to less of a visionary.

Lilibet is not a fool. She is not naïve. She knows that Philip is a man who needs other women. That does not mean that he needs to sleep with them. But it does mean that he needs them in his life. Lilibet is his wife and he loves her devotedly and completely. However, he was the golden boy who grew up surrounded by adoring women, and he has retained all his life a need to surround himself with adoring women. The fact that he is adorable means that their adoration is completely justified. Some would say he is vain; I would say he has always had strong emotional needs that require spreading his tentacles in various directions, giving and receiving love, not only from his female companions, but also from his male, for the one thing that people who believe him to be a Lothario forget is that he has always had equally strong and intense relationships with men.

Lilibet has always understood Philip and his need for human companionship, for amusement, for dedication, passion, and his quest in a variety of ways to bring meaning into his life. He has always been far more emotionally connected than she has; she understands this and accepts it. She even relishes this quality in him, knowing that it brings emotional and spiritual wealth into her life in a way that few other men would have been able to achieve.  As Pat Kirkwood observed in 1948, and many others have noticed since, Philip is one of those rare human beings who is completely alive.  He needs to make connections with an intensity that few others do. Lilibet understands this, and 'gives him a lot of leeway' according to Sacha Abercorn.  Her father, being a naval man, understood Philip, and warned Lilibet not to throttle him with too much control. 'Remember, he's a sailor. They come in on the tide.' Had Princess Margaret adopted a similar approach with Tony Snowdon, she might well have retained his interest.  Instead, her possessiveness pushed him away.

Another indication that Philip might well be speaking the truth when he denies ever having strayed is the way he behaved when his children's marriages got into trouble.  Not only was he understanding of his children as well as their spouses, but he also clamped down forcefully at any suggestion of sexual incontinence.  He lambasted Sarah for being 'like Edwina', his aunt by marriage whose sexual antics were legion.  This was high condemnation indeed, and suggests that he would not have been castigating her so openly, in front of the family who know him well and knows what he has and has not got up to, had he had skeletons in his own closet.

Of course, the world has changed beyond recognition in the nearly hundred years since Philip was born.  When he was young, marriage was for life.  If marriages, such as his parents', did not work, the couple in question found satisfaction elsewhere, in whatever form they wished.  His father did, with the Comtesse Andrée de La Bigne, and his mother did too, though through her religious faith.  He respected their choices, and has never condemned either, though their separation was unusual for the times.

Under the old, traditional ways of civilised conduct, a couple that remained together might have to adjust to different sexual tempi.  Andrew (11th Duke of) Devonshire and his wife Debo did.  My own parents and grandparents did, my grandmother moving her lover into the family home under a pretext, but never even touching him, much less kissing him, in front of anyone, whether it be husband, child, grandchild, friend, relation or servant.  My father, like all the other men in his family, had mistresses, but he conducted that aspect of his life away from the family.  He always maintained to us children that he had never looked at another woman once he had married our mother, and while we knew that that was not actually accurate, he was not trying to deceive us.  Men who respected their wives denied the existence of their mistresses.  They made declarations of faithfulness, not out of hypocrisy, but because it was a way of showing their wives respect.  What they were really saying was, 'Your position is inviolate. No one is threatening it.' This was not hypocrisy, but consideration.

# Chapter X

While it is possible that Philip has been doing all his adult life what my father, who was only five years his senior and therefore brought with the same mores, did, I doubt it. When asked whether she believed that Philip slept with his other playmates, Sacha Abercorn responded, 'I doubt it very much,' before asserting that she was 'sure not'. However, when pressed, she conceded that 'he's a human being. Who knows? I don't.'

The truth is, no one knows for sure except the people concerned. On the balance of probabilities, however, when everything is considered, it is likely that Philip has spoken the truth when he says that he has never cheated on Lilibet. Had he been a more ordinary individual, one might well have concluded that he was protecting the wife he loved by refusing to humiliate her as he sought his satisfaction elsewhere. However, the fact that he is such an extraordinary individual leads one to conclude that his denials are credible. While other, more mundane, men, my own father included, have channelled their energies into affairs, his have been absorbed by a host of interests, starting with the environment, taking in sport, philosophy, psychology, and theology, to name but a few of the range of subjects which have fascinated him.

He and Lilibet are nearing their end. Some fifteen months ago, he was at a party when someone mentioned that they had been diagnosed with pancreatic cancer. 'That's what I've got,' he said, and proceeded in his own, matter-of-fact way to provide hope for them. At his age, life itself is a terminal condition. Pancreatic cancer is a condition that affects the very old somewhat more generously than those who get it when they are younger. He has now lived with it for some years. It is being managed well, but Philip knows that no one is immortal, himself included. He has his faith to sustain him, and the knowledge that his has been an extraordinary life well lived. According to Lilibet, he is modest, and resists compliments, but he must know, in his darkest as well as his lightest moments, that both he and she have lived their lives to the best of their abilities and have, in the process, made invaluable contributions to millions of people all over the world.

As his grandmother Victoria said, 'What will live in history is the good work done by the individual & that has nothing to do with rank or title.' Both Philip and Lilibet have, throughout their long lives and their long marriage, sought to do good work. Even republicans concede the good they have done. Ultimately, their epitaphs will be the good they have done, and the millions of lives which have benefitted as a result of their existence. Their existence would have been nowhere as positive as it has been, had they not come together. By that yardstick alone, theirs has indeed been not only a long and successful marriage, but an exceptionally worthwhile shared existence.

The evidence suggests that theirs has indeed been the successful marriage they believed it to have been.

Philip retired from public life in 2017. Although he still accompanies Lilibet on the occasional official engagement, he has retired to Wood Farm on the Sandringham estate. This is the house which was converted for tragic Prince John and has remained a firm favourite within the family, being large enough to be spacious for a limited number of people, but small enough to be cosy. This has been converted for them and has become their 'home'. As their ends near, such time as they have left is being spent in the cosy domesticity that both of them, being descendants of the bourgeois Danish Grandfather of Europe, relish. Couples who elect to spend their final days together in such domestic surroundings do so because they enjoy each other. Greater testament to the depth of their feelings, and the success their marriage has been, does not exist.

# Chapter XI

THE PRIMARY PURPOSE of all royal marriages is securing the crown through the perpetuation of the line. In this respect also, Philip and Lilibet's marriage has been successful. They have produced four children, who in turn have produced two children each. They are now great-grandparents five times over, with another grandchild due later this year.

If the primary purpose of all royal marriages is the production of children, the primary purpose of the monarchy is perpetuation of the system. To achieve that, the monarchy must grow and change while remaining sufficiently the same to provide a link between the past and the future. Heirs to the throne are therefore nurtured from birth to provide good, solid leadership within constitutional parameters. Lilibet has been coaching William in constitutional ways for years now, ever since he was a pupil at Eton College. He used to come over to Windsor Castle on weekends to have tea with his grandmother, visits reminiscent of when she was a girl of her grandson's age and Henry Martens used to make the same journey to school her in Britain's constitution. The relationship between the present and the future monarch, however, was not merely that of tutor and pupil, for Lilibet has also taken care to play the role with William that her beloved granny, Queen Mary, played with her. She has therefore not only taught him about the constitution, but how a good monarch functions within it.

In that, Lilibet has been as successful as Queen Mary was with her. He has been as receptive to her wisdom, experience and beliefs as she was to her own grandmother's. One royal told me, 'The monarchy is ultimately in safe hands. William has been well schooled by his grandmother. They have very similar approaches and you will see, when he ascends the throne, her imprimatur all over the way he does things.'

According to this royal, Lilibet and Philip have been outstandingly successful grandparents to all their grandchildren. They have poured love and concern into all of them, and all the grandchildren, 'adore both grandparents. The Queen has become a lot more relaxed with children as she has got older. Prince Philip was always good – very good – with children and with the passage of time, she has become a lot more like him than she used to be when she was young.'

Martin Charteris once told me that the 'great misfortune' of Lilibet and Philip's lives has been the strains in their relationship with their firstborn. He recounted how Lilibet said that, 'Charles resents me because I taught him his ABCs,' while Philip was of the opinion that, 'Charles thinks me an unfeeling brute if I encourage him to put his personal feelings to one side and just get on with the job in hand without making himself miserable while doing so. I mean, if you have to do it, you may was well just do it and not moan about it.'

Charles simply cannot see that both his parents have had to make sacrifices, unlike Anne, who 'appreciates the burden her parents have functioned under and made the allowances that he should be making too.' Lord Charteris observed that Charles is a 'world-class moaner' but one whose 'heart is in the right place. He really does want to do good. He just can't seem to stop licking wounds he wouldn't have if he'd just stop licking them all the time.'

Colin Glenconner thought that this predilection of Charles's was inculcated and fostered by Queen Elizabeth the Queen Mother, who deliberately played upon it to drive a wedge between Charles and his parents. 'She was determined to shape Charles and did so. She was intent on undermining his parents so that she would have influence into the next reign. She loved power; loved wielding it; loved being near it and loved feeling that she was influencing events,' he believed. He observed that Elizabeth was 'a golden granny' to Princess Margaret's two children, 'not only because she enjoyed being the fairy grandmother – she was terribly vain and would do whatever it takes to shine – but also because this was her way of undermining PM. She knew PM didn't have a good word to say about her, and she hoped that, by playing up to David and Sarah, they would think PM and not Queen Elizabeth was the one at fault.' Colin did concede that Elizabeth was also a loving grandmother to her other grandchildren, and observed that 'Charles was the only one she wreaked havoc with.'

When I broached Colin's opinion to Lord Charteris about Elizabeth undermining Charles's parents' influence to his, and their own, detriment, he did not shy away from saying that, while Colin 'has a tendency to the histrionic,' he too was of the opinion that 'Queen Elizabeth's influence has not always been helpful.' She had 'mollycoddled' Charles all his life and 'encouraged aspects of his character which would have been left to wither and die of their own accord.' Whether Elizabeth's motives were quite as selfish as Colin thought they were, or whether they were simply the 'sentimental indulgence' of an 'overprotective granny', the effect of her 'encouragement'

was to drive a wedge between Charles and his parents, by nurturing characteristics which ultimately precluded sympathy between parents and child.

Elizabeth encouraged Charles to be an extravagant and a luxury-loving
sybarite like her. This had also caused conflict with his parents, both of
whom were thrifty by nature, but what really perturbed them was that he
seemed in danger of refusing to be limited by the constraints and boundaries
of constitutional monarchy, and might, when his day came, confront issues
which were best circumvented until a propitious moment came to deal with
them. Charteris was full of admiration for the way both Lilibet and Philip
had coped with, then safely untied, the binds placed upon them in the early
days of their public lives. He hoped that Charles would one day see that,
'sometimes the surest way between two points is not the quickest one, but
the slower one,' something that might not be tested for a long time, if ever,
as there is no guarantee that Charles will outlive his mother. Even if he
does, his reign will not be a long one, which is possibly why he forged a
path which has been, in some respects, divergent from both his parents. He
has taken full advantage of the constitutional freedom a Prince of Wales can
create for himself, and as long as he does not confront elected politicians once
he becomes king, who is to say that the divergence between his ways and his
parents will be more onerous than Edward VII's was from his mother Queen
Victoria's? She too dreaded her heir's more luxurious approach, dreading
that it would undermine the monarchy, but when Edward VII's time came,
his reign, though short, turned out to be a howling success.

Maybe it is in the nature of monarchy that friction exists between the
future monarch and the present one. After all, Lilibet and Philip also, in
their day, had ambitions to change the system, though it has to be said, Colin
Glenconner was of the view that Charles rather than Lilibet is the one who
harkens back to a past way of conduct, to days when the crown was more
powerful than it now is, when intervention was more acceptable than it now
is.

Traditionally, in Lilibet's family, few heirs to the throne have had easy
relationships with their parents. The fact that Charles and his parents
sometimes see things from different perspectives does not alter the fact that,
in many ways, their objectives are similar. Many of Charles's charitable
objectives can be traced back to his father's influence. His concern for
society's downtrodden, for making a difference, for creating initiatives which
will provide meaningful assistance, are all outgrowths of his parents' earlier
initiatives, his father's especially. As one of Philip's close relations said to me,
'It is ironic that Prince Charles can seem so resentful of his father when they
are so similar in so many ways. Except that Prince Philip is pragmatic and

doesn't complain, while Prince Charles is romantic and has no compunction about complaining when the urge takes him.'

Charles aside, Lilibet and Philip have enjoyed good relationships with all their other children. According to relations, Philip's favourites are Anne and Edward, while Lilibet's is Andrew. Nevertheless, they are close to all of them, and to their children. Lilibet is especially fond of Edward's wife Sophie, who has become something of a model daughter-in-law as well as a model princess. She quietly, self-effacingly, graciously and glamorously keeps her head below the parapet as she works to support her parents-in-law and the monarchy. One day she will be the Duchess of Edinburgh, and Philip has already placed Edward, the next duke, in the driver's seat at his main charity, The Duke of Edinburgh's Award scheme.

Lilibet and Philip also enjoyed good relations with their other two daughters-in-law, at least while both women were married to their sons. Diana herself told me that she loved the Queen dearly and never had a word to say against her, though she found her mother-in-law 'peculiarly ineffective' when dealing with Charles. According to Diana, 'the Queen thinks he's hopeless. One simply can't do a thing with him, she says.' Philip, on the other hand, tried his level best to encourage both of them to preserve their marriage, if only in name, and expressed both sympathy and understanding for Diana's predicament. Only when she tried to dislodge Charles from the line of succession did they lose patience with her, though, even then, they always treated her with kindness and encouraged her to bring any concerns she had to them. The fact that she chose not to, was her choice, not theirs.

Sarah York, on the other hand, did not enjoy quite so smooth an exit as Diana. The manner of her fall was not technically of her own making, though she was blamed for it as if it had been. She was photographed through a long lens having her foot kissed by her lover while around the swimming pool of a private villa in the South of France. She could never have imagined that a photographer would be able to snap pictures of her, but when they were published, Philip took against her, accused her of being like Edwina Mountbatten – no greater insult was possible - and thereafter refused to have anything to do with her. Although in the last year or two the interdict has softened slightly, and Philip now allows her access to the outer periphery of the royal circle, it is unlikely that he will ever allow her back into the sanctum sanctorum. In the early days of her marriage, he thought she was a 'breath of fresh air' and thoroughly enjoyed her down-to-earth jollity. Indiscretion after indiscretion, however, eroded his tolerance, though he has remained close to her two daughters.

Lilibet's approach to Sarah has shown how she maintains her independence of mind even within the family, despite Philip being its acknowledged head. Sarah herself confirms that her mother-in-law has continued to see her and lend her support throughout her years in the wilderness, though she has had to do so away from Philip's presence.

In reality, both Philip and Lilibet acquitted themselves with graciousness and understanding as each of their children's marriages unravelled. I used to see Mark Phillips from time to time at parties in the late eighties and early nineties. It was an open secret that he and Princess Anne's marriage was over, but it was also well known that the Lilibet and Philip took an enlightened and sophisticated approach to their daughter's marital difficulties. Only when Phillips fathered a child out of wedlock did it become impossible to maintain an illusion of normality, by which time Princess Margaret's divorce had opened the door to the unthinkable. Only too soon, not only Princess Anne, but also Prince Andrew and Prince Charles would walk through those portals. Charles, however, had to wait until his beloved granny, Queen Elizabeth the Queen Mother, was dead, before he could marry the woman he loved. There was no way he could ever have married Camilla while his grandmother was alive. She simply would not have allowed it. And so strong was her influence, that it not only would never have happened, but it didn't happen until she was no longer around to prevent it. Queen Elizabeth the Queen Mother's death also proved liberating for Lilibet. As long as her mother was alive, Lilibet functioned within her shadow. Once Elizabeth died, her daughter was finally free to step out of the shadows and take her rightful place centre stage. She visibly blossomed, jazzing up her wardrobe, slightly expanding her hairstyle, even indulging her sense of fun. There is no doubt in royal circles that the James Bond spoof which went down so well during the jubilee celebrations would never have been possible had Elizabeth still been alive. She would have squelched the idea on the grounds of dignity and, in so doing, would have deprived her daughter and the nation of a moment which even endeared her to detractors.

Families are all the same in that each one is unique. Each one is different. Each one has its bugbears, its positive and negative dynamics. Most families, of course, have the luxury of privacy. But this is something royal families do not have. For better or for worse, their private lives enter the public domain, and the real person can sometimes be lost amidst the flotsam and jetsam of fallacy passing itself off as fact. The Queen and Prince Philip have had to contend with their share of that phenomenon. The great philosopher Arthur Schopenhauer made the observation that, 'All truth passes through three stages: First, it is ridiculed. Then it is violently opposed. Finally, it is accepted as self-evident.'It is to be hoped that the public will ultimately accept the Queen and Prince Philip's verdict on their marriage. It has been a success, and one which has not only added to their own lives, but has enriched their public positions and thereby enhanced the lives of the millions they have touched in the seven decades they have been together.

*The End*

# Partial Bibliography

Palace Walk by Naguib Mahfouz (English translation 1990 Anchor Press)

One Leg Over by Robin Dalton (Text Publishing 2017)

Prince Philip by John Dean (Henry Holt Co., 1955)

Young Prince Philip: His Turbulent Early Life by Philip Eade (HarperPress 2011)

The Royal Marriages by Lady Colin Campbell (St Martin's Press 1993)

The Duke: A Portrait of Prince Philip by Tim Heald (Hodder & Stoughton 1991)

Philip and Elizabeth: Portrait of a Marriage by Gyles Brandreth (Century 2004)

The Untold Life of Queen Elizabeth The Queen Mother by Lady Colin Campbell (Dynasty Press 2012)

The Queen: A Biography of Elizabeth II by Ben Pimlott (John Wiley & Sons 1998)

Royals and the Reich: The Princes von Hessen in Nazi Germany (Oxford University Press 2006)

Memoirs of HRH Prince Christopher of Greece (The Right Book Club 1938)

The Little Princesses by Marion Crawford (Harcourt Brace 1950)

Past Forgetting by Veronica Maclean (Review 2002)

Elizabeth The Queen by Sally Bedell Smith (Random House 2012)

Elizabeth: A Biography of Her Majesty The Queen by Sarah Bradford (Heinemann 1996)

The Road to Abdication by Frances Donaldson (Weidenfeld & Nicolson 1978)

The Sleepwalkers: How Europe Went to War in 1914 by Christopher Clark (Harper Collins 2013)

The Fall of the Ottomans: The Great War in the Middle East 1914-1920 by Eugene Rogan (Allen Lane 2015)

The Kaiser: Warlord of the Second Reich by Alan Palmer (Weidenfeld & Nicolson 1978)

Once a Grand Duke by HIH Grand Duke Alexander Mikhailovitch of Russia (Farrar & Rinehart 1932)

A Family of Kings: The Descendants of Christian IX of Denmark by Theo Aronson (Thistle Publishing 2014)

APAPA: King Christian IX of Denmark and his Descendants by Arturo E. Beéche (eurohistory.com 2014)

The Last Courts of Europe: A Royal Family Album 1860-1914 by Jeffrey Finestone (JM Dent Sons 1981)

Marie Bonaparte: A Life by Celia Bertin (Harcourt Brace Jonavovich 1982)

Drives, Affects and Behaviour: Essays in Honor of Marie Bonaparte by Rudolf Poewenstein (1952)

An Outline of Psychoanalysis by Sigmund Freud (W.W. Norton & Co 1949)

Freud and the British Royal Family by D. Cohen (The Psychologist, Vol 26, No. 6, June 2013)

Princess Louise: Queen Victoria's Unconventional Daughter by Jehanne Wake (Collins 1988)

Towards Disaster: The Greek Army in Asia Minor in 1921 by HRH Prince Andrew of Greece (John Murray 1931)

Alice, Princess Andrew of Greece by Hugo Vickers (Hamish Hamilton 2000)

War Diaries by Harold Macmillan (Macmillan 1984)

Kings of the Hellenes by John van der Kiste (Alan Sutton Publishing 1994)

A Short History of Modern Greece by Richard Clogg (Cambridge University Press 1979)

Louis and Victoria: The Family History of the Mountbattens by Richard Hough (Weidenfeld & Nicolson 1984)

Prince Louis of Battenberg by Mark Kerr (Longmans, Green & Co 1934)

Mountbatten by Philip Ziegler (Collins 1985)

The British Admirals of the Fleet by Tony Heathcote (Haverton: Pen & Sword 2002)

# Partial Bibliography

Daughter of Empire: My Life as a Mountbatten by Lady Pamela Hicks (Weidenfeld & Nicolson 2012)

Queen Mary by James Pope-Hennessy (George Allen & Unwin 1959)

Thatched with Gold by Mabell Airlie (Hutchinson 1962)

King George V by Kenneth Rose (Weidenfeld & Nicolson 1983)

The People's Princess: Portrait of Princess Mary, Duchess of Teck by S.W. Jackman (Kensal Press, 1984)

Balfour: A Life of Arthur James Balfour by Max Egrement (Collins 1980)

Darling Loosy by Elizabeth Longford (Weidenfeld & Nicolson 1991)

For my Grandchildren by Princess Alice, Countess of Athlone (Evans Bros 1966)

HRH The Princess Margaret: A Life Unfulfilled by Nigel Dempster (Quartet Books 1981)

Snowdon: The Biography by Anne de Courcy (Weidenfeld & Nicolson 2008)

George VI by Patrick Haworth (Hutchinson 1987)

The Heart Has Its Reasons: Memoirs of the Duchess of Windsor by The Duchess of Windsor (Michael Joseph 1956)

A King's Story: The Memoirs of HRH The Duke of Windsor by The Duke of Windsor (Putnam 1951)